Picking Winners

Books by Andrew Beyer

Picking Winners
My $50,000 Year at the Races
The Winning Horseplayer
Beyer on Speed

Picking Winners

A Horseplayer's Guide

ANDREW BEYER

HOUGHTON MIFFLIN COMPANY
Boston New York

To my mother

Library of Congress Cataloging in Publication Data

Beyer, Andrew.
Picking winners.
1. Horse race betting. I. Title.
SF331.B45 798'.401 74-34311
ISBN 0-395-39379-5 (pbk.)

Printed in the United States of America

AGM 19 18 17 16 15 14 13

Contents

Foreword

SEVENTEEN YEARS AFTER the original publication of *Picking Winners,* the methods in this book received their ultimate vindication. In April 1992, the *Daily Racing Form* began to include Beyer Speed Figures in the record of every racehorse in North America. Casual horseplayers became speed handicappers and regularly based betting decisions on these figures, which translate each previous performance of a horse into a numerical rating. Handicappers writing for the *Racing Form* also acknowledged the importance of speed figures, making comments such as this: "Beyer Boys will form flying wedge to betting windows to play this standout." Even owners, trainers, and breeders started to define their horses in terms of figures. An advertisement for the stallion Housebuster listed his career victories according to the speed figures that he had earned.

To anyone who has become interested in horse racing in recent years, this keen awareness of horses' speed may seem unremarkable. Surely it doesn't require much imagination to conclude that races will often be won by the fastest horse. Yet in 1975, this idea was considered heterodox, even preposterous. Horseplayers believed in class, not speed, and experts would frequently pose a hypothetical question like this one: A $10,000 horse runs six furlongs in 1:11. A $20,000 horse runs the same distance in 1:11⅗. Now they are matched against each other; who will win? The overwhelming majority of people involved in American racing would have answered without hesitation that the $20,000 animal's superior class would enable him to prevail. Even Tom Ainslie, the most astute and literate author of handicapping books, espoused the supreme importance of class.

Of course, there were in America some bettors who recognized the importance of speed and profited handsomely by betting on the $10,000 horse who could run faster than his $20,000 rival. In the 1950s, the handicapper Jules Fink and his associates enjoyed legendary success at the betting windows and became known as the Speed Boys. A gambler named Harry Ragozin hired a statistician to help him analyze the times of races; his son, Len, would later sell figures based on his father's methods to a coterie of trainers, owners, and high-rolling gamblers. So when I started experimenting with figures in the early 1970s, and was exhilarated to learn that I could make a profit with them, I was merely reinventing the wheel.

But unlike other gamblers who were understandably close-mouthed about their successful methods, I was also a journalist, and I wanted to write a book about horse racing. While I was an undergraduate at Harvard, the most widely read book of my generation was not *The Iliad* or *Hamlet,* but *The Education of a Poker Player,* by Herbert O. Yardley, which combined sound, sophisticated strategy for the game with wonderful stories depicting the unique characters who populated the world of high-stakes poker. It made the reader want to hop on the nearest riverboat. Even as a college student I had envisioned writing a book that would do the same for horse-race betting, but then, of course, I was still learning the fundamentals of the game. But after discovering the usefulness of speed figures, I had the basis for a possible book, and when a former classmate became an editor at Houghton Mifflin, I had the opportunity to write *Picking Winners.*

The book made the intellectual case for speed handicapping but, even so, I thought that only a handful of readers would be willing to wade through the complicated chapters that form its core and then devote the considerable time and effort necessary to calculate a set of figures. Yet the racing world was filled with a surprising number of bettors who were ready and eager to do whatever was necessary to succeed at the track; they needed only to be shown the way. And as the computer era was dawning, more and more people with a mathematical bent were attracted by the idea of using numerical methods to analyze this complex game. When an increasing number of bettors recognized the great usefulness of figures, speed handicapping finally received wide acceptance, culminating with the *Daily Racing Form*'s inclusion of them.

With speed figures now so accessible, most horseplayers will conclude that there is little need to grapple with the complexities involved in making their own — just as students armed with calculators don't need to worry about the basics of arithmetic. But it will be a pity if making figures becomes a lost art, because the process can be an exciting one. It is also important for bettors who use the Beyer Speed Figures in the *Racing Form* to understand what the numbers mean and how they are made. Too many readers want to view the published figures as holy writ, when in fact many speed figures may be tinged with ambiguity and will involve a good deal of subjective judgment by the person who calculates them.

The method of making figures that I explain in *Picking Winners* has changed very little over the years. The basic speed-rating charts have been revised, and the ones I now use appear in the Appendix, along with par figures for various tracks. But the principles behind them are the same.

And, surprisingly, in a game that has undergone so many profound changes, much of the rest of *Picking Winners* has stood the test of time, too — particularly the chapters on track bias, trainer patterns, and physical appearance. (Although these concepts now are viewed as fundamental subjects of handicapping, they had been ignored in racing literature before *Picking Winners.*) But there were at least two subjects whose importance I did not recognize in 1975: pace and trips.

In the original edition of *Picking Winners,* I had dismissed the importance of pace and declared that horses' performance — and their speed figures — were unaffected by the early fractions of a race. (To spare the reader from being misled and me from being embarrassed by my youthful ignorance, this short section has been expunged.) Nor had I begun to grasp the concept that the way a horse runs his race — his "trip" — will affect his performance, and that a handicapper must watch and interpret races skillfully to judge a horse's ability fully. I devoted the better part of two subsequent books, *The Winning Horseplayer* (1983) and *Beyer on Speed* (1993), to this subject. But the central thrust of *Picking Winners* has remained relevant and highly effective because it deals with the most fundamental aspect of handicapping. As I quoted an old-time speed handicapper in 1975: "Time is the one immutable truth in the game." And immutable it remains.

1

The Joy of Handicapping

From time to time, every confirmed horseplayer is racked by doubts about what he is doing with his life. He is playing the toughest game in the world, one that demands a passionate, all-consuming dedication from anyone who seriously wants to be a winner. Even a winner will necessarily experience more frustrations than triumphs, and when the frustrations come in rapid succession he may wonder if the struggle is worth it.

As I drove to Liberty Bell Race Track on the morning of December 9, 1970, I was beset by more than the usual doubts about my obsession with betting. For months I had been suffering through an unbroken series of racetrack disasters — a worse losing streak than most horseplayers will ever endure. I was beginning to question the assumptions that had encouraged me to devote so much of my energy to studying the *Racing Form:* Can the races be beaten consistently? And even if the game can ultimately be beaten, is it worth spending years of effort to reach a goal that most members of society would view as a trivial achievement? I remembered a conversation I had once had with a seventy-year-old horseplayer who felt he had wasted his life at the racetrack. "Son," he told me, "if I'd spent the time studying law books that I've put into the *Racing Form*, I'd probably be on the Supreme Court now."

I would be better able to answer my own questions after the second race at Liberty Bell that afternoon. It was an ordinary maiden-claiming race — for cheap horses who had never been able to win — but it was the most important race of my life. A week earlier I had been riding the Gray Line bus to Laurel, studying the *Racing Form* intensely. The past performances for the ninth race at Laurel happened to appear next to those for the first race at Liberty Bell, and the record of a horse on the also-eligible list at the out of town track leaped out of the page at me. His name was Sun in Action. His record was superficially dismal: In the only two starts of his career, he had finished fifth and seventh while competing at the rock-bottom level of horsedom. But Sun in Action had done something very unusual in those two races. In his debut he had broken slowly and rallied strongly, passing six horses and making up nine lengths in the last quarter mile. The next time he showed a burst of early speed and then tired. This change of running styles had produced many winners for me — including a 148-to-1 shot — but I had never seen a horse embody the pattern as clearly as Sun in Action.

Sun in Action was scratched from the race in which I

discovered him; he would not be entered again until the next week. During that week I scrutinized every aspect of his record a hundred times. I became obsessed. I could neither think nor talk of anything else. I did not merely hope or suspect that he was going to win his next race. I knew. Sun in Action was going to be my salvation.

When his name finally appeared in the entries for a mile-and-one-sixteenth maiden race, I could not contain my excitement. Three months earlier I had been hired to write a horse-racing column for the Washington *Daily News*. On the day of the race I wrote about Sun in Action, unconditionally advising the paper's readers that he was "the betting opportunity of the year." If I was going to go broke that day, I might as well be publicly humiliated, too.

I took all of my dwindling bank account to Liberty Bell. Sun in Action was 23 to 1 when I walked to the $50 window a few minutes before post time. He was 20 to 1 when I left, after betting $200 to win for myself and another $200 for friends who had been infected by my enthusiasm for the horse. Sun in Action broke quickly and he was running second when the field reached the first turn. But then he started dropping back. And back. And back. After three-quarters of a mile he was fourteen lengths behind the leader. I lowered my binoculars with resignation and told the friend who had accompanied me on the trip, "No chance. Sorry."

As I conceded defeat, Sun in Action was beginning to gain some ground on the last turn, running so wide that his jockey had to lean left in the saddle to prevent him from going to the outside fence. As he reached the stretch he was still an impossible eight lengths behind the leader, Birchcrest. Sun in Action continued gaining momentum through the stretch, but with only a sixteenth of a mile to run he still didn't seem to have a chance. In those final yards, however, Birchcrest began to tire perceptibly, and Sun in Action was flying at him. The finish was too close to call.

During the agonizing minutes while the photo was being developed I consoled myself with the thought that, even if Sun in Action had lost, I had not been disgraced. My judgment and my confidence in the horse had been vindicated. But who wants a moral victory? Put up number five!

They put up number eight, Birchcrest, the winner by a nose. And a few seconds later they put up a red sign that said OBJECTION. It was a stewards' inquiry, against the winner. Moments later the track announcer said that Sun in Action's jockey, Martin Fromin, had also claimed foul against the winner.

I sat hypnotized by the tote board, where the numbers eight and five were blinking as the stewards pondered their decision. A man near me was holding a $2 ticket on Birchcrest and he looked very unhappy. "There's no chance," he said. "They'll take him down." He was right. Birchcrest was disqualified for crowding Sun in Action on the first turn, forcing Fromin to check his horse sharply so he wouldn't stumble over Birchcrest's heels. The result was now official and the tote board said Sun in Action paid $43.20 to win. I had won more than $4000 for myself, the same amount for friends who had given me their money, and an unknown sum for readers who had wagered with their bookmakers that morning. I was a minor celebrity when I got back to Washington.

Sun in Action's victory meant more to me than $4000. It convinced me, for the last time, that the races could be beaten. And the exhilaration of that triumph persuaded me that mastering the art of handicapping was a goal worth pursuing, no matter how much time and energy it required. The mental attitude with which a man approaches gambling can determine whether he will succeed or fail. I did not have all the necessary skills yet, but I now had the self-confidence and determination to become a winning horseplayer.

This was not exactly the life's calling for which I had been programmed. I had once been destined to be respectable. The son of a college professor and product of a good middle-class upbringing in Erie, Pennsylvania, I was a model student in high school and went off to Harvard, where I expected to become a scholar and write learned essays on the poetry of T. S. Eliot. I was diverted.

Even in my early childhood I displayed a natural affinity for games of chance that my father and mother noted with some chagrin. My first gambling experience came at the age of five when I hit the jackpot on a slot machine. When I was twelve I persuaded my parents to take me to Randall Park in Cleveland, where I caught my first glimpse of that wonderful, esoteric set of statistics known as the *Daily Racing Form*. I was hooked. By the time I was fifteen I was buying the *Form* every weekend, studying it from cover to cover and placing $2 bets with an indulgent bookmaker. My fondest memory of Strong Vincent High School was sitting in the physics class of grim-faced, humorless Mr. Armagost when a messenger came into the room and handed the student council president a note reading, "Your parlay at Aqueduct paid $74." Mr. Armagost was not impressed.

When I went to college my resolution to become a diligent scholar was undermined by the discovery that four racetracks lay within easy commuting distance of Harvard Square. I managed to dabble at both academic and equine pursuits for the better part of four years, until an irreconcilable conflict arose two weeks before graduation. My final examination in Chaucer was scheduled on the same day that Kauai King would be trying to win the Triple Crown at Belmont Park. I knew nothing about the *Canterbury Tales* but I did know something about Amberoid in the Belmont Stakes. So I went to the track. Although I blew a $12,000 education, I did collect a $13 payoff on Amberoid, cutting my losses for the day to $11,987.

Having been reared to become an intellectual, I was seduced by horse-race betting because it offers more mental challenge and stimulation than any subject in the formal academic world. Few people ever master it. Men who are successful in every other facet of their lives — in school, in their jobs, in their financial affairs — can tackle racing and be frustrated, bewildered, or even ruined. It is maddening to serious students of handicapping that society confers its blessings on traditional academic pursuits but views the study of horse racing as utter frivolity. If you are writing a thesis on religious symbolism in the poetry of Sir Thomas Wyatt the elder, you are a respectable scholar. If you are studying the symbolism in the *Daily Racing Form*, you're a bum.

Horseplayers have to be content with the private satisfaction that comes from mastering the art of handicapping. The gratification is especially great because success at the racetrack is completely unambiguous. A man who writes a book may have to wait a lifetime for the judgment of history; a man who studies the stock market may have to wait for months or years to learn if a particular investment was a good one. A horseplayer can see his opinion validated — or contradicted — in a matter of seconds. At the end of a race meeting or a calendar year he can total his results and measure the extent of his success or failure. If there is a plus sign on the bottom line he will know unequivocally that he has achieved a goal that eludes almost everyone who pursues it. Even the money is secondary to that satisfaction.

The cerebral stimulation of handicapping, and the ego gratification that comes from doing it well, are only part of the attraction of playing the horses. The act of betting itself, as the legendary plunger Nick the Greek once said, "improves the flavor of living." Most solid citizens think gamblers are in the same psychological league as dope fiends and child molesters, but they don't understand and they don't know what they're missing.

A friend of mine from Boston was obsessed by playing the horses. He would awaken at dawn so he could study the races all morning, spend the afternoon at the track, and devote his evening to a stack of yellowing *Racing Forms*, searching for new handicapping techniques. He didn't have much money but his life was a joy. Every day was a new challenge, a new adventure. My friend didn't think there was anything abnormal about his passion. "I am thankful," he said once, "that God gave me the capacity to enjoy. And let's face it: there's nothing more enjoyable than gambling."

The capacity to enjoy: so few people have it. Most citizens live lives of such routine and drudgery and are so concerned about security that they cannot imagine how delicious uncertainty is. A gambler may have as many periods of pain and frustration as he does of exhilaration, but at least he knows he's alive.

I remember a day when I fell in love with a horse named Sandlot at Bowie Race Track. He was shipping in from New York, where in his most recent race he had encountered an astounding amount of bad luck but still managed to finish second in excellent time. I went to the track in a state of high excitement, prepared to make a killing. As the seventh race approached and the tension increased, it occurred to me that most people are completely reliant on external forces for this sort of stimulation. They fall in love, they get a promotion, they inherit money — but they must wait for these momentous events to happen. A horseplayer can will them. I bet Sandlot at 5 to 1 and watched ecstatically as he broke from the gate quickly, took the lead, and steadily increased his advantage. With a sixteenth of a mile to go, he was four lengths in front and I shouted, "Mark him up!" The words had barely escaped my lips when a gray horse named Zadig came streaking from out of nowhere and caught Sandlot in the last stride to win by a nose. I was stunned and silent for the rest of the day, and as I left the track a friend asked me how I felt. I thought of a scene in the movie *Patton* in which George C. Scott walks through a battlefield where fighting has raged all night long. He sees that many of his men are dead, hears the moaning of the wounded, and says, "God help me, but I love it so."

To reach this advanced state of lunacy, most horseplayers travel down similar paths. They are initially lured to the racetrack by greed, perhaps believing the blandishments of tipsters, system peddlers, and glib how-to-beat-the-races books that say there is easy money to be made at the track. They may be further encouraged by a stroke of beginner's luck. But all horseplayers soon learn that it is enormously difficult to win at the track consistently. In casino games, players are destined to lose and the house will get rich because it has a 1 or 2 percent advantage in its favor. In racing, the state and tracks extract more than 17 percent of every betting dollar. So the vast majority of horseplayers will inevitably be losers. It is a testimony to the unique lure of racing that once a man has discovered it and starts losing money — as he surely will, for a while at least — he usually doesn't abandon the sport and put his capital into municipal bonds. His appetite will be whetted by his initial failures.

Some people who become addicted horseplayers remain

dilettantes all their lives. They do not truly believe that the races can be beaten so they do not make a determined effort to learn. They live not for the day when they will be expert handicappers but for the one big lucky hit that will change their lives.

Serious students of handicapping are driven by the desire to learn so that someday they will have the skills to win consistently. In most areas of human knowledge a reasonably intelligent person with the will to become an expert can become one. If he wants to learn about Byzantine history or ancient philosophy or Elizabethan drama, he can spend years reading every book in the library, assimilating all the accumulated worldly wisdom on the subject. But in the field of horse racing this kind of intense study probably won't turn a horseplayer into a winner.

Most published material on handicapping is based on the assumption that horseplayers are looking for an easy, untaxing way to beat the horses and make a fortune overnight. The pages of racing magazines used to be filled with advertisements for systems that virtually assured the reader he would be able to retire to a life of ease by sending $25 for the secret of beating the races. These systems all consisted of a few simple rules: "Bet only horses who have finished out of the money in their last race while finishing within 5¼ lengths of the winner, and are racing within nine days of their last start." They all had exotic names: the Trainer's Overlay Profit System, the Investor's Dependable Earnings Accumulator. And they were all advertised with powerful pitches. I will confess that I succumbed to the come-on for something called the Master Key System. The brochure advertising it described the life of J. K. Willis, a telegraph operator who devoted years of effort to understanding the mysteries of handicapping. "Month after month," he wrote, "I studied, investigated, analyzed and experimented. Time after time it seemed as if I had solved the riddle, only to have my hopes dashed by some incurable flaw. And then, when I was almost convinced that I was wasting my time, I discovered the long-sought solution, the secret of beating the races — a simple wonder-working formula of figures . . . that provided the surest thing in Turfdom." Not long after making this momentous breakthrough, Willis was stricken and crippled by an acute form of rheumatism and ordered by his doctors to an area of the country where there was no racing. "Killing time is a problem," he wrote. "To help pass the slowly moving hours and divert my mind from my physical condition, I decided to teach my system to others." Who could resist? I raced for the nearest mailbox with my check for $25. I did not subsequently retire to a life of ease.

In the last few years systems have become passé and have been displaced by gadgets — nifty plastic slide rules like the Smart Money Detect-O-Meter, the Harvard Concentric Selector, and the Kel-Co Calculator. I succumbed to the propaganda for the latter device, which was said to have been developed by an aerospace scientist who is an expert on statistics and probabilities, and tested it on paper during a two-week period at Hialeah. It produced a 42 percent loss.

The systems and the gadgets are all based on the same assumption: that the complexities of horse racing, which have baffled men for centuries, which involve hundreds of factors, can be resolved by the application of a few simple rules or calculations. The assumption is a seductive one. I spent many hours tinkering with systems and once even created one that worked spectacularly. Armed with the Beyer Miracle System, I looked for horses who had shown early speed and tired in their next to last race, then ran at a longer distance, showed early speed again and tired less drastically. During one month at Bowie Race Track, system horses were winning nearly 50 percent of the time, at odds as high as 71 to 1. And then, just as abruptly as it had started working, it stopped. There is probably a time and place where any simple system will be profitable, even if it consists of betting horses with three-syllable names that begin with the letter *A*. But in the long run there is no way to circumvent the complexities of handicapping. A bettor who wants to win must come to grips with them.

When a horseplayer recognizes the shortcomings of systems and slide rules, he will probably turn to books to learn the art of handicapping. But he will find that most writers display the same mentality as the system peddlers. They try to make winning at the track sound as easy as possible. They present their readers either with a compilation of systems or with a set of inflexible rules to guide them when they handicap.

This approach is epitomized in *Lawrence Voegele's Professional Method of Winner Selection*, a book that was made a spectacular financial success by a nationwide advertising blitz. Voegele bases his "method" on a statistical study of 5000 races. It tells him, for example, that 84.3 percent of winners run within fourteen days of their last race. So Voegele turns this statistic into a dictum: Never bet a horse who has not started within the past fifteen days. Even though this is a sound guideline — a recent race suggests that a horse is in decent physical condition — there are many cases in which a layoff is a positive sign. If a horse has been racing frequently and his form begins to deteriorate, his trainer may give him a rest to revivify him. Then he brings the horse back into racing condition with a series of good workouts. If the trainer is competent the animal may be ready to run his best race after a layoff. But Voegele would summarily dismiss this or any other exception to his rule. He knows it will be much easier for his reader to operate with an inflexible method that dictates what he should do rather than with an approach that calls for him to use his intelligence and judgment at every stage of the handicapping process.

I read most of the literature on handicapping and it didn't make me a winner. Nor do I know any consistently successful bettor who acquired most of his knowledge from books. After recognizing the limitations of writings on the subject, a horseplayer who is still hungering for knowledge may try to discover the truths of handicapping through his own research. I know one Harvard-educated horseplayer, dubbed by a *Look* magazine article as "the Wizard of Odds," who plans to feed into an IBM 360 Model 65 computer the past performances for every race run in New York over a two-year period — some 30 million digits of information. His problem is finding $100,000 to finance the project. It would require an undertaking of this magnitude for a single person to unravel many of the mysteries of horse racing. Most of us are fortunate to have a few small but original insights into handicapping during the course of our careers as horseplayers.

Many aspiring handicappers, unable to master the game after reading all the books and conducting their own research, give up the quest in despair without realizing that there is a body of knowledge that could show them how to win at the track. This knowledge is transmitted not by the printed word but by an oral tradition.

Good horseplayers learn from each other. Contrary to the popular image of them as close-mouthed loners, serious bettors like to talk, argue over theories, and exchange ideas with people who share their obsession. They don't possess great secrets of handicapping any more than the system peddlers do. But winning horseplayers do know the areas of handicapping that are important and worth study, ones that the majority of bettors overlook because the handicapping books ignore them.

Without exception every successful horseplayer I know is keenly aware of the importance of the trainer when judging a horse's record and his chances in a race. He knows he must familiarize himself with the trainers at the track where he operates. He must learn who is competent and who is not. He must learn the specific strengths and weaknesses of individuals. A handicapper in New York, for example, ought to know that Frank Whiteley wins a high percentage of the time with horses making the first start of their careers; Elliott Burch, a trainer of comparable stature, seldom wins with them. But a horseplayer who has acquired his knowledge from books would be only dimly aware that this is a vital part of handicapping. The trainer factor does not lend itself to simplistic rules or dogmatic assertions. The writers don't want to tell their readers that the only way to learn about trainers is to sit down with a stack of *Racing Forms* and analyze their records. So they ignore the subject.

Because my job with the Washington *Star-News* brings me into contact with many fellow horseplayers, I have been fortunate enough to meet other serious handicappers who contributed greatly to my own knowledge. Sheldon Kovitz, a college classmate, taught me how to evaluate, with remarkable precision, the real meaning of horses' times. Clem Florio, probably the best handicapper for a newspaper in America, showed me how to relate a horse's speed figures to his current physical condition. Steve Davidowitz, an editor of *Turf and Sport Digest*, convinced me to view all handicapping factors in light of the racing surface over which the horses are competing.

There was no dramatic flash of insight, accompanied by a lightning bolt from the heavens, by which I learned how to beat the races. I began to study in the uncharted areas that these successful handicappers had suggested to me. At first I used these new techniques in a somewhat disorganized fashion. I finally ordered them, in my mind, to form a logical, coherent method of handicapping. And then I took the most important step of all. Frustrated by the realization that I was still not maximizing my winnings, I formulated a betting strategy and learned how to manage my money and my emotions. The process took years and it is still continuing, because no serious horseplayer ever stops learning. But I can now say, with much satisfaction and with no equivocation, that I beat the races. I do not claim that my method is the one and only true path to enlightenment, but I do know that it works.

I would like to be able to suggest that the reader will be able to finish this book, proceed directly to the nearest racetrack, and amass a fortune. But he can't. This book is only a shortcut to mastering the art of handicapping. The reader will not have to spend years, as I did, simply learning which directions to pursue so he can understand the game, but he will have to study so he can apply the important principles of handicapping to the track at which he operates. And he will need experience and judgment to use the principles properly. There are no neat lists of "dos and don'ts" in this book, no dogmatic pronouncements to make handicapping sound easy. If a man is looking for easy money, he is horribly misdirected if he looks for it at the racetrack.

2

A Handicapping Primer

I HAVE STOOD on street corners in the midst of blizzards and rainstorms waiting for the *Daily Racing Form* to be delivered to the corner newsstand. I have burst into paroxysms of rage because a friend or loved one inadvertently wrinkled a copy of my precious newspaper. I have accumulated thousands of old *Racing Forms* in my basement because I cannot bear the thought of throwing them away, even after they have yellowed and mildewed with age and the horses whose records they contain have long since retired or died.

The *Racing Form* occupies the place in the existence of a horseplayer that a Bible does in the life of a fundamentalist. It is the source of our knowledge, the basis of our decisions, the repository of our memories. Although bettors are fond of criticizing it for its high price and its occasional inaccuracies, the *Form* is the best publication of its type in the world. An American horseplayer who visits England and tries to handicap with that country's comparable publication, the *Sporting Life*, will inevitably return home with a renewed appreciation for the vast quantities of information jammed into every line of the *Form*.

For the benefit of uninitiated readers I have included in this chapter an explanation of the symbols in the *Racing Form* and the handicapping principles that underlie them. Learning how to analyze the data in past performances is an absolutely essential skill, though it alone is rarely enough to make a horseplayer a consistent winner. Handicapping is a competition among bettors. Because the betting dollar is so heavily taxed, only a small percentage of the people at a racetrack can possibly win. They are usually the people with superior knowledge.

A horseplayer who relies solely on the information in the past performances will know only what everybody else does. So the emphasis in this book will be placed upon the areas of handicapping that the *Form*'s past performances do not cover explicitly and that most bettors therefore ignore: the methodology of trainers, the influence of the track on the outcome of races, the importance of horses' physical appearance, and the accurate measurement of the times of races. But before a reader can venture into these uncharted areas, he must first master the fundamentals.

CONSISTENCY

The figures in the upper right-hand corner of a horse's past performances summarize his record for the last two years and paint an overall picture of his ability and reliability. In 1973 Jacques Who raced twenty times. The letter *M*

Jacques Who * **117** **Gr. c (1970), by Grey Dawn II.—Lady D**
Breeder, J. D. Wimpfheimer (Ky.).

1973	20	M	13	1	$26,470
1972	10	M	0	0	$960

Owner, J. D. Wimpfheimer. Trainer, W. Sedlacek.

Date/Race/Track	Course	Dist.	Time/Track	Odds	Wt.	1st	2nd	Str.	Fin.	Jockey	Class	Speed	Company	Field
Sep19-73^{2}Bel		7 f	1:24$\frac{2}{5}$ft	$4\frac{1}{2}$	120	$6^{4\frac{1}{2}}$	5^{4}	$3^{1\frac{1}{2}}$	$2\frac{1}{2}$	VasquezJ^{7}	Mdn	79	P'ceMissi	
Aug30-73^{1}Bel	[T]	$1\frac{1}{4}$	2:03$\frac{1}{5}$fm	$3\frac{3}{4}$	115	$2^{1\frac{1}{2}}$	$3\frac{1}{2}$	3^{nk}	$5^{1\frac{3}{4}}$	VasquezJ^{1}	Mdn	92	Harbor Pilot 105 Pistolet WaltherF.	9
Aug23-73^{1}Sar	(T)	$1\frac{1}{8}$	1:49$\frac{3}{5}$fm	6-5	▲115	6^{7}	4^{4}	3^{3}	$2^{3\frac{1}{2}}$	BaezaB^{3}	Mdn	79	Getthru 115 JacquesWho Pistolet	10
Aug11-73^{3}Sar		1 1-8	1:52$\frac{4}{5}$ft	$2\frac{1}{2}$	115	4^{5}	4^{6}	$5^{3\frac{1}{4}}$	$4^{3\frac{3}{4}}$	BaezaB^{8}	Mdn	73	Noble Indian108 Pistolet B.W.'sL'rk	8
Aug 1-73^{1}Sar	(T)	$1\frac{1}{8}$	1:48 fm	$2\frac{3}{4}$	115	8^{5}	$8^{6\frac{1}{2}}$	$6^{5\frac{1}{2}}$	4^{4}	BaezaB^{9}	Mdn	87	Remagen122 B.W.'sLark NobleIndian	11
Jly 21-73^{3}Aqu		1	1:38$\frac{4}{5}$sy	7-5	▲113	$5^{1\frac{3}{4}}$	1^{h}	$2\frac{1}{2}$	2^{1}	BaezaB^{5}	Mdn	72	R'lR's'n113 J'cq'sWho G'tl'm'n'sWord	7
Jly 7-73^{2}Aqu		1	1:36 ft	$3\frac{1}{2}$	113	$5^{5\frac{1}{2}}$	4^{6}	$3^{2\frac{1}{2}}$	2^{h}	VeneziaM^{1}	Mdn	87	Y'wH'wJ'nct'n113 J'cq'sWho Reasoric	12
Jun30-73^{2}Aqu		1	1:35$\frac{2}{5}$ft	3	111	4^{2}	2^{3}	2^{5}	2^{8}	VeneziaM^{5}	Mdn	82	PleaseDon't111 JacquesWho Pistolet	8
Jun 9-73^{1}Bel		$1\frac{1}{16}$	1:43$\frac{4}{5}$ft	3	111	4^{6}	$2\frac{1}{2}$	2^{h}	2^{4}	VeneziaM^{7}	Mdn	80	K'y to theK'gd'm112 J'sWho Br'yBeau	8
Jun 1-73^{2}Bel	(T)	$1\frac{1}{16}$	1:43$\frac{3}{5}$fm	$6\frac{3}{4}$	111	$4^{4\frac{1}{2}}$	$1\frac{1}{2}$	2^{h}	$2\frac{3}{4}$	VeneziaM^{8}	Mdn	83	Mist'rF'nt'y122 Jacq'sWho SkyK'gd'm	10

Aug 20 Sar trt 3f ft :38b

means he is a maiden, a horse who has never won a race. He finished second thirteen times and third once, compiling earnings of $26,470.

Jacques Who's record made him a legend in his own time with New York bettors and a source of utter bewilderment to his trainer, Woody Sedlacek. After the colt suffered through a dismal season in 1972, Sedlacek straightened out his physical problems, prepared him for what he thought would be a winning effort, and presumably made a bet. Jacques Who broke slowly, rallied, opened a lead in mid-stretch, and looked like a winner. But when another horse challenged him, he gave up entirely and lost by a head. He kept behaving like this throughout the year, establishing a remarkable record of futility.

Jacques Who was the classic embodiment of the type of animal known as a "sucker horse," one who seemingly refuses to win under any conditions. This behavior is usually inexplicable, but Jacques Who's bad tendencies may have been hereditary. His half sister, La Basque, was also running during the 1973 season; she finished third seven times in the first nine starts of her career but was unable or unwilling to win.

Most horseplayers seem to have a fatal weakness for sucker horses. The betting public at the New York tracks sent Jacques Who to the post at odds of 3 to 1 or less almost every time he ran, reasoning, no doubt, that he was overdue to win a race. The reasoning always proved to be wrong.

Handicappers should view with skepticism any horse who displays a chronic inability to win, no matter how strong his credentials may appear otherwise or how weak his opposition may be. In maiden races that are teeming with sucker horses, a bettor can sometimes hit extreme longshots by the process of elimination — by disregarding all the perennial losers and taking a chance on a lightly raced horse who has shown virtually nothing but has not yet proved himself to be a hopeless case.

Just as persistent losers are bad bets, horses with excellent winning percentages are often good bets. A handicapper cannot play consistent horses blindly, because their successes will eventually propel them to a level of competition where they are overmatched. But when such horses fulfill all the important handicapping requirements, they will usually find a way to win because they possess the determination and competitive spirit that animals like Jacques Who do not have.

BREEDING

Exemplary **115** B. g (1967), by Fleet Nasrullah—Sequence, by Count Fleet.
Breeder, L. Combs II. & B. Combs (Ky.). 1974 . . 9 0 2 2 $2,650
Owner, W. L. Miller. Trainer, W. L. Miller. $4,250 1973 . . 2 0 0 0 (——)

Apr23-741Kee	6 f	1:13⅕	ft	23	112	55½	55½	33½	2¾	Patt'sonG3	4000	75	Mark'sRing113	Exemplary	TaulHill	12
Apr17-741Kee	6½ f	1:18	ft	19f	112	89¾	1015	1219	1217	Valdiz'nF4	6250	71	F'rm'lCount114	Mr.Ex'c't'n'r	G'l'tFl'r	12
Mar12-746Lat	5½ f	1:09	sy	7¾	117	1111	108	1012	98¾	BeechJJr1	5000	64	Allur'gLady112	AlibiFella	Pressitback	11
Mar 5-748Lat	5½ f	1:08⅗	gd	14	117	94¼	97	86¼	86	BeechJJr2	7500	69	Bay Do Do 110	Perennial	Misty Too	10
Feb21-746Lat	5½ f	1:08	ft	9-5	▲117	31	53½	68½	614	WeilerD4	7500	64	Andy'sM'yC'p122	E'b'y'sT'in'	R'd'sB'n	6
Jan31-746Lat	1	1:42	gd	7-5	▲117	11	1h	2½	36½	WeilerD2	7500	62	HeavenlyHero113	BBsPride	Exemplary	7
Jan26-748Lat	6 f	1:15⅗	sm	8¾	117	2h	31	43	413	WeilerD4	Alw	57	Big Spade 124	Gray Page	Nadarko	7
Jan12-747Lat	6 f	1:11⅘	ft	3¼	115	3½	1h	2h	3½	BrambleC2	Alw	88	NativeSh's109	T'sBigGem	Exemplary	8
Jan 7-748Lat	6 f	1:10⅕	ft	11	112	15	11½	22	21	Ten'b'mM1	Alw	96	Maj'sticN'dle109	Exempl'ry	Mike'sPal	10

The breeding line in a horse's past performances identifies his sire, dam, and maternal grandsire. Exemplary is a son of Fleet Nasrullah, out of the dam Sequence, who was a daughter of Count Fleet. Though this information may be largely academic to horseplayers, it is the basis of the highest-stakes gambling in the racing world.

The owners and breeders who pay astronomical prices for unraced one-year-old horses on the basis of pedigree and conformation are taking what the man who runs the Saratoga Yearling Sales concedes is "a crapshooter's gamble." Exemplary was a roll of the dice that came up craps. He was sold at Saratoga in 1968 to the Ada L. Martin Stable for $280,000, which at the time was the highest price ever paid for a yearling colt. He wound up running in $4000 claiming races, unable to win.

If even the breeding experts can make mistakes of such proportions, horseplayers are fortunate that they do not have to pay much attention to bloodlines when they are handicapping. Once a horse has acquired a racing record, his pedigree matters very little. When a man encounters Exemplary in a $4000 claiming race, it doesn't matter whether he is an ill-bred plug or a horse who was once destined to be great.

There are, however, a few circumstances in which bettors may be helped by a rudimentary knowledge of breeding. In two-year-old-maiden races, bloodlines can provide clues about the ability of first-time starters. Certain sires, like the great Bold Ruler, consistently beget precocious sons and daughters. Other sires, like Sea-Bird, usually produce offspring who are late bloomers, if they bloom at all.

When a sprinter attempts to run a mile or more for the first time, his breeding may determine his capability at the longer distance. A horse would probably perform well at a route if he were a son of Gallant Man, who usually transmits stamina to his offspring. A horse would not be likely to fare so well if he were a son of Loom, whose progeny are usually gasping for breath after they have run three-quarters of a mile.

Of all the characteristics of thoroughbreds, the one that seems to be carried most often from generation to generation is the ability to run well on the grass. The following sires were all excellent turf runners who usually pass on this talent to their sons and daughters:

Assagai	Round Table
Herbager	The Axe II
Mongo	Tom Rolfe
Prince John	Vimy Ridge

When a scion of one of these horses makes his debut on the grass, I will give him serious consideration no matter how dismal his record on the dirt may be. But even this application of breeding will at best produce only a few winners for a handicapper during the course of a year. A horseplayer trying to learn the game would be advised to concentrate his study in more productive areas.

SEX

Laughing Bridge **120** **Dk. b. or b. f (1972), by Hilarious—Brookbridge, by Ambehaving.**
Breeder, N. Hellman (Fla.). **1974 7 4 1 1 $51,635**
Owner, N. Hellman. Trainer, A. A. Scotti.

Aug12-748Sar	6 f	1:10⅘ft	1-3	▲120	31½	11½	13	15	Pin'yLJr4	ScwS	8[illegible]	Ⓕ [illegible]augh'gBr'ge120	Stulc'r S'eSwing'r	6
Jly 29-748Sar	6 f	1:09⅘ft	3-5	▲117	1½	15	18	113	BaezaB1	AlwS	9[illegible]	Ⓕ [illegible]'gh'gB'dge117	M'yB'l'tine FairW'd	7
Jly 10-748Aqu	5½ f	1:02⅘ft	3½	115	21	23	26	29	BaezaB1	AlwS	9[illegible]	Ⓕ [illegible]uff'n118	L'gh'gB'dge OurD'c'gGirl	4
Jun20-744Bel	5½ f	1:04⅖ft	2¼	117	11	12	12½	14¼	BaezaB4	Alw	9[illegible]	Ⓕ [illegible]aughingBridge117	Suzest ACharm	6
Jun 3-746Bel	5½ f	1:04⅕gd	7-5	117	11½	1½	24	37	TurcotteR5	Alw	8[illegible]	Ⓕ [illegible]opernica117	ACharm L'hingBr'ge	7
Apr16-744Aqu	6 f	:58⅘ft	2-3	▲116	13	14	17	17¾	Turc'tteR3	Mdn	9[illegible]	Ⓕ [illegible]'gBr'ge116	Wh't's theR's'n B'dV'e	6
Mar22-743Hia	5 f	:59 ft	2½	▲117	1½	13	13	12½†	TurcotteR2	Mdn	94	Ⓕ [illegible]'gh'gB'ge117	M't'yM'd F'rY'gM'd	12

†Disqualified from purse money.
Aug 19 Sar 5f gd :59⅕h **Aug 10 Sar 3f ft :33⅘h** **Aug 5 Sar 5f ft :59⅖h**

The sex of a thoroughbred is indicated in the breeding line of his past performances. A male is a colt (c) until he reaches the age of five and becomes a horse (h). A castrated male of any age is a gelding (g). A female is a filly (f) until she turns five and becomes a mare (m). The symbol Ⓕ describes races limited to fillies and mares.

Most horseplayers consider this to be important handicapping information, perhaps because sexism is so deeply ingrained in the American racing scene. Female jockeys are held in low esteem; female trainers are practically nonexistent; and female horses are considered the natural inferiors of their male counterparts.

The folly of the latter notion was demonstrated during the 1974 racing season, when the crop of two-year-old fillies was vastly superior to the colts. Ruffian was one of the greatest two-year-olds in history. The fillies she was beating, Laughing Bridge and Hot N Nasty, would have been champions in a normal year.

I saw Laughing Bridge win two stakes at Saratoga during the summer of 1974 and was convinced that she could defeat males in the track's big two-year-old race, the Hopeful Stakes, if she got the chance. I relished the prospect: Laughing Bridge's odds would be generous because of the public's reluctance to bet on fillies against colts. So I sought out trainer Al Scotti and asked him if he planned to nominate Laughing Bridge for the Hopeful.

Scotti looked at me as if I were a madman. "I don't run fillies against colts," he said.

"Why?"

"They're the weaker sex," Scotti said. "A good filly can't beat a good colt."

"That just isn't true," I protested. "The reason fillies don't beat colts very often in this country is because trainers are afraid to run them. But look at Europe. Fillies beat colts all the time over there. Dahlia's a filly, and she's the best horse in Europe now. It's nothing unusual for a filly to win the Arc de Triomphe — the biggest horse race in the world."

"You're right about one thing," Scotti conceded. "Trainers don't like to run fillies against colts because they don't like to be second-guessed. But that doesn't bother me. Hell, I'm not going to get into the Hall of Fame anyway."

I pressed on: "Laughing Bridge ran six furlongs here in 1:09⁴⁄₅. The last stake for colts was run in 1:10²⁄₅. She'd kill those colts in the Hopeful."

"Well, I don't know," Scotti said. "She might open four lengths out of the gate, get to the head of the stretch, and start thinking that woman's place is in the home."

Laughing at the absurdity of his own argument, Scotti said he wanted to consult an official of the New York Racing Association before deciding on his course of action. He went to the official's office and emerged a few minutes later shaking his head. "He thought I'd be crazy to run a filly against colts," Scotti said.

Scotti did not enter Laughing Bridge in the Hopeful. Instead, he ran her against other members of the "weaker sex" in Saratoga's big filly race, the Spinaway Stakes. Ruffian blew Laughing Bridge off the track, winning by nearly thirteen lengths and running the second-fastest six furlongs in Saratoga's long history. The difference between second-place money in the Spinaway and the winner's share of the Hopeful was $29,000.

Sexism can be costly, and a horseplayer should not let himself succumb to it. He may occasionally cash a bet on a filly who has been competing against colts and is now entered against members of her own sex, because this move is often a signal that the trainer thinks he has his filly ready for a winning race. But most of the time a handicapper should pay little attention to the sex of horses. He should consider them as individuals and try to evaluate their relative merits without letting prejudice against females cloud his judgment.

THE RUNNING LINE

J. R.'s Pet **122** **B. c (1971), by Subpet—Island Fair, by Noor.**
Br., J. J. DiGrazia & P. J. DiVito (Fla.). **1974 5 4 1 0 $135,910**
Owner, W. C. Partee. Trainer, H. Tinker **1973 9 2 1 1 $15,575**

Date / Track	Dist.	Time / Cond.	Odds	Wt.	1st	2nd	Str.	Fin.	Jockey	Class	Speed	First	Second	Third	Field
Apr 6-74^{9}OP	1 1-8	1:50⅗ft	2½e▲	123	12^{17}	$6^{6½}$	$2^{2½}$	1^{h}	McH'eD^{11}	AlwS	90	J.R.'sPet 123	SilverFlorin	NicksFolly	17
Mar30-74^{8}OP	1-70	1:43⅕ft	1-2e▲	119	[illegible]	[illegible]	[illegible]	[illegible]	McHar'eD^{7}	Alw	80	J.R.'sPet119	BoldClarion	PerfectAim	7
Mar16-74^{9}OP	1-70	1:42⅘ft	4-5e▲	121	6^{6}	6^{8}	$4^{3½}$	$2^{¾}$	McH'eD^{1}	HcpO	81	PerfectAim111	J.R.'sPet121	OfficeK'g	11
Mar 2-74^{9}OP	6 f	1:11⅕ft	6-5e▲	118	$5^{3½}$	$4^{1½}$	$3^{2½}$	1^{h}	McH'eD^{2}	HcpO	89	J.R.'sPet 118	Satan'sHills	Tisab	9
Feb16-74^{8}OP	6 f	1:12⅕sl	2¾e	113	$6^{4¼}$	4^{2}	$1^{2½}$	1^{7}	McH'eD^{5}	HcpO	84	J.R.'sPet113	BigLatch	Brunate	10
Aug25-73^{8}Haw	6½ f	1:15⅘ft	8	110	$7^{8¼}$	6^{7}	4^{4}	$2^{2¼}$	BroganG^{6}	AlwS	92	Be aNative114	J.R.'sPet	TrojanBr'nze	8
Aug17-73^{8}Haw	6 f	1:10⅕ft	6¾	116	$9^{9¾}$	$8^{8½}$	$6^{5½}$	$5^{5¾}$	SibilleR^{5}	AlwS	89	Be aNative122	PrincelyPl's're	Br'sB'l	10
Aug 6-73^{3}Haw	5½ f	1:04⅘ft	9¾	115	$7^{9½}$	7^{11}	6^{5}	$4^{2½}$	SibilleR^{3}	Alw	91	Be aN'tive121	Pr'c'lyPl's're	BrassBall	7
Jly 5-73^{8}AP	5½ f	1:04 ft	8	119	6^{6}	6^{6}	$3^{5½}$	$3^{5½}$	GavidiaW^{2}	Alw	89	Beau Groton 122	Hula Chief	J.R's Pet	8

April 25 CD 5f ft 1:01h **April 21 CD 5f ft 1:01⅘h** **April 4 OP 5f ft 1:03⅖b**

The *Racing Form*'s past performances vividly describe the way a horse has run his previous races. They indicate his position in the field and the number of lengths by which he was leading or trailing at four different stages of the race.

In sprints from six to seven furlongs, the *Form* shows a horse's position at the quarter-mile mark, the half mile, the stretch, and the finish. In routes from one mile to one and three-sixteenths, it shows his position at the quarter, three-quarters, stretch, and finish.

The most recent race of J.R.'s Pet — the top line of his past performances — was at 1⅛ miles. After a quarter mile he was running twelfth, 17 lengths behind the leader.

After three-quarters of a mile he was sixth, 6½ lengths behind the leader.

As he came into the stretch he was second, 2½ lengths behind.

At the finish, he was the winner by a head. (A margin of a nose would have been abbreviated "no." A margin of a neck, "nk.")

A horse's running line and finishing position are obviously the crucial part of his past performances. Many handicappers concentrate on it, trying to find patterns and clues in the running line alone that indicate how a horse is likely to perform in his next race. The popular author Tom Ainslie says to discount the chances of an older horse whose last two running lines look like this:

$$3^{3} \quad 2^{1} \quad 2^{1/2} \quad 1^{no}$$
$$2^{1} \quad 1^{nk} \quad 1^{hd} \quad 2^{nk}$$

Ainslie reasons that the horse exerted himself so much in these head-and-head battles that he is likely to go off form the next time he runs.

Almost every handicapping book illustrates the way horses round into form by citing a pattern like this:

$$3^{3} \quad 2^{1} \quad 1^{1} \quad 1^{3}$$
$$5^{4} \quad 4^{3} \quad 4^{2} \quad 2^{1}$$
$$6^{9} \quad 6^{9} \quad 5^{8} \quad 4^{6}$$
$$10^{11} \quad 10^{12} \quad 10^{10} \quad 9^{10}$$

In the bottom line of his past performances, this horse ran a thoroughly dismal race. He came to life in his next start, finishing fourth, and continued to improve. His sharp second-place finish signaled that he was ready for a winning effort.

One of the most positive signs in a horse's running line is an unprecedented flash of speed:

$$2^{nk} \quad 3^{5} \quad 6^{8} \quad 8^{13}$$
$$9^{10} \quad 10^{12} \quad 10^{13} \quad 10^{16}$$
$$6^{7} \quad 8^{13} \quad 8^{13} \quad 8^{14}$$

This brief burst of speed for a quarter mile — after which the horse was running second by a neck — can be a harbinger of a dramatic wake-up. Horses with such records can and do win at enormous odds.

A more reliable sign of imminent improvement comes

when a horse manages to carry his speed to the stretch for the first time:

$$\begin{array}{llll} 1^{1} & 1^{1} & 2^{nk} & 6^{7} \\ 2^{nk} & 3^{4} & 5^{8} & 9^{13} \\ 2^{1/2} & 5^{7} & 8^{13} & 12^{20} \end{array}$$

An animal with a record like this is very likely to lead all the way in his next start.

Every horseplayer has his own notions of what running lines should and shouldn't look like. But whatever his preferences may be, they will cost him money if he views horses' form patterns as phenomena independent of other handicapping factors. The textbook notions about a horse rounding to form or exerting himself too much in previous efforts may be valid in theory. They would be useful if a horse's physical condition never changed, if he ran all his races against the same opposition, at the same distance, over identical tracks. But past performances never take such a conveniently pure form. A handicapper must view running lines in the context of the dozens of factors that influence a horse's performances, not as independent entities that by themselves will reveal how a horse will run in the future.

CLASS

Horses are judged by the company they keep. Most handicappers assess the relative ability of thoroughbreds by observing the quality of the opponents they have faced and beaten. Measuring class demands some fairly sophisticated techniques, which will be discussed in Chapter Ten, but before a horseplayer can use them he must first acquire a basic understanding of the different types of races.

Sharp Gary **126** **Dk. b. br br. g (1971), by Carry Back—Token of Love, by Prince John.**
Breeder, E. R. Scharps (Fla.). **1974 6 3 0 1 $53,932**
Owner, E. R. Scharps. Trainer, J. T. Diangelo. **1973 8 1 0 1 $7,230**

Date/Race/Track	Dist.	Time/Track	Odds	Wt.				Fin.	Jockey	Race	PP	Winners	Str.
Apr20-74 7Aqu	1 1-8	1:51 2/5ft	23	126	11 17	9 12	6 4 1/2	3 2 1/2	Vel'q'zJ5	ScwS	5	Flip Sal 126 Triple Crown Sharp Gary	11
Mar23-74 9FG	1 1-8	1:51 1/5ft	15	120	7 8 3/4	7 3 1/4	8 7 3/4	7 8 3/4	V'n'ziaM9	AlwS	9	Sellout 118 Buck's Bid Beau Groton	12
Mar 9-74 8GS	1 1/16	1:46 3/5m	8-5	▲121	3 3 1/2	6 7	6 12	6 21	MapleE3	HcpS	1	C'p'teH'd'che111 W'gS'th N'bleMich'l	7
Feb18-74 8Bow	1 1/16	1:46 3/5ft	7	122	5 3 1/4	3 2	3 1/2	1 1	BarreraC5	AlwS	5	SharpGary122 JollyJohu GroundBr'k'r	10
Jan26-74 8Lib	1 1/16	1:47 3/5gd	3 3/4	112	3 2	3 3	2 1/2	1 nk	BarreraC4	AlwS	8	Sh'pG'ry112 W'gS'th M'm'sD's n'Mine	9
Jan13-74 6Lib	1-70	1:43 4/5gd	2 1/2	120	2 1	1 2	1 1/2	1 no	BarreraC6	Alw	7	SharpGary120 RestlessRoad Ribopeak	8
Dec26-73 4Aqu	6 f	1:10 4/5gd	8 3/4	118	6 8 1/2	3 4 1/2	3 1	1 4	V'ziaM1	M20000	9	SharpGary118 Molt Unanim'sVerdict	7
Dec 7-73 1Aqu	6 f	1:10 2/5ft	11	118	10 12	12 14	11 16	9 15	V'iaM11	M25500	6	Ev'nSh'r's118 M'reH'p'f'l Un'm'sV'd't	12
Dec 1-73 2Aqu	6 1/2 f	1:17 4/5ft	24	122	11 9 3/4	12 12	11 14	8 18	Ven'aM12	Mdn	9	Watersc'pe122 H'v'nF'rbid S'rfC'tch'r	14
Nov24-73 1Aqu	6 f	1:11 1/5ft	12	122	8 5 1/4	10 12	10 13	10 9 1/4	VeneziaM9	Mdn	8	Nostrum122 I'llmakeitup Rube theGr't	12
Sep15-73 3Bel	6 f	1:09 3/5sy	7 3/4	121	5 9	5 8	5 14	7 18	C'd'oAJ10	Mdn	7	C'm'loN'b's121 H'r to t'eL'e Chr't'f'ro	12
Sep 8-73 3Bel	6 f	1:10 3/5ft	11	120	3 2	3 1/2	3 2	3 6 1/4	RiveraMA4	Mdn	4	St'n'w'lk120 Sp'rkl'gPl's're Sh'rpG'ry	11
Aug29-73 2Bel	6 f	1:10 3/5ft	17	119	7 5 3/4	5 3 1/2	6 5 1/4	5 6	RiveraMA2	Mdn	4	TripleCrown119 Accipiter R'ghMarch	11
Apr23-73 3Aqu	5 f	:59 3/5ft	13	117	4 2	4 3	3 4	4 7	BaezaB6	Mdn	10	WhoD'zit117 Jov'lJudge T'mp't'rSw'n	7

April 29 CD 5f ft 1:02b **April 13 Aqu 1m ft 1:38 3/5h** **April 6 Bel 5f sy 1:01 3/5b**

About two-thirds of all the races run in America are claiming races, in which each entrant is up for sale for a designated price. If a horse is entered in a $10,000 claiming race, any owner or trainer at the track can acquire him for that sum by filling out the appropriate form and depositing it in a box in the racing secretary's office fifteen minutes before post time. After the race the buyers take the horse to his new stable. If the animal drops dead on the track, the new owners are responsible for disposing of the carcass. The claiming system is a wonderfully effective way of insuring that the entrants in most races will be evenly matched. The trainer of a $15,000 horse could, of course, enter him in a $5000 race with a virtual certainty of winning. But he would have to be crazy to do it because no rational man is going to sell a horse for $10,000 less than he is worth.

If a trainer considers his horse too valuable to run in claiming races he can enter him in allowance races — a category that bewilders most beginning horseplayers. In claiming races a handicapper can evaluate class rather easily: an animal who runs for a $15,000 price tag is presumably superior to one who competes at the $8500 level. Although there can be enormous variation in the quality of allowance races, the past performances simply say "Allowance" for all of them.

Every allowance race has conditions limiting the eligibility of the entrants. The conditions may be straightforward: "For 3-year-olds who have never won two races." Or they may be terribly abstruse: "For 3-year-olds and upward which have not won $6800 twice since July 14 other than maiden or claiming."

Sometimes the conditions will suggest the relative quality of allowance fields. An event for "fillies and mares who have never won three races" will usually be superior to one for "fillies and mares who have never won two races." When the conditions are confusing, the purses will usually suggest the strength of allowance fields. Horses running for prize money of $10,000 will usually be better than those who compete for a $9000 purse. Since the past performances indicate neither the conditions nor the purses of allowance races, a handicapper should keep a set of result charts, in which this information is listed.

Stakes races, so named because owners must pay a fee to enter, offer the biggest purses and attract the best horses. Many stakes are handicaps, for which the track racing secretary assigns the weight that the horses will carry, theoretically to give each one an equal chance of winning.

Starter handicaps are an odd breed of race, open to horses who have run for a certain claiming price since a certain date. For example: "For horses who have started for a claiming price of $3500 or less since July 15." These races usually attract horses who have improved greatly since they started for the designated claiming price. A $3500 starter handicap may actually be the equivalent of a $10,000 claiming race.

Maiden races are limited to horses who have never won. Maiden-special-weight events may draw fields of highly regarded young horses; even a little Secretariat has to start his career somewhere. Maiden-claiming races, on the other hand, usually are composed of the dregs of horsedom — animals bad enough that they haven't been able to win and cheap enough that their trainer is willing to lose them. The claiming price on such races is frequently inflated. A horse who wins a $5000 maiden claimer is likely to be overmatched in bona fide $5000 competition.

These are the symbols used by the *Racing Form* to describe different classes of races:

5000	$5000 claiming race
M5000	$5000 maiden-claiming race
H5000	$5000 starter handicap
c5000	Horse was claimed for $5000
Mdn	Maiden-special-weight race
Alw	Allowance race
AlwS and ScwS	Stakes races in which weights are determined by various conditions
HcpS	Handicap stakes
HcpO	Overnight handicap: one that is not a stake

Racing's classification system is complex. But when a horseplayer understands and learns to use the class factor, he is equipped to answer the central question of handicapping: who is better than whom?

COMPANY LINE

When a handicapper becomes familiar with the horses who run at a track he can judge their class by recognizing

Gay Pierre **112** Ch c (1969), by Chateaugay—La Bonne Mouche by Bold Ruler.
Breeder Mr. & Mrs. J. W. Galbreath (Ky.). 1973 14 2 1 3 $ 31,480
Owner, Mrs. L. W. Knapp, Jr. Trainer, S. Di Mauro. 1972 16 3 3 1 $23,210

Dec18-73^{8}Aqu	1	1:35⅗ft	15	114	1^{1}	$3^{1\frac{1}{2}}$	3^{5}	$3^{8\frac{3}{4}}$	MapleE^{5}	Alw 8[illegible]	Onion117 Champ'gneCharlie GayP'rre	5
Dec 4-73^{8}Aqu	1	1:34⅘ft	2½	119	$2^{1\frac{1}{2}}$	3^{6}	3^{9}	3^{12}	BaezaB^{1}	Alw 8[illegible]	Everton II. 116 GentleSmoke G'yPierre	5
Nov23-73^{8}Aqu	1	1:35 ft	11	116	$1^{1\frac{1}{2}}$	1^{2}	$1^{1\frac{1}{2}}$	$1^{4\frac{1}{2}}$	PincayLJr^{6}	Alw 92	GayPierre116 PassenM'd Gall'ntKn've	7
Nov16-73^{8}Aqu	6 f	1:11 ft	19	111	$4^{4\frac{1}{2}}$	3^{6}	$4^{4\frac{1}{4}}$	$6^{5\frac{1}{2}}$	MapleE^{5}	Alw 82	Gov'rn'rM'x113 L'tleBigCh'f Cheriepe	7
Nov 6-73^{7}Aqu	6 f	1:10⅖ft	35	112	8^{15}	$8^{8\frac{1}{4}}$	7^{7}	$4^{4\frac{1}{2}}$	MapleE^{1}	Alw 86	Cutlass 112 Angle Light Busted	8
Oct26-73^{7}Aqu	7 f	1:22⅘ft	29	116	5^{5}	$8^{8\frac{1}{2}}$	9^{10}	$9^{5\frac{3}{4}}$	MapleE^{1}	Alw 81	Cutlass 113 Plum Bold Jazziness	11
Oct10-73^{8}Bel	6 f	1:08⅘ft	21	112	$4^{6\frac{1}{2}}$	$6^{6\frac{1}{2}}$	6^{12}	4^{11}	MapleE^{2}	Alw 88	Whatabreeze 118 My Gallant Busted	7
May30-73^{6}Bel	7 f	1:22⅗ft	10	112	1^{1}	1½	3^{2}	$4^{9\frac{1}{2}}$	Cast'daM^{6}	Alw 84	D'deeM'm'l'de118 ZuluTom C'ri'sC'se	7
Apr21-73^{5}Aqu	6 f	1:09⅗ft	37	112	1^{1}	3^{nk}	4^{1}	3^{6}	Cast'daM^{5}	Alw 89	Petrograd 112 Banderlog Gay Pierre	6

Dec 11 Bel trt 4f gd :50⅖b **Nov 22 Bel trt 3f ft :36⅖b** **Nov 12 Bel trt 4f ft :50b**

the names of the opponents they have been facing. The *Racing Form*'s past performances list the first three finishers in a race. A horseplayer trying to evaluate Gay Pierre's most recent allowance race might not know what its conditions or purse value were, but he could see that the winner of the race was Onion, who had conquered Secretariat in the Whitney Stakes earlier in the year. The second-place finisher was Champagne Charlie, also a stakes-caliber animal. Gay Pierre's loss in this company was no disgrace, and he would have a reasonable chance to win if he were entered against moderate allowance horses.

DATES OF PREVIOUS RACES

Head Table * **116** Ch. c (1969), by Prince John—Birthday Cake, by Swoon's Son.
Breeder, Happy Hill Farm (Ky.). 1973 12 9 1 2 $49,030
Owner, L. J. Miller. Trainer, E. W. King. **$22,500** 1972 11 2 2 0 $16,000

Dec 5-73^{5}Aqu	6½ f	1:16 ft	2¾	116	1^{1}	1^{2}	$1^{2\frac{1}{2}}$	1^{2}	AmyJ^{3}	16000	96	Head Table 116 Extra Hand Fota	7
Dec 1-73^{9}Aqu	6 f	1:11⅕ft	2	▲116	3^{nk}	1^{h}	$1^{2\frac{1}{2}}$	$1^{1\frac{1}{4}}$	C'oAJr^{10}	c8000	87	HeadT'ble116 WitnessSt'nd B'uReav'r	12
Oct22-73[illegible]Aqu	6 f	1:10⅘ft	6-5	▲116	$4^{1\frac{1}{2}}$	5^{2}	$4^{\frac{3}{4}}$	1^{nk}	Pin'yLJr^{2}	11000	89	HeadTable116 Messmate IrishMate	12
Sep27-73^{4}Bel	6 f	1:10⅘ft	9-5	▲120	3^{1}	$3^{1\frac{1}{2}}$	3^{nk}	$3^{1\frac{3}{4}}$	Tur'tteR^{5}	15000	87	DeltaTraffic116 BoldMerit HeadTable	10
Sep20-73^{5}Bel	6½ f	1:17⅕ft	6-5	▲116	1^{h}	1^{h}	1^{h}	1^{h}	Pin'yLJr^{5}	12500	90	HeadTable116 B'g ofWind SilentR'm'r	9
Aug 6-73^{2}Sar	6 f	1:11 ft	6-5	▲116*	$3^{1\frac{1}{2}}$	$3^{3\frac{1}{2}}$	$3^{2\frac{1}{2}}$	$3^{1\frac{1}{2}}$	WallisT^{4}	c15000	83	Long Hunt 116 Palm Pago Head Table	8
Jly 28-73^{4}Aqu	7 f	1:22⅖ft	6-5	▲124	1^{h}	1½	1^{2}	2^{h}	Bel'nteE^{5}	16000	89	NavyBlueBl'd114 H'dTable ArcticCh'f	7
Jly 13-73^{3}Aqu	6½ f	1:17⅕ft	1	▲121	2^{h}	$1^{1\frac{1}{2}}$	1½	1^{1}	Bel'nteE^{6}	18000	90	Head Table 121 Irish Mate Suspected	7
Jun30-73^{1}Aqu	7 f	1:22⅗ft	2¼	116	$1^{2\frac{1}{2}}$	$1^{2\frac{1}{2}}$	1^{4}	1^{5}	MapleE^{2}	15000	88	HeadTable116 OdieBob JestaDreamer	8
Jun11-73^{2}Bel	6 f	1:10⅕ft	7-5	▲111*	$3^{2\frac{1}{2}}$	$3^{1\frac{1}{2}}$	1^{h}	1^{2}	WallisT^{3}	15000	93	HeadTable111 RidingTune Span'hFl't	7
Jun 1-73^{8}Bel	7 f	1:23⅖ft	2¼	▲111*	$6^{5\frac{3}{4}}$	3^{4}	$1^{1\frac{1}{2}}$	1^{2}	WallisT^{8}	c11000	90	H'dT'ble111 N'vyBlueBl'd N'bleVict'ry	12

Nov 8 Bel trt 5f ft 1:02h

A generation ago, one of the most positive signs in a horse's past performances was a very recent race. Horses in that bygone era were handled cautiously and raced sparingly, and when one like Head Table was entered just four days after his previous start it was an almost certain indication that his trainer thought he was physically fit and ready to win.

Since the racing industry has expanded so greatly — with an overabundance of tracks and an undersupply of thoroughbreds — horses are asked to run much more frequently. At cheap tracks, especially, they may run every week until they are so infirm that they cannot walk to the starting gate.

So a recent race isn't as much of a guarantee of a horse's sharpness as it used to be. But it is still a generally positive sign. If a horse ran well a week ago, that evidence is fresh enough to provide a good indication of what he is likely to do today. If a horse has been idle for several months, a handicapper will have to analyze his workouts, his previous performances after layoffs, and his trainer's methods in order to assess his chances.

TRACK CONDITIONS

Riva Ridge * 127 **B. c (1969). by First Landing—Iberia, by Heliopolis.**
Breeder, Meadow Stud Inc. (Ky.). **1973 3 2 0 0 $43,632**
Owner, Meadow Stable. Trainer, L. Laurin. **1972 12 5 1 1 $395,632**

Jun17-73[9]Suf	1 1-8	1:48[illegible]	ft	2-5	▲125	1^{1}	$1^{2\frac{1}{2}}$	1^{3}	$1^{3\frac{3}{4}}$	T'rc'teR[5]	HcpS	100	RivaRidge125	CraftyKhale	Loud	7
May28-73[7]Bel	1	1:35	sy	$2\frac{1}{4}$	127	$5^{4\frac{1}{2}}$	$5^{8\frac{1}{2}}$	5^{11}	7^{17}	Tur'tteR[2]	HcpS	80	Tentam116	Key to theMint	K'g'sB'h'p	8
May12-73[3]Aqu	6 f	1:08[illegible]	ft	1-3	▲121	$2^{1\frac{1}{2}}$	1^{2}	1^{4}	1^{4}	TurcotteR[1]	Alw	99	RivaRidge121	Dr'm ofK'gs	Silv'rM'llet	5
Nov11-72[7]Lrl	Ⓣ $1\frac{1}{2}$	2:38[illegible]	sf	$4\frac{1}{4}$	120	1^{h}	5^{19}	6^{26}	6^{38}	Velas'zJ[8]	InvSp		Droll Role 127	Parnell	Steel Pulse	9
Oct28-72[7]Aqu	2	3:21[illegible]	ft	2	119	2^{2}	3^{17}	3^{20}	3^{18}	Vel'q'zJ[3]	WfaS	71	A't'b'gr'hy124	K'y to theM't	RivaR'ge	7
Sep30-72[7]Bel	$1\frac{1}{2}$	2:28[illegible]	sy	7-5	▲119	$2^{\frac{1}{2}}$	2^{h}	2^{3}	$4^{6\frac{1}{4}}$	Turc'teR[5]	WfaS	85	K'y to theMint119	S'm'rG'st	A't'b'gr'y	10
Sep20-72[7]Bel	1 1-8	1:46[illegible]	ft	2-3	▲123	1^{1}	1^{h}	$2^{\frac{1}{2}}$	2^{5}	Turc'teR[1]	HcpS	98	Canonero II. 110	Riva Ridge	Loud	5
Aug 5-72[8]Mth	1 1-8	1:50	ft	1-3	▲126	3^{3}	2^{h}	2^{3}	4^{6}	Turc'tteR[3]	InvH	84	Freetex117	King'sBishop	CloudyDawn	8
Jly 1-72[8]Hol	1 1-4	1:59[illegible]	ft	3-5	▲129	$1^{\frac{1}{2}}$	1^{h}	$1^{1\frac{1}{2}}$	1^{nk}	Tur'teR[4]	AlwS	95	Riva Ridge 129	Bicker	Finalista	8
Jun10-72[8]Bel	1 1-2	2:28	ft	3-5	▲126	$1^{1\frac{1}{2}}$	1^{3}	1^{7}	1^{7}	Turc'teR[1]	ScwS	93	RivaRidge126	Ruritania	CloudyDawn	10
May20-72[8]Pim	$1\frac{3}{16}$	1:55[illegible]	sy	[illegible]-3	▲126	4^{3}	2^{2}	2^{4}	4^{6}	Tur'tteR[2]	ScwS	86	BeeBeeBee126	NoLeH'e	K'y to theM't	7
May 6-72[9]CD	1 1-4	2:01[illegible]	ft	[illegible]-2	▲126	$1^{\frac{1}{2}}$	$1^{1\frac{1}{2}}$	1^{3}	$1^{3\frac{1}{4}}$	Tur'teR[9]	ScwS	91	RivaRidge126	NoLeHace	H'ldY'rPeace	16

July 2 Bel 3f ft :33⅘h **June 28 Bel tc 6f fm 1:13h** **June 24 Bel 6f ft 1:13b**

The condition of tracks can take a variety of forms, but the *Racing Form*'s past performances manage to describe most of them.

Fast tracks (fst) are dry and hard.

Sloppy tracks (sly) have puddles of water on the surface but still may be firm on the bottom.

Good tracks (gd) are the intermediate stage between fast and sloppy, when rain is falling or the racing strip is drying out.

Muddy (my), slow (sl), and heavy (hy) describe conditions when moisture has accumulated and permeated the racing surface, making it progressively more deep, tiring, and messy.

Firm (fm) and soft (sf) describe conditions of a grass course.

Certain types of horses usually do well on certain types of tracks. Front runners win frequently in the slop, because horses who try to come from behind are hindered by mud kicked in their faces. Stretch runners usually have an advantage on deep, tiring tracks. But it is dangerous to generalize too much about the effects of track conditions on horses because individual racetracks differ so much. A sloppy track at Aqueduct is nothing like a sloppy track at Garden State. (The influence of racing surfaces will be discussed in detail in Chapter Four.)

The most important consideration on an off track is simply whether a horse has demonstrated either a fondness or a dislike for running in mud. Riva Ridge was one of the best horses in America from 1971 to 1973 but he never won in the mud. As his past performances show, he was often humiliated on off tracks. Riva Ridge had a stablemate with the opposite tendencies. Spanish Riddle was just a decent allowance-class horse under most conditions, but if a few drops of rain fell on a track there wasn't a sprinter in America who could beat him.

As important as track conditions may be for horses like Riva Ridge and Spanish Riddle, many handicappers pay too much attention to this factor. When they go to the track on rainy days they abandon their normal procedures and bet automatically on mudders or, worse yet, on absurd longshots, assuming that the results will be wild and unpredictable. This is usually a costly mistake. The fundamentals of handicapping do not become any less important in the mud.

TURF RACES

Court Road **116** **Dk. b. or br. h (1966), by Day Court—One Lane, by Prince John.**
Breeder, Elmendorf Farm (Ky.). **1972 4 1 0 0 $5,400**
Owner, Elmendorf. Trainer, V. J. Wickerson. **$20.000** **1971 10 3 1 1 $33,450**

Date/Race		Dist.	Time	Track	Odds	Wt.					Jockey	Class	Speed	First	Second	Third	Starters
Aug 9-72 ^{8}Sa	Ⓣ	1 1/16	1:40	fm	6½	112	8^{9}	8^{8}	$5^{6½}$	$5^{8½}$	C'pedesR^{8}	40000	88	Nevado 116	Shadow Brook	Jogging	10
Aug 1-72 ^{2}Sa	Ⓣ	1 3/16	1:53⅕	hd	3½	116	$4^{2½}$	$2^{1½}$	1^{3}	1^{4}	B'zarC^{3}	17000	116	Court Road 116	Tradesman	Delver	8
Jly 15-72 ^{9}Aqu		1	1:35⅖	ft	4	115	$4^{5½}$	$4^{6½}$	7^{11}	7^{12}	Bal'zarC^{5}	30000	78	Proj'ctive120	DanP'tch	NavyL'uten'nt	7
Jly 6-72 ^{7}Aqu		7 f	1:21⅗	ft	31	112	1^{h}	2^{h}	$5^{5½}$	$5^{6¼}$	BaltazarC^{6}	Alw	87	Beaukins 112	Accohick	Swift Passage	7
May 8-71 ^{6}Hol	Ⓣ	1 3/8	2:13⅖	fm	7-5	▲120	$3^{6½}$	1^{1}	1^{3}	$1^{3¾}$	Pin'yJr^{5}	A20000	91	CourtRoad120	GrayPower	Twogie	8
Apr27-71 ^{6}Hol	Ⓣ	1 1/16	1:42⅕	fm	2	114	4^{3}	3^{1}	$2^{½}$	1^{2}	Pin'yLJr^{3}	20000	88	CourtRoad114	GreatDescretion	Secolo	6
Apr16-71 ^{8}Hol	Ⓣ	1 1/16	1:42	fm	3¾	▲122	5^{10}	$8^{6¼}$	$9^{7¾}$	8^{6}	Pin'yLJr^{3}	AlwS	83	TheField122	TripleAxe	Aggressively	10
Apr 8-71 ^{8}SA	Ⓣ	1½	2:25⅕	fm	3¾	118	5^{5}	$5^{2½}$	5^{5}	$4^{4½}$	Pin'yLJr^{3}	HcpS	84	Pleas'ntH'rbour115	B'titu	Azinc'rt II.	9
Mar20-71 ^{5}SA	Ⓣ	1¼	2:02⅖	fm	4-5	▲114	$4^{3½}$	2^{h}	$1^{½}$	1^{1}	PincayLJr^{6}	Alw		Court Road 114	Born Wild	Makor	6
Mar13-71 ^{8}SA		1 1-4	2:03	sl	19	109	$7^{6½}$	9^{15}	9^{20}	9^{25}	D'ss'uLJ^{4}	HcpS	58	Ack Ack 130	Cougar II.	The Field	10

July 28 Aqu 5f ft 1:02h **June 30 Aqu 1m sy :48b** **June 25 Aqu 5f sy 1:01⅕h**

Racing on the grass — indicated in the past performances by the symbol Ⓣ — is a game completely different from racing on the dirt. Horses who couldn't win claiming events on the main track can become turf champions. Horses who tire badly in sprints on the main track may become capable distance runners on the grass. And, conversely, many horses with championship credentials on dirt have been utter flops when they have attempted to negotiate a turf course.

A horseplayer trying to pick the winner of a turf race should be guided by a four-word precept: class on the grass. He should almost always prefer horses who have proved their turf ability and ignore, for the most part, their dirt form. A handicapper analyzing the record of Court Road at Saratoga on August 1, 1972, would have observed that the horse had been a very capable turf runner the year before.

He had two races on the main track in 1972 in which he showed some slight signs of life but was beaten soundly. Then he was entered in his proper milieu. The year-old evidence about Court Road's grass-running ability would have made him an excellent wager. He won by four lengths, set a track record, and paid $9.20.

Only in races where no horse has shown any particular aptitude for grass running should a handicapper consider betting an entrant who is making his debut on the turf. Even in these cases a horse's dirt form is not as important as other factors. Certain sires produce offspring who like the turf and certain trainers, such as Mac Miller, T. J. Kelly and Allen Jerkens, are especially adept at developing turf specialists. Workouts on the grass may often suggest that a horse is ready to win in his first try over the different terrain. But none of these indications is unfailingly reliable, and a handicapper should not bet serious money on a horse unless he has already run on the grass and liked it.

DISTANCE

Mio Host **107** **B. g (1970) by Gallant Host—Mia Sorella, by Mr. Hemisphere.**
Br., May Stock Farm & E. L. May (Cal.). **1974 9 3 1 0 $8,850**
Owner, S. Galt. Trainer, P. Briones. **$8.500** **1973 21 3 2 1 $8,090**

Apr19-74 5Pim	6 f	:12⅕ft	23	114	10^{11}	9^{15}	8^{12}	8^{11}	Marq'zR3	10500	74	Erezev114	CharlieJr.	BigDevil	10
Mar30-74 9GS	$1\frac{1}{16}$	:48⅖sy	3	112	$3^{2\frac{1}{2}}$	3^{6}	4^{7}	5^{11}	FantiniP8	H3500	52	Watawopper114	PositivePete	Built	8
Mar19-74 6Pim	6 f	:12⅕ft	24	114	$7^{6\frac{1}{4}}$	$7^{7\frac{1}{4}}$	$5^{6\frac{3}{4}}$	2^{5}	McC'onG1	8500	80	RoyalEmperor114	MioHost	OsageJac	9
Feb23-74 9Bow	1 1-4	:08 ft	8	109	$1^{\frac{1}{2}}$	3^{4}	5^{8}	5^{14}	WalshE2	H4000	69	Cont'tedCl'wn110	EightEasy	Riv'rAb'd	8
Feb13-74 7Bow	7 f	:25⅗ft	2¼	114	$10^{6\frac{3}{4}}$	$8^{6\frac{1}{4}}$	$3^{\frac{1}{2}}$	$1^{2\frac{1}{4}}$	HawleyS1	6500	77	MioHost114	River Idol	NoblePromise	11
Feb 2-74 9Bow	$1\frac{1}{16}$	:48 ft	9	108	1^{h}	2^{h}	2^{h}	5^{4}	Jim'ezC3	H4000	64	Faber'sChoice111	Riv'rAbroad	Magoni	9
Jan22-74 3Bow	$1\frac{1}{16}$	:47⅗m	3¼	114	2^{h}	1^{h}	4^{2}	$6^{7\frac{1}{4}}$	Fel'noBM5	6500	63	DaintyDick114	Fo'c'sleFiend	Riverld'l	9
Jan12-74 1Bow	7 f	:26⅘m	2¼	119	$2^{\frac{1}{2}}$	1^{3}	1^{8}	1^{10}	GinoL5	c3000	71	MioH'st119	Ch'rgeR't	H'ckl'b'ryFr'nd	10

How would a handicapper evaluate the chances of Mio Host in a $7500 claiming race? It would depend. Mio Host would be viewed differently if he were entered at six furlongs, seven furlongs, $1\frac{1}{16}$ miles, or $1\frac{1}{4}$ miles. (A furlong is an eighth of a mile.) Like most horses, Mio Host's capabilities vary drastically according to the distance he runs.

If today's race were at six furlongs, a handicapper would note that Mio Host had tried the distance twice without success. He broke slowly and rallied insufficiently. He wasn't completely ill-suited at six furlongs, but he would have to face cheaper opposition to win at the distance.

A seven-furlong race would suit Mio Host perfectly, giving him an extra eighth of a mile in which to continue his rally. He won impressively in both of his starts at the distance.

One might suppose, because of his stretch-running style, that Mio Host would like 1¹⁄₁₆ miles even better than seven furlongs. But he doesn't. He never managed to finish in the money at a route. On March 30, when he was obviously in form, he showed brief speed and tired at 1¹⁄₁₆ miles. He would obviously have to be dropped in class to win at this distance.

In a demanding mile-and-a-quarter race, Mio Host could be eliminated at almost any class level. He tried to go that far only once, on February 23, and after taking the early lead he collapsed and suffered the worst defeat in his past performances.

A handicapper should always try to determine whether a horse has been entered at an appropriate distance. The best evidence of his suitability is a victory, or at least a strong performance, at the distance in the past. If a horse has previously tried today's distance and failed when he was in condition and entered at the right class level, he can usually be disregarded.

When a horse is trying a new distance — particularly in the case of a sprinter attempting to go a route for the first time — a handicapper should view him as a risky proposition and realize that his running style in sprints may be very deceptive. Horses who finish powerfully in short races, like

Mio Host, will often show early speed and tire at a longer distance. And some rare horses who habitually tire in sprints will improve when they run farther because they can better cope with the slower, less demanding pace of route races. Generally, however, the sprinters most likely to succeed in routes are the ones who have shown that they can lay within striking distance of the leader and finish strongly, with a running line like this:

3^3 3^2 2^{nk} 1^3

Routers entered in sprints can usually be eliminated, unless they have shown high speed in the early stages of their races, or unless their records show that they have been able to win sprints in the past.

A trainer will sometimes purposely enter his horse at an inappropriate distance in order to prepare him for a future race. The trainer of a faint-hearted sprinter might put him in a route race to build his stamina. The trainer of a plodding router might enter him in a sprint to sharpen his speed. If horses have been prepped in this way, they may be excellent bets when they are entered again at the right distance.

TIME AND SPEED RATINGS

Triple Crown * **126** **Ch. c (1971), by Hawaii—Belle Jeep, by War Jeep.**
Breeder, T. Gentry (Ky.).
Owner, S. Lehrmann. Trainer, W. P. King.

1974	7	2	3	1	$110,132
1973	6	2	1	0	$18,742

Date/Track	Dist.	Time	Odds	Wt.					Jockey	Class	Speed	Company	
Apr20-74^{7}Aqu	1 1-8	1:51⅖	9-5	▲126	1^4	1^2	2½	$2^{1\frac{1}{4}}$	BaezaB^{10}	Scw	77	Flip Sal 126 Triple Crown Sharp Gary	11
Mar31-74^{8}SA	1 1-8	1:48⅘	3	120	4^1	$5^{2\frac{1}{2}}$	$3^{1\frac{1}{2}}$	$6^{8\frac{1}{2}}$	BaezaB^7	Spw	79	Destroyer 120 Aloha Mood Agitate	8
Mar17-74^{8}SA	1 1/16	1:42⅖	4¼	124	$5^{2\frac{1}{2}}$	$6^{2\frac{3}{4}}$	$4^{3\frac{1}{2}}$	$3^{\frac{3}{4}}$	BaezaB^7	Hcp	89	AlohaM'd118 MoneyLender TripleCr'n	10
Mar 3-74^{8}SA	[illegible]	1:38⅘	5	122	2½	2^h	1^h	1no	BaezaB^2	Alw	75	TripleCrown122 AlohaMd M'n'yL'nd'r	9
Feb10-74^{8}SA	7	1:22⅗	3½	114	3^1	$4^{2\frac{1}{2}}$	4^1	1no	BaezaB^6	Alw	90	TripleCrown114 El Esp'leto Destroy'r	8
Jan23-74^{8}SA	6	1:11⅖	2	114	2½	3½	3^{nk}	2no	BaezaB^3	Alw	84	Mon'yLend'r122 TripleCr'n ElEspan'o	6
Jan 9-74^{8}SA	6½	1:20⅖	1	▲120	3½	$1^{2\frac{1}{2}}$	1½	2^h	BaezaB^9	Alw	71	GoldStand'd 120 TripleCr'n FastP'ppa	10
Dec31-73^{5}SA	6	1:10⅕	1	▲114	5^3	$4^{2\frac{1}{2}}$	2^h	2½	BaezaB^2	Alw	89	MerryFellow117 TripleCrown ElArish	7
Nov17-73^{8}CD	[illegible]	1:36⅘	6¼	116	$5^{1\frac{3}{4}}$	$2^{1\frac{1}{2}}$	$4^{5\frac{1}{2}}$	8^{18}	BaezaB^1	Alw	67	C'nonade119 S'tan'sHills D'tBeL'eJim	15
Oct13-73^{8}Bel	[illegible]	1:36	10	122	1½	1^h	3^{nk}	$4^{1\frac{1}{4}}$	BaezaB^3	Scw	87	Pr't'g'nist122 Pr'ce ofR'son C'nn'nade	10
Sep29-73^{4}Bel	6	1:10⅖	9¾	120	$4^{1\frac{1}{2}}$	2½	1^4	1^5	BaezaB^1	Alw	91	TripleCrown120 Kurt theN'tive Toth'd	10
Sep11-73^{4}Bel	7	1:24	9-5	▲121	1^h	1^h	3^3	$7^{9\frac{3}{4}}$	BaezaB^8	Alw	72	Hosiery 119 Flip Sal Cannonade	11
Aug29-73^{2}Bel	6	1:10⅗	13	119	2^h	2^h	1½	$1^{1\frac{1}{2}}$	BaezaB^7	Md	90	TripleCrown119 Accipiter R'ghMarch	11

May 2 CD 4f [illegible]h   **April 29 CD 6f ft 1:14h**   **April 26 Bel 6f ft 1:11⅘h**

Time is the most precise measurement of a horse's ability. Triple Crown's last race was run in $1:51\frac{2}{5}$ for a mile and one-eighth. This is the winner's time; Triple Crown was beaten by a length and a quarter. According to a universally accepted rule of thumb, one length equals one-fifth of a second. So Triple Crown's actual time was $1:51\frac{3}{5}$.

If another horse had run a mile and an eighth in 1:52 on the same day and was now meeting Triple Crown, the advocates of speed handicapping would religiously bet on Triple Crown, concluding that he was two-fifths of a second, or two lengths, superior to his rival. Unfortunately, times can seldom be so easily compared, because horses run at many different distances, over racing surfaces that are constantly changing.

To help its readers resolve these difficulties, the *Racing Form* computes a numerical speed rating for each of a horse's previous races. Its Eastern Edition also offers a track variant that purportedly indicates the speed of the racing surface over which he was running. But the *Form*'s figures are too crude for serious handicapping. A sophisticated and accurate method of making speed figures will be discussed, in excruciating detail, in Chapter Seven.

JOCKEYS

Smiling Jacqueline **120** **B. m (1969), by Hilarious—Fulfiliole, by Beau Gar.**
Breeder, Hobeau Farm, Inc. (Fla.). **1974 6 1 0 2 $8,650**
Owner, Green Mill Farm. Trainer, T. J. Gullo. **$25,000** **1973 16 1 0 2 $10,075**

Date/Track	Dist	Time	Cond	Odds	Wt				Fin	Jockey	Class	SR	Company line	Field
Mar12-74 6Aqu	1 1-8	1:52	ft	$2\frac{1}{2}$	112	2^6	2^1	1^5	$1^{8\frac{1}{2}}$	Vel'sq'zJ2	5000	75	Ⓕ Smil'gJ'q'line112 Hi-Mimi L'tleT'e	5
Mar 5-74 8Aqu	1	$1:35\frac{3}{5}$	ft	22	107*	7^9	7^{17}	6^{16}	6^{12}	SkinnerK5	Alw	77	Ⓕ Kl'pto110 Midni'':M'd'g'l Gr't'nM's	7
Feb20-74 8GP	Ⓣ a$1\frac{1}{16}$	$1:44\frac{3}{5}$	fm	$6\frac{3}{4}$	112	7^8	$8^{9\frac{1}{2}}$	$6^{9\frac{1}{2}}$	5^5	Velasq Z3	Alw	86	Ⓕ Instinctively114 TappedIn W't'rnld'l	8
Feb12-74 5GP	Ⓣ a$1\frac{1}{16}$	1:45	fm	$2\frac{3}{4}$	114	5^{12}	6^{11}	$6^{7\frac{1}{2}}$	$3^{1\frac{3}{4}}$	Vel'q'zJ4	35000	87	Ⓕ W'st'nld'l 116 C't'sV. Smil'gJ'qu'l'e	7
Feb 6-74 8GP	Ⓣ a1	$1:38\frac{1}{5}$	fm	$8\frac{1}{2}$	114	$8^{9\frac{1}{2}}$	8^{13}	8^{15}	8^{13}	TurcotteR2	Alw	77	Ⓕ Sh'rw't'r113 Inst'ctiv'ly D'gt'thV'l't	8
Jan23-74 8GP	Ⓣ a1	$1:41\frac{1}{5}$	fm	31	112	9^{14}	8^8	$3^{6\frac{1}{2}}$	3^3	C'rd'roAJr1	Alw	72	Ⓕ D'eCr'kL'y122 N'th ofV's Smil'gJ'e	9
Nov21-73 7Aqu	1	$1:36\frac{1}{5}$	ft	$9\frac{1}{2}$	115	7^7	8^{13}	8^{15}	7^9	BaezaB5	Alw	77	Ⓕ Ev'yEv'g112 M'ke anAt't L'r'neEdna	8
Nov 6-73 5Aqu	7 f	$1:24\frac{2}{5}$	ft	17	109‡	8^{13}	$8^{7\frac{1}{4}}$	5^{10}	$3^{5\frac{1}{4}}$	Skinn'rK3	30000	74	Ⓕ Jill theQ'n118 M'sNewb'y S'l'gJ'q'e	8

Feb 2 Hia 5f ft 1:00h

When his horse wins a race, a bettor will sing the praises of his jockey, citing him as a master strategist and a paragon of virtue. Half an hour later, the same horseplayer is likely to be denouncing the same jockey as a blind, incompetent little thief. The reactions are understandable — it is easier to pour out one's emotions on a human being than on a dumb animal — but they are often misdirected.

Jockeys usually win races because they are riding the best horses. Not even the giants in the history of the profession, men like Eddie Arcaro and Bill Shoemaker, could magically transform a horse's capabilities. If a great rider can make a horse improve by as much as a length over his performance in the hands of an average jockey, that is a notable achievement.

Yet horseplayers are so obsessed by jockeys that they often bet on them blindly. If the popular Sandy Hawley is riding a legitimate 4-to-1 shot in Maryland or Canada, that horse is likely to go to the post at odds of 2 to 1 or less. Because the superior jockeys attract an enthusiastic following and the odds on their mounts are so depressed, a handicapper will usually get a better value for his money by playing horses that are ridden by average, competent, unpopular jockeys.

I try not to let my handicapping of a race be influenced by any prejudices about riders — not even ones who have lost money for me in the past — unless I am convinced that certain jockeys are hopelessly inept. Every track has a few riders who can be counted on to be left at the post, blocked or boxed, or to commit some similar atrocity whenever they are aboard a horse who has a chance to win. There is no conceivable circumstance, for example, in which I would bet so much as $2 on a horse ridden by Kathy Kusner.

When a horse has been ridden in previous races by an incompetent, inexperienced, or unfashionable jockey and then gets the services of a top jockey, he deserves consideration — as Smiling Jacqueline did on March 12. She had been ridden in her previous start by Kenny Skinner, a little-known apprentice, and now was being ridden by the great Jorge Velasquez. Even though Velasquez couldn't be expected to improve upon Skinner's performance by 10 or 15 lengths, the rider switch was an important signal of the trainer's intentions. When a trainer employs Kenny Skinner, he is probably not taking his best shot to win a race. When he uses Jorge Velasquez, he probably is.

WEIGHT

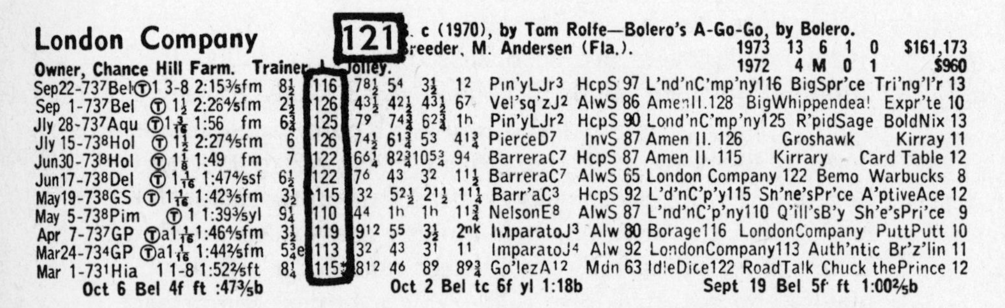

London Company **121** **. c (1970), by Tom Rolfe—Bolero's A-Go-Go, by Bolero.**
Breeder, M. Andersen (Fla.). 1973 13 6 1 0 $161,173
Owner, Chance Hill Farm. Trainer ... Jolley. 1972 4 M 0 1 $960

Race	Dist / Time / Cond	Odds	Wt	1st	2nd	Str	Fin	Jockey	Class	Sp	First three	Field
Sep22-73^{7}Bel Ⓣ	1 3-8 2:15⅗ fm	8½	116	$7^{8\frac{1}{2}}$	5^{4}	$3^{\frac{1}{2}}$	1^{2}	Pin'yLJr^{3}	HcpS	97	L'nd'nC'mp'ny116 BigSpr'ce Tri'ng'l'r	13
Sep 1-73^{7}Bel Ⓣ	1½ 2:26⅘ fm	2½	126	$4^{3\frac{1}{2}}$	$4^{2\frac{1}{2}}$	$4^{3\frac{1}{2}}$	6^{7}	Vel'sq'zJ^{2}	AlwS	86	AmenII.128 BigWhippendeal Expr'te	10
Jly 28-73^{7}Aqu Ⓣ	1 3/16 1:56 fm	6¾	125	7^{9}	$7^{4\frac{3}{4}}$	$6^{2\frac{3}{4}}$	1^{h}	Pin'yLJr^{2}	HcpS	90	Lond'nC'mp'ny125 R'pidSage BoldNix	13
Jly 15-73^{8}Hol Ⓣ	1½ 2:27⅘ fm	6	126	$7^{4\frac{1}{2}}$	$6^{1\frac{3}{4}}$	5^{3}	$4^{1\frac{3}{4}}$	PierceD^{7}	InvS	87	Amen II. 126 Groshawk Kirray	11
Jun30-73^{8}Hol Ⓣ	1⅛ 1:49 fm	7	122	$6^{6\frac{1}{4}}$	$8^{2\frac{3}{4}}$	$10^{5\frac{3}{4}}$	9^{4}	BarreraC^{7}	HcpS	87	Amen II. 115 Kirrary Card Table	12
Jun17-73^{8}Del Ⓣ	1 1/16 1:47⅘ sf	6½	122	7^{6}	4^{3}	3^{2}	$1^{1\frac{1}{2}}$	BarreraC^{7}	AlwS	65	London Company 122 Bemo Warbucks	8
May19-73^{8}GS Ⓣ	1 1/16 1:42⅗ fm	3½	115	3^{2}	$5^{2\frac{1}{2}}$	$2^{1\frac{1}{2}}$	$1^{1\frac{1}{4}}$	Barr'aC^{3}	HcpS	92	L'd'nC'p'y115 Sh'ne'sPr'ce A'ptiveAce	12
May 5-73^{8}Pim Ⓣ	1 1:39⅗ yl	9¼	110	4^{4}	1^{h}	1^{h}	$1^{1\frac{3}{4}}$	NelsonE^{8}	AlwS	87	L'nd'nC'p'ny110 Q'ill'sB'y Sh'e'sPri'ce	9
Apr 7-73^{7}GP Ⓣ	a1 1/16 1:46⅘ fm	3½	119	9^{12}	5^{5}	$3^{\frac{1}{2}}$	2^{nk}	ImparatoJ^{3}	Alw	80	Borage116 LondonCompany PuttPutt	10
Mar24-73^{4}GP Ⓣ	a1 1/16 1:44⅖ fm	5¾e	113	3^{2}	4^{3}	3^{1}	1^{1}	ImparatoJ^{4}	Alw	92	LondonCompany113 Auth'ntic Br'z'lin	11
Mar 1-73^{1}Hia	1 1-8 1:52⅖ ft	8¼	115*	8^{12}	4^{6}	8^{9}	$8^{9\frac{3}{4}}$	Go'lezA^{12}	Mdn	63	IdleDice122 RoadTalk Chuck thePrince	12

Oct 6 Bel 4f ft :47⅗b **Oct 2 Bel tc 6f yl 1:18b** **Sept 19 Bel 5f ft 1:00⅖b**

Every handicapper, and every handicapping book, has a theory about weight: Never bet a horse carrying more weight than he did in his last start. Five pounds of added weight slow a horse by one-fifth of a second. Weight is important in routes but not in sprints. The list is endless. It is also worthless.

Weight is a factor that seems to defy generalizations because every individual horse is affected by it differently. For most horses the effect of an increase in weight from 112 to 119 pounds would be imperceptible. In the case of the few who would be hampered by the extra burden, it is impossible to factor out weight from the countless other influences that determine horses' performances so that its effect can be measured.

I will discount a horse's chances when he is carrying very high weight only if his past performances unequivocally suggest that he cannot win with the burden he is now assigned. Such situations arise in handicaps, when good horses are steadily loaded with more weight until they are unable to win. The past performances of London Company indicate that his breaking point is 126 pounds, and I would not bet him carrying that weight.

I have found weight to be important in one other type of situation. When a three-year-old is asked to carry the top weight in a race against older horses, he will not win. Even if the weights by themselves are insignificant — with the younger horse carrying 113 and his elders 112 — the disparity will prevent the three-year-old from winning. The reasons for this phenomenon are utterly inexplicable to me.

WORKOUTS

Secretariat ✕ **126** **Ch. c (1970), by Bold Ruler—Somethingroyal, by Princequillo.**
Breeder, Meadow Stud, Inc. (Va.). 1973.. 3 2 0 1 $63,768
Owner, Meadow Stable. Trainer, L. Laurin. 1972.. 9 7 1 0 $456,404

Date/Track	Dist	Time/Cond	Odds	Wt				Fin	Jockey	Class	Speed	Comment			Field
Apr21-73 7Aqu	1 1-8	1:49⅘ft	1-3e	▴126	7 5½	5 5½	4 5½	3 4	T'rc'teR6	ScwS	83	Angle Light 126	Sham	Secretariat	8
Apr 7-73 7Aqu	1	1:33⅖ft	1-10	▴126	3 1	1 2	1 ½	1 3	T'rc'teR3	AlwS	100	Secret'riat126	Ch'mp'gneCh'rlie	Flush	6
Mar17-73 7Aqu	7 f	1:23⅕sy	1-5	▴126	5 6	5 3	1 h	1 4½	Tur'tteR4	AlwS	85	Sec'tar't126	Ch'pagneCh'lie	Impec'n's	6
Nov18-72 8GS	1 1/16	1:44⅖ft	1-10e	▴122	6 9½	3 3	1 1½	1 3½	Tur'teR6	ScwS	83	Secretariat122	AngleLight	StepNicely	6
Oct28-72 7Lrl	1 1/16	1:42⅘sy	1-10e	▴122	6 14	5 3	1 5	1 8	T'rc'teR5	ScwS	99	Secretar't122	St'p t'eM'sic	AngleL'ht	6
Oct14-72 7Bel	1	1:35 ft	2-3e	▴122	11 13	5 3½	1 ½	1 2†	Tur'teR4	ScwS	97	Secr'tar't122	St'p theM'sic	St'pNic'ly	12
†Disqualified and placed second.															
Sep16-72 7Bel	6½ f	1:16⅖ft	1-5	▴122	6 5½	5 3½	1 2	1 1¾	Turc'teR4	ScwS	98	S'cr't'r't122	St'p t'eMusic	Sw'tC'rier	7
Aug26-72 7Sar	6½ f	1:16⅕ft	1-3	▴121	9 6½	1 h	1 4	1 5	Turc'teR8	SpwS	97	Secretariat121	Fl't toGl'y	St'p theM'c	9
Aug16-72 7Sar	6 f	1:10 ft	3-2	121	5 4	4 2	1 ½	1 3	Turc'teR2	SpwS	96	Secr't'riat121	L'da'sCh'f	N'thst'rD'c'r	5
Jly 31-72 4Sar	6 f	1:10⅘ft	2-5	▴118	7 3¾	3 ½	1 h	1 1½	TurcotteR4	Alw	92	Secretariat 118	Russ Miron	Joe Iz	7
Jly 15-72 4Aqu	6 f	1:10⅗ft	6-5	▴113*	6 6½	4 3	1 ½	1 6	Felic'noP8	Mdn	90	Secret'riat113	M'sterAch'v'r	BetOn It	11
Jly [illegible]	[illegible]	[illegible]	3	▴113*107	[illegible]	[illegible]	[illegible]	[illegible]	[illegible]	Mdn	87	Herbull [illegible]	[illegible]	[illegible]'y'l	12

May 2 CD 5f sy :58⅗h **April 27 CD 6f sy 1:12⅗h** **April 17 Bel 1m ft 1:42⅖b**

Secretariat went into the 1973 Wood Memorial Stakes at Aqueduct with a streak of ten straight victories and the reputation of a budding superhorse. He came out of it with his credentials tarnished and his chances to win the Kentucky Derby two weeks later in serious doubt. His loss in the Wood Memorial appeared to be a shocking upset, but an astute student of workouts might have foreseen it.

Secretariat always trained like the champion he was. Before his first two victories of the 1973 season he recorded workouts that left the clockers rubbing their eyes in disbelief — three furlongs in 32$\frac{3}{5}$ seconds, and a mile in 1:35$\frac{2}{5}$. But in the two-week period before the Wood Memorial something had changed. Secretariat went a half mile in 49 seconds and a mile in 1:42$\frac{2}{5}$ — times that would have been unimpressive for a claiming horse. This was a tipoff that something was wrong with Secretariat, and he verified that suspicion by running the dullest race of his life.

Nobody knew whether Secretariat would run another mediocre race in the Kentucky Derby or would revert to his best form. His workouts again provided a clue. Before the Derby he zipped six furlongs in 1:12$\frac{3}{5}$ and five furlongs in :58$\frac{3}{5}$, both over sloppy tracks. He confirmed the impression that he was the old Secretariat again by winning the fastest Derby in history.

A horse's condition will often change from race to race, causing many handicappers to moan about his inconsistency or the unpredictability of the sport. But good handicappers can often foresee reversals of form by reading the workout line carefully.

While there are some morning glories who invariably train fast and run poorly in actual competition, most horses who work well are signaling their readiness to run a good race. These workout times would be considered good for a top-class horse:

Three furlongs in :35.
Four furlongs in :47.
Five furlongs in 1:00.

Six furlongs in 1:13.
Seven furlongs in 1:26.
One mile in 1:39.

Workouts slower than these might still be very impressive if the track were dull, if the horse were cheap, if he worked from the gate (indicated in the *Form* by the letter g) instead of from a running start, or if he were not urged by his exercise rider. The letter *b* after a horse's workout time indicates that he was breezing, that he was under heavy restraint. *H* means handily: he was being moderately urged by his rider.

Good workouts are especially meaningful if a horse shows something in them that he hasn't shown in his races. When a fast-breaking sprinter works four furlongs in 47 seconds, that does not reveal anything new about his capabilities. But if he works a mile in 1:38, displaying uncharacteristic stamina, that may be a tipoff that his condition is improving sharply.

The best judges of workouts are the people who see them: the clockers. With the possible exception of politicians and television repairmen, no occupation group has a greater reputation for larceny. When a horse turns in a significant, fast workout, the clockers may keep it as their own private information and tell the *Racing Form* that he worked five furlongs in an indifferent 1:03. Horseplayers in Maryland are so justifiably suspicious that the clockers lack integrity that they pay close attention to any horse who has been idle for several months and shows no workouts in his past performances. They figure that the horse must have been training somewhere and that sinister forces are making an effort to conceal his workout information.

At the major league tracks in New York, Florida, and

BELMONT PARK (Track Fast)

3 FURLONGS							
		Path to Peace	:37⅗b	Java Moon	:50⅖b	Fleetferd	1:04⅖b
Arum Lily	:38 b	**PROD**	**:34⅖h**	Lead Line	:48 h	First Slice	:59⅖h
Boston Peggy	:37 bg	Ravage	:35⅘bg	Mush Mouse	:47⅘hg	High Steel	1:00 h
Blue Cross	:36⅖h	Self Importance	:38 bg	Our Dancing Girl	:47⅘h	Halo	1:01⅗b
Blue Bush	:36⅖b	Set the Style	:37 b	Old Vic	:50⅖b	Idle Answer	:59⅗h
Continuation	:37 b	Sylvan Place	:38 b	On His On	:48 h	Imperator	1:01⅕b
Drollery	:35 h	Summ'rtime Pr'mise	:35⅘h	Posterity	:50⅖b	Left End	1:02⅕h
Easter Chorus	:36⅖h	Take a Bride	:36 h	Powerful Minn	:48 h	Lefty	1:02⅕b
Foolish Pleasure	:36 h	Weather Well	:36⅕b	**PRINCE DANTAN**	**:46⅕b**	Marry In Haste	1:02⅕h
French Rule	:37 bg	You Will Like It	:37 bg	Pilots Son	:46⅗h	Paradise Lost	1:01⅖hg
Game Tim	:36 b	**4 FURLONGS**		Rock Music	:49⅘b	Permanent	1:04⅕h
Good Marks	:38 b	Amberalero	:52⅖b	Sky Island	:50 b	Riverbank	1:01⅖h
Handsome Ghost	:37⅕bg	All Stirred Up	:48 h	Sound of the Bell	:47 h	Rain Again	1:03⅕h
Jack Sprat	:35 h	Breezy Gal	:49⅘hg	With Devotion	:50⅗bg	Spunky Princess	1:01⅗h
Let Me Count	:37 b	Clio Maroon	:48⅗hg	Wild Land	:49⅕b	Tropical Sea	1:01⅗hg
Life of the Party	:37⅗b	Century Gold	:50⅖bg	**5 FURLONGS—:57⅕**		Trainer Mickey	1:01 hg
Lake Montauk	:38⅗bg	Camelford	:47⅕h	Alfie G.	1:01⅖hg	**6 FURLONGS—1:08⅗**	
Magical Lady	:38 b	Dr. Yana	:47⅕h	Bold Review	1:04⅕b	Majority Ruler	1:14 h
Motto	:35 h	El Bailador	:47⅘h	Bussento	1:01⅖hg	Piaster	1:14 h
McCorkle	:35⅕h	Fashionable Girl	:50⅖b	Cornish Castle	1:01 bg	**1 MILE—1:33⅗**	
Nopalito	:36 b	Relio Rise	:49⅕b	Crystal Gaze	1:04⅕b	Certain Vote	1:42 h
Othris	:40 bg	Hello Goodbye	:49⅘h	Corrugation	1:02 h	**NORTH BR'DWAY**	**1:39⅗h**
Parlor Game	:35⅘bg	Instaneaneously	:50⅖b	Earlville	1:02⅖b	True Knight	1:41⅗b

PROD (3 furlongs) had good speed. PRINCE DANTAN (4 furlongs) continues to train well. HIGH STEEL (5 furlongs) acts sharp. NORTH BROADWAY (1 mile) had jockey Wallis up.

California the clockers tend to be honest as well as competent. And their footnotes to the daily workout listings make valuable reading (see above). Positive comments like "Prod had good speed" and "High Steel acts sharp" are worth remembering.

I keep a complete set of the daily workout listings so I can get more information about a horse's training than the past performances provide. This is especially helpful for evaluating first-time starters. While the past performances list only a horse's last three workouts, a first-time starter may work fifteen or twenty times before he makes his debut in actual competition. By checking these workouts, a studious handicapper can get a complete picture of the horse's preparation, and perhaps locate swift workouts that give a better indication of his capabilities than the ones listed in the *Form*.

OTHER PAST PERFORMANCE SYMBOLS

Sham × **126** B. c (1970) **by Pretense—Sequoia, by Princequillo.**
Breeder, Claiborne Farm (Ky.). **1973 . . 6 4 1 0 $140,528**
Owner, S. Sommer. Trainer, F. Martin. **1972 . . 4 1 2 1 $9,2**

Date / Race	Dist.	Time	Track	Odds	Wt.					Jockey	Class		First	Second	Third	Field
Apr21-73 7Aqu	1 1-8	1:49⅘	ft	$2\frac{1}{2}$	126	2^{1}	$2^{1\frac{1}{2}}$	$2^{1\frac{1}{2}}$	2^{h}	Vel'q'zJ2	ScwS	87	Angle Light 126	Sham	Secretariat	8
Mar31-73 SA	1 1-8	1:47	ft		120	3^{3}	$2^{1\frac{1}{2}}$	1^{2}	$1^{2\frac{1}{2}}$	Pin'yLJr	SpwS	97	Sham 120	Linda'sChief	Out of theEast	6
Mar17-73 8SA	$1\frac{1}{16}$	1:41⅘	ft	6-5	123	6^{6}	$6^{4\frac{1}{2}}$	6^{5}	$4^{7\frac{3}{4}}$	Pin'yLJr3	HcpS	85	Lind'sCh'f126	Anc'tTitle	O't of theE'st	9
Feb12-73 8SA	$1\frac{1}{16}$	1:45	m	1-10	▲118	3^{2}	5^{2}	3^{2}	$1^{2\frac{1}{2}}$	Pin'yLJr3	SpwS	77	Sham 118	Out of the East	Scanting	5
Feb 2-73 8SA	$1\frac{1}{16}$	1:41⅖	ft	1-3	▲118	4^{5}	3^{3}	$1^{\frac{1}{2}}$	1^{6}	PincayLJr2	Alw	95	Sham 118	Table Run	Untangle	6
Jan 1-73 6SA	$1\frac{1}{16}$	1:42	ft	1-2	▲118	5^{5}	4^{1}	1^{8}	1^{15}	PincayLJr7	Alw	92	Sham118	D'bleVar'ty	QuantumJump	7
Dec 9-72 2Aqu	1	1:37	m	9-5	▲121	1^{4}	1^{3}	1^{4}	1^{6}	Vel'quezJ6	Mdn	82	Sham 121	Water Wheel	Radnor	13
Sep23-72 3Bel	1	1:37⅘	ft	$2\frac{3}{4}$	118	5^{2}	$1^{\frac{1}{2}}$	1^{1}	2^{h}	GustinesH5	Mdn	83	Dicks Boots 118	Sham	Drollery	8
Sep13-72 3Bel	7 f	1:24	ft	9-5	▲120	2^{h}	$1^{\frac{1}{2}}$	2^{h}	$2^{2\frac{1}{2}}$	GustinesH1	Mdn	84	BroadwayPlayboy120	Sham	D'ksBoots	13
Aug28-72 3Bel	6 f	1:11	ft	28	120	9^{13}	9^{15}	5^{10}	$3^{7\frac{3}{4}}$	Gust'esH4	Mdn	81	AngleLight120	TimelessM'ment	Sham	11

April 30 CD 6f ft 1:11⅕h **April 17 Bel 5f ft :58h** **April 12 Bel 1m ft 1:37⅖h**

"7 Aqu" indicates that Sham ran in the seventh race at Aqueduct. A complete list of track abbreviations appears in most issues of the *Racing Form.*

"2½" reveals that Sham's odds were approximately 2½ to 1. The symbol *e* in this column means he was part of a stable entry; the symbol ▲ indicates he was the favorite.

"2," the number next to his jockey's name, was Sham's post position.

"8," in the right-hand column of the past performances, was the number of horses in his last race.

"B. c (1970)" in the breeding line indicate Sham's color, sex, and year of birth. The colors of thoroughbreds are bay (B.), black (Bl.), brown (Br.), chestnut (Ch.), roan (Ro.), and gray (Gr.).

READING CHARTS

Thorough handicappers should keep a set of result charts, which describe the running of individual races and contain more information about them than the past performances.

EIGHTH RACE Aqu Dec'mb'r 26, 1973	1⅛ MILES. (1:47). ALLOWANCES. Purse $11,000. 3-year-olds and upward which have not won a race other than maiden, claiming or starter. 3-year-olds, 119 lbs.; older, 122 lbs. Non-winners of $6,000 at a mile or over since Nov. 10 allowed 3 lbs.; maidens, 5 lbs. 3-year-olds which have never won at a mile or over allowed 3 lbs.; older, 5 lbs. (Winners preferred.)

Value to winner $6,600; second, $2,420; third, $1,320; fourth, $660. Mutuel Pool, $240,079. Off-track betting, $60,026.

Last Raced	Horse	EqtAWt	PP	St	¼	½	¾	Str	Fin	Jockeys	Owners	Odds to $1
12- 8-73^{7} Aqu^{4}	Bold Play	b3 119	6	5	3^{h}	3^{1}	2^{4}	2^{4}	1$^{2\frac{1}{2}}$	PAnderson	Willwynne Stable	4.00
12-20-73^{8} Aqu^{5}	Bold Merit	b3 113	2	1	1$^{2\frac{1}{2}}$	1$^{3\frac{1}{2}}$	1^{2}	1^{h}	2$^{\frac{3}{4}}$	EMaple	S Lehrman	7.70
12-15-73^{8} Aqu	Dream With Me	b3 108	4	4	6	6	4$^{2\frac{1}{2}}$	4^{10}	3^{1}	DMontoya^{5}	C Rosen	8.00
12- 8-73^{7} Aqu^{3}	Sacred Soul	b3 114	1	2	4^{h}	2^{h}	3^{h}	3^{h}	4^{12}	RTurcotte	Shinrone Farm	1.30
12-12-73^{5} Aqu^{2}	Sentimentalist	b3 119	3	6	5^{5}	5^{2}	5^{h}	6	5$^{4\frac{1}{2}}$	JVelasquez	G R Gardiner	2.80
12-17-73^{2} Aqu^{1}	Scrooge Kelley	3 114	5	3	2^{h}	4^{h}	6	5$^{\frac{1}{2}}$	6	JCruguet	Mrs J L Cotter	16.00

Time, :24⅖, :48⅖, 1:13⅘, 1:40, 1:53⅖ (no wind in backstretch). Track sloppy.

$2 Mutuel Prices:				
	6-BOLD PLAY	10.00	6.20	3.80
	2-BOLD MERIT		8.80	4.80
	4-DREAM WITH ME			5.00

B. c, by Chieftain—Thimbleful, by Needles. Trainer, W. C. Stephens. Bred by Mr. and Mrs. J. W. Stone (Fla.).

IN GATE—3:23. OFF AT 3:23 EASTERN STANDARD TIME. Start good. Won driving.

BOLD PLAY, prominent while forced to stay wide around the clubhouse turn, moved nearest the pace leaving the backstretch, responded outside BOLD MERIT when set down in the drive, got the lead leaving the eighth-pole and drew off. BOLD MERIT bore out slightly immediately after the start, remained well away from the rail throughout and could not resist the winner while tiring in the final furlong. DREAM WITH ME checked on BOLD MERIT's heels soon after the start, rallied on the rail leaving the backstretch and finished with good courage. SACRED SOUL had no apparent excuse. SENTIMENTALIST also checked behind BOLD MERIT after the start, had brief early speed, but did not appear to handle the going very well.

Overweight—Sacred Soul, 1 pound; Scrooge Kelley, 1; Bold Play, 3.

Most of the symbols in the charts are self-explanatory. The one significant difference between them and the past performances is in the running line. Instead of showing the number of lengths by which a horse was trailing the leader at each stage of a race, the charts show how far he was ahead of the horse behind him. In the race above, Bold Play finished first, 2½ lengths ahead of Bold Merit, who was three-quarters of a length ahead of Dream with Me, who was one length ahead of Sacred Soul, who was 12 lengths in front of Sentimentalist. A chart reader has to add these numbers to learn that Sentimentalist lost by 16¼ lengths.

Charts are especially useful because they indicate the conditions of the race. A handicapper who encountered Bold Play in a subsequent start would know from the past performances only that he had won an allowance race. The chart would reveal that he had won an event for "3-year-olds and upward which have not won a race other than maiden or claiming" — the lowest form of allowance race.

The footnotes in charts provide a detailed description of the way the race was run. A handicapper who reads them would know he could disregard Sentimentalist's bad defeat: "Sentimentalist checked behind Bold Merit after the start, had brief early speed but did not appear to handle the going very well."

There are many other valuable uses for the result charts, involving more sophisticated handicapping techniques, and they will be discussed in later chapters.

3

Larceny and Betting Coups

IT WAS IN a Miami telephone booth, of all places, that a young man named Mark experienced something every horseplayer dreams about. He stumbled onto a bit of genuine inside information about a betting coup.

Mark was an undergraduate at Georgetown University, majoring in equine studies. He spent much of his time gambling at Laurel, Bowie, Pimlico, and Charles Town, though he should have known better. The son of a bookmaker, he was having his education financed by the unsuccessful investments of his father's clientele. But Mark was a manic horseplayer anyway, and one winter he decided to take a break from the rigors of academe and fly to Hialeah for a week. It was a disaster. Mark went broke, borrowed money, and went broke again. Because of his father's professional standing he was able to get enough credit to go $3000 in debt to one bookie, $1500 to another.

After a climactic catastrophe at Hialeah, Mark went to a phone booth a couple blocks from the track to stall off his creditors and raise more capital. It was a double phone booth, and a man on the other side of the glass partition was on the phone. Mark heard him place a call to a famous movie star. Mark knew the actor was an enthusiastic horseplayer, and he strained to listen. "He's ready," the caller said. "Tomorrow's the day."

There was no mention of any horse's name, but Mark was not going to let this opportunity pass. He fixed in his mind the face of the man in the phone booth, and at six the next morning he was in the Hialeah stable area, tromping from barn to barn under the pretext of looking for a job as a groom. When Mark finally spotted his man, he noted the name of the stable where he was working, learned in the *Racing Form* that the stable had a horse entered in the third race, and went to a phone to bet as much as he could. The credo of bookmakers, of course, is to give their customers enough rope with which to hang themselves. Mark was able to place more than $1000 in bets and went to the track feeling serenely confident. His horse won at odds of 20 to 1. Mark collected nearly $25,000 from his bookmakers the next day, and returned to Washington with all the clichéd trappings of success: He was sporting a new wardrobe, driving a gold Cadillac, and displaying a decorative blonde on his arm.

All horseplayers envision a stroke of fortune like this, and many come to believe it is the only way they can beat the races. After a man has learned the rudiments of handicapping, he will inevitably be frustrated when he cannot immediately convert his new knowledge into consistent winnings at the track. He may think that the fault lies not within himself but in the nature of the game. Many crucial elements of horse racing do not appear in black and white in the pages of the *Daily Racing Form.* A horse's condition and capabilities may change drastically from one race to the next — and only insiders will know. A trainer may be manipulating his horse's form with drugs; a jockey may be losing deliberately with a horse — and only insiders will know. Perhaps the only ways to beat the game are either to become an owner or trainer, or to discover what the insiders are doing.

I was leaning toward this point of view during my frustrating fledgling years as a horseplayer. My inclinations were turned into convictions on a train ride from Boston to Narragansett Park one summer night in 1963. I could not have guessed, from his outward appearance, that the man sitting next to me would exert more of an influence on my mind than would any of my professors at Harvard. Wearing a rumpled suit and an ancient straw hat, he looked like a typical racetrack bum. But when I caught a glimpse of the *Racing Form* he was studying so intensely, I got a different impression of the man. The paper was completely covered with esoteric symbols and notations, utterly incomprehensible to me, that suggested the man was a very serious student of the game.

I asked the stranger his opinion of the horse I liked in the second race that night; he had finished second by a nose in his most recent start and looked like a solid favorite. The man glanced at the horse's record and said, in a faintly foreign accent, "I wouldn't touch him." He pointed toward the upper right-hand corner of the past performances, where it was noted that the horse had raced ten times during the year with one victory, three seconds, and three thirds. "The stable is always trying to win with this horse," he said, "and he doesn't get the job done. Whenever a horse runs second or third, I consider it a black mark against him. It means he was trying to win and couldn't. The crazy public loves to lose its money on horses like this. Not me."

I asked the man whom he preferred in the second race. He pointed to the name of a horse that had raced twice in his career, losing both starts by 20 lengths. He was a maiden running against winners — a type of horse that every handicapping book says can be automatically eliminated. By what logic did he pick such a hopeless animal?

"The logic of illogic," the man said, and did not elaborate. He was obviously not prepared to share all his wisdom with a stranger. I was not sure if my companion was a genius or a madman, but I was fascinated and I stayed with him as we got off the train. My faith was slightly shaken when his maiden in the second race was beaten by 20 lengths again; the horse I had liked finished second, as usual. After eight races neither of us had cashed a ticket, but the man was confident and enthusiastic about an animal named Carbreuse in the ninth race.

I couldn't imagine what virtues he saw in a horse who had managed to win only once in his last forty attempts, and that had lost each of his last eight races by ten lengths or more. The man pointed out that Carbreuse had been racing in $3000 company for most of the year. He was dropped to $1500 and was beaten badly at 8 to 1. In his next race for $1500, he was beaten badly at 21 to 1. "They weren't trying in those races," the man said. "They've been waiting until the price is right. And I think tonight is the night." He told me to study Carbreuse's running line in his most recent race, which looked like this:

6^{9} 8^{12} 9^{16} 7^{12}

This, the man explained, was what he called the *Z* pattern. Carbreuse had dropped back steadily throughout most of the race but had come on at the end, gaining four lengths in the stretch. It was the jockey and trainer's way of testing him. They had let him run only during the stretch, giving him a workout-within-a-race. Carbreuse had responded, and now the stable was ready to cash a bet.

I bet my last $5 and watched in ecstasy as Carbreuse went to the front, led all the way, and held on to win by a neck. He paid $119.60 to win. My hands were trembling as I collected more money than I had ever won in my life. I knew that I had had the remarkable fortune to encounter a genius who marched to the sound of a different drummer.

On the train ride home, the man introduced himself as Mr. D. He said he had come to Boston to serve as the consul for a South American country, and occupied the dull hours in his office by studying the *Racing Form*. When the government of his native country was overthrown by a left-wing coup, Mr. D. was out of a job and started betting the horses full-time.

A horseplayer's temperament will often influence his betting. Mr. D.'s political views — his convictions about the treachery and duplicity of the Communists — helped shape his philosophy of handicapping. He believed in the conspiracy theory of horse racing. Only naive bettors looked for the best horse in a race; Mr. D. wanted to know who was trying to win and who wasn't. He viewed all horses as tools that were manipulated by their trainers. The trainers were ruthless, calculating, omnipotent. Their mission in life was to deceive the public, to orchestrate a horse's form until they could cash a bet at the proper odds. Horse racing was a larcenous game, and to be a successful bettor a man had to be able to detect the larceny. To a struggling handicapper who had been baffled by the intricacies of the sport, Mr. D.'s philosophy was very seductive. I became his protégé.

Mr. D. taught me that the cornerstone of his handicapping method was consistency. He wanted horses who had a high winning percentage and, even more important, had a "clean record" — a minimal number of second- and third-place finishes. If a horse had ten races, three wins, no seconds, and no thirds, Mr. D. would conclude that he was a perfect betting tool. The trainer had tried to win three times, and had succeeded three times.

To discover when a horse would be trying to win, Mr. D. looked for various signs in the way he had run his most recent race, and invented his own private language to describe them — "the *Z* pattern," "middle flashes," "convats." One of his discoveries, the change of pace, brought me my triumph on Sun in Action years later. It is the most brilliant single tool I have ever seen for detecting horses who are ready to wake up, seemingly out of the blue, and win at long odds.

A horse who dramatically changes his usual running style — for example, a confirmed stretch runner who inexplicably shows early speed and tires — will often improve mysteriously the next time he runs. After Mr. D. taught me about the change of pace, I encountered a classic embodiment of the pattern in the past performances of a horse named Parma Town at Thistledown Race Track on June 16, 1965. His recent running lines looked like this:

$3^{2\frac{1}{2}}$	6^{8}	5^{5}	$4^{2\frac{1}{4}}$
1^{h}	3^{3}	$7^{5\frac{1}{2}}$	8^{11}
$1^{\frac{1}{2}}$	3^{2}	$4^{4\frac{1}{2}}$	$10^{7\frac{1}{4}}$
4^{2}	$3^{3\frac{1}{2}}$	$3^{4\frac{1}{2}}$	$4^{6\frac{1}{4}}$

Parma Town had displayed a consistent running style throughout his career: he would always show early speed and tire. In his next to last race, he had taken the early lead and faded to finish far out of the money. In his most recent race he had started to drop back as usual. After a half mile he was running sixth by eight lengths. Then, uncharacteristically, he rallied to finish fourth, 2¼ lengths behind the winner. Regardless of the time of the race or the quality of his competition, Parma Town had managed to do something he had never done before, and it was a meaningful sign. He won and paid $57.20.

I cashed one of my most memorable $2 bets on a change of pace in 1967 in Toronto, where I had been dispatched to cover a soccer game. I had left Washington a day early so I could make a detour through Chester, West Virginia, where Waterford Park was offering a nineteen-race double-header. After losing disastrously, I arrived in Canada without enough money for my plane fare back home, so I naturally made an excursion to Woodbine Race Track in an effort to recoup. A horse named M.J.'s Boy was entered in the first race with these past performances:

M. J.'s Boy **110** **B. g (1964), by Royal Visitor—Jenny, by Firethorn.**
Breeder, R. Harvey (Can.). **1967 2 M 0 0 (——)**
Owner, Serbert R. Lihou. Trainer, Wilfrid L. Sayles. **$3,000** **1966 0 M 0 0 (——)**
May25-67 ^{1}WO 6 f 1:13$\frac{1}{5}$ft 99f 116 $14^{12}12^{12}10^{10}10^{7\frac{1}{2}}$ Val'laS^{11} M3000 71 C'ntFerd116 RunA'dSue106 St'd'leLeo 14
May 1-67 ^{2}F.E 6 f 1:12$\frac{4}{5}$ft 50 106* 4^{5} 9^{15} 9^{21} 9^{21} GriffoP^{2} M3000 64 LandyDee110 HelenM'ry117 Or'ntVeil 12
May 30 WO 2f ft :24$\frac{3}{5}$h **May 24 WO 3f ft :37$\frac{2}{5}$h** **May 18 WO 4f ft :48$\frac{3}{5}$h**

M.J.'s Boy had broken fourth and tired badly in his racing debut. The next time he ran he broke fourteenth and managed to finish tenth. This was, technically, a change of pace, and I felt obliged to bet $2. M.J.'s Boy paid $298.50, the second-biggest win price in North America that year.

In addition to his various wake-up signs, Mr. D. talked a lot about "the logic of illogic." He explained it simply:

"When a horse is entered in a race where he obviously doesn't belong, watch out!" If a chronically unsuccessful $5000 horse were one day entered in a $10,000 claiming race, most handicappers would dismiss him summarily, but Mr. D. would ask, "What is he doing here?" He would suspect that the horse had been entered in a seemingly impossible spot to deceive the public and let the trainer execute a massive betting coup. Sometimes the logic of illogic would point toward horses so absurd that even Mr. D.'s most devoted disciple couldn't take them seriously.

We were at Lincoln Downs one night, handicapping a cheap claiming race at a mile and one-sixteenth. One of the entrants, Tiki of Maori, was a hopeless bum. In his last four starts, all at seven-eighths of a mile, he had shown brief speed and tired to lose by at least 20 lengths each time. I eliminated him at first glance. Mr. D. asked, "What is he doing here? This horse has been showing speed and tiring. It would make sense for the trainer to enter him at a shorter distance. Why a longer distance? This may be a betting coup." It was always necessary for the disciple to treat the master with reverence, so I said, "Mr. D., you know I have the greatest respect for you and your methods. But I think this horse is just a little far-fetched." We argued about the horse's merits or lack thereof until post time, when it was too late for Mr. D. to get a bet down. Tiki of Maori won by six lengths and paid $89. Mr. D. didn't let me forget about that race for years; he was less distressed about the $89 than he was about the apostasy of his pupil.

The logic of illogic is a very dangerous technique for an inexperienced handicapper to use because it requires him to bet horses who are clearly bad ones. Sometimes a horse will be entered in an inappropriate spot because he is merely out for the exercise or because his trainer is stupid. More often a horse will be put in the wrong kind of race because the racing secretary has put pressure on the trainer to enter him so that the race will have a field of adequate size. But occasionally a bettor will encounter a horse entered under such suspicious circumstances that he deserves a second look.

A very implausible horse named Parted Seas was entered in a race at Saratoga in 1970. The animal had run only once in his career, in a $3000 maiden-claiming event at Lincoln Downs. At this rock-bottom level, he had gone off at 50-to-1 odds and finished sixth. A week later he was running against winners in a $3500 claiming race at Saratoga. Why had the trainer gone to the trouble and expense of shipping a horse from Rhode Island for a race in which he presumably didn't stand a chance? Maybe he was crazy. Maybe he wanted to take the waters at the spa. Or maybe he wanted to cash a bet. The answer came on the tote board two minutes before post time, when a flood of money poured onto Parted Seas and drove his odds down to 7 to 1. He won in a gallop.

Mr. D. believed that betting action is very important, that the tote board has the same significance in horse racing that the ticker tape does in the stock market. There is a school of thought on Wall Street that holds that it doesn't matter whether a company makes a profit or, indeed, whether it makes anything at all. The ticker tape tells everything. If a stock is being actively traded and its price fluctuates in certain ways, shares are probably being accumulated by knowledgeable insiders and the company is probably a good investment. Similarly, the tote board can often indicate where the smart money is going on a horse race.

An inexperienced horseplayer will frequently be misled by the tote board, because some of the most obvious types of betting action are the least meaningful. Sometimes an unlikely looking horse will be heavily bet in the first few minutes of wagering and open as an odds-on favorite. When this happens, it isn't the stable betting. The money probably comes from a bookmaker who has been overloaded with action on a particular horse and wants to reduce his liability in case the horse wins.

Another form of betting action can trigger an outburst of mass hysteria at the racetrack. A horse is a legitimate 20-1 shot in the early wagering but his odds begin to drop steadily. He goes to 15-1, 10-1, 8-1, 5-1, 7-2, 5-2, as more money pours in with each flash of the tote board. Everybody at the track observes the betting action, and as post time approaches bettors are rushing frantically to the windows, knocking over little old ladies in their paths, to cash in on the hot horse. Nobody knows how these stampedes begin, but they are seldom caused by genuine stable betting. And these obvious hot horses do not win with great frequency. When insiders are really betting on a horse whose virtues are well concealed, they will do so as subtly as possible so that the masses will not jump on the bandwagon.

A sharp trainer may do all his betting in the last minute or two before post time. When a horse plummets from 15-1 to 10-1 in the last flash of the tote board, that betting action is usually significant. More often, though, there will be no eye-catching fluctuations in the price of a horse who is being bet by knowledgeable insiders. He will receive steady support throughout the betting and go to the post at odds much lower than his record would seem to warrant. There is no easy or systematic way to detect this subtle betting action. A horseplayer must have the experience to know the sort of horses that the public does and doesn't bet.

A handicapper who wants a quick (and probably costly) education in betting action and racetrack larceny ought to visit Churchill Downs during the week of the Kentucky Derby. The Kentucky tracks seem to have more sharpies to the square inch than any other area of the country, and they all save their best tricks for Derby Week, when the out of town suckers come to Louisville to be fleeced. The 163,628 people who attended the centennial Derby in 1974 also got to witness a betting coup of classic proportions. These were the past performances for the third race that day:

3rd Churchill Downs

7 FURLONGS (chute). (1:21⅖). CLAIMING. Purse $6,500. 4-year-olds and upward. Weight, 122 lbs. Non-winners of two races since March 15 allowed 3 lbs.; a race, 6 lbs.; in 1974, 10 lbs. Claiming price, $16,000; 2 lbs. for each $1,000 to $14.000.

Mild Joker **110** Ch. g (1970), by Jester—Ultimate Weapon, by Bold Ruler.
Breeder, R. L. Carter (Ky.). 1974 5 0 1 0 $800
Owner, R. N. Hardin. Trainer, G. Hild. **$15,000** 1973 17 1 3 2 $10,280

Apr25-74^{3}Kee	6½ f	1:18	ft	9½	116	2^{3}	2^{3}	2^{3}	2^{5}	Pat'nG^{1}	c10000	82	R'sh aBet116 MildJ'ker MamasH'eN'w	9
Apr19-74^{2}Kee	6 f	1:10⅖	sft	15f	113	5^{4}	7^{8}	$7^{8\frac{3}{4}}$	8^{9}	Cam'lRJ^{7}	14000	81	Et'rn'lL'k116 L'ngD'cis'n J.Finxpilter	12
Apr 9-74^{2}Kee	7 f	1:24⅕	ft	25	112	1^{h}	1^{h}	$4^{1\frac{1}{2}}$	6^{11}	Pat'sonG^{5}	13000	74	Aerodrome116 D'b'n'reHost Ind'nSp'd	10
Mar23-74^{6}Hia	6 f	1:10⅖	sft	48	108‡	$4^{3\frac{1}{2}}$	10^{11}	10^{17}	11^{14}	Sag'iaR^{7}	15000	77	IrishSweep'r117 ChiefTamao Cliff'rdR.	12
Feb 7-74^{6}GP	6 f	1:09⅖	sft	61	112	$9^{9\frac{3}{4}}$	10^{12}	12^{19}	12^{16}	Gallit'oG^{2}	18000	76	P'tEverg's116 Br'ssC'n G.Ham'nOwen	12
Oct15-73^{6}Atl	6 f	1:12	ft	2¾	116	2^{1}	4^{6}	$5^{5\frac{1}{2}}$	$5^{7\frac{1}{2}}$	Sol'neM^{2}	18000	74	SundaySupper116 StillFlying AlsoJoe	8
Sep29-73^{7}Atl	6 f	1:11	ft	7¼	115	$5^{2\frac{3}{4}}$	$7^{9\frac{1}{4}}$	$7^{7\frac{1}{4}}$	$7^{9\frac{1}{4}}$	Solom'eM^{3}	Alw	78	MovingTarget116 Buck a'dWing Kilt'g	7
Sep22-73^{5}Atl	6 f	1:11	ft	6¾	115	$2^{\frac{1}{2}}$	2^{h}	3^{nk}	3^{nk}	Solo'neM^{7}	Alw	87	Myst'ryR'l'r113 M'v'gT'rg't MildJ'k"r	7
Sep11-73^{7}Atl	6 f	1:10⅖	sft	3e	115	4^{1}	$4^{\frac{3}{4}}$	2^{h}	3^{1}	Solom'eM^{8}	Alw	89	HomeJerome116 OurTown MildJoker	8
Aug21-73^{7}Mth	6 f	1:10⅖	sft	6½	114	$2^{1\frac{1}{2}}$	$3^{1\frac{1}{2}}$	$3^{2\frac{1}{2}}$	1^{nk}	Solom'eM^{7}	Alw	90	MildJoker114 BestJiminto StillFlying	7

April 17 Kee 4f ft :50b **April 14 Kee 3f ft :36b** **April 7 Kee 3f ft :36⅗b**

Rush a Bet **119** Dk. b. or br. g (1969), by Narushua—Besbet, by Ballydonnell.
Breeder, J. W. Mecom (Tex.). 1974 7 2 2 0 $7,200
Owner, Audley Farm Stable. Trainer, D. Smith. **$16,000** 1973 15 1 4 1 $10,049

Apr25-74^{3}Kee	6½ f	1:18	ft	6-5	▲116	1^{3}	1^{3}	1^{3}	1^{5}	Br'f'ldD^{2}	10000	87	R'sh aBet116 MildJ'ker MamasH'eN'w	9
Apr13-74^{3}Kee	6 f	1:11⅗	sft	5	116	1^{2}	1^{2}	$1^{1\frac{1}{2}}$	$2^{\frac{1}{2}}$	Val'zanF^{1}	10000	83	Chief Intent 120 Rush a Bet HastyBay	10
Mar17-74^{8}FG	1-40	1:41	ft	3¾	116	$2^{\frac{1}{2}}$	9^{15}	9^{15}	Eas.	And'nJR^{5}	13000		Sea ofF'rt'ne116 S'ndyR'j'ct FluteBoy	9
Feb26-74^{5}FG	6 f	1:11⅕	sft	3	114	$8^{4\frac{3}{4}}$	8^{13}	$8^{5\frac{1}{2}}$	7^{12}	Copl'gD^{8}	15000	80	JohnJet113 ModestMorn SatinLark	8
Feb16-74^{3}FG	6 f	1:11	gd	15	114	$5^{2\frac{3}{4}}$	5^{5}	3^{2}	$2^{1\frac{1}{2}}$	CoplingD^{2}	15000	91	R'll a'dT'ss120 R'sh aB't B'ck t'eS't'm	6
Jan28-74^{6}FG	1-40	1:41⅗	sy	14	113	3^{nk}	8^{19}	8^{19}	8^{22}	Rub'coP^{8}	14000	63	TommyG.118 PunkinTime Ch'm'gT'rry	8
Jan 5-74^{5}FG	$1\frac{1}{16}$	1:45⅗	gd	2¼	116	1^{2}	1^{2}	$1^{1\frac{1}{2}}$	$1^{3\frac{1}{2}}$	An'nJR^{2}	c10000	87	Rush A Bet116 SpeakOut FairFlight	7
Dec29-73^{5}FG	6 f	1:12⅘	sy	3¼	111	$2^{\frac{1}{2}}$	$2^{1\frac{1}{2}}$	2^{3}	$5^{2\frac{3}{4}}$	BreenR^{1}	12500	81	UncleZip116 SatinLark K'nt'ckyFlip'r	8
Oct24-73^{5}Atl	6 f	1:11⅗	sft	6½	115	1^{h}	$3^{2\frac{1}{2}}$	3^{2}	3^{4}	UsseryR^{8}	12500	80	IrishHighball 119 Dillprince Rush aBet	8
Oct13-73^{4}Atl	6 f	1:11⅕	sft	7½	115	7^{4}	$3^{2\frac{1}{2}}$	3^{3}	2^{3}	Sol'neM^{10}	11000	83	IrishHighb'll 115 R'sh aB't B'nitaBl'e	10
Oct 6-73^{5}Atl	$1\frac{1}{16}$	1:45⅕	sft	7½	116	3^{3}	$1^{1\frac{1}{2}}$	1^{2}	$2^{\frac{3}{4}}$	UsseryR^{10}	10000	80	Fall Rush 108 Rush aBet He'sSolid	12

May 2 CD 4f sy :49b

(cont'd on next page)

Daring Baby **111** Dk. b. or br. f (1970), by Daring Knight—Plea's Baby, by Gallahadion.
Breeder, R. E. Rapp (Cal.). 1974 7 0 0 3 $4,005
Owner, H. E. Sutton. Trainer, C. E. Welch. $16,000 1973 21 2 3 5 $23,180
Apr20-747Kee 6½ f 1:17⅕ft 25 112 1113 1012 911 79¾ FiresE2 20000 83 FavoriteRoad116 Aerodr'me JodiPete 11
Mar24-742SA 6½ f 1:17⅕ft 3½ 117 64 65 56½ 57¼ Cam'sR5 c16000 80 ⒻKamadora 112 Celary RubySatan 7
Mar15-745SA 6 f 1:10⅗ft 10 118 65 54½ 53 3¾ Camp'sR5 20000 87 Morn'sBest112 LastMinute DaringBoy 8
Feb28-746SA 1 1/16 1:44⅘gd 9½ 114 77½ 63½ 54½ 58 CampasR3 Alw 70 ⒻReputat'n117 St'telyG'me DearInt't 9
Feb17-742SA 6 f 1:11⅖ft 37 117 1111 79¼ 95¼ 33½ CampasR6 20000 80 ⒻK'lb'sF'ly118 Maur'n'sB't D'r'gB'by 12
Feb 8-745SA Ⓣ 1⅛ 1:49⅘fm 20 114 63¼ 63½ 99¼ 916 ValdezS2 Alw 64 ⒻGrasp'g115 Sultan'sB'ty JollyAng'l 9
Jan18-749SA 1 1/16 1:46⅖sl 20 114 22 21½ 21½ 33½ ValdezS3 Alw 66 ⒻWistfully115 Met'poMiss Dar'gBaby 9
April 7 SA 5f ft :59⅗h April 5 SA 4f ft :48h

Not So Well **112** B. g (1970), by He Jr.—Dottisan, by Dotted Swiss.
Breeder E. Lowrance (Okla.). 1974 7 0 0 2 $3,510
Owner, E. Lowrance. Trainer, J. Eckrosh. $16,000 1973 13 0 2 4 $5,955
Apr20-747Kee 6½ f 1:17⅕ft 31f 116 87¼ 88¾1015 1020 C'b'llRJ9 20000 72 FavoriteRoad116 Aerodr'me JodiPete 11
Apr 5-747OP 6 f 1:12⅕ft 14 123 1111 109 86 54¾ Campb'lRJ8 Alw 79 MaryDugan112 GayG'her Bo's andOh's 12
Mar27-748OP 1-70 1:42⅗ft 50 113 46 33 35 36¾ SpindlerL3 Alw 76 OfficeK'g113 D'mondH'shoe N'tSoW'l 8
Mar20-747OP 1-70 1:41⅕ft 26 118 1119 1112 1015 1016 UsseryR9 Alw 59 BoldDave113 FragileFolly S't'n'sS'try 11
Mar 6-747OP 6 f 1:12⅖ft 6¼ 123 76¼ 65 74¼ 74¼ UsseryR11 Alw 78 CountryTradition113 Peeber BoldDave 11
Feb27-747OP 5½ f 1:06⅕ft 12 117 812 711 53 3nk UsseryR6 Alw 87 Delin't'n124 F'rnl'ghC't'ge NotSoW'll 9
Feb18-747OP 6 f 1:13 sy 5½ 123 716 711 69½ 49½ Patt'sonA1 Alw 70 DanielB'ne123 Peeber CountryTr'dit'n 9
May25-738CD 7 f 1:26 sy 2-3 ▲113 46½ 42¼ 34 24 B'rqueK2 15000 73 Junie F. 112 Not So Well Podaco 6
April 29 CD 5f ft 1:03⅗b April 16 Kee 4f ft :51⅕b Mar 17 OP 4f ft :48⅖b

Lover's Flight * **112** B. g (1967), by Certain Flight—Hallie Dear, by Aera.
Breeder, Far Cry Farm, Inc. (Ky.). 1974 6 0 2 2 $7,254
Owner, J. E. O'Bryant. Trainer, J. E. O'Bryant. $16,000 1973 10 2 2 3 $16,860
Apr 6-745OP 1 1/16 1:45⅘ft 9¼ 115 46½ 33½ 2h 2h LivelyJ3 17500 79 SolidMist118 Lover'sFlight WrightD'l 9
Mar23-747OP 1-70 1:43⅘ft 3 113 65½ 42 5¾ 54¾ LivelyJ2 17500 72 RedTamao114 StevieW'vie BruteForce 10
Mar16-7410OP 1-70 1:44 ft 4½ 115 45 43 24 22½ LivelyJ4 17500 73 BruteForce119 L'v'r'sFl't Pr'cePresto 9
Mar 2-7410OP 1-70 1:43⅕ft 3¾ 115 75 75½ 45½ 35 LivelyJ2 17500 75 NobleKingd'm116 RedT'm'o Lov'sFli't 9
Feb20-748OP 1-70 1:42⅖ft 5½ 115 56 84¼ 79½ 79¼ Wh'dDE7 20000 75 OurT'deW'ds111 P'l'zEnc're R'dT'mao 11
Feb15-747OP 6 f 1:12⅗sy 3¾ 115 88¾ 914 55¼ 33½ UsseryR5 15000 78 ToolinAr'nd110 Pr'mR'ss L'v'r'sFlight 10
Aug21-736Lib 1-70 1:44⅘ft 4-5 ▲120 64 56 46 410 BlackAS6 14000 66 Petrous113 Sport'gly YouPickedAb'ty 6
Jly 26-737Lib 1 1:39⅗ft 2¼ 122 43½ 43½ 43 33 UsseryR5 25000 73 GunWadding116 S'cessR'd Lover'sFl't 7
Jly 17-738Lib 1-70 1:42⅘ft 9-5 ▲118 1½ 12 14 17 UsseryR1 22500 86 Lover'sFli't118 Trop'lSuns't Intrav'n's 6
May 1 CD 5f ft 1:02⅘b April 25 CD 3f ft 1:03b March 22 OP 4f ft :50b

Hasty Departure **115** B. g (1970), by Wallet Lifter—Opium Den, by Indian Hemp.
Breeder, Loma Rica Ranch (Cal.). 1974 4 1 2 9 $4,925
Owner, Mr. & Mrs. W. Hicks. Trainer, L. Niles. $14,000 1973 14 4 3 0 $8,758
Apr27-745CD 6 f 1:12⅖ft 13 113 63½ 89¼ 43½ 12¾ TauzinL3 7000 84 H'tyD'p't're113 R'nd'lsB'sin H'pyCl'wn 12
Mar12-744OP 6 f 1:13⅖ft 5¾ 116 69 46 52¾ 21¼ UsseryR5 6250 77 BigK'g116 HastyDep't'e H'mb'g'rP'tie 9
Feb27-743OP 6 f 1:12⅘ft 3½ 115 44 43 1h 2no ZakoorW2 c4500 81 Sunburn117 H'tyDep't're Pr'ceH'bert 11
Feb11-742OP 5½ f 1:06⅗ft 12 117 108 96½ 97¼116¼ ZakoorW11 5000 79 B's'nsF'lc'n117 How-Tum Kr'ks InS'k 12
Nov17-734CD 6 f 1:12⅘ft 5 114 52¾ 41¼ 2h 2h ZakoorW4 4750 82 B'd ofTh'ria119 H'styD'p't'e F'rB'g'r 9
Nov 2-735CD 6 f 1:13⅖ft 5 119 4½ 1½ 2h 1½ ZakoorW6 3750 79 H'styD'p'rt'e119 St'mpyJ'e P'goT'rio 11
Sep24-734Det 6 f 1:12⅗ft 6-5 ▲118 3nk 1h 1½ 13 EngleJ8 3200 77 HastyDep't're118 Haw'iBoy D'naL R'n 8
Sep 7-732Det 6 f 1:14 ft 3-2 ▲116 65¼ 31 11½ 16 EngleJ8 2500 70 HastyDeparture116 MiniSk'ny Sw'sT'l 12
April 26 CD 3f ft :37b April 20 CD 5f ft 1:03b Mar 11 OP 3f sy :37b

Red Hot Tamale * **116** Ch. rig (1968), by Tamao—Miss Tahiti, by Tahitian King.
Breeder, W. B. Robinson (Ky.). 1974 12 2 1 2 $11,637
Owner, S. Jones & J. Stebbins. Trainer, C. E. Picou. $16,000 1973 13 3 4 2 $24,225
Apr20-747Kee 6½ f 1:17⅕ft 38 118 53¼ 43½ 56½ 68¼ M'lloM10 20000 84 FavoriteRoad116 Aerodr'me JodiPete 11
Apr10-747Kee 6 f 1:09⅗ft 22 116 21 58 58 713 S'l'monG5 25000 82 Str'ngSide122 C'lMeJ'die G'ld'nGreek 8
Mar30-746Lat 5½ f 1:07 sy 12 119 44½ 45 47½ 411 Mang'loM4 Alw 72 Pop'l'rD'm'nd115 CariC'ty B'teR'axt'n 6
Mar16-748Lat 1 1/16 1:47⅗m 44 115 33½ 38 36 413 FriarJW2 HcpS 59 B'tleg'r'sPet116 L't'r'sJ't'r B'b't'sl'ge 8
Mar 9-748Lat 6 f 1:15 ft 9½ 122 52¼ 54 45 37½ SolomonG7 Alw 62 FleetTudor119 LuckAh'd R'dH'tT'm'le 8
Mar 2-748Lat 1 1:45 sy 3½ 119 21 16 18 1½ SolomonG1 Alw 54 R'dH'tT'male119 Mr.Ch'mp L'tt's'nse 7
Feb23-748Lat 1 1:41⅕m 7½ 119 31 21½ 24 49 SolomonG5 Alw 64 BigSpade122 Bab'gton'slm'e Mr.Ch'p 9
May 1 CD 4f ft :49b April 19 Kee 3f ft :36h April 16 Kee 5f ft 1:01h

Native Shoes **116** **Ch. g (1969), by Native Charger—Silver Shoes, by Goya II.**
Breeder, L. Savage (Fla.). **1974 . . 9 2 3 1 $9,172**
Owner, R. E. Harris. Trainer, R. E. Harris. $16,000 **1973 . . 5 0 0 1 $1,105**

Apr17-74^{6}Kee	6½ f 1:16⅖ft	50	114	9^{14}	9^{14}	7^{10}	7^{10}	WhitedDE^{9}	Alw	86	StrongSide121	Br'stigert	P'rlezEnc're	9
Apr 1-74^{8}Lat	1 1:42⅗sy	13	122	6^{17}	6^{17}	6^{11}	5^{11}	McKn'htJ^{4}	Alw	55	BigSpade122	Lester'sJester	Voyage	7
Mar11-74^{8}Lat	1 1:43⅖sy	3-2	▲115*	8^{33}	5^{22}	5^{15}	2^{2}	MorganM^{1}	Alw	60	AngelMissy 115	NativeShoes	Voyage	8
Feb21-74^{8}Lat	1$\frac{1}{16}$ 1:49⅘sy	7	119	6^{28}	6^{9½}	3½	1no	SmithsonG^{1}	Alw	61	NativeShoes119	BigParty	Once Irish	7
Feb 7-74^{8}Lat	1 1:43 ft	2½	117*	6^{8}	4^{6}	3^{7}	3^{4½}	MorganM^{4}	Alw	59	Mr.Champ115	AngelMissy	NativeSh'es	6
Jan31-74^{8}Lat	6½ f 1:20⅗gd	6¾	117*	6^{2½}	2^{4}	2^{7}	2^{2½}†	MorganM^{6}	Alw	79	RedH'tTam'le115	Mr.Ch'p	N've Shoes	7
†Dead heat.														
Jan19-74^{8}Lat	1 1:47 m	3½	▲114*	Fog.			2^{5}	MorganM^{2}	Alw	39	SnowFacePat117	NativeSh's	Nadarko	8
Jan12-74^{7}Lat	6 f 1:11⅘ft	8¾	109*	7^{8½}	5^{5¾}	3^{1½}	1^{h}	MorganM^{6}	Alw	89	NativeSh's109	T'sBigGem	Exemplary	8

April 30 CD 4f ft :50⅘b **April 24 CD 5f ft 1:04⅖b** **March 23 Lat 6f ft 1:19⅗b**

Federal Ruler ✻ **115** **Ch. h (1969), by Irish Ruler—Vala, by Cosmic Bomb.**
Breeder, Farnsworth Farm (Fla.). **1974 . . 10 2 1 0 $6,870**
Owner, R. Cotb. Trainer, A. Montano. $14,000 **1973 . 18 2 3 1 $11,156**

Apr22-74^{9}Aqu	7 f 1:24⅖ft	3¼	114	9^{5½}	8^{8}	9^{8}	9^{5}	Cor'roAJr^{7}	7750	74	Pembles112	MoreL'dings	Old'stMich'l	12
Apr11-74^{9}Aqu	1 1:37⅗ft	2¼	▲118	7^{9½}	3^{4½}	2^{3}	1½	Velasq'zJ^{1}	5000	79	F'd'r'lR'l'r119	Old'st Mich'l	RioT'n'y'n	9
Apr 4-74^{9}Aqu	6 f 1:10⅗sy	5	116	7^{8}	7^{9¾}	8^{11}	8^{14}	Cas'daM^{3}	10000	76	JollyD'cer116	J'hnDegr't	E'rlyJ'd'm't	8
Mar27-74^{5}Aqu	6 f 1:11⅕ft	10	116	5^{3¼}	3^{1½}	2½	2^{nk}	C'roAJr^{12}	10500	87	Corporat'n116	F'd'lRuler	WitnessSt'd	12
Mar19-74^{2}Aqu	1 1-8 1:52 ft	2¾e	118	4^{1}	1^{h}	3^{1½}	6^{5½}	Vel'quezJ^{1}	8500	69	PatrolPrince116	Penetrante	Pr'ceB'lo	7
Mar 6-74^{6}PR	1$\frac{1}{16}$ 1:49⅕ft	3½	115	5^{5½}	6^{9½}	5^{7}	6^{4½}	VelezH^{5}	Alw		IncaWarrior114	Catbette	Alumchorus	7
Feb24-74^{8}PR	1$\frac{1}{16}$ 1:49⅗ft	3	115	3^{1½}	1^{h}	1^{h}	1^{1¼}	VelezH^{9}	10000		FederalRul'r115	Sense ofD'ty	Classico	9

March 23 Bel trt 3f ft :35⅕h

The public figured to concentrate its betting on two horses in this field. Lover's Flight had lost his most recent race by only a head, and now was dropping slightly in class. Rush a Bet had beaten cheaper horses very convincingly, leading all the way to win by five lengths. But neither of these horses was favored. Daring Baby — who was a filly running against males, who was winless in seven starts during the year, who had been badly beaten at 25 to 1 in her last race — was bet steadily and heavily, and went off at 9 to 5. The untutored Derby Day crowd could not possibly have made her the favorite; the smart money was responsible. Just a few days before, the same stable had won a race with a horse named Gaelic Coffee who came from California to Kentucky, ran one dismal race, dropped slightly in class, went off as an inexplicable 9-to-5 favorite, and won by seven lengths. Now Daring Baby showed the identical pattern. An outsider could not know what the stable was doing with the horse and why it was so confident, but any perceptive conspiracy theorist had to bet Daring Baby out of sheer, blind faith. Blocked for a quarter mile, she came four horses wide entering the stretch and won going away.

Sometimes the most meaningful betting action is of a negative variety: a horse who has obvious handicapping virtues, who is sure to be heavily supported by the public, will go off at a suspiciously high price that suggests the smart money is avoiding him completely. A handicapper usually should not be frightened because he is getting generous odds on a horse he likes. But when the odds are too generous, he should be wary.

Even an untutored handicapper could have spotted a standout in the ninth race at Saratoga on July 30, 1974. Monetary Principle, a maiden, had run impressively against allowance horses in his last start, losing by a nose. Since that race he had worked six furlongs in a phenomenal 1:10$\frac{2}{5}$. He looked like a potential stakes horse. And now he was entered in a maiden race.

Because his credentials were so obvious, Monetary Principle figured to be an odds-on favorite. He wasn't. His odds hovered around 5 to 2 until a few minutes before post time. Then the public, thinking it was being offered a bargain, drove his price down to 7 to 5. The lukewarm support that Monetary Principle had received through most of the betting, and his suspiciously high final odds, suggested that something was wrong with him. And something was. He was trounced by 15 lengths.

A week later Monetary Principle was entered in the same sort of race. Despite his bad loss he received strong betting action and went off the favorite. This time he won by 11 lengths.

Any observant horseplayer can cash good bets periodically by trying to divine the intentions of trainers and detect betting coups. For a long time, while I was operating at the larcenous New England tracks under Mr. D.'s influence, I thought this was the only way to beat the races. But when I started covering horse racing for a newspaper and learned more about the sport and the people in it, I recognized the fallacy of this approach to handicapping. When a horseplayer is betting on the basis of thievery, coups, and inside information, he is betting on the trainer's judgment. He must assume that the insiders are all-knowing and all-powerful; when they bet, their horse is going to win.

As I became acquainted with many trainers, owners, and jockeys, I learned that this notion conflicts head-on with reality. The insiders are just as fallible as any horseplayer. The mysteries of handicapping are mysterious to them, too.

Very often, when a longshot wins and conspiracy-minded horseplayers assume his victory was the product of a well-planned betting coup, the owner and trainer will be utterly surprised by their horse's performance. When I bet Sun in Action, I took it for granted that trainer Ron Bateman had been manipulating the horse's form and was now ready to gamble on him. After Sun in Action won, I asked jockey Martin Fromin if he thought the trainer had cleaned up on the race. "No," Fromin said. "He'd probably laugh at you if you asked him. Normally trainers will tell you if they're betting their money. They'll lay a story on you about why his last races were bad. But Bateman just said he didn't know much about the horse and told me to ride the way I wanted."

A good trainer will usually know his own horse and know when he is ready to run his best race. But even when the trainer has laid the groundwork for what he thinks will be a winning performance, he still has to beat a field of other horses, many of whose trainers have done the same thing. Because they are so committed to their own horses, trainers and owners can seldom handicap a race with objectivity and frequently misjudge their opposition drastically. Every day I go to the track I hear tips and tidbits of information from insiders who are genuinely convinced their horses will win. The insiders' batting average is no better than that of average horseplayers who rely on the *Racing Form* for all their information.

As skeptical as I am about tips, I sometimes find them irresistible. No rational man could have resisted trying to capitalize on the piece of inside information I heard at Saratoga in the summer of 1973. The source of it happened to be the best trainer in America.

One Sunday afternoon I was visiting the stable of Allen Jerkens, where a friendly touch football game was being played. After the game, Jerkens strolled around his barn talking about his horses. He came to one stall and said, "This horse is so good now that I get scared every morning when I come to look at him." The animal's name was Triangular. An old stakes-class grass horse, he had been out of competition for six months. But he was training beautifully under the master's tutelage, and Jerkens was contemplating a gamble. He could, of course, enter Triangular in an allowance race where he would be facing tough competition. But Jerkens was thinking about putting him in a high-priced claiming race, where he would surely outclass his opposition. I waited anxiously for the big day. And finally, on the next to last day of the Saratoga meeting, Triangular was entered in a $45,000 claiming race. I bet with confidence.

Triangular broke last, made one ineffectual move on the last turn, and faded to finish last. On the same afternoon, Jerkens also saddled a horse named Prove Out, that he had bought just a week earlier. He didn't know much about the horse yet. Prove Out won by six lengths, shattered the track record, and paid $11.80. Jerkens was as stunned by his victory as by Triangular's defeat. If the best horseman in America can be so wrong, the typical trainer who tries to concoct betting coups is certainly apt to be wrong much of the time.

A horseplayer who pays too much attention to larceny and inside information is likely to lose, not only because betting coups often fail, but because this preoccupation will wreck the rest of his handicapping. There was one season in Maryland when I became totally paranoid about jockeys, suspecting that most of them were holding horses — that is, deliberately losing races — with great frequency. As a result, I couldn't evaluate a horse's previous races with any confidence; I always wondered if the jockey had been trying to win. If I did find a horse who looked like an excellent bet, I feared that the jockey might be holding him today. When I lost a bet on a horse I liked, I would ascribe the defeat to the rider's moral turpitude. At every stage of the handicapping process, my judgment had been undermined. I didn't handicap properly; I didn't bet my solid selections with confidence; I didn't analyze races after they had been run and try to learn from them.

I finally decided that my mental attitude was so self-defeating that the only way to function properly was to assume that the game is honest and that the results of races are true. By viewing the sport logically instead of conspiratorially, I found that the outcome of most races did seem to be the product of logical factors rather than conspiracies.

I consider the possibility of larceny in a race only when I am confronted by powerful evidence of it — such as unmistakable betting action, the suspicious presence of a horse in a race in which he shouldn't be entered, or a pattern of thievery in a horse's past performances that his trainer has employed with success before. But even under these circumstances, I still handicap the race. There are many times when I will conclude that the stable is trying to execute a betting coup, but I will still not bet the horse because I think he is not good enough and the trainer's judgment is faulty. Betting primarily on the basis of a trainer's intentions, or on inside information, is for people who don't have the knowledge to handicap properly. When I put my money on a race, I don't want to bet on anybody's judgment but my own.

4

Track Biases

BEFORE I MET Steve Davidowitz, I had spent some fifteen years looking for the elusive Secret of Beating the Races. I knew that it would not be easy to find but I knew it existed: the great principle that underlies the science of handicapping, that would work any time, anywhere.

I found the answer by pure chance when I sat on a bench near the paddock at Saratoga Race Track. A young man sitting a few feet away struck up a conversation with me and we compared notes on the day's races. It didn't take me long to sense that Steve Davidowitz was the most brilliant student of handicapping I had ever met. As we conversed, we saw that our lives as horseplayers had developed along parallel lines. We had both become addicted to racing in college, had both suffered through a lot of losers, and had both experienced one great betting triumph that had changed our lives. But I still had not found the Secret, and Steve had.

Steve's obsession as a youth had not been horses, but baseball. He was a high-school hotshot in New Jersey, pitching one no-hitter after another. He was offered a $30,000 bonus by the Milwaukee Braves but turned it down so he could go to college. In his freshman year at Rutgers University he wrecked his arm in a pick-up basketball game and saw his hopes for a major league baseball career shattered. At the time of this personal disaster, Steve was enrolled in a statistics class for which the teacher had assigned him a term project: Analyze the effect of post positions on races at Garden State Park. The sport fascinated him immediately, and it also provided him with an outlet for some of the self-destructive urges he was feeling after his injury. He started going to Garden State every day, and losing every day. He borrowed money from friends. He bet on credit with bookmakers. And he soon found himself $1500 in debt with no way to extricate himself.

Steve drove the 100 miles from school to his father's business, sat in front of his desk, and broke into tears as he related the whole story. His father listened impassively and then reached for his checkbook. "I'll give you the money you need," he said. "But I want you to promise that you'll never gamble again."

Steve promised. But gambling was already too much in his blood and not long afterward he found himself back at Garden State Park. He walked to the daily-double window but stood there unable to speak, unable to violate his pledge and place a bet. He sat through nine races and still couldn't bring himself to bet. Yet he couldn't abandon his interest in racing, and so he plunged into a chaste, academic study of the sport. He pored over the *Morning Telegraph* every day, learning all he could about handicapping. He became especially interested in workouts as indications of horses' conditions, and he studied the workout listings in the *Telegraph* diligently. As he did, he noticed a name that kept reappearing: Flying Mercury. This old horse had been such a fast sprinter that he had once outbroken Intentionally, who had then been considered the fastest horse in America. Flying Mercury had been idle for a long time, but his steady workouts at Garden State suggested that he was returning to top condition. Finally, his name appeared in the entries — in a mile-and-a-quarter handicap. This was an obviously inappropriate spot for a horse whose specialty was running three-quarters of a mile. But Steve was so intrigued that he went to see the race. Flying Mercury broke alertly but his jockey eased him back, and the horse finished 40 lengths behind the winner.

A few days later Flying Mercury was entered in a six-furlong race at Aqueduct, and Steve knew that this was the race for which he was being prepared. Steve drove to New York for that one race and bet $20 to win, $20 to place. Flying Mercury flew out of the gate, opened a five-length lead, and won with ease at odds of 38 to 1. Steve collected $1200 and drove directly to his father's office. He handed him the money and said, "I won this betting a horse." His father understood. And Steve understood, almost immediately, that Flying Mercury had changed his life.

"It made me know, for an absolute certainty, that there was logic behind this game and that it could be beaten," Steve said. "I never had really believed that you could know how a horse was going to run unless you walked up to his trainer before the race and asked him. But I was convinced by that one victory that I could know — that I could go up to a trainer before the race and tell him what his horse was likely to do."

The triumph of Flying Mercury did not immediately transform Steve into a winning horseplayer. Just as he had done during his disastrous losing streak, he would often bet on horses he thought had solid credentials and then watch them lose badly. This happens to every horseplayer, of course, but most of them chalk up the defeat to the inscrutability of the game. It confirms their deep-seated belief that nobody can beat the races. But Steve now believed that he could and would beat them, and whenever a seemingly outstanding horse was beaten he tried to comprehend what had happened. He didn't find the explanation in any one dramatic flash of insight. The answer crept into his consciousness slowly.

During his ill-fated betting binge at Garden State Steve had noticed, without recognizing the implications, that horses with inside post positions won an unusually high percentage of the races and that the best jockeys at the track tried to steer their horses toward the rail whenever they could. When he started going to Saratoga every August he witnessed an opposite phenomenon: Most of the winners were horses who broke from outside post positions and rallied in the middle of the track. As he handicapped at Saratoga he found himself thinking along these lines: "Here's a horse with early speed and an inside post position. He doesn't have much of a chance. But if they were running this race at Garden State, this horse would be a strong contender."

In order to pursue his interest in horses full-time, Steve went to work as a handicapper for the *Racing Form*, where his duties called for him to make selections in all the races at six or seven tracks a day. Here he confirmed his impressions about the diversity of the sport. When he was handicapping a race at Garden State, he preferred horses who had early speed, an inside post position, and a recent race over the track. When he was studying the Fair Grounds in New Orleans, he observed that horses trained by the brilliant Jack Van Berg would win countless races even though they defied all conventional handicapping wisdom. When he doped out races in New England, he saw that horses recently acquired by trainer Richard L. Barnett won a high percentage of the time. When he was dealing with a mile-and-one-eighth race at Aqueduct, he knew that horses with inside post positions would win most of the time.

Here it was, the Secret of Beating the Races: There was no one secret! The horseplayers like me who searched for the great underlying truth of handicapping were as misdirected as the alchemists who spent their lives trying to find the philosophers' stone. The game is diverse and it is perpetually changing. Methods that work beautifully at Bowie are almost useless sixty miles away at Shenandoah Downs. Handicapping rules that sounded axiomatic a year ago are obsolete today. The winning horseplayer is not the man who holds the proper set of dogmatic beliefs, but the one who can observe and adapt to the ever-changing conditions of the sport.

These conditions take many forms. I remember a season at Suffolk Downs when horses wearing mud caulks—cleated shoes that gave them better footing—would win practically every race on a sloppy track. Steve told me about a meeting at the Fair Grounds when he enjoyed great success simply by betting on the horse who was warmed up most vigorously before the race. These dominant factors appear and disappear for no apparent reason. But there are two types of changing conditions that a good horseplayer must be aware of constantly. One of them is the influence of trainers. Certain men, with methods uniquely their own, will consistently win races with horses who don't conform to any sort of established handicapping logic. (The importance of trainers will be discussed in the next chapter.) The other important variables are those caused by the racing surfaces over which horses run.

The profound influence of the track condition on the outcome of a race is a relatively recent phenomenon. Handicapping books of previous generations rarely mentioned it as an important factor. But horseplayers of the past lived when there was a defined racing season, conducted during the temperate months of the year. They never experienced the dubious pleasures of year-round racing, never had to cope with the effects of the weather on a racetrack in Rhode Island in the middle of January. I visited Narragansett Park on one day that made the traditional designations of track conditions — fast, good, sloppy, muddy, and heavy — laughably irrelevant. There had been a heavy snowfall and the moisture in the Narragansett track had seeped toward the rail, turning that part of the racing strip into a virtual bog. On the stretch turn snow that had been piled up in the adjacent parking lot had begun to melt, and the outside part of the track had been converted into a small lake. In between the bog and the lake there was a narrow strip of the track that was frozen. The horse who stayed on this hard path was an automatic winner.

Old-time horseplayers were also spared the experience of dealing with the mentality of the new breed of track superintendents who unabashedly manipulate their racing surfaces. Before the 1971 Preakness Stakes, for example, everyone was saying that the horses in the Triple Crown event were a very mediocre group. So Pimlico took action to insure that its big race wasn't mediocre. Tons of soil were scraped from the track, making it extraordinarily hard and fast. Cheap horses were running more swiftly than they ever had in their lives, and Canonero II won the fastest Preakness in history, giving management the spectacular race that it had wanted.

Though there are many possible causes for aberrant track conditions, their effects will take only a few basic forms:

1. The track favors front-running horses. This will happen on very hard tracks, like the one at Pimlico. Horses with early speed will tire less quickly than they would under normal conditions, for the same reason that human runners can go farther and faster on asphalt than they can on a sandy beach. Speed horses usually have an advantage on sloppy tracks, too, because come-from-behind horses are hampered by the mud that is kicked in their faces.
2. The inside part of the track is harder and faster than the outside. This usually helps front runners because they can outbreak their opponents and get to the good footing along the rail. A stretch runner, even if he starts from an inside post position, may have to move outside for running room.
3. The inside part of the track is deep and slow. Under these conditions, speed horses with inside post positions can rarely win. Horses breaking from outside posts have a distinct advantage, although stretch runners with inside posts can move off the rail and try to win by circling the field.

In theory, knowledgeable horseplayers should win a fortune whenever they encounter one of these types of track biases. When speed horses breaking from inside post positions are winning all the races, an observant gambler should be betting speed horses with inside post positions. But this is not as easy as it sounds. Even after meeting Steve Davidowitz, absorbing and intellectually accepting his ideas about adapting to the changing conditions of the sport, it took me years before I could capitalize properly on track biases.

To become successful horseplayers, most of us spend years studying and learning about class, condition, speed, and the other classic principles of handicapping. I have devoted a large part of my life to the creation and refinement of my speed figures, and I believe in them with an almost religious devotion. It is not easy for me to disregard the principles I believe in and the methods that have worked for me in order to bet a horse simply because he is breaking from post position one on a day when the inside part of the track is fast. I feel like an apostate turning his back on the faith in which he was raised.

It wasn't until the summer of 1973 that I was able to make money from a track bias, and I owe the breakthrough partly to my mother (who still can't quite grasp the difference between win, place, and show). I went to visit her in Erie, where a brand-new track, Commodore Downs, had opened just a few weeks before. The citizens of Erie were curious but uninformed about the new game in town, and numerous family friends had asked my mother to arrange an outing to Commodore, with me as their private tout. My mother, of course, was quite willing to show off her son the horse-player. But I knew I was going to look like a bumbling incompetent. Commodore Downs offers the rock-bottom level of races that are usually undecipherable even under optimum conditions. And since the track had been open for only a brief time, it would be impossible to do much worthwhile research into the handicapping methods that might work there.

When I visit an unfamiliar track I try to discover if any track biases exist. I calculate the percentage of front-running winners at each distance. I go through the *Racing Form* charts and list, in a separate column for each distance the track offers, the winning post position and the number of horses in the field. My compilation of the results of four-furlong races at Commodore Downs over a two-week period looked like this:

FOUR FURLONGS

Winning Post	*Horses in Field*
5	7
6	6
6	10
2	8
8	8
8	8
6	7
8	8
7	8
5	8
9	9
3	7
3	10
4	9
6	9
4	6

Then I added the number of winners and the number of starters from each post position and calculated the percentage of winners from each post. These were the results:

FOUR FURLONGS

Post	*Winners*	*Starters*	*Percent*
1	0	16	0
2	1	16	6
3	2	16	13
4	2	16	13
5	2	16	13
6	4	16	25
7	1	14	7
8	3	11	27
9	1	5	20
10	0	2	0

The results of my calculations for other distances were much the same, and they couldn't have been more fruitful. Horses breaking from outside post positions had an enormous advantage at Commodore Downs. Horses in posts one and two could be eliminated almost automatically, regardless of their credentials. It looked too good to be true, and so on my first night at the track I resolved to bet with restraint and concentrate on watching what was happening. Whenever a horseplayer suspects the existence of a track bias, he should study the early races on the card diligently, decide who is likely to show speed, who is likely to rally, who is likely to win, and then compare the actual running of the race with what he thinks should have happened.

The first race I saw at Commodore was, typically, a $1500 claiming event for horses that had not won a race in the last two years. There were only four horses in the field with records that suggested they might be bona fide members of the thoroughbred family. Brent's Tiger had early speed and post position one. Jocantry was dropping from the $2000 level and had post two. Roses of Mentor and Mr. Teal, breaking from posts four and five, had both run sharp races over the track against similar opposition. But none of these horses ever got into serious contention. Morie Pie, a 52-to-1 shot who had never been close to the lead in two years, broke from the No. 6 post and blew past all the contenders inside him on the turn. In the stretch, an equally unimposing-looking horse named Conscientious Lad, who had broken from post eight, circled the field and finished second. In the one minute five and two-fifths seconds that it had taken these plugs to negotiate five-eights of a mile, I had learned all I needed to know about handicapping at Commodore Downs. For the rest of the week I confidently disregarded any horse starting from the two inside post positions. I would have thrown out Secretariat if he had been on the rail in a $1500 claiming race. By concentrating on exactas and using horses in favorable post positions who had shown a glimmer of ability, I was hitting an average of five races a night.

An important lesson dawned on me during this winning streak. If I had known more about handicapping at Commodore Downs, if I were more aware of the methods of the trainers and the relative merits of the horses, I probably wouldn't have done nearly so well. I would have been bewildered whenever I encountered a horse with solid credentials who was breaking from an inside post position. But with no other tools to work with, I let the track bias dictate the horses I bet. I learned that whenever I see such a powerful bias — even at a track where I know all the angles — I should subordinate all my other handicapping ideas to it.

When I encounter a race in which the best horse — the

one with my top speed figure — is disadvantaged by the track bias, I will usually make a moderate bet against him. If his merits look so strong that I cannot resist, I will make a moderate bet on him, knowing that I probably shouldn't be doing it. But when I find a race where the best horse also has the track bias in his favor, I am inclined to bet all I can and then some. Such horses offer the best gambling opportunities in all of racing.

Unfortunately, these clear-cut situations don't arise often enough. But during my stay at Commodore Downs I hoped I would find at least one obviously superior animal who would be helped by the track bias. On my last day in Erie, I did. The opportunity came in an unlikely spot — a $2500 claiming race for maidens. Almost every how-to-beat-the-races book ever written has unconditionally advised its readers to avoid races for cheap horses who have displayed a chronic inability to win. Personally, I don't believe in any of these absolutist dicta about handicapping. While it is true that cheap maiden races are usually unbettable, the first race at Commodore Downs on June 22, 1973, was a classic exception. These were the past performances of the nine horses in the field (see pages 78–79).

Baldwin Twister was the favorite. She had sprinted to big early leads in six-and-a-half-furlong races at Jefferson Downs in Louisiana. She had collapsed every time, but now she was running only five-eighths of a mile, and the shorter distance would help her. If this race were being run on a typical half-mile track, where horses with inside post positions and early speed win with high frequency, Baldwin Twister probably would have been a standout. But this was Commodore Downs, and Baldwin Twister epitomized the type of horse that almost never could win at this track: a speedster breaking from the No. 1 post position.

Bullet Lady had run well to finish second in a four-furlong race at Commodore though she hadn't been able to gain in the stretch. She had weakened in her previous start at four and a half furlongs. Five furlongs seemed to be a bit too far for her. And even if she had shown ability to handle the distance, she would still have been a speed horse breaking from the No. 2 post, and thus a likely loser at Commodore.

Grand Lou Ann, No. 3, had never shown any ability and could be instantly eliminated. The same was true of Miss Bush Ahead, Gomesa's Baby, Lay Arms, and Milk Bottle.

Edwards Country, breaking from post position five, had run in a $2500 maiden race a week before. After starting from an advantageous outside post position, he made a move at the leaders on the turn, but weakened slightly in the stretch of a four-furlong race. In his previous attempts to go five furlongs or more, he had tired badly. Edwards Country figured to have an edge over Baldwin Twister and Bullet Lady simply because of their post positions, but his credentials were otherwise unimpressive.

Wembley Legend had raced only once, which in itself is a recommendation in a maiden race. The other horses in the field had established themselves as losers; Wembley Legend at least had not yet shown that she was a hopeless bum. Her racing debut on June 8, in which she broke ninth and rallied to finish fourth, was much better than it appears on the surface. The winner of that race, Lonesome Sailor, stepped up in class and won an allowance race by four lengths the next time he ran; he was obviously much better than the typical winner of a $2500 maiden race. Makemeadeal, who had finished a length in front of Wembley Legend, had also come back to win his next start, as we can see in the top line of Edwards Country's past performances. Makemeadeal had destroyed Edwards Country by eight

1 COMMODORE

5 FURLONGS COMMODORE START FINISH

5 FURLONGS. (.59⅗) MAIDEN CLAIMING. Purse $1,500. Weight, 3-year-olds, 120 lbs. Claiming Price $2,500.

Baldwin Twister

B. f. 3, by Metier—Kitty Sue, by George Gains
$2,500 **Br.—Rester M L (Ala)** **Tr.—Delahoussaye J**
Own.—Noullet M

115

	St.	1st	2nd	3rd	Amt.
1973	3	M	0	0	$192
1972	2	M	0	1	$165

Date	Track	Dist	Fractions	Race	PP	St	1/4	Str	Fin	Jockey	Wt	Odds	Comment
26May73- 4JnD	fst 6½f :23		:47⅘ 1:21⅕	3↑ Md 5000	5 4 1^{3}	$1^{1}_{\frac12}$ 2^{2}	6^{12}			Terre J E Jr	b 107	19.00	67-15 Mr. Ideal 120^{6} Wailing Wind 113^{1} Corporals Guard 115^{1} Speed, tired 10
14May73- 1JnD	fst 6½f :23		:48⅕ 1:23	3↑ ⒻMd 2500	3 4 1^{5}	1^{hd} $1^{1\frac12}$	$4^{2\frac12}$			Terre J E Jr^{5}	b 110	7.70	67-20 Terriwin 120^{hd} Jab MyBubble $113^{1\frac12}$ GrandmammaSugar 115^{1} Weakened 10
10May73- 1JnD	fst 6½f :22⅘		:47⅗ 1:22⅘	Clm 1500	5 2 1^{5}	1^{4} 2^{1}	$4^{6\frac14}$			Terre J E Jr	b 110	19.90	66-18 Miss Jet Princess $112^{\frac34}$ Chart East 112^{2} Graceful Grace $110^{3\frac12}$ Weakened 10
15Nov72- 4JnD	fst 6½f :23⅕		:48 1:22⅘	Clm 4000	4 7 9^{15}	10^{24} 10^{29}	—			Tauzin L	114	14.70	— — King Rocks $112^{\frac34}$ Tison Quemado 112^{2} Ozone Queen 108^{nk} Eased 10
3Nov72- 1JnD	sl 4f		:23⅗ :48⅘	Md Sp Wt	4 9	3^{3} 3^{3}	$3^{2\frac14}$			Tauzin L	b 116	17.00	81-17 Zel's Gal $116^{1\frac12}$ Social Debutante $116^{\frac34}$ Baldwin Twister 116^{1} Rallied 10

LATEST WORKOUTS Jun 19 Com 3f gd :39 b

Bullet Lady

B. f. 3, by Abashed—Bullet Baby, by Paul H
$2,500 **Br.—Maxwell A (Okla)** **Tr.—Maxwell A D**
Own.—Maxwell A D

110^{5}

	St.	1st	2nd	3rd	Amt.
1973	3	M	1	0	$397
1972	0	M	0	0	

- 13Jun73- 5Com fst 4f :23⅗ :47⅘ 3↑ Md 2000 3 4 $2^{\frac12}$ $3^{\frac12}$ 2^{2} Maxwell J 115 4.30 — — Flag Flyer 120^{2} Bullet Lady 115no Executrix $117^{2\frac34}$ Gamely 8
- 26May73- 9Com gd 4½f :24 :49⅗ :55⅗ Md 2500 4 2 2^{3} $3^{3\frac12}$ $4^{2\frac14}$ Maxwell J 115 6.50 — — Sweet Market 115^{2} Hall's Hero 120^{hd} Swift Signal 115^{nk} Speed, tired 6
- 10Apr73- 2HP sl 4f :23⅗ :48⅕ 3↑ Md 3500 5 8 6^{6} 9^{12} 9^{15} Snyder D 110 9.00 69-16 Swift Tune 120^{1} Right Trail $120^{3\frac12}$ Third Thrill 111^{2} No speed 10

Grand Lou Ann

Ch. f. 3, by Aber Roussel—Miss Grand, by Quick Reward
$2,500 **Br.—Spiroff G Jr (Mich)** **Tr.—McNerney W D**
Own.—Crenshaw H

115

	St.	1st	2nd	3rd	Amt.
1973	5	M	0	0	$209
1972	4	M	0	0	$228

- 15Jun73- 2Com fst 4f :23 :47⅖ Md 2500 1 7 5^{8} 6^{11} 4^{13} McNerney T b 115 15.70 — — Makemeadeal $120^{5\frac12}$ Swift Signal $115^{2\frac12}$ EdwardsCountry $120^{4\frac34}$ No mishap 8
- 8Jun73- 9Com fst 4½f :23⅗ :48⅖ :54⅗ Md 2500 3 4 9^{11} 8^{15} 7^{19} McNerney T b 115 20.10 — — Lonesome Sailor 120^{3} Bab's Flash $115^{1\frac34}$ Makemeadeal 120^{1} No factor 10
- 25May73- 4Com sl 4½f :23⅖ :49⅗ :55⅘ 3↑ Md 1500 7 2 $4^{5\frac12}$ $5^{8\frac12}$ $6^{9\frac12}$ McNerney T b 114 5.20 — — Prince Placid $115^{\frac34}$ Dr. Swafford 120^{4} Rival Mark $115^{\frac12}$ Tired 7
- 4Apr73- 3HP gd 6f :24⅖ :50⅖ 1:18⅘ 3↑ Clm 3500 10 10 10^{15} 9^{17} 9^{25} 9^{20} Low S b 105 183.40 38-36 Error Not 106^{nk} No Mustard $113^{\frac12}$ Carters Match 110^{2} No factor 10
- 28Mar73- 4HP gd 4f :23⅗ :48 3↑ ⒻClm 2500 3 10 10^{13} 10^{17} 10^{18} Paugh C D b 105 113.20 67-14 Lucy Beatrice 111^{4} Teebee $110^{1\frac12}$ No Mustard $113^{1\frac12}$ Trailed 10
- 14Nov72- 3Det my 6f :25⅗ :51⅘ 1:20⅗ Md Allow 5 4 2^{2} 6^{11} 9^{23} 9^{32} Bacon M b 117 12.70 — — Ronbar $120^{3\frac12}$ Twiddley De 117^{6} Small Fortune $117^{2\frac12}$ No speed 12
- 7Nov72- 3Det my 6f :24 :49⅖ 1:19⅗ ⓈMd 5000 1 6 4^{12} 4^{9} 7^{9} $5^{9\frac14}$ Strauss R b 117 8.90 33-49 Loonsong 117^{nk} Jean's Music 117^{2} Whimsical Lass 117^{2} No threat 8
- 3Nov72- 1Det my 5½f :24⅖ :49⅕ 1:10⅘ Md 3200 9 4 1^{hd} 3^{4} 3^{8} 4^{10} Snyder D b 112 *1.50 53-34 Flying Gal 110^{2} Little Beth 112^{7} Miss Hiccups 117^{1} Weakened 11

LATEST WORKOUTS May 18 Com 5f fst 1:03⅘ b May 15 Com 3f fst :38⅕ b

Miss Bush Ahead

B. f. 3, by Bush Ahead—Admiral Louise, by Beauguerre
$2,500 **Br.—Rapp F (La)** **Tr.—Molero V A**
Own.—Molero V A

108^{7}

	St.	1st	2nd	3rd	Amt.
1973	3	M	0	0	$30
1972	5	M	0	1	$242

- 15Jun73- 2Com fst 4f :23 :47⅖ Md 2500 3 8 8^{13} 5^{10} 5^{13} Jett J^{7} 108 19.10 — — Makemeadeal $120^{5\frac12}$ Swift Signal $115^{2\frac12}$ Edwards Country $120^{4\frac34}$ No threat 8
- 21May73- 5JnD fst 5f :23 :48⅕ 1:00⅖ Clm 3000 7 7 $7^{7\frac12}$ 8^{17} 8^{20} 8^{36} Young J F 112 121.30 56-16 Wayward Winner 112no Meisje 107^{2} Bab's Hill 110^{nk} No factor 8
- 5May73- 2JnD fst 4f :22⅘ :47⅕ Clm 2500 9 8 $8^{9\frac12}$ 9^{16} 9^{19} Keller E D 112 104.20 72-09 Jo's Bad Girl 109^{1} Two Tonco 114^{8} Witch Of Benevinto 117^{2} No factor 9
- 27Dec72- 4FG fst 6f :22⅘ :47⅖ 1:14⅖ ⓈMd Sp Wts 7 5 7^{5} 9^{8} 11^{20} 11^{21} Young J F 115 32.70 55-20 Intaner B. 118^{4} Easy Pic $110^{2\frac12}$ Rayburn's Red $118^{\frac12}$ No speed 12
- 7Dec72- 1FG sl 6f :22⅘ :47⅖ 1:14⅘ ⒻⓈMd Sp Wt 2 11 1^{hd} 3^{4} $5^{8\frac12}$ 7^{12} Young J F 119 33.10 62-23 NitNevergivesin $119^{\frac12}$ Dode'sRequst 119^{1} MidofOsiris 119^{6} Sluggish start 12
- 14Nov72- 1JnD gd 4f :23⅗ :48⅕ ⒻⓈMd 3500 2 5 $6^{5\frac12}$ $6^{8\frac14}$ 6^{9} Menard N 119 11.70 77-14 Honey Hook $119^{1\frac12}$ Little Jean Swaps 114^{5} Angie M. $114^{1\frac12}$ No threat 10
- 12Oct72- 1JnD fst 4f :23 :48 Md Sp Wt 9 10 7^{11} 6^{13} 6^{13} Martinez J U 116 5.00 74-08 Greek Bay 116^{2} Star Of Sunla 113^{4} Lea Joe $119^{2\frac12}$ No mishap 10
- 29Sep72- 3JnD fst 4f :23 :47⅘ Md Sp Wt 5 5 $5^{7\frac12}$ 3^{6} 3^{9} Martinez J O 116 6.30 79-10 Charley He Ran 119^{6} Melrose Girl 116^{3} Miss Bush Ahead $116^{\frac12}$ Rallied 10

Edwards Country

B. g. 3, by Rellim S W—Anns Time, by Time Signal
$2,500 Br.—Bateman A L (La) Tr.—Sider L
Own.—Sider A

120

	St.	1st	2nd	3rd	Amt.
1973	5	M	1	1	$555
1972	0	M	0	0	

15Jun73- 2Com fst 4f :23 :47⅗ Md 2500 7 4 6^{11} 3^5 3^8 Tanner D b 120 *2.30 — — Makemeadeal $120^{5\frac12}$ Swift Signal $115^{2\frac12}$ Edwards Country $120^{4\frac34}$ Evenly 8
19May73- 1JnD fst 6½f :22⅘ :47⅕ 1:22 3 ♦ Md 5000 1 1 1^{hd} $3^{2\frac12}$ 6^{12} 8^{24} Young J F b 112 8.70 51-15 I Can Dance 114^{hd} Concentrate 107^2 [D]Hurrican Harley $109\frac12$ No mishap 10
12May73- 7JnD fst 6½f :23⅗ :47⅕ 1:20⅖ [S]Clm 6000 2 6 7^5 8^{12} 8^{16} 8^{21} Keller E D b 112 19.60 62-18 Tracey Own 112^2 She's Tight $109\frac34$ Manchac Pass $112\frac34$ No speed 8
30Apr73- 5JnD fst 5f :22⅘ :47⅘ 1:01 [S]Clm c-3500 3 4 $2^{1\frac12}$ $6^{8\frac34}$ $8^{7\frac14}$ $8^{4\frac12}$ Menard N b 115 *1.20 84-14 Speedy P. D. $115\frac12$ Spinella 110^2 Windburner 110^1 Brief speed 8
19Apr73- 1JnD gd 4f :22 :47⅕ 3 ♦ Md 2500 1 10 $3^{4\frac12}$ $2^{1\frac12}$ 2^{nk} Domingue J^5 b 107 *1.30 91-07 WitchOfBenevinto 107^{nk} EdwrdsCountry $107\frac34$ Bib'sAngel $109^{1\frac12}$ Bad start 10
LATEST WORKOUTS Jun 12 Com 3f fst :38⅘ h

Gomesa's Baby

Ch. f. 3, by Laugh Aloud—Gomesa, by Nadir
$2,500 Br.—Clark R H (Va) Tr.—Rhoton N L
Own.—Rhoton N L

115

	St.	1st	2nd	3rd	Amt.
1973	7	M	0	0	$147
1972	3	M	0	1	$272

13Jun73- 5Com fst 4f :23⅖ :47⅘ 3 ♦ Md 2000 6 6 $7^{5\frac12}$ $4^{1\frac12}$ $5^{5\frac34}$ Mills B 110 30.00 — — Flag Flyer 120^2 Bullet Lady 115no Executrix $117^{2\frac34}$ Tired 8
2Jun73- 3Com gd 6½f :23⅘ :49 1:21⅗ Md 2500 5 6 $2\frac12$ $5^{3\frac12}$ 6^8 6^{16} Montesanto P 115 23.50 — — Waygoer $120^{4\frac14}$ Elgin Kitty 115^{hd} Hall's Hero 120^5 Early speed 6
26May73- 9Com gd 4½f :24 :49⅖ :55⅗ Md 2500 5 5 5^5 $6^{7\frac34}$ $6^{6\frac34}$ Montesanto P 115 9.70 — — Sweet Market 115^2 Hall's Hero 120^{hd} Swift Signal 115^{nk} No factor 6
5May73- 5Pen fst 5f :23⅗ :48⅘ 1:02 Md 2500 8 6 $11^{8\frac12}$ 11^7 $11^{9\frac34}$ 9^{13} Sheppard D 118 19.90 — — Rose Tat 115no Furiant 118^1 Help's Barry 113^3 No factor 11
1May73- 2Wat fst 5½f :23⅖ :47 1:06⅖ 3 ♦ Md Sp Wt 3 5 $3^{2\frac12}$ $5^{5\frac12}$ $6^{8\frac14}$ 7^{17} Masters K 112 9.20 68-17 Dr. Jasper $122^{2\frac12}$ Jodi's Go Go 109^6 Martin's Boy 116^1 Fell back early 8
25Apr73- 1ShD sly 3½f :23⅕ :35⅗ :42 3 ♦ Md 2500 1 8 $8^{7\frac14}$ 8^5 9^{11} Finnefrock R 115 35.40 74-14 Gin Money 114^1 Hy Way Joy 112^5 Jeanie Kelly 109^{hd} No factor 10
6Apr73- 2Dov fst 3½f :23⅕ :41⅘ 3 ♦ Md 1500 5 2 $2\frac12$ $4^{4\frac12}$ $4^{4\frac34}$ Whitemen P 109 4.55 84-09 Nautical Nymph $107^{2\frac12}$ Eagle's Pilot $123^{2\frac14}$ Zozo Johnny 123no Weakened 9
3Aug72- 3Poc fst 5½f :23⅖ :47 1:07 Md Sp Wt 2 1 $4^{2\frac34}$ 4^7 3^{10} 3^7 Reynolds L 117 9.70 83-11 Flaming Nail 113^2 Siempre's Melody 120^5 Gomesa's Baby 117^{13} Fair try 6
LATEST WORKOUTS Apr 30 Wat 3f fst :38⅖ b

Lay Arms

B. f. 3, by Open Arms—Taylor, by Royal Clove
$2,500 Br.—Locke G E (Ark) Tr.—Laffargue G J
Own.—Harris D

105^{10}

	St.	1st	2nd	3rd	Amt.
1973	2	M	0	0	$60
1972	0	M	0	0	

15Jun73- 2Com fst 4f :23 :47⅗ Md 2500 4 5 4^3 4^8 7^{20} Theall S b 120 38.10 — — Makemeadeal $120^{5\frac12}$ Swift Signal $115^{2\frac12}$ Edwards Country $120^{4\frac34}$ Tired 8
8Jun73- 9Com fst 4½f :23⅗ :48⅖ :54⅗ Md 2500 7 5 $6^{6\frac12}$ 7^{10} 8^{19} Theall S b 120 30.20 — — Lonesome Sailor 120^3 Bab's Flash $115^{1\frac34}$ Makemeadeal 120^1 No factor 10
LATEST WORKOUTS Jun 5 Com 2f fst :25 hg

Wembley Legend

Ch. f. 3, by Jersey Legend—Miss Wembley, by Old Rockport
$2,500 Br.—Corkran Dr T R (Md) Tr.—Starkey J H
Own.—Barnard C F

115

	St.	1st	2nd	3rd	Amt.
1973	1	M	0	0	$60
1972	0	M	0	0	

8Jun73- 9Com fst 4½f :23⅗ :48⅖ :54⅗ Md 2500 6 9 7^8 5^7 $4^{5\frac34}$ Heim K b 115 13.80 — — Lonesome Sailor 120^3 Bab's Flash $115^{1\frac34}$ Makemeadeal 120^1 Belated rally 10
LATEST WORKOUTS Jun 20 Com 3f fst :39 b Jun 16 Com 5f fst 1:03⅘ b ● Jun 5 Com 3f fst :37⅗ b May 30 Com 3f sly :39⅕ bg

Milk Bottle

B. g. 3, by Cyclotron—Mesmerizer, by Jet's Date
$2,500 Br.—Cartimiglia L A (La) Tr.—Douglas J
Own.—Douglas J

110^{10}

	St.	1st	2nd	3rd	Amt.
1973	4	M	0	0	$30
1972	0	M	0	0	

15Jun73- 2Com fst 4f :23 :47⅗ Md 2500 6 1 7^{12} 8^{18} 8^{37} Baratinni D^{10} b 110 33.80 — — Makemeadeal $120^{5\frac12}$ Swift Signal $115^{2\frac12}$ Edwards Country $120^{4\frac34}$ Far back 8
8Jun73- 9Com fst 4½f :23⅗ :48⅖ :54⅗ Md 2500 4 10 10^{15} 10^{20} 10^{28} Dupre T b 127 30.20 — — Lonesome Sailor 120^3 Bab's Flash $115^{1\frac34}$ Makemeadeal 120^1 Trailed 10
23May73- 1JnD fst 4f :23 :47⅘ 3 ♦ [S]Md 2500 1 9 9^{13} 9^{15} 9^{23} Baratinni D^5 b 107 37.60 65-11 Skeeter Jacobs $112^{1\frac12}$ Steady Juror $107^{1\frac12}$ Spinella 112^5 Far back 9
5May73- 1JnD fst 6½f :23⅖ :48 1:22⅘ 3 ♦ Md 5000 9 9 9^{15} 10^{21} — — Derouen G b 111 22.20 — — Miss Poker Chip $111\frac12$ I Can Dance $114\frac12$ I'll Be OnTime $120\frac34$ Outdistanced 10
LATEST WORKOUTS Jun 21 Com 3f fst :39⅗ b

lengths — and Edwards Country looked like Wembley Legend's strongest opponent in today's race.

Wembley Legend was the best horse in the field. He would be helped by the No. 8 post position. Two of his chief rivals would probably be eliminated from contention by their inside post positions. Before the race I announced to my mother and our companions at Commodore Downs that Wembley Legend was a cinch. And she was. She ran away with the race, winning by five lengths and paying $9.40 to win. "Son, you may have chosen the right calling," my mother conceded as she headed toward the cashier's window.

If situations like the Wembley Legend race arose on a regular basis, I would have retired to a villa in Marrakesh long ago. But they don't. Whenever I am operating at a track with a powerful bias — say, speed on the rail — I can wait for days or weeks without finding a horse who has my top figure, early speed, and an inside post position. The gods who oversee horse racing do not intend that this game be too easy. But there is another application of track biases that does produce many winners, whose virtues are usually so subtle that they go off at excellent odds.

One of the most pronounced track biases I ever saw came at Bowie in mid-February, 1973. There had been several days of heavy rain in the Washington-Baltimore area. The Bowie racing strip was inundated, and because of its drainage system all the moisture seeped toward the rail. The rains were followed by a fast freeze, which trapped the moisture on the inside part of the track. The soil on the Bowie track is usually kept in a granular condition, but the water made these granules adhere to each other so that the inside part of the track was as hard as a superhighway. As a result, practically every winner was a horse that raced along this narrow path. There was a day when six of the nine races were captured by a horse breaking from post position one. Here are the *Racing Form* charts for the first three races at Bowie on one of the days during this extraordinary speed-on-the-rail period:

Official Racing Charts

Bowie Race Course

BOWIE, MD., SATURDAY, FEBRUARY 17, 1973—BOWIE RACE COURSE (1 mile)
Meeting scheduled for sixty days (January 2 to March 16). (Four dark days to be announced.)
Southern Maryland Agriculture Association. President, F. George Tucker. American Totalisator. United and Puett Starting Gates. Teletimer, automatic timing. Film Patrol. Complete finish of each race confirmed by Jones Precision Photo Finish, Inc. Trackman, Dick Carroll.
Weather clear. Temperature 23 degrees.
Length of stretch from last turn to finish, 1,080.15 feet.

Steward representing Maryland State Racing Commission, J. Fred Colwill. Stewards, Merrall MacNeille and J. Melvin Mackin. Placing Judges, J. Heislen, F. G. Gabriel and Lawrence R. Lacey. Patrol Judges, C. Blind, P. O'Dell, P. Pitts, Jr. and T. J. Baker. Paddock Judge and Timer, E. T. McLean. Clerk of Scales, S. Young. Starter, Edward Blind. Identifier, J. W. Gogel Sr. Racing Secretary and Handicapper, Lawrence J. Abbundi. Assistant Racing Secretary, E. Litzenberger.

Racing starts at 1:00 p. m. Eastern Standard Time. Percentage of winning favorites corresponding meeting 1972, .29; current meeting, .35. Percentage of favorites in the money, .66. Daily Double wagering on first and second races. Exacta, third, fifth, seventh and ninth races. No entries or field horses permitted in Daily Double or Exacta races. Mutuel take, 15 per cent (State, 5.34; track, 8.91; Improvement Fund, .50; Pension Fund, .25).

The superior figure following the jockey's name indicates the number of pounds apprentice or rider allowance claimed, s spurs, b blinkers. NOTE: All riders are equipped with whips unless otherwise designated in footnote below chart.

FIRST RACE
Bow
February 17, 1973

6 FURLONGS (chute). (1:08$\frac{3}{5}$). CLAIMING. Purse $3,500. 4-year-olds and upward. Weight, 122 lbs. Non-winners of two races since Jan. 6 allowed 3 lbs.; a race, 6 lbs.; a race since Dec. 30. 9 lbs. Claiming price, $3,000.
Value to winner $2,100; second, $770; third, $420; fourth, $210. Mutuel Pool, $64,392.

Last Raced		Horse	EqtAWt	PP	St	¼	½	Str	Fin	Jockeys	Owners	Odds to $1
1-29-73^{2}	Bow^{3}	Brave Gem	4 113	1	8	1^{h}	1$^{1\frac{1}{2}}$	1^{3}	1^{2}	CCooke	R F Cicala	3.50
12- 2-72^{1}	Lrl^{11}	Reaction	b6 113	10	2	8^{3}	6^{3}	5$^{\frac{1}{2}}$	2^{1}	ORosado	C E McDonald	25.80
1-31-73^{1}	Bow^{4}	William de Great	b7 113	5	5	2^{h}	4^{h}	6^{4}	3no	JArellano	R E Dutrow	4.90
2-12-72^{2}	Bow^{11}	Apache Way	b6 113	8	1	3^{3}	3^{1}	2^{h}	4^{3}	VBraccialeJr	Pacesetter Stable	4.80
1-13-73^{1}	Bow^{2}	Bard of Cornwall	b4 113	2	9	4$^{\frac{1}{2}}$	2^{h}	4^{h}	5no	ASBlack	R T Stokes	5.20
2-10-73^{6}	CT^{6}	Right Risk	b6 113	11	4	6^{h}	5$^{\frac{1}{2}}$	3^{h}	6^{1}	WJPassmore	D E Reckart	109.00
1-30-72^{2}	Bow^{1}	Bal K.	b5 119	6	6	5^{h}	7	7^{2}	7^{2}	EWalsh	F D Vechery	3.10
1-20-73^{1}	Bow^{8}	Dawning Sun	b4 110	4	12	9^{h}	9^{6}	8^{7}	8^{8}	GMcCarron	C C Unglesbee	15.30
1-30-73^{2}	Bow^{9}	War Parade	7 123	3	7	12	12	10^{4}	9^{1}	TBarnes	J Costew	44.70
1-20-73^{1}	Bow^{10}	Brise de Mer	b6 113	9	11	7$^{\frac{1}{2}}$	8$^{\frac{1}{2}}$	9^{2}	10^{3}	JCanessa	Ida Geller	41.60
1-27-73^{2}	Bow^{12}	Rated M.	4 113	12	3	11$^{1\frac{1}{2}}$	10^{1}	11^{h}	11$^{2\frac{1}{2}}$	RStovall	W M Backer	101.50
1- 6-73^{1}	Bow^{10}	Mr. Judex	b10 113	7	10	10^{2}	11^{h}	12	12	DRWright	R E Vogelman Jr	16.90

Time, :23$\frac{3}{5}$, :45$\frac{4}{5}$, 1:11$\frac{4}{5}$. Track fast.

(cont'd on next page)

Official Program Numbers ↘

$2 Mutuel Prices:

1-BRAVE GEM	9.00	6.20	4.40
10-REACTION		20.00	10.80
5-WILLIAM DE GREAT			4.20

Dk. b. or br. g, by Big Brave—Ginnygem, by Road House. Trainer, M. Angelastro. Bred by Hopkins & Smith (Md.).

IN GATE—1:00. OFF AT 1:00 EASTERN STANDARD TIME. Start good. Won driving.

BRAVE GEM had room inside to take the lead, then continued gamely through the stretch run to win as the best. REACTION, never far back, rallied inside and between horses in the stretch and beat the rest in the late stages. WILLIAM DE GREAT vied for the early lead and, after being headed, kept going willingly while saving ground. APACHE WAY, outside of horses, went gamely to the end. BARD OF CORNWALL, hustled along early, began to weaken entering the final eighth. RIGHT RISKY, widest, hung after getting close to the lead. BAL K. could not keep a contending position after the midway mark. DAWNING SUN went evenly. WAR PARADE and the rest were outrun.

Overweight—War Parade, 1 pound; Dawning Sun, 2.

Apache Way claimed by M. Miller, trainer H. E. Worcester III.

Scratched—Navy Coach, Bow Shannon, Gwanadier, Windward Passage, Kathy's Pet, Chariot Race.

SECOND RACE
Bow
February 17, 1973

$1\frac{1}{16}$ MILES. (1:41⅗). CLAIMING. Purse $4,000. 4-year-olds and upward. Weight, 122 lbs. Non-winners of two races since Jan. 6 allowed 3 lbs.; a race, 5 lbs.; a race since Dec. 30, 8 lbs. Claiming price, $4,000; 1 lb. for each $250 to $3,500. Value to winner $2,400; second, $880; third, $480; fourth, $240. Mutuel Pool, $102,153.

Last Raced	Horse	EqtAWt	PP	St	¼	½	¾	Str	Fin	Jockeys	Owners	Odds to $1
1-13-73^{2} Bow^{4}	Royal Choice	b4 114	1	2	1½	1^{h}	1^{h}	1^{1}	$1^{1\frac{1}{4}}$	VBraccialeJr	A P Bovello	2.70
2-10-73^{9} Bow^{6}	Huapango	b8 117	6	11	6^{2}	3^{1}	3^{3}	$3^{1\frac{1}{2}}$	2^{nk}	JKurtz	Margaret A Jacobs	9.40
2-10-73^{9} Bow^{4}	Better Bee Quick	5 114	7	10	8½	7½	4^{h}	4^{4}	$3^{3\frac{1}{2}}$	CJimenez	Audley Farm Stable	4.60
2- 3-73^{9} Bow^{6}	Parenteral	4 114	12	12	12	11^{1}	$8^{1\frac{1}{2}}$	5^{2}	4¾	ASBlack	R Staszak	23.70
2- 6-73^{3} Bow^{8}	Mafufski	b4 114	2	4	2^{3}	2^{3}	2^{3}	2½	$5^{3\frac{3}{4}}$	GMcCarron	C Unglesbee	4.10
1-29-73^{9} Bow^{5}	Flashmaster	5 113	9	4	$9^{1\frac{1}{2}}$	9^{2}	9^{h}	7^{2}	$6^{3\frac{1}{2}}$	CCooke	R Stephano	12.10
2- 3-73^{2} Bow^{8}	Fields of Eton	b6 119	11	8	7^{1}	8^{2}	7^{1}	$6^{1\frac{1}{2}}$	7½	EWalsh	E F Schoenborn	22.60
2- 3-73^{9} Bow^{8}	Colony Prince	4 114	10	9	10^{2}	6^{2}	6^{h}	9^{4}	$8^{2\frac{1}{2}}$	BMFeliciano	Jean B Bradley	48.90
2-12-73^{2} Bow^{6}	Dixie Doctor	4 114	5	5	5½	4^{2}	5^{2}	8^{h}	9^{1}	AAgnello	G Radford	15.40
2- 5-73^{2} Bow^{8}	Super Amber	b4 114	8	7	11^{1}	12	11^{12}	11	$10^{1\frac{1}{4}}$	AGomez	P Jacobson	30.20
2- 5-73^{1} Bow^{4}	Adaptive	8 114	3	3	3^{h}	5^{1}	10^{5}	10^{2}	11	JDavidson	C H Harding	6.00
2-12-73^{5} Bow^{10}	Star Bama	b5 113	4	6	4^{h}	10^{1}	12	Eased.		WJPassmore	Helen Barabas	33.60

Time, :25, :49⅕, 1:14, 1:40⅕, 1:46⅘. Track fast.

$2 Mutuel Prices:

1-ROYAL CHOICE	7.40	5.00	3.20
6-HUAPANGO		9.80	5.20
7-BETTER BEE QUICK			4.40

Dk. b. or br. c, by Alternative—Heritage Cave, by Blue Heritage. Trainer, J. Tammaro. Bred by A. P. Bovello (Md.).

IN GATE—1:28. OFF AT 1:28 EASTERN STANDARD TIME. Start good. Won driving.

ROYAL CHOICE raced inside, held MAF UFS KI off nicely to the last eighth, then was able to handle the others with authority. HUAPANGO, well placed and never far back, tried hard but was no match for the winner. BETTER BEE QUICK, smoothly ridden into a striking position, lacked a good rally thereafter while continuing wide. PARENTERAL, without early speed, was able to get through inside in his rally. MAFUFSKI had no excuse. FLASHMASTER went evenly. FIELDS OF ETON raced wide. COLONY PRINCE made his run on the outside but faltered entering the stretch. DIXIE DOCTOR and ADAPTIVE could not keep pace. SUPER AMBER lacked speed. STAR BAMA was eased while being badly outrun.

Overweight—Star Bama, 1 pound.

Adaptive claimed by C. I. Frock, trainer C. I. Frock.

Claiming Prices (in order of finish)—$4000, 4000, 4000, 4000, 4000, 3750, 4000, 4000, 4000, 4000, 4000, 3500.

Scratched—Arctic Pole, Prince Joker, Drink Up, Mayhem, I Ching, Last Ripple.

Daily Double (1-1) Paid $42.60; Double Pool, $152,048.

THIRD RACE
Bow
February 17, 1973

$1\frac{1}{16}$ MILES. (1:41⅗). CLAIMING. Purse $5,000. 4-year-olds and upward. Weight, 122 lbs. Non-winners of two races at one mile or over since Jan. 6 allowed 3 lbs.; one such race, 5 lbs.; such a race since Dec. 30, 8 lbs. Claiming price, $6,500; 1 lb. for each $250 to $6 000. (Races where entered for $5,000 or less not considered.)

Value to winner $3,000; second, $1,100; third, $600; fourth, $300. Mutuel Pool, $83,201.

Last Raced	Horse	EqtAWt	PP	St	¼	½	¾	Str	Fin	Jockeys	Owners	Odds to $1
2- 8-73^{4} Bow^{1}	T. Fred	b5 114	6	4	1^{3}	1^{3}	1^{2}	1^{3}	$1^{3\frac{1}{2}}$	JDavidson	Row Farm	2.00
2- 3-73^{5} Bow^{11}	Dasha Bitters	b5 113	4	11	$10^{1\frac{1}{2}}$	$8^{1\frac{1}{2}}$	3^{2}	2^{h}	2^{4}	GMcCarron	E A Roller	40.30
2-10-73^{7} Bow^{7}	Seven Sails	5 114	1	2	5^{1}	5^{h}	2^{h}	3^{5}	$3^{2\frac{1}{4}}$	AAgnello	L F Wilcox	50.70
2- 8-73^{5} Bow^{8}	Lord Luvus	b6 114	3	3	7^{2}	11	9^{3}	6^{3}	$4^{\frac{1}{2}}$	CJimenez	Starlight Farm	10.80
2- 2-73^{5} Bow^{7}	Plucky Star	4 110	7	7	$9^{1\frac{1}{2}}$	7^{h}	$6^{\frac{1}{2}}$	4^{1}	5^{1}	BMFeliciano	M Martin	26.30
2- 6-73^{3} Bow^{4}	Shy Moment	6 115	5	6	11	9^{h}	$7^{1\frac{1}{2}}$	5^{1}	6^{5}	RPlatts	J D Cochrane	6.00
1-22-73^{5} Bow^{3}	Powder Peddler	5 114	8	10	8^{h}	$6^{\frac{1}{2}}$	5^{2}	7^{h}	7^{h}	GCusimano	N E Rinaldi	4.70
2-10-73^{6} Pen^{1}	Royal 'n Nimble	4 119	2	1	2^{h}	$2^{\frac{1}{2}}$	4^{h}	8^{1}	8^{1}	AGomez	Double B Stable	10.40
2- 6-73^{3} Bow^{2}	Angle Right	b7 119	9	5	$4^{1\frac{1}{2}}$	3^{1}	8^{h}	9^{8}	9^{9}	RHoward	J J Kaminski	4.00
2- 6-73^{3} Bow^{6}	Wolf It Down	4 109	11	8	3^{h}	4^{2}	10^{4}	$10^{\frac{1}{2}}$	10^{3}	SNeff^{5}	Audley Farm Stable	55.80
1-22-73^{7} Bow^{5}	Doux Go	b4 114	10	9	6^{h}	$10^{\frac{1}{2}}$	11	11	11	JKurtz	R Mascuilli	13.10

Time, :24⅘, :48⅗, 1:13⅕, 1:38⅗, 1:45⅗. Track fast.

$2 Mutuel Prices:			
6-T. FRED	**6.00**	**4.40**	**3.80**
4-DASHA BITTERS		**22.00**	**14.60**
1-SEVEN SAILS			**14.80**

Dk. b. or br. h, by Rip 'n Skip—Spent Money, by Auditing. Trainer, R. E. Dutrow. Bred by R. J. Turcotte (N. Y.).

IN GATE—2:01. OFF AT 2:01 EASTERN STANDARD TIME. Start good. Won handily.

T. FRED sprinted to a good lead early, made the pace on his own courage, stopped bid approaching the stretch, then was in command again. DASHA BITTERS, unhurried early, was able to slip through inside once rallying and, although no match for the winner, easily beat the rest. SEVEN SAILS saved ground, held well until inside the last eighth, then weakened. LORD LUVUS had a mild rally to pass beaten horses. PLUCKY STAR went wide to pull within striking distance, then leveled off. SHY MOMENT lagged back half the race, moved on the outside thereafter, but could not get close. POWDER PEDDLER made a brief rally, then stopped. ROYAL 'N NIMBLE had no excuse. ANGLE RIGHT raced forwardly to the far turn, then gave way. WOLF IT DOWN and DOUX GO were outrun.

Overweight—Shy Moment, 1 pound; Plucky Star, 1.

Claiming Prices (in order of finish)—$6500, 6250, 6500, 6500, 6500, 6500, 6500, 6500, 6500, 6500, 6500.

Scratched—Swapping Doctor, Quill Pen, Sing Man Sing, Shining Royal, Chinihue, Scotch Broth.

Exacta (6-4) Paid $187.00; Exacta Pool, $119,285.

A serious handicapper should scrutinize the charts of each day's races at the track he follows, especially when a bias exists. Even if he had not been at Bowie on February 17, a reader of these charts would have been able to comprehend what the track was like. The first winner, Brave Gem, broke from post position one and, according to the footnotes, "had room inside to take the lead, continued gamely through the stretch to win as much the best." In the second race, Royal Choice broke from the inside post position and led all the way. In the third race, the first three finishers all raced on the inside. T. Fred opened an early three-length advantage and led all the way; although the footnotes do not specify it, we can assume he was on the rail. The second-place finisher, Dasha Bitters, "was able to slip through inside once rallying." The third horse, Seven Sails, "saved ground."

These charts, and the other ones for the same day, indicate clearly that horses who possessed early speed and could get to the rail had a tremendous advantage. When these horses run again, we must remember that their good performances on February 17 were more the result of the aberrant track condition than of their own ability. Even if a horse wins by a huge margin and earns a speed figure like Citation's, we should discount his performance. But the betting public doesn't do this. When Royal Choice ran a week later over a normal track, the Bowie patrons were impressed by his wire-to-wire victory and made him the 6-to-5 favorite. With no track bias to help him, he finished fifth. When T. Fred ran again, the bettors saw his 3½-length victory on February 17 and made him the 8-to-5 favorite. He was beaten. Brave Gem was a 5-to-1 shot in his next start and was trounced by 23 lengths. In my early experiences handicapping with speed figures, I lost a lot of money on horses like Brave Gem, T. Fred, and Royal Choice. I was hypnotized by the impressive times in which they had won, and was oblivious of the conditions under which they had earned their big figures. Now when I evaluate a horse who ran well with the track bias in his favor, I discount that performance almost completely and handicap the animal off his prior races on a normal track.

Just as horses that have benefited from the track bias should be viewed with skepticism when they run again, the chances of horses who were disadvantaged by the bias should be upgraded. We must watch races carefully, or at least study the charts meticulously, and make a list of horses that showed some sign of life but couldn't run their best race because of the bias. In the first three races on February 17, there were many horses that gave strong indications of being able to win over a normal track. Better Bee Quick was one of the favorites in the second race, going off at 9-to-2 odds. But he was a stretch runner breaking from the No. 7 post position; an observant handicapper at the track that day would have eliminated him without a moment's hesitation. But Better Bee Quick ran well under the circumstances and finished third. The footnotes say, "Better Bee Quick, smoothly ridden into a striking position, lacked a good rally thereafter while continuing wide." The reason he lacked a good rally was that he was running on the part of the track where no horses could accelerate. In his next start, over a normal racetrack, Better Bee Quick was entered against similar opposition and won by 3½ lengths, paying $7.40.

Angle Right had come into the third race on February 17 with two excellent efforts behind him and was second choice in the betting at 4 to 1. He showed early speed from the No. 9 post, but two horses from inner post positions outbroke Angle Right and prevented him from getting to the rail. After a half mile, Angle Right gave up. He retreated to finish ninth, 17 lengths behind the winner. A week later Angle Right was entered in a weak $6500 claiming race. He figured to be an easy winner if he ran his good race, but he went off at 7-to-2 odds because of that dismal 17-length defeat. Handicappers who knew that they could discount that loss because of the track bias collected a $9.80 payoff.

Of all the horses who raced during the speed-favoring period at Bowie, there was one who had by far the most intriguing dope. His name was Right Risk, and the chart of the first race on February 17 tells the whole story. Right Risk had been running at Charles Town, where his record had been atrocious. He was justifiably a 109-to-1 shot at Bowie. His already remote chances of winning were rendered nonexistent by his No. 11 post position. Right Risk was running sixth after a quarter mile, fifth after a half mile, third entering the stretch, and finally finished sixth by six lengths. The footnotes of the chart said, "Right Risk, widest, hung after getting close to the lead." It was easy to visualize what had happened. Right Risk was trying hard to win; he made a big move on the outside, the sort of move that usually wins races. But he was virtually running on a treadmill in the middle of the track and couldn't overcome the disadvantage. Almost all the horses who finished in front of him had either broken from favorable post positions or had made their moves along the rail.

When I spot a horse like Right Risk, who ran well against a track bias, I don't go wild with enthusiasm until I evaluate the time of the race. Maybe he got into contention only because his rivals were so slow. But the Teletimer indicated that Right Risk had been pitted against exceptionally good $3000 horses. His race was run in 1:11 $\frac{4}{5}$. The only other six-furlong event that day was an allowance race that served as a prep for Bowie's biggest race of the year, the $100,000 John B. Campbell Handicap. The classy horses in that allowance race had run in 1:11 flat — a mere four-fifths of a second faster than the $3000 claiming race.

Right Risk was the sort of horse I have fantasies about but never encounter in real life. He had run a remarkable race, trying to overcome insurmountable obstacles in an exceptionally fast race. But the next time he ran, his past performances would suggest that he was a terrible horse who had finished an indifferent sixth in his most recent effort. I waited anxiously for his name to reappear in the Bowie entries.

Seven days later, Right Risk was entered in the first at Bowie. He had drawn the inside post position. His opposition was negligible. The *Racing Form*'s morning line listed him at 30 to 1. I went to the track that day with unshakable confidence that I was going to win a small fortune. I didn't. Right Risk had been scratched. I couldn't imagine why. Perhaps the horse had been hurt. Or perhaps the trainer was looking for an easier race. I didn't know where he could find one, though one remote possibility did cross my mind. Dover Downs, a little track in Delaware that was a two-hour drive from Bowie, offered a cheaper brand of racing than the Maryland tracks. Trainers based in Maryland, New Jersey, and Pennsylvania would often ship their horses to Dover on Saturday or Sunday in search of easy pickings. These superior out of town horses would almost always win. Steve Davidowitz had observed this phenomenon, and we had spent the two previous weekends at Dover betting almost exclusively on these horses, who had a clear class advantage over the locals.

Steve was out of town on the weekend that Right Risk had been scratched at Bowie, and I planned to forgo the long trip. But I did wake up early Sunday morning to check the Dover entries and see if Right Risk, or any other horses I recognized, was entered that afternoon. The information was not in the edition of the *Racing Form* that was delivered to my front door. The *Racing Form* had recently started publishing a Special Sunday Edition that was the only place to find Dover entries. It was sold at one newsstand on the other side of Washington. So I went back to bed. This, it turned out, may have been a $35,297 mistake.

The next day I glanced at the Dover Sunday results in an afternoon newspaper and the name leaped out of the page at me: Right Risk had won the eighth race and paid $13.10 to win. The race had been an extremely weak field of six $2500 claimers, the sort of spot where I could have bet Right Risk with absolute confidence. And the eighth race had been part of the Big Exacta, a gimmick requiring bettors to select the one-two finishers in two consecutive races. Nobody at Dover had it that day. It would have been worth $35,297. I briefly contemplated self-destruction, but finally convinced myself that an understanding of track biases would present me with other opportunities in the future that would be just as clear and just as lucrative as Right Risk would have been. I am still waiting.

5

Trainers

LUCIEN LAURIN AND ELLIOTT BURCH traveled very different paths before they became archrivals in the upper echelon of the training profession. The son of a laborer in a Quebec paper mill, Laurin quit school at the age of sixteen to become a jockey. When he became too heavy to ride anymore, he turned to training. He got his first modest bankroll with a mare he had bought for $30, and he managed to live from hand to mouth by campaigning a stable of a few cheap horses on the leaky-roof circuit. It was a long struggle before he moved up into the big leagues of racing and finally earned national fame as the trainer of Secretariat and Riva Ridge.

Burch was born to be a successful horseman. His father

and grandfather had both earned niches in the Racing Hall of Fame for their accomplishments as trainers. After attending Lawrenceville, Yale, and the University of Kentucky, Burch worked for eight years as his father's assistant and took over his job with the Brookmeade Stable when he retired. Two years later he trained Sword Dancer to win the Horse of the Year title. Since becoming the trainer for Paul Mellon's Rokeby Stable in 1966, he has developed two more Horses of the Year, Arts and Letters and Fort Marcy. While Laurin can be alternatively cocky, sullen, and combative, Burch is always cool, rational, and articulate, the perfect patrician.

The paths of the two men began to cross regularly in 1972, when Laurin was training Riva Ridge and Burch was handling Key to the Mint. Riva Ridge had won the Kentucky Derby and had seemed destined to win the three-year-old championship until he suffered a stunning defeat in the Preakness. Laurin was shaken. He lashed out at his jockey, Ron Turcotte, irrationally blaming him for the loss. Many second-guessers thought that Laurin was so rattled by the Preakness that he wasn't going to be able to train his horse properly for the Belmont Stakes, the final leg of the Triple Crown. Burch, who may have shared this view, honed Key to the Mint into razor-sharp condition for the Belmont, working him six furlongs in 1:10 three days before the race. But Laurin confounded all his critics when he sent out a perfectly prepared Riva Ridge to win the Belmont by seven lengths, while Key to the Mint struggled home fourth.

After the race, Burch did something that is rare for members of his profession. He did not blame his jockey for Key to the Mint's defeat; he blamed himself. The fast workout just before the Belmont had been a horrible mistake. For a grueling mile-and-a-half race, a trainer must try to build up a horse's stamina, not sharpen his speed.

Burch had learned his lesson when Key to the Mint met Riva Ridge again in the fall, in Belmont's mile-and-a-half Woodward Stakes, a race that would determine the three-year-old championship. During the month leading up to the Woodward, Burch prepared his horse with workouts that were designed to build up his stamina. He sent Key to the Mint a mile and an eighth in competition with two stable-mates that were running at him in shifts. He followed that with a rare mile-and-a-half workout four days later. While Burch was concentrating all his energies on this project, Laurin may have been distracted. He had been upset to find himself in the midst of a controversy when Riva Ridge's owner, Penny Tweedy, made a baseless public charge that her horse had been drugged before a midsummer defeat at Monmouth Park. And Laurin was also becoming increasingly preoccupied with another horse in his barn, a two-year-old named Secretariat. Whatever the reason, Riva Ridge ran dismally in the Woodward, and Key to the Mint ran away with the race and the three-year-old championship.

Burch's training of Key to the Mint for the Woodward had been a masterpiece, but the heavens did not reward him for his expertise the next year. Instead it was Laurin who was blessed to be training Secretariat, the first Triple Crown winner in twenty-five years and one of the great horses of all time. After his sweep of the three-year-old classics, Laurin decided to give Secretariat his first test against older horses in the Whitney Stakes at Saratoga. His strongest possible rival looked like Key to the Mint, who was in excellent form at the time. But Burch didn't enter his horse in the Whitney. He did not want to lose a big one to Lucien Laurin. He made a bad calculation, for this was one of the few times in his career that Secretariat was vulnerable. The superhorse had been running a fever at Saratoga and he hadn't been acting right in his workouts. But Laurin made an even worse calculation. He entered Secretariat in the Whitney despite his below-par condition and was the victim of a stunning upset by an unknown named Onion.

Having blown a golden opportunity to beat Secretariat, Burch got his chance six weeks later in the ballyhooed $250,000 Marlboro Cup. Secretariat had not raced since his Saratoga debacle, and Laurin was trying to bring his horse back from an illness to face the greatest challenge of his career. Burch didn't think that he could do it. He said publicly, the day before the race, that he didn't even consider Secretariat to be Key to the Mint's most formidable rival.

But Laurin had demonstrated many times before that he thrives on adversity. When his horse's prospects look bleak, when he is being subjected to intense scrutiny and criticism, he does his best work. He had done it before the Belmont in 1972 and he did it in the Marlboro Cup. Secretariat won and set a world record for a mile and one-eighth. Key to the Mint finished last, demonstrating perhaps that when a trainer is too obsessed by another man's horse he cannot properly train his own.

Laurin and Burch had as much to do with the outcome of the big races of 1972 and 1973 as the horses they were training. They are two of the most astute members of their profession, but they are also flesh and blood beings who can have lapses as well as strokes of brilliance, who can experience self-doubt, overconfidence, jealousy, and self-deception. Every horse, whether he is a champion or a lowly claimer, may be affected by similar human influences. Horseplayers who want to understand the game and beat the races must recognize the enormous importance of trainers. It is not enough merely to evaluate the ability of horses; we must evaluate the men behind them as well.

Before trying to deal with the nuances of different trainers' methods, a handicapper should first know which horsemen in his area are generally competent and which are not. Their overall records usually provide a reasonable guideline. A trainer who wins with 20 percent of the horses he sends onto the track has to have some virtues.

During the 1973–74 Maryland season, I compiled statistics on most of the trainers in the state and found that the best winning percentage belonged to a small-time operator whose name I didn't even recognize: George J. Burns. His two-horse stable had compiled a 5-for-6 record. Claiborne Reed, a filly, had won all four of her races. Burns had handled her gingerly, running her only in appropriate spots when she was in peak condition. The other half of his stable, a cheap claimer named Potestas, was 1-for-2. Not long after discovering Burns's remarkable rate of success, I encountered Potestas in a $4000 claiming race at Bowie. The horse looked like a standout, except for one thing: he had not raced for twenty-six days and had had no workouts since his last start. Normally I would be very hesitant about betting a horse whose record gave no indication of his current condition. If he were trained by a man with a 1-for-40 record, I would be doubly skeptical. But even though I knew nothing else about the man, I knew that George J. Burns would not have entered Potestas in this race unless he were ready. I bet with confidence, and Potestas paid $7.20.

If a trainer wins with 20 percent of his starters during the course of a year, that does not mean that he will win at the same rate every week and every month. Like other types of competitors, trainers have hot streaks and cold spells. Sometimes these streaks will be caused by factors completely extraneous to racing — ill health or marital troubles, for instance — but usually they will fall into patterns that a handicapper can analyze and even predict. When the 1972 Maryland racing season began at Laurel, two of the men who were expected to dominate the trainer standings were John Tammaro and King Leatherbury. Their individual talent and the quality of their stables were comparable. Leatherbury had brought his horses from Delaware Park, where he had enjoyed a sensational meeting, running his horses often and winning often. By the time he reached Laurel, many of his horses were tired. Their form was starting to deteriorate. The higher-class horses in his barn had won so much that they were no longer eligible for allowance races with restrictive conditions, such as "nonwinners of three races since February 15." Tammaro had brought his stable from Atlantic City, where during the last few weeks of the meeting he had not won many races. He had been making a conscious effort to prepare for Laurel. He rested and recycled some of his campaigners who had already had a hard season and had begun to decline. He claimed fresh new horses who would help him in Maryland. During the first month of the Laurel meeting, Leatherbury suffered through a terrible slump. His horses all seemed to run worse than the past performances suggested they should. Tammaro was red hot. Even his horses who showed dismal form at Atlantic City were coming to life. A horseplayer must not only recognize which trainers are generally successful. He must know which ones are winning *now*.

Many of the qualities that make a winning trainer are invisible to the public. A successful horseman will work hard. He will hire competent people to work for him and oversee them carefully. He will know each of his horses as individuals and will be able to sense the day to day changes in their conditions. He will understand horses' physiology, so he can detect problems and ailments just as they are developing instead of after they have become critical. Most of the virtues that a trainer displays in his behind the scenes activities will ultimately be reflected in the past performances of his horses. A handicapper can easily recognize certain signs of a trainer's competence.

A good trainer knows how to prepare a horse to win a specific race. Any second-rate horseman can put an animal onto the track, run him until he gets into shape, and win a purse or two. But it takes expertise to aim for a certain objective and find the optimum way to prepare a horse for it. Burch did it in the 1972 Woodward Stakes when he concluded that the best way to approach the race was to train Key to the Mint with a series of long, stamina-building workouts. A trainer with an unraced two-year-old of moderate ability might give his horse a couple of races for exercise against maiden-special-weight company, then drop him into a maiden-claiming race and equip him with blinkers. A trainer might prepare a sluggish router for a winning effort by entering him first in a sprint race that will sharpen his speed. The possibilities are endless. But whenever a handicapper sees an intelligent plan underlying a horse's past performances, he can usually conclude that the trainer knows what he is doing.

A good trainer will not race his horse when the animal's form is beginning to deteriorate. "When horses run hard five or six times in a row they'll generally tail off," says Allen Jerkens. "If a horse is a good eater and then stops eating as much, or if his coat starts looking duller, that's the key that tells you he's about to go off form. We are all tempted to go to the well once too often, but if you run them when they're tailing off it's much tougher to bring them back."

A good trainer will seldom run his horses in races where they don't belong — against competition that is too tough or at a distance beyond their capabilities. George Getz, a young Chicago-based horseman, says he has learned this lesson many times. Before he became a trainer, Getz had been a hotshot bowler. He carried a 200 average, but he couldn't resist head to head money matches with rivals who could always hit 210. Getz blew his paycheck every week. Instead of seeking weaker opponents, he became discouraged and depressed. His average dropped, and he finally gave up the sport completely. Years later Getz would realize that horses respond the same way when they face competition that they cannot handle. In 1971 Getz had a three-year-old colt named Royal Leverage who he thought was going to develop into a nice allowance-class runner. His owner wanted to run in the Kentucky Derby, and Getz complied with his wishes. Royal Leverage was soundly trounced, of course, and when he returned to Chicago he seemed totally discouraged by that defeat. The horse lost all his enthusiasm for training. He developed a phobia about the starting gate and wouldn't break from the gate without considerable prodding. "He finally broke down at the eighth pole at Sportsman's Park," Getz said. "I guess they burned him in the incinerator.

"This is no theory. It is a fact. If you run a horse way over his head, where he doesn't belong, he'll get discouraged or lose interest. And when you drop him back to his proper level, he won't run. I think this is what makes a good trainer. We all take care of our horses. We all call up the vet when they get sick. The thing that distinguishes the good ones from the bad ones is that they take time with their horses."

When a horseplayer has a realistic sense of what training is about, he should study every horse's past performances with the trainer in mind. Has he managed the horse intelligently? Is he preparing him for a specific race? By asking and answering these questions, a handicapper will begin to learn which trainers are competent and which are not. And he will often uncover good bets when he understands the trainer's intentions with a particular horse. A handicapper who scrutinized the past performances of the filly Poker Night in the Bed of Roses Handicap at Aqueduct on April 18, 1973, would have learned, even if he had never heard of the man before, that Allen Jerkens is a great trainer, and he would have found an excellent wager.

Poker Night * **110** **Lt. b. f (1970), by Poker—Vault, by On Trust.**
Breeder, C. E. Mather II. (Ky.). **1973 6 5 1 0 $43,330**
Onwer, Hobeau Farm. Trainer, H. A. Jerkens. **1972 7 2 1 1 $10,140**

Apr18-73^{7}Aqu	1	1:35⅖	ft	3e	108	$3^{5\frac{1}{2}}$	$1^{1\frac{1}{2}}$	1^{3}	$1^{1\frac{1}{2}}$	W'dh'eR^{4}	HcpS	90	Ⓕ P'k'rNight108 Number'dAc'nt Ferly	6
Apr10-73^{7}Aqu	6 f	1:09⅖	gd	7-5	112	$4^{3\frac{1}{2}}$	$3^{3\frac{1}{2}}$	2^{2}	2^{1}	W'dh'seR^{5}	Alw	95	Ⓕ W'dy'sD'ht'r118 P'k'rN't H'l'yH'n'h	6
Apr 3-73^{7}Aqu	6 f	1:10⅕	gd	2-3	▲110	3^{1}	$1^{1\frac{1}{2}}$	1^{3}	$1^{\frac{1}{2}}$	W'dh'seR^{3}	Alw	92	Ⓕ PokerNight110 Krislin LuckyPayd'y	6
Mar10-73^{5}Aqu	7 f	1:22⅗	ft	1	▲113	5^{2}	2^{h}	1^{h}	1^{2}	W'dh'seR^{5}	Alw	88	Ⓕ P'kerNight113 G'dedMissile Sumba	6
Mar 6-73^{6}Aqu	6 f	1:10⅘	gd	2¼	▲118	3^{nk}	1^{1}	1^{5}	$1^{4\frac{1}{2}}$	W'dh'eR^{9}	27500	89	Ⓕ PokerNight118 TikiTie D'c'nMind'd	10
Feb16-73^{8}Hia	7 f	1:27	sl	4½	114	$7^{7\frac{3}{4}}$	4^{5}	3^{2}	$1^{1\frac{1}{2}}$	W'dh'seR^{10}	Alw	72	Ⓕ PokerNight114 SelfDefense TikiTie	11
Dec 7-72^{6}Aqu	1	1:37⅕	ft	21	116	$6^{5\frac{1}{2}}$	$5^{7\frac{1}{2}}$	$3^{3\frac{1}{2}}$	2^{3}	W'dh'seR^{1}	Alw	78	Ⓕ Tr'pic'lH't116 Pok'rN'ht F'milyPr's	9
Nov30-72^{6}Aqu	6 f	1:12⅕	ft	18	116	10^{10}	$8^{8\frac{1}{2}}$	9^{10}	$9^{6\frac{1}{4}}$	W'dh'seR^{2}	Alw	76	Ⓕ H'rl'yH'n'h120 F'm'neT'ch Tr'p'lH't	11
Nov20-72^{3}Aqu	6 f	1:13	gd	3½e	116	6^{11}	$5^{5\frac{1}{2}}$	$2^{1\frac{1}{2}}$	$1^{1\frac{1}{4}}$	W'dh'eR^{5}	17000	78	Ⓕ PokerNight116 Biscay'sBaby L'mp	7
Nov 1-72^{2}Aqu	6½ f	1:19⅕	ft	6½	120	$8^{4\frac{1}{2}}$	$8^{3\frac{3}{4}}$	2^{1}	1^{2}	T'tteR^{1}	M16000	82	Ⓕ PokerN'ht120 Prop's'l StiffComp't'n	13
Oct25-72^{2}Aqu	6 f	1:14⅘	ft	7½	120	$11^{5\frac{1}{4}}$	$10^{9\frac{1}{4}}$	7^{9}	3^{5}	W'h'eR^{4}	M13000	64	Ⓕ M'sNewb'ry118 Cobul'sC't P'k'rN'ht	14

Jerkens had handled Poker Night rather cautiously and unambitiously throughout most of her career. Even after the filly had won two claiming races in 1972 and an allowance race at Hialeah in early 1973, Jerkens did not view her as anything special. On March 6 he had entered her in a claiming race and had been willing to lose her for $27,500. Four days later she won an allowance race in very fast time, and Jerkens evidently concluded here that the filly was going to be more than a run-of-the-mill sprinter. He took her out of competition from March 10 to April 3 and gave her a pair of mile workouts during this period, presumably to prepare her for distance races. After running Poker Night in two more sprints he entered her in the Bed of Roses, a mile stakes race. Usually, if a horseplayer encounters an allowance-class sprinter in a route states race, he must conclude that the trainer is being overly ambitious and that he is probably guessing about his horse's capabilities. But Jerkens had already demonstrated that he was realistic about Poker Night; he had never entered her in a race where she didn't belong. He obviously felt that she belonged in stakes company now. Nor was he guessing when he entered Poker Night at a mile. Jerkens had tested her in workouts at the distance. If he had not liked what he had seen, he could have found a six-furlong stakes race for his filly. Jerkens had managed Poker Night intelligently through all her races; now he was preparing her specifically for the Bed of Roses Handicap. She was a very logical bet and, as the past performances indicate, Poker Night won by 1½ lengths at 3-to-1 odds.

Quality horses are usually handled with more finesse than cheap ones, but sometimes a trainer will display comparable expertise in his management of a low-grade animal.

Mr. Janin * **114** **Dk. b. or br. h (1967), by Restless Native—Valerie J., by Great Circle.**
Breeder, C. W. Hancock (Md.). **1974 3 1 0 2 $5,088**
Owner, R. R. Brooks. Trainer, R. W. Dillon. **1973 2 1 1 0 $3,224**

Date	Dist.	Time	Odds	Wt.				Fin.	Jockey	Class	Sp.				
Mar23-74 9Pim	$1\frac{1}{16}$	1:46⅖ft	6	112	$6^{3\frac{3}{4}}$	1^{1}	$1^{\frac{1}{2}}$	1^{nk}	Alb'rtsB4	H5000	73	Mr. Janin112	Mendelson	River Aboard	8
Mar 6-74 2Bow	6 f	1:12⅘ft	25	115	10^{10}	$10^{7\frac{3}{4}}$	$7^{7\frac{1}{4}}$	$3^{4\frac{1}{4}}$	Alb'rtsB11	5000	75	SirJig119	Hail'sSong	Mr.Janin	12
Jan 1-74 10Lrl	1	1:42⅕sm	10	116	$4^{4\frac{1}{2}}$	2^{h}	$2^{1\frac{1}{2}}$	3^{4}	AlbertsB3	8000	58	GhostTrain 120	DaintyDick	Mr.Janin	7
Dec 7-73 9Lrl	1	1:40 ft	8¼	116	$6^{3\frac{1}{2}}$	1^{h}	1^{1}	1^{1}	AlbertsB11	4000	73	Mr. Janin 116	Big Vin	Potestas	12
Nov20-73 2Lrl	6 f	1:12⅖ft	27	115	4^{3}	3^{3}	$4^{4\frac{3}{4}}$	$2^{1\frac{1}{4}}$	AlbertsB6	3000	86	BoldUmber117	Mr.Janin	ChargeRight	12
Oct 3-72 1Lrl	6 f	1:14 ft	8½	106‡	$5^{3\frac{1}{2}}$	3^{5}	4^{3}	$6^{8\frac{1}{2}}$	Mart'zJA9	3000	71	Priam B. 113	It Do	V Day	11

March 17 Pim 1m gd 1:41⅖h **Feb 27 Pim 7f ft 1:33b**

Trainer R. W. Dillon had won a race with Mr. Janin in the

winter of 1973, and he would not forget how he had done it. The gelding had been idle for more than a year but Dillon brought him back to the races in fairly sharp condition. He finished second in a $3000 claiming event at six furlongs, and that was all the preparation Mr. Janin needed. In his next start he stepped up in class and won at a mile.

Dillon rested Mr. Janin for another two months and then repeated this pattern. He worked the horse seven furlongs — evidence that he was aiming to win a distance race again. He entered Mr. Janin in a six-furlong race as a prep and the horse ran creditably, closing strongly to finish third. He worked the horse a mile in 1:41⅖ — excellent time for a cheap claimer. Now he entered Mr. Janin at a mile and one-sixteenth. A handicapper who had analyzed the horse's record closely would have observed that Dillon had handled this animal very patiently, had found the way to set him up for a winning effort, and was now repeating the pattern.

Mr. Janin paid $13.80.

Scrutiny of a horse's record will often disclose that a trainer does not know what he is doing.

Akrotiri **115** **Dk. b. or br. c (1971), by Tambourine—Originality, by Laugh Aloud.**
Breeder, Orme Wilson, Jr. (Va.). 1974.. 9 M 0 1 $1,260
Owner, J. L. Parrish. Trainer, S. T. Payne.

Jun26-74 5Del	1-70	1:44⅕ft	11	115	$11^{8\frac{1}{4}}$	$9^{9\frac{3}{4}}$	$7^{7\frac{3}{4}}$	$6^{6\frac{3}{4}}$	McCar'nG 2	Mdn	68	MarketKing115	BrightLust	Sagetown	12
Jun16-74 8Del	Ⓣ 1 1/16	1:47⅖sf	83	110	$9^{8\frac{1}{4}}$	13^{15}	12^{22}	9^{16}	McC'nCJ 8	AlwS	50	SilverFl'rin122	Gr'dBr'ker	ClydeWil'm	13
Jun11-74 2Del	6 f	1:12⅘ft	9¾	106**	12^{18}	12^{21}	10^{18}	9^{13}	G'rgeDD 10	Mdn	68	Forb'y'sRuler116	JaySq'red	BrightL't	12
Jun 2-74 8Del	Ⓣ 1	1:40⅘sf	35f	108	12^{22}	12^{13}	8^{9}	$6^{7\frac{1}{2}}$	AgnelloA 2	AlwS	63	Sp't'gH'd'he120	M'l'aB'y	ClydeWill'm	12
Apr26-74 5Pim	Ⓣ 1 1/16	1:46 fm	20	114	10^{12}	$9^{4\frac{1}{4}}$	$5^{5\frac{1}{2}}$	$3^{4\frac{1}{2}}$†	AngelloA 2	14500	76	C'zinsJimAndy109	ClydeWil'm	Akr'tiri	10
†Dead heat.															
Apr18-74 3Pim	1 1/16	1:46⅖ft	58	112	10^{15}	12^{11}	8^{14}	8^{9}	AgnelloA 10	Mdn	64	LateLateShow112	LatinHumor	Jetstat	12
Apr 4-74 5Pim	1 1/16	1:47 sy	4¾	120	9^{13}	7^{12}	7^{13}	8^{14}	Hart'ckW 9	Mdn	56	Illegal Pass 115	Micaster	Flashy Tee	9
Mar27-74 3Pim	6 f	1:14⅖ft	9½	114*	9^{13}	$9^{9\frac{1}{4}}$	$7^{4\frac{3}{4}}$	4^{5}	M'tinR 8	M15500	69	Gilboa120	C'ntOnClem	SusieCuc'mb'r	9
Mar19-74 3Pim	6 f	1:11⅗ft	22	113*	$8^{9\frac{3}{4}}$	8^{11}	5^{10}	4^{13}	M'tinR 7	M14500	75	Wide Berth 108	Gilboa	S. S. Houston	9

July 8 Del 5f ft 1:02b

Akrotiri had run dismally in all his races over the main track, when trainer Shirley Payne decided to experiment and enter him on the grass. Akrotiri finished third in a $14,000 claiming race against winners — and his effort was much better than it appears on the surface. The winner of the race, Cuzzins Jim Andy, came back to win twice in allowance company on the grass. The second-place finisher, Clyde William, captured an allowance race and then finished third in a stake on the grass. Two other horses in the field, who had finished behind Akrotiri, also won subsequently on the turf. Payne had discovered his horse's proper milieu: Akrotiri figured to beat just about any field of maidens on the turf. But Payne did not enter him in a maiden race. He ran him instead in a stakes race at Delaware Park, where he was totally overmatched but still ran creditably. Then he ran him at six furlongs on the dirt, a type of race that Akrotiri had already demonstrated he could not win. And Payne continued to go out of his way to lose with a horse who was in sharp condition and was ready to win in an appropriate spot. I don't need much further evidence about his capabilities. When I encounter a horse trained by Shirley Payne in the future, I am going to view it with a great deal of skepticism. If the horse is entered in a difficult-looking spot, I certainly will not assume (as I would with Jerkens) that he is there because the trainer knows what he is doing.

Of course, no trainer is perfectly good or completely bad. Even the most successful men in the business have areas of strengths and weaknesses. A trainer who wins 20 percent of his races overall may win only 10 percent of the time with two-year-olds and 30 percent of his starts in grass races. Many of the factors in handicapping that horseplayers tend to view in absolute, dogmatic terms are actually variables that depend largely on the trainer.

Should a horseplayer bet on first-time starters? If the trainer is Frank Whiteley, he may. If the trainer is Elliott Burch, he shouldn't.

Should a horseplayer bet a sprinter who is going a distance for the first time? If the trainer is Allen Jerkens, he may. If the trainer is Laz Barrera, he shouldn't.

Should a horseplayer bet a claiming horse who is dropping precipitously in class? If the trainer is Frank Martin, he may. If the trainer is Dick Dutrow, he shouldn't.

A horseplayer will slowly acquire a knowledge of different trainers' talents and shortcomings in the course of his day to day handicapping. But sometimes he will have to undertake a hard, rigorous study to understand a man's method of operation.

During the 1972 meeting at Saratoga Steve Davidowitz and I were astounded and confounded by the training of Allen Jerkens. He won nineteen races during the twenty-four-day meeting, a performance that would have been good anywhere but was especially brilliant at a track that offers the most intense competition among top-class trainers. As much as Steve and I respected Jerkens, we could never seem to bet him at the right time. When his horses seemed to figure best, they often lost. When they figured second- or third-best, they would win. Before our excursion to Saratoga in 1973 I vowed that we wouldn't be fooled by Jerkens any more. I took all the *Racing Forms* from the previous season and tried to analyze his performance carefully. I listed all his winners and beaten favorites on a large chart and wrote down, next to their names, the class in which they were running, the distance they were running and the distance of their previous race, the number of days since their last race, their recent workouts, their odds. On the next page is the record of Jerkens' winners.

The statistics disclosed that Jerkens won mostly in allowance races. He was adept with fillies and with grass horses. He didn't win a single race with a two-year-old. He won

Name	*Class*	*Last Distance*	*Today's Distance*	*Days*	*Works*	*Odds*
Wakefield Miss	Alw (fillies)	6f	6f	4	none	5–1
Bill Boland	Allowance	7f	6f	13	3f 34$\frac{4}{5}$	1–1
Blessing Angelica	Alw (fillies)	1$\frac{1}{16}$	7f	8	3f 34$\frac{4}{5}$	8–5
Never Confuse	Clm 40,000	1$\frac{1}{16}$	6f	6	3f 36	7–2
Red Orange	Mdn 14,000	6f	7f	53	7f 1:27$\frac{3}{5}$	9–5
Blooper	Clm 35,000	6f	6f	65	3f 35$\frac{4}{5}$	7–1
Wakefield Miss	Alw (fillies)	6f	6$\frac{1}{2}$f	8	none	3–2
Lucky Pants	Allowance	6$\frac{1}{2}$f	7f	12	6f 1:12$\frac{3}{5}$	7–1
Onion	Allowance	1m	7f	15	5f 1:02$\frac{2}{5}$	3–1
Beaukins	Allowance (turf)	1m	1$\frac{1}{8}$	15	5f 59	5–2
Bill Boland	Allowance (turf)	6$\frac{1}{2}$f	1$\frac{1}{16}$	5	none	9–2
Wakefield Miss	Alw (fillies)	6$\frac{1}{2}$f	1$\frac{1}{8}$	8	none	3–1
Garland of Roses	Maiden (turf)	6$\frac{1}{2}$f	1$\frac{1}{8}$	6	none	7–1
Whale	Allowance	7f	6f	6	4f 50$\frac{2}{5}$	5–2
Blessing Angelica	Stake (fillies)	1$\frac{1}{4}$	1$\frac{1}{8}$	8	3f 35$\frac{3}{5}$	4–5
Onion	Allowance	7f	7f	10	6f 1:12$\frac{4}{5}$	2–1
Blooper	Clm 25,000	6f	6f	4	none	7–2
Tunex	Allowance	7f	1$\frac{1}{8}$	9	5f 57$\frac{3}{5}$	3–5
Red Orange	Allowance (turf)	1$\frac{1}{16}$	1$\frac{1}{16}$	7	none	3–1

often with horses stretching out to a longer distance, and also won with horses going at a shorter distance. He won at all kinds of odds. But there was one pattern that fit eighteen out of his nineteen winners. Jerkens' winners either had raced within the last eight days, or else showed a recent workout so fast that it left no doubt about their current condition. Wakefield Miss, his first winner of the 1972 meeting, was coming back four days after her most recent start. Bill Boland had been away thirteen days but had worked three furlongs in a sizzling 34⅘ seconds since his last race. Blessing Angelica was coming back after eight days. And so on.

In 1973 at Saratoga Jerkens was the leading trainer of the meeting again and almost all his winners fit the pattern. But there was one glaring exception. His sprinter Onion had been laid off for more than two months, showed a succession of indifferent workouts — a half mile in 53 seconds, three furlongs in :38⅘, a mile in 1:47 — but won big, setting a track record. A few days after his victory I was interviewing Jerkens for a newspaper story and couldn't resist trying to learn why Onion had contradicted his pattern.

"I did a lot of homework on your training methods and thought I found a pattern that was pretty reliable," I said, "but Onion didn't fit it."

"I don't have any pattern," Jerkens answered, explaining that every horse is an individual, and a good horseman has to treat him as an individual instead of operating with some preconceived formula.

"I guess you're right," I conceded. "According to my research, Onion should have had a very fast workout before he ran."

Jerkens said, "He did. Two days before the race, on Sunday, he worked a half mile in forty-six flat on the training track. The clockers missed it."

Trainers may have patterns that they don't even recognize themselves. A horseplayer who learns their methods will have knowledge more valuable than any inside information he could receive from a stable. Trainers' opinions about their horses are usually very subjective and often wrong. But a handicapper can possess objective evidence that will tell him when a trainer is likely to be right or wrong.

Nowhere is an understanding of trainers' methods more important than in Maryland. During the 1973–74 season there was widespread suspicion that some trainers were using drugs illegally and indiscriminately on their horses, and that racing officials either weren't testing for these sophisticated medications or weren't enforcing the rules. As a result, the time-honored principles of handicapping seemed almost irrelevant.

Harvey Pack, a horseplayer friend of mine from New York, visited Bowie one Saturday and stopped by the press box to get a few pointers. "Is speed holding up here?" he asked. "Is the rail fast?" The Maryland regulars chuckled at his naiveté. At Bowie, we explained, we don't handicap horses. We look for horses trained by Dick Dutrow, King Leatherbury, John Tammaro, and Raymond Lawrence, Jr., and try to guess which ones will be waking up today.

In the second race Dutrow had entered a horse whom he had recently claimed. Redeem Battle had tired in the stretch of every one of his races, and had lost to $9500 rivals in his last start. Now he was facing $12,000 opposition. Harvey protested that no rational handicapper could bet this horse, but Redeem Battle closed strongly for the first time in his life and won at 5-to-2 odds.

Lawrence had a horse in the third race whom he had claimed nine days before. Flint Castle had been soundly beaten for $12,000 and now was stepping up to $17,000. "This one's impossible," Harvey said. "He'd have to improve seven or eight lengths to win here."

When Flint Castle won at 16 to 1, Harvey put his *Racing Form* aside. "Hey, it's Leatherbury's turn now," he said. "Does he have any horses in the next race?" Harvey had learned how to handicap, Maryland style.

Even though I understood the importance of trainers, I

was maddened and frustrated by what was happening in Maryland. Races were not being won by horses that had been trained in any definable, analyzable way. They were being won by horses who were improving overnight by five or ten lengths, mysteriously and unpredictably. It seemed that a rational sport had been turned into a guessing game. Without much hope of succeeding, I undertook detailed studies of all the leading trainers' records over a period of several months, trying to learn if there was any way to predict their horses' sudden form reversals. I found that even under these difficult conditions I could discover the hole card of most trainers.

Lawrence had unbelievable success winning with horses in their first start after he had claimed them or purchased them privately. He won with 50 percent of his new acquisitions, often under the most improbable circumstances. Bobpat had lost four races in a row by 20 lengths or more when Lawrence bought him. He promptly won at odds of 40 to 1, raising suspicions that his trainer may have been giving him something stronger than carrots. Whatever the reason for Lawrence's success, a handicapper could profit by betting automatically and blindly on the horses he had just claimed.

J. J. Lenzini had an uncanny ability to win distance races with faint-hearted sprinters. He would take a horse who had been tiring repeatedly at six furlongs and enter him at a mile and one-sixteenth, where the usual principles of handicapping would suggest that he had no chance. But these horses would win for Lenzini, and they made excellent bets at good prices.

The most remarkable pattern, perhaps the most reliable trainer pattern I have ever seen, belonged to King Leatherbury. It was not easy to detect because it had four components. Leatherbury would lay off a horse and drop him in class. The horse would show no workouts that would suggest he was in condition, but he would receive strong betting action and he would win. Leatherbury trained a filly named Moore Sassy who was a solid $7500 animal when she was in form. But she began to run poorly, descending the class ladder to $5000, where she was still unable to win. Leatherbury rested her for a month, corrected her problems, and entered her for $4000. Running a $7500 animal in a $4000 race is like shooting fish in a barrel, but most horseplayers could not deduce that she was ready on the basis of one nondescript three-furlong workout. Somebody knew, however. Moore Sassy was 8 to 1 in the morning line and was bet down to 5 to 2. She won impressively. The Leatherbury horses with a similar pattern win about 50 or 60 percent of the time. A horseplayer who recognizes them can bet them blindly.

As I wrote in an earlier chapter, I don't like to bet horses exclusively on the basis of a trainer's intentions and judgment. But, realistically, I know that the best horses I can select with my own handicapping are not going to win much more than 50 percent of the time. If I know that a trainer wins that often with horses who conform to a particular pattern, I will wager on them regardless of what I consider to be their handicapping merits and demerits. The ego gratification for a horseplayer may not be so great when he bets on the basis of a trainer's judgment rather than his own, but the money is just as green.

6

The Horses' Appearance

ON THE DAY BEFORE the Gulfstream Park Handicap in 1965, the track management staged a press breakfast at which newspapermen could direct questions to the trainers of horses in the race. As is customary at such affairs, the writers asked innocuous questions and the trainers responded with innocuous answers. They did, at least, until Clem Florio of the Miami *News* rose to interrogate Eddie Neloy, who trained Gun Bow, the fastest horse in America and the odds-on favorite for the Gulfstream race.

"Mr. Neloy," he asked, "what's wrong with Gun Bow?"

The room suddenly fell silent; then Neloy smiled and said, "Don't scare me like that. As far as I know, he's all right."

"When he worked six furlongs the other day," Clem said,

"he went all right for half a mile and then he started to waddle."

Clem had watched the workout, and as Gun Bow came through the stretch he thought he noticed that, instead of reaching forward with both his legs, the horse was reaching off slightly to the side with his right leg — a sign that something might be ailing him.

The other journalists in the room started hissing, booing, and yelling, "Sit down!" but Clem persisted: "You've always said that Gun Bow has beautiful action. Can you explain what that waddling is?"

"I never noticed that he did it," Neloy said. "I think I should know my own horse."

The next afternoon Clem watched intently through his binoculars as the horses came onto the track for the $100,000 race. Gun Bow looked good in the post parade; he wasn't sweating and he was striding smoothly. But as he warmed up Clem noticed that his head was turned down and sideways — another sure sign, he thought, that something was bothering the champion. He also observed that a long-shot named Ampose looked extraordinarily fit and energetic on the track. Clem bet Ampose and saw his judgment fully confirmed as Ampose rallied to win and pay $33.40, while Gun Bow struggled to finish third.

To the vast majority of horseplayers at the track, the outcome of the Gulfstream Park Handicap defied explanation. No handicapper could have studied the *Racing Form* and logically concluded that Ampose was going to defeat Gun Bow. But horse races are not run on paper. They are run by flesh and blood creatures who are susceptible to hundreds of ailments. There is probably no horseplayer in America who can match Clem Florio's astuteness at judging a horse's appearance. I have watched him for several years in the Maryland press boxes, where he now works as a handicapper for the Baltimore *News-American*, and I know that he is almost unfailingly right when he says a horse is sore or lame, when he says a horse is developing a physical problem that will bother him one or two races hence, when he says that a horse has been hopped up.

Clem's background prepared him uniquely to deal with the appearance and condition of racehorses. A former professional boxer, known somewhat hyperbolically as "the Ozone Park Assassin," he had a first-hand knowledge of physical conditioning. As a groom for the legendary trainer Sunny Jim Fitzsimmons, he acquired an understanding of horses and their ailments. As a serious handicapper, he could intelligently relate this understanding to horses' performances.

Clem grew up in the Ozone Park section of New York, just a few blocks from Aqueduct Race Track, where betting the horses was a way of life. Clem worked at Aqueduct during the summer when he was ten, learned the principles of handicapping from older men who hung out in the neighborhood coffee shops, and started betting with a bookmaker on 100th Street when he was thirteen. He quickly began thinking like all the other horseplayers in his neighborhood: When a horse figured to win but didn't, he would blame the defeat on the jockey, concluding that the thieving little rat had lost intentionally.

After Clem began attending the track regularly he sensed that there might be another way to explain the losses of horses who had figured to win. He noticed many times that a horse would look good on the track and win, then come back the next week, looking terrible, and lose. He couldn't understand why the condition of a horse would change so frequently, but he had observed a similar phenomenon in his own training as a fighter. He would often do his roadwork over the Aqueduct track. One day he might breeze through a mile in six minutes; the next day he would struggle to the finish line in seven minutes.

Clem finally began to comprehend the reasons for the changing condition of equine athletes when he went to work for Fitzsimmons. He saw that the strain of racing took a physical toll on horses — especially in their ankles and knees. When a horse's ankle started to swell, his performance on the track would deteriorate. Not only was the horse hurting, but his ailment had prevented him from being trained properly for his races. Clem noticed that horses with physical problems behaved in ways that were perceptibly different from the manner in which healthy horses acted. They showed many of the same characteristics that Clem, as a bettor, had already noticed were signs of a horse about to run a poor race.

When he learned to judge all aspects of a horse's appearance and to relate this appearance to the *Racing Form*, Clem found that he could understand the game and explain many of its apparent contradictions as he had never been able to do before. One spring when he was injured and out of work, he took a $46 compensation check to the track and launched a winning streak that lasted the entire year. Every day he would study the *Racing Form* in depth before he went to the track. Before each race he would go to the paddock, observe the horses, and make preliminary notes on his program. Then he would dash to the grandstand, where he could get a topside view of the animals as they warmed up and approached the starting gate. He would dash to the windows to make his bet, dash back to his seat and watch the race, looking for horses who got into trouble. One day toward the end of the season Clem's brother came to the track and watched him go through this grueling routine. He saw Clem peering through his binoculars at the horses, saying, "Come on, you son of a bitch, warm up . . . That's right . . . Now let me see what you're going to do . . . Now turn around so I can get a good look at you." Sensing that it was not altogether healthy for a grown man to be talking to animals, Clem's brother grabbed his arm, told him, "The referee is stopping this contest," and dragged him home.

Observing and judging the appearance of horses is perhaps the most demanding facet of handicapping. And, for me at least, it is the most difficult to learn and master. I don't have the knowledge or the instincts to sense when a horse is feeling good. I can barely distinguish a Secretariat from a battle-scarred $1500 claimer. To teach this backward pupil, Clem tried to break down the different components of a horse's appearance that he observes before a race.

Overall Appearance: "You look for a quiet horse — quiet, but with a controlled energy. If he has a stable pony with him, as most horses do, he looks like he wants to outrun the pony. He might try to thrust his head in front of the pony or over the pony's neck. You can tell there's power there. But when a horse is fractious — champing at the bit, tossing his head from side to side, stamping his feet — he's too nervous, and he's dissipating his energy before the race."

Wetness: "On a cold day, it's very negative when you see a horse wet, lathered up around the neck, loins, in behind his tail. He definitely won't run his best race. This isn't so important on a hot day, when you could expect anybody to sweat."

Fluidity of Motion: "When I ran and got tired my legs would get stiff; later I came to realize the explanation — that oxygen is not feeding into the muscles properly. When a horse is stiff-legged in a warm-up, if he's not striding out properly, if his movements are choppy, there's something wrong. What you look for is a fluidness of movement. You look for a horse's ankles and knees to curl — bend, if you will — the way a weight lifter's arms and legs curl when he lifts a weight."

Feet: "You want a horse who puts his feet down squarely, grabs the ground, and takes a full stride. When they pick their feet up real fast, with a short jerky motion, it's a sign something in the foot is stinging them."

Ears: "One of the worst signs a horse can show is when he has his ears pinned back as he's going to the post. Forget about him. When he gets to a point in a race where he puts a little pressure on himself, he'll stop. When a horse is feeling good he'll usually have his ears pricked, like he's trying to hear something. And when a horse has been drugged, you can usually tell it by the rigidity of the ears. He looks like a bird dog who's pointing when he's got a bird spotted. The ears won't flop, won't wiggle."

Tail: "A horse who swishes his tail going to the post, with a straight up-and-down swish, is telling you that he's feeling good."

Head: "You want a horse to go to the post with his head straight. When he turns his head to the side and down, and it stays that way, something's wrong. He's hurting. This is infallible."

Bandages: "I don't put too much emphasis on bandages, but if a horse has bandages on his front legs for the first time, it's probably negative. There's probably something wrong with his tendons."

Seeing the Gate: "When a horse gets to the starting gate a couple minutes before post time, you can see if he's willing. If he kind of challenges the gate, charges it, that's a real good sign — especially with older horses who have already shown you they're feeling good. This is one of the best indications I've ever seen that a horse is going to run well."

The Jiggle: "This is something that has to be seen. It's a very special look that you see maybe once or twice a year when a horse is going to the post. You get the feeling that if you got next to the horse you'd almost hear him screaming to run. The horse will give constant short starts; he's not fractious, but it's almost as if he's saying, 'Please turn me loose.' "

A handicapper may occasionally cash bets on the basis of appearance alone, but he should learn to relate this factor to the horse's form. It is not a good policy to bet on a slow chronic loser just because he looks healthy. Appearance is most important when it represents a change from the way a horse usually looks. When a horse habitually looks good — like Gun Bow — and one day comes onto the track displaying negative signs, he can be eliminated. Or at least his chances can be greatly downgraded. When a horse who usually looks bad comes onto the track exuding energy, it is one of the best betting situations in racing.

One of the most gifted horses of the sixties was the Wheatley Stable's Reviewer, a colt whose talent was matched by his physical problems. Reviewer always looked terrible in the post parade. He would be drenched in sweat and would be taking choppy strides. Because of his various ailments he could never be trained properly. Yet he consistently managed to run first or second against the best horses in the country.

Clem saw Reviewer win a race at Belmont Park one day and noticed that the colt looked slightly better than usual. A week later, he read in the *Racing Form* that Reviewer had worked a mile in 1:36 — a time that would be brilliant for any horse and was unbelievable for one that had never been able to withstand rigorous training. When Reviewer was entered in the Nassau County Handicap, Clem went to Belmont to see if the horse's seemingly improved condition was reflected in his appearance. He could barely believe what he saw. The horse was so full of energy that the jockey had trouble restraining him on the way to the post. This was a classic betting opportunity, and Clem took advantage of it. Reviewer not only won easily, but he also covered a mile and an eighth in a breathtaking 1:46$\frac{4}{5}$, shattering Belmont's track record.

Looking at horses on the track before a race is only one of the ways in which a handicapper's visual skills can help him. An observant student of the game will learn to watch the running of races — to follow all the horses in the field instead of just the one he has bet on — and try to spot horses that encounter bad racing luck. One September day Clem called me and told me to come to Timonium, where he had "an absolute cinch." When I arrived at the track and looked at the past performances of the cinch, I thought I had wasted a trip. Boogaloo Dancer was 0-for-15 for the year; in his last start, against similar opposition, he had rallied to finish an indifferent third. Clem explained that the horse had broken last, started to make a move, was blocked and knocked back to last again. He tried to make another move, and was knocked back again. He finally circled the field and finished third. Yet the *Racing Form* charts didn't mention a word about any trouble in the race. The chart-makers are only human and therefore fallible. Boogaloo Dancer came back to win by six lengths at 6-to-1 odds.

Sometimes a horseplayer with a keen eye will see and profit from things that he isn't even looking for. One day at Laurel Clem was watching the post parade before a cheap claiming race and exclaimed, "Hey! He just hit that horse with a joint!" — meaning a battery, an electrical device used to stimulate a horse illegally. Clem had seen a jockey jab a horse with the base of his whip, where batteries are often concealed, and the horse responded with a sudden lunge forward. I suggested to Clem that maybe he was a bit punchy after eighty-five middleweight fights. The horse won and paid $91.

Clem's visual perceptiveness paid off in another way during a summer when he was working as a clocker in Chicago. He would arrive at Arlington Park each morning at dawn, cut across the infield, and take his position to time the horses' workouts. One morning he was walking across the track and observed a fresh set of hoofprints in the dirt. Clem was intrigued, for trainers do not work their horses under the cloak of darkness unless they have larceny in their hearts.

Clem began reporting to the track before sunrise, waiting for a reappearance of the night rider. Five days after his initial discovery he was shivering in the early morning cold when he heard a sound that sent further chills down his back. The sound went clip-clop, clip-clop, and Clem saw a dark bay horse with a small patch of white at his heel running around the track — fast. He had never seen the horse before, so he stealthily followed him to the stable area and watched him being led to the barn of a trainer named Jones. Clem raced back to his files and looked up all of Jones's horses that had raced at the meeting. None of them was a dark bay with a patch of white over the heel.

A couple of weeks later Clem saw that Jones had entered a horse named John's Bouquet, who hadn't raced for two years, in the sixth at Arlington. He went to the paddock before the race and there was the mystery horse. John's

Bouquet looked fit and energetic, and Clem bet with enthusiasm. The horse ran like a thief in the night and won at 7 to 1.

"The next day," Clem recalled, "I had to go to the bank. I walk in and who's there but Jones. He's got a big manila envelope under his arm. It's sort of rounded and bulging. I went up to him and said, 'Hi, what you got there?' He said, 'Oh, just some papers.' We had a laugh, and then he disappeared into the vault."

7

Speed Handicapping: I

AMONG SERIOUS HANDICAPPERS there are two major schools of philosophy. In one intellectual camp are the empiricists, who view every race as a unique problem to be solved by intuition and analysis. They evaluate horses' records by weighing many factors and subtleties, and reject the notion that a horse's ability can be measured in any precise, concrete way. In the other camp are the rationalists, the speed handicappers, who believe that a horse can be measured by how fast he runs. Speed handicappers perform various arcane calculations to translate a horse's ability into a number. If an animal earns a figure of 99, he is superior to a rival who earns a 92. His age, sex, class, breeding, and even his name is irrelevant.

No area of handicapping inspires more passion or controversy. The advocates of speed figures share the view of Pat Lynch, an astute New York handicapper, who says, "Time is the one absolute truth in the game." The critics — who include the writers of most books on betting the races — view speed handicappers as madmen looking for certainty and easy answers in a game in which they don't exist. Author Tom Ainslie approvingly quotes a horseplayer who says, "Very few speed handicappers are lolling in loot. In fact, one of them we know is rarely let out of the attic, and steadfastly maintains he is Martin Van Buren."

For most of my career as a horseplayer, I shared this skepticism. But when I finally became acquainted with a few bettors who believed in speed handicapping, I was infected by their messianic fervor. I started making my own figures. I proceeded gingerly at first, with the caution of a bather dipping one toe in a cold lake. But soon I was completely immersed. Discovering figures was one of the momentous events of my life.

I became more enraptured by the technical process of computing figures than I was by the sport of racing itself. I relied on them religiously, disregarding almost everything else I knew about handicapping, and managed to win modestly. When I finally learned to put the figures in proper perspective and used them in conjunction with the other important principles of handicapping, I became confident, for the first time in my life, of my ability to win consistently at the track.

Speed figures clarified mysteries, subtleties, and apparent contradictions of the sport that I had always thought were beyond human understanding. I realized that all other handicapping tools, even the most sophisticated ones, fail to attack what should be the central question in any race: Who is better than whom? A horse may be perfectly prepared for a race by an outstanding trainer, but if he is inherently ten lengths inferior to his opposition, that preparation probably won't help him win. A horse may have a powerful track bias in his favor, but if he is a much slower animal than his rivals, the bias may not make him win. To handicap a race intelligently a horseplayer must know, above all else, which horse has superior ability. Time is the one way to measure this ability with precision. It is by far the most important factor in handicapping.

The most difficult part of speed handicapping is making the initial commitment to learn it. The virtues of other aspects of handicapping that have been discussed in this book — such as trainers' methods and track biases — are self-evident. A serious horseplayer should be able to perceive readily that these are subjects worthy of study and mastery. But an uninitiated horseplayer cannot know if speed handicapping is useful until he tries it. He will suspect that a lengthy study of speed figures may only lead him up a blind alley. When he confronts the inevitable initial difficulties and confusion, when he takes a look at all the charts and technical material on the ensuing pages, he will undoubtedly wonder if it is worth the effort.

So the reader must accept this on faith for the time being: Speed figures are the way, the truth, and the light. And my method of speed handicapping is, I believe, without equal. If a man truly wants to learn how to beat the races, the answer is contained in these next three chapters.

Speed handicapping would not be at all complex if horse races were conducted on artificial surfaces that never changed from day to day. Any bettor could look at horses' final times and correctly conclude that an animal who runs six furlongs in 1:11 is superior to one who runs the distance in 1:12. But the conditions of racetracks change constantly. Rain may make them deeper and slower. Sunny, windy weather may dry them out and make them faster. The movement of the tides may affect tracks located near an ocean, like Suffolk Downs and Gulfstream Park. Track superintendents may, at their whim, add or remove soil to make a racing surface slower or faster. So a horse who runs six furlongs in 1:11 one day may very well run in 1:13 the next. Times cannot be taken at face value.

To gauge the condition of a racetrack, a horseplayer could probably take daily samples of the soil and have them analyzed by a professional agronomist. But a more practical way to judge the speed of a track on a given day is to look at the times of the races that were run over it. If a $5000 claiming race was run in 1:15, and a stakes race was run in 1:12, the track was relatively slow. If $5000 claimers ran in 1:12 and stakes horses in 1:09, the track was obviously very fast.

To judge any horse's time, a speed handicapper views it in the context of the times that other horses ran on the same day. By doing this, even a novice could have found a superb bet in the sixth race at Bowie on January 19, 1973, a $13,000 claiming race in which there were only two strong contenders.

Prez's Son had run on January 8 in a $13,000 claiming race, finishing second by four lengths. The winner's time was 1:10 for six furlongs. According to the rule of thumb that says one length equals one-fifth of a second, then Prez's Son's time was 1:10$\frac{4}{5}$.

Sandlot had last run in a $10,000 claiming race on January 5, losing by a neck. His time was 1:12. At first glance, Prez's Son appeared to be $1\frac{1}{5}$ seconds faster than Sandlot, but an analysis of the tracks over which they had run previously told a different story.

These were the times of the six-furlong races on January 8, the day Prez's Son ran:

$3000 claiming race for three-year-olds	1:11$\frac{4}{5}$
$7500 maiden-claiming race	1:12
Allowance race for three-year-olds	1:10
Low-grade allowance race	1:10$\frac{3}{5}$

Prez's Son had obviously raced over a lightning-fast track. His time of 1:10$\frac{4}{5}$ was not spectacular, considering that it was only one second faster than the time of a race for rock-bottom three-year-old claiming horses.

These were the six-furlong times on January 5, when Sandlot ran:

$5000 maiden-claiming race	1:16$\frac{1}{5}$
$3000 claiming race for three-year-olds	1:15$\frac{3}{5}$
$5000 maiden-claiming race	1:15$\frac{3}{5}$
Maiden-special-weight race	1:14
$16,000 claiming race	1:12$\frac{3}{5}$

This track was extremely slow. A $3000 claiming race for three-year-olds was run in 1:15$\frac{3}{5}$—nearly four seconds slower than horses of the same class had run on January 8. Sandlot's race was by far the best of the day. Although he was running for a $10,000 claiming price, he had run three-fifths of a second faster than the winner of a $16,000 claiming race.

The majority of the fans at Bowie were impressed by the apparently fast time of Prez's Son and made him the 6-to-5 favorite. But speed handicappers, who evaluate horses' times by considering the track over which they ran, knew that Sandlot was the superior horse. They collected a $5.80 payoff after he beat Prez's Son by four lengths.

Horses like Sandlot are, unfortunately, all too rare. In most cases, a cursory examination of previous days' result charts will not disclose the winner of a race. It is not enough for a handicapper to know merely that certain days were very fast, others were very slow, and others were roughly average. He must be able to measure the condition of a racetrack with some precision. If a track was two-fifths of a second faster one day than the next, a speed handicapper has to know it.

A numerical measurement of the speed of a racing surface is called a track variant. The *Daily Racing Form*'s past performances include a variant for each of a horse's previous races. It is calculated by averaging the difference between the time of each winner on a day's program and the track record for the distance he ran. If the times on a particular day average 3⅕ seconds — or sixteen-fifths of a second — slower than the track records, the variant is 16. A track with a variant of 16 would be four-fifths of a second faster than a track with a variant of 20. Theoretically.

The *Racing Form*'s track variants contain one fatal flaw that makes them practically useless for serious speed handicapping. They don't take into consideration the quality of the horses who were running on a given day. A typical racetrack may offer, on a Friday, a run-of-the-mill program with many cheap claiming races, and the winners will be covering six furlongs in 1:12 and 1:13. The racing strip could be identical the next day, but the higher class horses who are traditionally entered on Saturday programs will be running in 1:10 and 1:11. The *Racing Form* variant will therefore be much lower for Saturday than Friday, suggesting that the track was considerably faster, when in fact it only means that faster horses were running on Saturday.

If a handicapper knew the average times in which horses of different classes were to run, he could make a more accurate track variant. He could compare the time of a

$3000 claiming race with the average for $3000 claiming races, the time of a stakes race with the average for stakes races, instead of comparing them both with the same track record.

Average times for the various classes of horse races are not published anywhere, so a would-be speed handicapper must compile them himself. The procedure is the one phase of making figures that is excruciatingly boring. When I am tackling an unfamiliar track, I closet myself in my handicapping room with a minicalculator, a set of the charts of all the races run at the track during the previous year, several big sheets of poster paper, a few sharp pencils, a bottle of Jack Daniel's, and a belief that the ensuing hours of drudgery will eventually pay off. I mark on the poster paper columns for each class level offered at the track — all the prices of claiming races, all the prices of maiden-claiming races, maiden-special-weight races, stakes races, and allowance races. Since there are many species of allowance races, I divide them either according to their conditions or their purse value. I establish separate categories for races limited to two-year-olds or three-year-olds. After listing in the appropriate column the time of every race that was run over a fast track, I average the times in each class. These were my averages for older horses running six furlongs during one season in New York:

CLAIMING RACES

$3000	1:13
$4000	1:12⅘
$5000	1:12⅕
$6–7000	1:12
$8–10,000	1:11⅘
$11–14,000	1:11⅗
$15–20,000	1:11⅖

MAIDEN-CLAIMING RACES

$5000	1:13⅖
$6–7000	1:13⅕
$8–11,000	1:13
$12–15,000	1:12⅘

MAIDEN-SPECIAL-WEIGHT RACES

All ages	1:12

ALLOWANCE RACES

Nonwinners of one race other than maiden or claiming	1:11⅗
Nonwinners of two races other than maiden or claiming	1:11⅖
Nonwinners of three races other than maiden or claiming	1:11
$15,000 purses	1:10⅗
$20,000 purses	1:10⅖

STAKES RACES AND HANDICAPS	1:10

(Races limited to fillies and mares are, on the average, one-fifth of a second slower than the above times.)

When a horseplayer has compiled such a set of par times for the track at which he operates, he is equipped to analyze the results of a day's races and measure the condition of the racetrack with reasonable accuracy. On a hypothetical day at Belmont Park, a $7500 claiming race is run in 1:11⅖, a $15,000 claiming race in 1:11⅕, a maiden-special-weight event for fillies in 1:11⅕, an allowance race with a $15,000 purse in 1:10⅕, a stakes race in 1:10⅖. How fast is the track? A speed handicapper can analyze it systematically:

CLASS	PAR TIME	ACTUAL TIME	DIFFERENCE
$7500 claiming	1:12	1:11⅖	fast by ⅗
$15,000 claiming	1:11⅖	1:11⅕	fast by ⅕
Maiden (fillies)	1:12⅕	1:11⅕	fast by 5/5
$15,000 allowance	1:10⅗	1:10⅕	fast by ⅖
Stake	1:10⅕	1:10⅖	slow by ⅕

We average the figures in the right-hand column — the difference between the par times and the actual times of the races — and find that the average race on this day was run two-fifths of a second faster than it should have been. The track variant is +⅖. When horses who raced on this day are entered again, we can adjust their times accordingly. A horse who ran six furlongs in 1:12 will be credited with an adjusted time of 1:12⅖. By performing these simple calculations every day, we can build up a set of track variants that will enable us to evaluate the speed of every horse we encounter in our handicapping.

Without expending an unreasonable amount of energy, a casual racing fan can use the par-time method to make usable track variants. But for a serious speed handicapper the par-time method is not precise enough; it is only the first step toward making a perfect variant. While a large sampling of $3000 claimers may run six furlongs in an average time of 1:13, some races in this class will draw strong horses who run in 1:12; others may contain a bunch of candidates for the glue factory who have trouble running in 1:14. To make his variants as accurate as possible, a speed handicapper must take into account the abilities of individual horses. He may be computing a variant for a day when the par times and actual times look like the table on page 126.

Most of the evidence suggests that the track was only

CLASS	PAR TIME	ACTUAL TIME	DIFFERENCE
$3000 claiming	1:13	1:12$\frac{4}{5}$	fast by $\frac{1}{5}$
Maiden	1:12	1:11$\frac{4}{5}$	fast by $\frac{1}{5}$
$4000 claiming	1:12$\frac{4}{5}$	1:12$\frac{3}{5}$	fast by $\frac{1}{5}$
$10,000 claiming	1:11$\frac{4}{5}$	1:10	fast by $\frac{9}{5}$

one-fifth of a second faster than normal, but a $10,000 claiming horse ran 1$\frac{4}{5}$ seconds faster than the par for his class. What happened?

To understand the race, we examine the records of the horses in the field, the times in which they have run recently (adjusted by a track variant), and the way they finished. We find that the first three finishers — Horses A, B, and C — had all run their recent races in 1:11$\frac{3}{5}$. Horse A won by seven lengths, with Horses B and C a nose apart for second.

It is possible that Horse A ran his normal race, in 1:11$\frac{3}{5}$, and that B and C went off form drastically. Or else Horses B and C may have run their usual races, with Horse A improving sharply to beat them by seven lengths. If we see signs in A's past performances that he was ready to improve — perhaps he had just been claimed by a top trainer; perhaps he had been running against a track bias in his most recent start — we may deduce that this is what happened. Horse A figured to run in 1:10$\frac{1}{5}$ to beat B and C by seven lengths while they were running their usual 1:11$\frac{3}{5}$. So instead of using the par time for $10,000 claimers of 1:11$\frac{4}{5}$, we use this projected time of 1:10$\frac{1}{5}$. Comparing it with the actual race time of 1:10, we see that the track was one-fifth of a second fast, as the other results on the same day had suggested.

When I started making track variants, I relied largely on par times and would project a time only when I encountered a race that glaringly contradicted the other results of the day. But now I use par times only for the first two weeks or so of a new racing season, when I have no prior results with which to project times. Then I start using the projection method for every race, and I believe that the track variants it produces are the best that man can devise.

To project the running times of races requires a good deal of practice and knowledge. There are no easy rules to simplify the process, because judging whether horses have improved, deteriorated, or stayed the same since their last race requires all of a man's handicapping skills.

We are trying to make a track variant for a day on which the following hypothetical race is being run. It is a six-furlong event for $12,000 claimers, and these are the leading contenders:

Horse A, who won his last race in 1:11. He has been laid off for a month, with no good workouts during that time.

Horse B, who ran his last race in 1:12. He is a paragon of consistency who almost always records the same time.

Horse C, who ran his last race in 1:12$^{2}/_{5}$. He is trained by the leading trainer at the track.

Horse A wins by a length over B, with Horse C another length behind. What should the time of the race be?

It is conceivable that Horse A ran in 1:11 again. But if he did, the horses behind him had to improve sharply and implausibly, with B running in 1:11$^{1}/_{5}$ and C in 1:11$^{2}/_{5}$. It is more likely that A ran slower because of his recent inactivity, allowing B and C to finish close to him.

If A ran in 1:11$^{4}/_{5}$, B would have run in 1:12, his usual performance. Horse C's time would have been 1:12$^{1}/_{5}$, a slight improvement that might be due to his trainer's competence.

So we project a time of 1:11$^{4}/_{5}$ for A's victory: it is the most logical way to explain the way the horses finished. Now we can compare the projection with the actual time of the race. If A were clocked in 1:12$^{2}/_{5}$, we would conclude from this piece of evidence that the track was three-fifths of a second slow. If his actual time was 1:11$\frac{2}{5}$, the track would be two-fifths of a second fast.

Occasionally, even the most astute practitioner of this method of making track variants will encounter a race or a day's program that doesn't make sense. For example:

RACE	PROJECTED TIME	ACTUAL TIME	DIFFERENCE
1	1:13	1:13$\frac{3}{5}$	slow by $\frac{3}{5}$
2	1:12$\frac{1}{5}$	1:13	slow by $\frac{4}{5}$
3	1:12$\frac{4}{5}$	1:13$\frac{4}{5}$	slow by $\frac{5}{5}$
4	1:12	1:10$\frac{2}{5}$	fast by $\frac{8}{5}$
5	1:12	1:12$\frac{4}{5}$	slow by $\frac{4}{5}$

The fourth race is a bewildering mystery. All the other evidence seems to suggest that the track is somewhat slow, but this one race was run much faster than it should have been. Suspecting that my projection was an error, I would reanalyze the race, trying to interpret the horses' past performances in a way that would enable me to project a time of about 1:09$\frac{4}{5}$, which would jibe with the other results. But if the race still defied explanation, I would disregard it entirely for purposes of computing my track variant. And I would watch closely how the horses in this field perform when they run again. If one or two of them come back and run in the vicinity of 1:09$\frac{4}{5}$, I know the time of the race was legitimate. But if they subsequently run in 1:12, I disregard their extraordinarily fast time as a fluke, caused by freaky track conditions, atmospheric conditions, or perhaps a malfunctioning Teletimer. It happens sometimes.

Another problem that can arise in making a track variant might take a form like that shown on page 129. The condition of a racetrack will occasionally change suddenly during the middle of a day's program. It may happen because rain starts to fall during the afternoon. It may happen for no apparent reason at all. In the case above I would make a separate variant for the first four races (fast by 4/5 of a second) and another for the last five races (slow by

RACE	PROJECTED TIME	ACTUAL TIME	DIFFERENCE
1	1:12	1:11 2/5	fast by 3/5
2	1:13	1:12 1/5	fast by 4/5
3	1:12 1/5	1:11 1/5	fast by 5/5
4	1:11	1:10 1/5	fast by 4/5
5	1:11 3/5	1:12 1/5	slow by 3/5
6	1:12	1:12 1/5	slow by 1/5
7	1:10 4/5	1:11 3/5	slow by 4/5
8	1:11	1:11 2/5	slow by 2/5
9	1:13	1:13 1/5	slow by 1/5

2/5). There will be other perplexing days in which the track variant may be different at different distances; sprints may be fast but route races run around two turns will be slow.

If we lived in a kinder world, racetracks would card nine races a day at six furlongs, and the task of speed handicappers would be relatively easy. But every thoroughbred track offers at least two different distances. Belmont Park confounds speed handicappers with races at five, five-and-a-half, six, six-and-a-half, and seven furlongs, and one mile, 1 1/16, 1 1/8, 1 1/4, and 1 1/2 miles. Rarely will a horseplayer be treated to an easy race in which all the entrants do all their running at the same distance. Most speed handicappers approach the problem by translating a horse's time, at whatever distance he runs, into a numerical rating, so that they can more easily compare horses' performances at different distances.

The *Racing Form* past performances include speed ratings for each of a horse's races, and they are as ill-conceived as the *Form*'s track variants. The *Form* equates the track record for each distance with a rating of 100, and deducts one point for every fifth of a second slower than the record that a horse runs. Suppose a horseplayer were trying to compare two thoroughbreds at Aqueduct, one of whom ran six furlongs in 1:10$\frac{4}{5}$, the other, seven furlongs in 1:23. The Aqueduct track record for six furlongs used to be 1:08$\frac{4}{5}$. A horse who ran in 1:10$\frac{4}{5}$ was two seconds (or ten-fifths) slower than the record. So he would earn a rating of 90 (100 minus 10). The Aqueduct record for seven furlongs was 1:21$\frac{1}{5}$. So the horse who raced in 1:23 would get a rating of 91. He is one length superior to the six-furlong horse.

The fallacy of this method was exposed when the great horse Dr. Fager won Aqueduct's Vosborgh Handicap in the sensational time of 1:20$\frac{1}{5}$ for seven furlongs, breaking the record by a full second. Now a horse who raced seven furlongs in 1:23 would earn a rating of 86. Overnight he had become, under the *Racing Form*'s speed ratings, four lengths inferior to a rival who had raced six furlongs in 1:10$\frac{4}{5}$ and earned a rating of 90. This is patently absurd. There has to be some kind of logical relationship between times and six and seven furlongs, but it is ridiculous to base this relationship on the performance of one exceptional horse who sets a track record.

When a speed handicapper has compiled a set of average times for various classes to help him make track variants, he has accumulated evidence that will enable him to compare horses' performances at different distances. In Maryland, the most common races are $3000 claiming events for older horses. They are run practically every day of the season, at every distance. The average time for $3000 claimers may be based on as many as fifty or a hundred individual races. This large sampling provides a much more substantial basis for comparing times at different distances than the track records. At Laurel, for example, the average times of $3000 claimers are:

Six furlongs	1:13
Seven furlongs	1:26⅕
1⅛ miles	1:54

The difference between the average times at six and seven furlongs is 13⅕ seconds. If we are handicapping a seven-furlong race in which one horse has run the distance in 1:26⅗, and is meeting a rival who ran six furlongs in 1:12⅘, we add 13⅕ seconds to the latter's time and find that his effort equals 1:26 at the longer distance. He is three lengths superior to his opponent.

There is no universal set of comparative times that will work at every racetrack. The relationship of times in sprint races doesn't vary much — six furlongs in 1:13 will equal seven furlongs in 1:26⅕ at virtually every track that is at least a mile in circumference — but route races are different everywhere. At Pimlico, the average $3000 claimer runs six furlongs in 1:13 and a mile and an eighth in 1:53. At Aqueduct, where the short run to the first turn in route races prevents horses from getting into high gear quickly, a six-furlong time of 1:13 is equivalent to a mile and an eighth in 1:54⅖. At Bowie, where the first turn is traditionally much deeper and slower than the rest of the track, six furlongs in 1:13 equals a mile and an eighth in 1:55⅕. At Belmont, where all races shorter than a mile and a half are run around only one turn, six furlongs in 1:13 equals a mile and one-eighth in 1:52⅗.

Purists will object that comparing the efforts of horses at different distances is an exercise in futility and further indication of the warped mentality of speed handicappers. Every thoroughbred, from the humblest claimer to Secretariat, has a distance that he likes the best. Many horses who are crackerjacks at six furlongs would be gasping for air if they attempted to run seven furlongs, let alone a mile and one-eighth. This is quite true, and speed handicappers should resist the temptation to think that, just because six furlongs in 1:13 equals seven furlongs in 1:26⅕, a horse will cooperate and run precisely as fast as he should. These comparative times do not magically predict a horse's performance at a new distance. They only measure the level of his performance in previous races. But these comparative times are still very useful if a horseplayer evaluates them intelligently. If we are handicapping a mile-and-one-eighth race at Laurel, which pits a sprinter who runs in 1:13 against a router who runs 1⅛ miles in 1:54, we know that the horses' times are equivalent and we will probably prefer the one who has proved himself at the long distance. If a 1:13 sprinter were facing a 1:55 router, the decision would not be so easy. We would know that the sprinter's performance had been superior, and we would have to decide if he could do as well at a mile and an eighth. If his record showed that in the past he had the ability to negotiate a route, he might be a good bet.

To help horseplayers compare times at different distances, almost every tract on speed handicapping contains what is known as a parallel-time chart. As the name implies, the times for different distances are listed in parallel vertical columns. The handicapper using the chart simply looks across a horizontal line to relate a time at one distance to another. The parallel-time chart usually also includes a numerical rating for each time. We can construct one easily enough for Laurel, where we know that six furlongs in 1:13, seven furlongs in 1:26⅕, and a mile and an eighth in 1:54 are equivalent. We arbitrarily assign each of these times a rating of 80, and the parallel-time chart looks like this:

RATING	SIX FURLONGS	SEVEN FURLONGS	1⅛ MILES
95	1:10	1:23⅕	1:51
94	1:10⅕	1:23⅖	1:51⅕
93	1:10⅖	1:23⅗	1:51⅖
92	1:10⅗	1:23⅘	1:51⅗
91	1:10⅘	1:24	1:51⅘
90	1:11	1:24⅕	1:52
89	1:11⅕	1:24⅖	1:52⅕
88	1:11⅖	1:24⅗	1:52⅖
87	1:11⅗	1:24⅘	1:53⅗
86	1:11⅘	1:25	1:52⅘
85	1:12	1:25⅕	1:53
84	1:12⅕	1:25⅖	1:53⅕
83	1:12⅖	1:25⅗	1:53⅖
82	1:12⅗	1:25⅘	1:53⅗
81	1:12⅘	1:26	1:53⅘
80	1:13	1:26⅕	1:54
79	1:13⅕	1:26⅖	1:54⅕
78	1:13⅖	1:26⅗	1:54⅖
77	1:13⅗	1:26⅘	1:54⅗
76	1:13⅘	1:27	1:54⅘
75	1:14	1:27⅕	1:55
74	1:14⅕	1:27⅖	1:55⅕
73	1:14⅖	1:27⅗	1:55⅖
72	1:14⅗	1:27⅘	1:55⅗
71	1:14⅘	1:28	1:55⅘
70	1:15	1:28⅕	1:56

Many casual racing fans cannot devote a great deal of their time to handicapping but still want to be able to bet intelligently when they go to the track. For them, the speed-handicapping methods described in this chapter will be especially useful.

The only time-consuming part of the process is the compilation of a set of average times for all the classes that a track offers. With these averages, a horseplayer can construct a parallel-time chart so that he can compare, at a glance, the performances of horses who have been running at different distances. With the averages he can use the par-time method and make track variants in only a few minutes a day. He will be able to assess, more accurately than the vast majority of bettors, the real meaning of horses' times.

8

Speed Handicapping: II

Sheldon Kovitz, my classmate at Harvard, became fascinated by horse racing while he was studying for his doctorate in mathematics. Not only did he calculate his own speed figures, but he tried to translate every facet of handicapping into mathematical terms.

If a horse appeared on the track with a bandage on his left foreleg that he had not previously worn, Sheldon had a figure with which to adjust his numerical rating. If a wind was blowing at Suffolk Downs, Sheldon would measure its velocity with his portable anemometer and adjust the horses' times with his wind figures, which he had devised with the aid of an IBM 360 Model 40 computer. His sophistication had certain drawbacks. "I get so busy tabulating all the various data and keeping up with the results," Sheldon complained once, "that I don't have time to handicap." He never became a winning horseplayer, and finally gave up the game to devote himself to academic pursuits.

Most of Sheldon's racetrack cronies dismissed him as a lunatic, an opinion that seemed to be confirmed by his chronic lack of success as a bettor. But I sensed that the way he calculated his speed figures was solidly grounded in logic, and urged him to teach me his method. After understanding the mathematics behind his approach, using it for a few years, and comparing it with the ways other horseplayers compute their figures, I belatedly recognized that Sheldon was a true genius as a handicapping theoretician.

Not long after undertaking his study of racing, Sheldon made a discovery that was as stunning to me as it was obvious to him. He recognized that all the conventional parallel-time charts, which are the backbone of practically all the systems of speed handicapping, contain the same flaw. The error is a serious one, and to correct it requires a speed handicapper to advance to a much higher plateau of sophistication — into the realm of figures.

According to my parallel-time chart in the previous chapter, it takes a horse who runs six furlongs in 1:13 another 13$\frac{1}{5}$ seconds to cover an additional furlong. Correct. But the chart also says that a much faster horse — one who can run six furlongs in 1:10 — will also require 13$\frac{1}{5}$ seconds to travel an extra furlong. And a very slow horse — one who runs six furlongs in a dawdling 1:15 — will also run another eighth of a mile in :13$\frac{1}{5}$. This is totally illogical, but the same fallacy appears in just about every piece of literature on speed handicapping. Tom Ainslie, in his generally astute *Complete Guide to Thoroughbred Racing*, publishes a parallel-time chart that says a horse who runs six furlongs in 1:10 will go seven furlongs in 1:22⅖, covering the extra furlong in a swift 12⅖ seconds, which a very fast horse can do. But the same chart says a miserable plodder who runs six furlongs in 1:16 will run seven furlongs in 1:28⅖, covering the last eighth of a mile in a miraculous 12⅖ seconds. No wonder Ainslie is skeptical about the usefulness of speed handicapping.

Sheldon found a way to resolve these inconsistencies. The starting point of his method was the same as for traditional parallel-time charts. We learn times at different distances that are equivalent and assign the same numerical rating to them. Six furlongs in 1:13 is an 80. Seven furlongs in 1:26⅕ is an 80. Now, if horses run one-fifth of a second faster than these times, how do their ratings compare? Parallel-time charts would say they are identical. But this is a fallacy, because a fifth of a second is proportionately more significant at a shorter distance.

To make this a bit clearer, let us imagine we were making speed figures for human runners. The world record for 100 yards is 9.0 seconds. The world record for one mile is 3:51.1. If a runner went one second slower than the 100-yard record, his time would be :10.0 and he would be no better than an average high-school sprinter. But if he ran one second slower than the mile mark, in 3:52.1, he would still be one of the great track stars of history. Obviously, a fraction of a second in a short race is more significant than a fraction of a second in a long race.

Sheldon performed a relatively simple calculation to assess the relative importance of a fifth of a second at the different distances in horse racing. If a horse runs six furlongs in 1:13, he has covered the distance in 73 seconds, or 365-fifths of a second. One-fifth of a second represents

1/365, or .28 percent of his entire race. When a horse runs seven furlongs in 1:26$\frac{1}{5}$, one-fifth of a second is 1/431, or .23 percent, of the whole race.

We now know how to weight a fifth of a second at six and seven furlongs. Moving the decimal point over one place to make the figures more manageable, we know that a fifth of a second should be worth 2.8 points at six furlongs, 2.3 points at seven furlongs. If we have assigned a rating of 80 to a six-furlong time of 1:13, a horse who runs in 1:12$\frac{4}{5}$ earns a rating of 82.8. A horse that runs seven furlongs in 1:26 earns a rating of 82.3. A portion of a parallel-time chart would now look like this:

SIX FURLONGS		SEVEN FURLONGS	
1:12	94.0	1:25$\frac{1}{5}$	91.5
1:12$\frac{1}{5}$	91.2	1:25$\frac{2}{5}$	89.2
1:12$\frac{2}{5}$	88.4	1:25$\frac{3}{5}$	86.9
1:12$\frac{3}{5}$	85.6	1:25$\frac{4}{5}$	84.6
1:12$\frac{4}{5}$	82.8	1:26	82.3
1:13	80.0	1:26$\frac{1}{5}$	80.0
1:13$\frac{1}{5}$	77.2	1:26$\frac{2}{5}$	77.7
1:13$\frac{2}{5}$	74.4	1:26$\frac{3}{5}$	75.4

Using this method, we can construct a speed-rating chart that assigns a numerical value for every time at every distance a track offers. These are the basic equivalent times for the various distances at Aqueduct and Belmont, and the value we assign to a fifth of a second at each distance (see chart on page 139).

5 furlongs	1:00	(one-fifth = 3.3 points)
5½ furlongs	1:06⅖	(one-fifth = 3.0 points)
6 furlongs	1:13	(one-fifth = 2.8 points)
6½ furlongs	1:19⅗	(one-fifth = 2.5 points)
7 furlongs	1:26⅕	(one-fifth = 2.3 points)
1 mile	1:39⅖	(one-fifth = 2.0 points)
1¹⁄₁₆ (Belmont)	1:46	(one-fifth = 1.9 points)
1⅛ (Belmont)	1:52⅗	(one-fifth = 1.8 points)
1⅛ (Aqueduct)	1:54⅖	(one-fifth = 1.8 points)
1½ (Belmont)	2:36	(one-fifth = 1.2 points)

We assign each of these times a rating of 80, and then construct the entire speed chart, removing the decimal points and rounding off the numbers.

FIVE FURLONGS		5½ FURLONGS		SIX FURLONGS	
57	130	1:03	132	1:09	136
57⅕	127	1:03⅕	129	1:09⅕	133
57⅖	123	1:03⅖	126	1:09⅖	130
57⅗	120	1:03⅗	123	1:09⅗	127
57⅘	117	1:03⅘	120	1:09⅘	124
58	113	1:04	117	1:10	122
58⅕	110	1:04⅕	114	1:10⅕	119
58⅖	107	1:04⅖	111	1:10⅖	116
58⅗	103	1:04⅗	108	1:10⅗	113
58⅘	100	1:04⅘	105	1:10⅘	110
59	97	1:05	102	1:11	108
59⅕	93	1:05⅕	99	1:11⅕	105
59⅖	90	1:05⅖	96	1:11⅖	102
59⅗	87	1:05⅗	93	1:11⅗	99
59⅘	83	1:05⅘	90	1:11⅘	97
1:00	80	1:06	87	1:12	94
1:00⅕	77	1:06⅕	84	1:12⅕	91
1:00⅖	73	1:06⅖	81	1:12⅖	88
1:00⅗	70	1:06⅗	78	1:12⅗	86

(cont'd on next page)

FIVE FURLONGS		5½ FURLONGS		SIX FURLONGS	
1:00⅘	67	1:06⅘	75	1:12⅘	83
1:01	63	1:07	72	1:13	80
1:01⅕	60	1:07⅕	69	1:13⅕	77
1:01⅖	57	1:07⅖	66	1:13⅖	75
1:01⅗	53	1:07⅗	63	1:13⅗	72
1:01⅘	50	1:07⅘	60	1:13⅘	69
1:02	47	1:08	57	1:14	66
1:02⅕	43	1:08⅕	54	1:14⅕	64
1:02⅖	40	1:08⅖	51	1:14⅖	61
1:02⅗	37	1:08⅗	48	1:14⅗	58
1:02⅘	33	1:08⅘	45	1:14⅘	55
1:03	30	1:09	42	1:15	53

6½ FURLONGS		SEVEN FURLONGS		ONE MILE	
1:15	138	1:21	140	1:34	134
1:15⅕	135	1:21⅕	138	1:34⅕	132
1:15⅖	133	1:21⅖	136	1:34⅖	130
1:15⅗	130	1:21⅗	133	1:34⅗	128
1:15⅘	128	1:21⅘	131	1:34⅘	126
1:16	125	1:22	128	1:35	124
1:16⅕	123	1:22⅕	126	1:35⅕	122
1:16⅖	120	1:22⅖	124	1:35⅖	120
1:16⅗	118	1:22⅗	121	1:35⅗	118
1:16⅘	115	1:22⅘	119	1:35⅘	116
1:17	113	1:23	117	1:36	114
1:17⅕	110	1:23⅕	115	1:36⅕	112
1:17⅖	108	1:23⅖	112	1:36⅖	110
1:17⅗	105	1:23⅗	110	1:36⅗	108
1:17⅘	103	1:23⅘	108	1:36⅘	106
1:18	100	1:24	105	1:37	104
1:18⅕	98	1:24⅕	103	1:37⅕	102
1:18⅖	95	1:24⅖	101	1:37⅖	100

6½ FURLONGS		SEVEN FURLONGS		ONE MILE	
1:18⅗	93	1:24⅗	98	1:37⅗	98
1:18⅘	90	1:24⅘	96	1:37⅘	96
1:19	88	1:25	94	1:38	94
1:19⅕	85	1:25⅕	92	1:38⅕	92
1:19⅖	83	1:25⅖	89	1:38⅖	90
1:19⅗	80	1:25⅗	87	1:38⅗	88
1:19⅘	77	1:25⅘	85	1:38⅘	86
1:20	75	1:26	82	1:39	84
1:20⅕	72	1:26⅕	80	1:39⅕	82
1:20⅖	70	1:26⅖	78	1:39⅖	80
1:20⅗	67	1:26⅗	75	1:39⅗	78
1:20⅘	65	1:26⅘	73	1:39⅘	76
1:21	62	1:27	71	1:40	74
1:21⅕	60	1:27⅕	69	1:40⅕	72
1:21⅖	57	1:27⅖	66	1:40⅖	70
1:21⅗	55	1:27⅗	64	1:40⅗	68
1:21⅘	52	1:27⅘	62	1:40⅘	66
1:22	50	1:28	59	1:41	64

1$\frac{1}{16}$ MILES		BELMONT 1⅛ MILES		AQUEDUCT 1⅛ MILES	
1:41	128	1:48	121	1:49	128
1:41⅕	126	1:48⅕	119	1:49⅕	126
1:41⅖	124	1:48⅖	117	1:49⅖	124
1:41⅗	122	1:48⅗	115	1:49⅗	122
1:41⅘	120	1:48⅘	114	1:49⅘	121
1:42	118	1:49	112	1:50	119
1:42⅕	116	1:49⅕	110	1:50⅕	117
1:42⅖	114	1:49⅖	108	1:50⅖	115
1:42⅗	112	1:49⅗	106	1:50⅗	113

(cont'd on next page)

		BELMONT		AQUEDUCT	
1 1/16 MILES		1⅛ MILES		1⅛ MILES	
1:42⅘	110	1:49⅘	105	1:50⅘	112
1:43	109	1:50	103	1:51	110
1:43⅕	107	1:50⅕	101	1:51⅕	108
1:43⅖	105	1:50⅖	99	1:51⅖	106
1:43⅗	103	1:50⅗	98	1:51⅗	105
1:43⅘	101	1:50⅘	96	1:51⅘	103
1:44	99	1:51	94	1:52	101
1:44⅕	97	1:51⅕	92	1:52⅕	99
1:44⅖	95	1:51⅖	91	1:52⅖	98
1:44⅗	93	1:51⅗	89	1:52⅗	96
1:44⅘	91	1:51⅘	87	1:52⅘	94
1:45	90	1:52	85	1:53	92
1:45⅕	88	1:52⅕	84	1:53⅕	91
1:45⅖	86	1:52⅖	82	1:53⅖	89
1:45⅗	84	1:52⅗	80	1:53⅗	87
1:45⅘	82	1:52⅘	78	1:53⅘	85
1:46	80	1:53	77	1:54	84
1:46⅕	78	1:53⅕	75	1:54⅕	82
1:46⅖	76	1:53⅖	73	1:54⅖	80
1:46⅗	74	1:53⅗	71	1:54⅗	78
1:46⅘	72	1:53⅘	70	1:54⅘	77
1:47	71	1:54	68	1:55	75
1:47⅕	69	1:54⅕	66	1:55⅕	73
1:47⅖	67	1:54⅖	64	1:55⅖	71
1:47⅗	65	1:54⅗	62	1:55⅗	69
1:47⅘	63	1:54⅘	61	1:55⅘	68
1:48	61	1:55	59	1:56	66

BELMONT 1½ MILES		BELMONT 1½ MILES	
2:29	125	2:29⅗	121
2:29⅕	124	2:29⅘	120

BELMONT 1½ MILES		BELMONT 1½ MILES	
2:29⅘	122	2:30	119
2:30⅕	117	2:33⅕	98
2:30⅖	116	2:33⅖	96
2:30⅗	115	2:33⅗	95
2:30⅘	113	2:33⅘	94
2:31	112	2:34	93
2:31⅕	111	2:34⅕	91
2:31⅖	109	2:34⅖	90
2:31⅗	108	2:34⅗	89
2:31⅘	107	2:34⅘	87
2:32	106	2:35	86
2:32⅕	104	2:35⅕	85
2:32⅖	103	2:35⅖	83
2:32⅗	102	2:35⅗	82
2:32⅘	100	2:35⅘	81
2:33	99	2:36	80

This chart resolves the problem of comparing times at different distances. When a horse runs six furlongs in 1:13, he should run seven furlongs in 1:26⅕, requiring 13⅕ seconds to travel the additional eighth of a mile. A fast horse who runs six furlongs in 1:09⅘ (a rating of 124) should cover seven furlongs in 1:22⅖ (also a rating of 124), running the extra furlong in 12⅗ seconds. A plodder who runs six furlongs in 1:14⅕ (a rating of 64) should go seven-eights in 1:27⅗ (also a 64), covering the last eighth in 13⅖ seconds.

Since we are now dealing with figures instead of actual times, we translate the other elements of speed handicapping — par times, track variants, and beaten lengths — into figures as well. They are much less cumbersome to use. We don't have to say, "This horse ran six furlongs in 1:12⅗ over a track that was three-fifths of a second slow, making his adjusted time 1:12, and today is running at seven furlongs, so his time for that distance translates to 1:25." Instead we can say, "This horse is a 94," which neatly summarizes his capabilities.

The chart of New York par times that appeared in the previous chapter would now look like this:

CLAIMING RACES	
$3000	80
$4000	84
$5000	91
$6000	93
$7000	94
$8000	96
$9–10,000	97
$11,000	98
$12–13,000	99
$14,000	100
$15–16,000	101
$17–18,000	102
$19–20,000	103
MAIDEN-CLAIMING RACES	
$4000	69
$5000	75
$6–7000	77
$8–11,000	80
MAIDEN-SPECIAL-WEIGHT RACES	
All ages	93

ALLOWANCE RACES

Nonwinners of one race other than maiden or claiming	99
Nonwinners of two races other than maiden or claiming	103
Nonwinners of three races other than maiden or claiming	109
$15,000 purses	113
$20,000 purses	116
STAKES RACES	119

(For races limited to fillies and mares, deduct three points.)

These par figures can be applied to any distance. To make a track variant with the par-time method, we compare these figures with the actual figures for the races, as on the following hypothetical day at Aqueduct.

CLASS	DISTANCE	PAR	TIME	ACTUAL FIGURE	DIFFERENCE
$10,000 claiming	1 mile	97	1:37 2/5	100	fast by 3
Maiden (fillies)	6 furlongs	90	1:11 4/5	97	fast by 7
$15,000 allowance	7 furlongs	113	1:23 2/5	112	slow by 1
Stakes	1 1/8 miles	119	1:49 3/5	122	fast by 3
$17,000 claiming	6 1/2 furlongs	102	1:17 3/5	105	fast by 3

Averaging the difference between the par figures and the horses' actual figures, we find that the track was fast by three points. So the track variant for this day was −3. When any horse who raced on this day runs again, we subtract three points from his figure. If the track is slower than normal, say by eight points, the track variant will be

+8, and this should be added to the figure of every horse who races on that day.

When we use the projection method, the procedure is much the same. In a seven-furlong race, Horses A, B, and C have each run a figure of 94 in their most recent starts. Horse A, whose past performances indicate that he is ready to improve, wins by three lengths, with B and C second and third, a nose apart. Three lengths equal roughly three-fifths of a second, and three-fifths of a second at seven furlongs equals about seven points. So we project A's winning figure as 101. If he actually ran in 1:25⅕ — a figure of 92 — the evidence suggests that the track was nine points slow, and the variant should be +9.

The equation of one length with one-fifth of a second is used almost universally, but it is not quite accurate. A fast horse running in a sprint will obviously cover a length more quickly than a plodder going a mile and a half. The discrepancies are minor, and a reader whose head is reeling from all the figures on the previous pages may ignore the following chart for converting beaten lengths into figures at varying distances.

BEATEN-LENGTHS ADJUSTMENT CHART

Margin	*5 Fur.*	*6 Fur.*	*7 Fur.*	*Mile*	*1$\frac{1}{16}$*	*1⅛*	*1½*
neck	1	1	1	0	0	0	0
½	1	1	1	1	1	1	1
¾	2	2	2	1	1	1	1
1	3	2	2	2	2	2	1
1¼	4	3	3	2	2	2	1
1½	4	4	3	3	3	2	2
1¾	5	4	4	3	3	3	2
2	6	5	4	4	3	3	2
2¼	7	6	5	4	4	4	3

Margin	*5 Fur.*	*6 Fur.*	*7 Fur.*	*Mile*	*1 1/16*	*1 1/8*	*1 1/2*
2 1/2	7	6	5	4	4	4	3
2 3/4	8	7	6	5	5	5	3
3	9	7	6	5	5	5	3
3 1/4	9	8	7	6	5	5	4
3 1/2	10	9	7	6	6	6	4
3 3/4	11	9	8	7	6	6	4
4	12	10	8	7	7	6	5
4 1/4	12	10	9	8	7	7	5
4 1/2	13	11	9	8	8	7	5
4 3/4	14	11	10	9	8	8	5
5	15	12	10	9	8	8	6
5 1/2	16	13	11	10	9	9	6
6	18	15	12	11	10	9	7
6 1/2	19	16	13	12	11	10	8
7	20	17	14	13	12	11	8
7 1/2	22	18	15	13	13	12	9
8	23	20	17	14	13	13	10
8 1/2	25	21	18	15	14	13	10
9	26	22	19	16	15	14	11
9 1/2	28	23	19	17	16	16	11
10	29	24	20	18	17	17	12
11	32	27	23	20	18	18	13
12	35	29	25	21	20	20	14
13	38	32	27	23	22	22	15
14	41	34	29	25	23	23	16
15	44	37	31	27	25	25	17

I won't go into the mathematics behind it, but the chart is more precise than the standard rule of thumb. If the winning figure for a six-furlong race is 102, and a horse is beaten by three lengths, what is his figure? The user of the chart looks down the left-hand column and finds three lengths, then moves his eye across to the column for six furlongs and finds the figure 7. He subtracts 7 from the winner's figure of 102, and finds that the horse's figure is 95.

9

Speed Handicapping: III

WHEN A HORSEPLAYER has learned how to make figures, he will inevitably start to believe that he is omniscient. He will suddenly be able to answer with ease the sort of questions that befuddle most handicappers: Can a three-year-old beat older horses? Can a sharp $3000 claimer step up to $5000 and win? He will be able to measure the capabilities of horses more accurately than their trainers can. He will win many bets almost effortlessly by wagering blindly on horses who earn his top figures. And, without realizing it, he will be falling into a trap.

It happened to me, as it happens to most newly converted speed handicappers. I became so entranced by my figures that I ignored the fundamentals of the game. I viewed the figures as gospel, as certain indicators of what horses were going to do today rather than as measurements of what they had done in the past. Instead of using them as a tool, I let them dictate my decisions.

Speed figures are neither magic nor infallible. A handicapper who played every race by betting the horse with the highest figure for his last start might cash 30 percent of his wagers and eke out a modest profit. He could improve his percentage by winnowing out horses who do not meet basic handicapping requirements. And he could improve it even further by developing the ability to recognize when superior figures may be misleading.

After some expensive lessons, I now know to distrust figures that horses achieve under certain conditions.

I discount figures that a horse has earned with the assistance of a strong track bias.

I discount figures that a horse has earned on a muddy track, especially if he is running on a fast track today.

I downgrade figures that a horse has earned when he opened a big early lead and maintained it from wire to wire. Many horses can run like champions when they don't get competition, but wilt when they are subjected to pressure.

Even if a horse has run a big figure in his last start under seemingly normal conditions, I will hesitate to bet him on the basis of just one exceptional performance. A $3000 claimer consistently runs in the same range — 70, 75, 69, 73 — and then improves sharply to earn a figure of 90. Most speed handicappers would bet him enthusiastically; I wouldn't, unless I can find a reason to explain his improvement. If, for example, he had been claimed by an outstanding trainer, I might credit the man for transforming his new acquisition into a horse who would now run regularly in the 90s. But if the horse had improved for no apparent reason, I would expect him to revert to his usual level of performance — in the 70s — rather than to duplicate his last race.

The figure for a horse's last race is, of course, the most important one in his past performances. But the best bets uncovered by speed handicapping are not horses who have run one recent extraordinary race. They are, instead, horses who consistently run at the same level, whose normal figures are good enough to beat the opposition they will be facing today.

When a horse runs 70, 90, 72, 71, 92, I don't know quite what to expect of him. But when a horse runs 86, 87, 90, 87, 85, I know he should win a race in which none of his rivals ever does better than an 84.

Here is a race in which a speed handicapper could make a bet with unshakable confidence:

7th Bowie Race Course

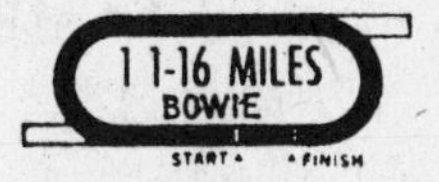

1 1/16 MILES. (1:41⅗). THE CROFTON HANDICAP. STARTER HANDICAP. Purse $6,500. 3-year-olds and upward which have started for a claiming price of $5,000 or less since June 30.

Sailor's Ace **107** B. g (1970), by Great Jimminy—Polly's Ace, by Ace Admiral.
Breeder, Rentie Hamilton (Tex.). 1973 18 3 2 2 $5,940
Owner, J. S. Zinman. Trainer, A. J. Delloso.

Dec29-73 9Lrl	7 f	1:29 sl	31	112	42½	54	711	714	Vasq'zG4	10000	52	Gray Idol 114	Hurtado	Tourforsure	8
Dec11-73 2Lrl	1	1:40⅗ gd	25	112	97¾	84¼	74¾	64¼	HowardR1	7500	66	Tight [illegible]ed113	[illegible]	NortherP'k	12
Nov27-73 7Lrl	Ⓣ 1	1:37⅖ fm	39	112	816	78¾	76¼	45	Hinoj'saH5	7500	78	Drum[illegible]	[illegible]ove	AtAGlance	9
Nov20-73 7Lrl	1	1:39⅘ ft	20	116	1112	97¾	1215	88¼	HowardR5	8000	66	AtaGlance115	Sh[illegible]D'sh	Beau o'S's'it	12

54 69

Mint Copy **110** Dk. b. or br. f (1970), by Bunty's Flight—Shakney, by Jabneh.
Breeder, Mr. & Mrs. J. Wilson (Can.). 1973 20 4 0 3 $12,290
Owner, J. M. Hardy. Trainer, J. M. Hardy. 1972 4 1 0 0 $2,015

Dec26-73 9Lrl	1	1:44⅕ sy	5¼	115	46	43	23	1no	McH'eDG2	7500	52	ⒻMintCopy115	EmaPo'chie	DatsYou	6
Dec15-73 7Lrl	1 1-8	1:52⅕ ft	17	112	49½	511	53½	54	McH'eDG2	H3500	82	Ghost [illegible]in 115	[illegible]in	Translator	7
Nov30-73 6Grd	1	1:40 m	12	111	77½	511	615	618	Dittf'hH6	HcpO	62	ⒻEm[illegible]d'g1[illegible]	S[illegible]reAng'l	R'y'lM's	7
Nov21-73 6Grd	7 f	1:27⅘ sy	2¾	112	58½	56½	12	16½	HawleyS2	Alw	78	MintCopy112	AlitreShaid	Lily'sPoint	6

76 82

Delta's Pia **116** Dk. b. or br. g (1970), by Pia Star—Delta Queen, by Bull Lea.
Breeder, Danada Farms (Ky.). 1973 11 2 2 1 $7,818
Owner, T. LaMarcra, Jr. Trainer, W. J. Lewis.

Dec19-73 9Lrl	1 1-8	1:53⅖ gd	37	112	616	64	43	1no	McC'ronG9	7000	80	Delta'sPia112	SilentJet	ShootN'Dash	9
Nov20-73 9Atl	1 1/16	1:46⅘ ft	10	112*	59½	212	28	26	TritsosP6	6500	67	Rigel 119	Delta'sPia	Larkel	7
Nov13-73 9Atl	1 1/16	1:46⅘ ft	21	117	89	710	59½	59½	BarreraC9	6500	63	Rige[illegible] 115	Sneakin'Deacon	Malvinas	10
Nov 6-73 9Atl	1 1-8	1:52⅖ gd	34	117	68½	510	34	38	BarreraC4	6500	68	Ph'nt'[illegible]Le[illegible]er119	Ca'nbert	D'lta'sPia	8
Oct22-73 3Atl	1 1/16	1:48 ft	9-5	▲117	3nk	1h	13	1no	T'teRL5	cM5000	67	D'lta'[illegible]117	Haw'nFlight	FairC'nty	8
Sep20-73 1Atl	6 f	1:12⅘ ft	33	117	72½	55¾	35½	24	Gr'mPl11	M5000	74	Trave[illegible]117	Delta'sPia	Hebbtide	11
Sep 6-73 1Atl	6 f	1:13⅗ ft	21	117	83	78	67	66½	B'leVJr7	M5000	67	TamiamiTr'l 117	C'perB'ch	Tr'v'linM'n	10
Aug30-73 1Atl	6 f	1:12⅗ ft	5¼	117	75½	510	69¼	611	HoleM5	M5000	68	DigThisDish117	HiN'Fast	TravelinMan	7

72

(cont'd on next page)

Son Diver 122 **Ch. h (1969), by Swoon's Son—Deep Blue Sea, by Nasrullah.**
Breeder, T. Gentry (Ky.). 1973 19 4 2 1 $24,870
Owner, H. V. Howley. Trainer, J. A. Licausi. 1972 3 1 0 2 $3,712
Dec28-739Aqu 1 1-8 1:53⅕ft 2¼ ▲120 13½ 12½ 12 12 C'roAJr10 c5000 69 SonDiver120 NavyNo MightlyBully 10
Dec 4-737Aqu 1 1-8 1:50⅕ft 6-5 ▲114 1h 1h 41 57 Vel'q'zJ2 11000 78 Bold Wit 113 Spread the Word Sig 7
Nov22-737Aqu 1 1-8 1:51⅕ft 8-5 ▲118 2h 11½ 13 13½ Vel'q'zJ2 c8500 80 SonDiver118 DoubleyRoyal Privado 9
Nov19-739Aqu 1 1-8 1:50⅗ft 14 113 1h 1½ 12½ 16 Vel'q'zJ5 10500 83 Son Diver 113 Never Or Now Chili II. 12
Nov13-732Aqu 6 f 1:11⅕ft 5½ 116 74¼ 53¾ 33½ 24¼ G'tinesH7 c6500 83 HolmesSmarty116 SonDiver BeR'stl'ss 12
Oct31-731Aqu 6 f 1:11⅕sy 23f 112 107¾ 88 77½ 76¼ Gusti'sH10 9000 81 Steal aDance116 StansStory Chili II. 13
Oct22-739Aqu 6 f 1:10⅘ft 19 116 129¾107 89¼ 86¾ GustinesH4 9000 82 HeadTable116 Messmate IrishMate 12
Oct11-731Bel 6 f 1:10⅗ft 35 114 51¾ 1h 1h 2nk GustniesH9 7500 90 SatansStory112 SonDiver NavyNo 11
Sep28-735Atl 1 1/16 1:45⅗ft 5½ 115 2h 11 56½ 617 Arist'neM6 8000 62 FallRush110 Enoc-A-Nee PlumGood 8

Shoot n' Dash 117 **Ch. g (1970), by Shoot Luke—Dash n' Splash, by Condiment.**
Breeder, Mrs. J. M. Branham (Tenn.). 1973 30 4 4 5 $20,944
Owner, W. Watts. Trainer, R. L. Maffay. 1972 17 2 2 2 $7,451
Dec31-735Lrl 1 1:42⅖sl 3¾ 120 713 46 32½ 2no Jimin'zC3 8500 61 At aGlance110 Shot n'Dash St'rtLittle 7
Dec19-739Lrl 1 1-8 1:53⅖gd 3 120 818 74½ 31½ 31 JimenezC8 8000 79 Delta's [illegible] Silen[illegible] ShootN'Dash 9
Nov27-737Lrl Ⓣ 1 1:37⅖fm 6 120 715 811 88¾ 86¾ Jim'nezC4 8500 76 Drum[illegible] Ex[illegible] AtAGlance 9
Nov20-737Lrl 1 1:39⅘ft 10 122 910 74¾ 21½ 2¾ StovallR9 8000 73 AtaGlance115 Sh'tn'D'sh Beau o'S's'it 12
Dec 30 Bow 3f my :40b

78 70

Cut the Deck * 111 **Gr. g (1967), by Sure Welcome—Last Slam, by Slam Bang.**
Breeder, M. Polinger (Md.). 1973 29 8 6 4 $19,740
Owner, Barbara Vranas. Trainer, M. Kuhn. 1972 17 1 5 2 $6,013
Dec 8-739Lrl 1 1:39⅖ft 8¾ 113 21 31 44 47¾ Stov'llR2 H3500 68 Hard[illegible] Flirtin'H'rt Bag ofMist 7
Dec 1-736Pen 1 1-8 1:52⅕ft 5 117 13 11½ 11 2¾ StovallR1 H3000 90 Wh't aWh'[illegible]109 C't theD'k H'lyH'me 6
Nov24-737Pen 1 1/16 1:46⅘sy 3 120 11 1h 2h 31 StovallR3 H3000 83 Cr'yB'[illegible] Wh't aWh'k'r C't theDeck 7
Nov17-733Lrl 1 1:37⅘ft 7 113 53½ 61¾ 44 47 St'vallR1 H4000 77 Hardboot122 HappyTank ArloMan 8
Jan 1 Bow 6f my 1:21b

72

Silly Buck 114 **Ch. c (1970), by Absurd—Sassy Deer, by Once A Year.**
Breeder, T. D. Bond, Jr. (Va.). 1973 12 2 1 3 $5,180
Owner, T. D. Bond, Jr. Trainer, H. E. Johnson.
Dec26-735Lrl 6 f 1:15 sy 6½ 116 64¼ 46½ 34½ 35½ LeeT3 14000 66 Time [illegible] Revitalize SillyBuck 8
Dec13-735Lrl 7 f 1:25⅗ft 41 116 11 12 11 33¼ Kot'koR2 10000 81 StrongL[illegible] Bunn[illegible] SillyBuck 12
Dec 6-734Pen 6 f 1:13⅗gd 3 111 11½ 14 15 19 KotenkoR4 5000 78 SillyBu[illegible] [illegible]'v'rLa[illegible] [illegible]mp'sAdmir'l 7
Nov20-737ShD 6 f 1:17⅖ft 3¾ 117 53½ 32 53 43½ Espin'saV10 Alw 63 Dayho[illegible]120 Mac'sKnight HillCrown 10
Jan 2 Bow 4f gd :50⅖b

78 72

Rapid Treat ⊗ 115 **Ch. g (1968), by Flaneur II.—Step Daughter, by Air Hero.**
Breeder, Mrs. H. Y. Haffner (Md.). 1973 11 2 2 2 $8,936
Owner, Double B Stable. Trainer, R. D. Ferris. 1972 27 3 5 2 $21,247
Dec27-733Lrl 1 1:44 m 2½ 119 43 2½ 11 14 BlackAS3 c5000 53 RapidTreat119 DontKnockMe BigVip 7
Dec20-739Lrl 1 1-8 1:54⅖sl 2½ ▲116 24 1½ 11½ 12¼ KurtzJ7 c4000 75 Rapi[illegible]116 Ma[illegible] Cont[illegible] 9
Dec12-739Lrl 1 1:38⅕ft 4½ 113 73¾ 58½ 411 411 KurtzJ7 5000 71 Am[illegible]13 Its[illegible] D'[illegible] 10
Nov28-733Lrl 7 f 1:26⅗ft 8¼ 116 86¾ 86 42½ 2nk BarnesT1 4000 78 BugleBuster120 RapidTreat KnockC'd 12

81 80 62

Dark Stone 119 **Dk. b. or br. g (1969), by Rablero—Nasmo, by Nasco.**
Breeder, L. & B. McDowell (Ky.). 1973 15 3 2 2 $12,234
Owner, The Cross Road Stable. Trainer, J. Tammaro. 1972 24 7 3 2 $23,534
Dec26-733Lrl 1 1:42⅘sy 12 116 1011 74½ 55½ 33¼†Br'eVJr10 12500 56 PictureFrame114 Octet DarkStone 11
†Disqualified and placed fifth.
Dec10-735Lrl 1 1:38⅖m 5 109* 98½ 48 37 34½ MartinR7 9500 76 Tha[illegible] A[illegible] D[illegible] 9
Dec 3-732Lrl 1 1:38⅖ft 10 115* 55½ 2h 2h 2nk MartinR10 8000 81 Hus[illegible]ppie116 D'kStone Sw[illegible] 10
Nov17-739Lrl 1 1-8 1:51⅗ft 7¾ 111* 44 46 32 1½ MartinR7 6500 90 D'kStone111 JoySmoke Vanderb'tAve. 9

84 86 83

The figures for each horse's last three starts are written on his past performances; none is given for races run on the turf, in the previous year, or on a different racing circuit. Sailor's Ace, for example, earned a 54 in his most recent start on December 29, and a 69 for the race before that. His third race back was a turf event, and no figure is listed for it.

Dark Stone's figures were, by a narrow margin, the best in this field. He had earned an 84 in his most recent race and was only about a length superior to Rapid Treat, who had run an 81. But Dark Stone had run in the mid-80s in every one of his recent races. He could certainly be expected to run a figure around 84 again. If so, who could beat him? Rapid Treat had never run better than an 81. Cut the Deck's best was an 81. Mint Copy had run an 82 in his next to last start. Shoot n' Dash's absolute best was a 78. The invader from New York, Son Diver, looked, on the surface, formidable, but his time of 1:53⅕ was very slow, by Aqueduct standards, on a track that was fairly fast. For Dark Stone to lose this race, he would have to run his worst race in months, or else one of his rivals would have to run his best race in months. At 8-to-5 odds he was an excellent bet, and the results of the race conformed to the figures. Dark Stone won by 1¾ lengths. Mint Copy ran back to his next to last race, his 82 figure, and edged out Rapid Treat for second place.

Speed figures help a handicapper evaluate the most troublesome and baffling sorts of horses — ones who are moving up or down in class. If a horse has been losing badly against $10,000 company and is now entered for $5000, will the class drop enable him to win? If a horse has been running very well for $5000 and is elevated to the $10,000 level, can he handle the rise in class? Speed figures provide an unambiguous answer. In the case of horses who are moving up in class, figures can often disclose lucrative betting opportunities because the vast majority of horseplayers shy away from animals stepping up to meet supposedly better opposition. This is what happened in the ninth race at Saratoga on August 10, 1974.

9th Saratoga

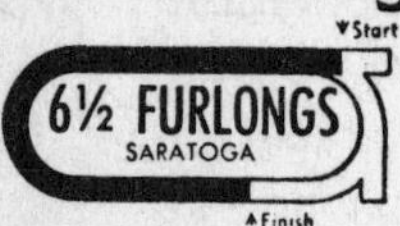

6½ FURLONGS (chute). (1:15). ALLOWANCES. Purse $9,500. 3-year-olds and upward which have not won a race other than maiden, claiming or starter. 3-year-olds, 119 lbs.; older, 124 lbs. Non-winners of $5,700 since July 15 allowed 3 lbs.; maidens, 5 lbs. (Winners preferred.)

Dark Encounter **116** Dk. b. or br. c (1971), by Cornish Prince—Karate Skill, by Cohoes.
Breeder, Tricorn Farms, Inc. (Ky.). 1974 4 1 0 1 $7,320
Owner, F. G. Allen. Trainer, S. Watters, Jr. 1973 2 M 0 0 (——)
Jly 4-747Aqu 6 f 1:10⅕ft 3¾ 117 53 52¾ 65½ 87¾ HoleM6 Alw 84 Nile Delta 114 Big Moses Bitache 8
Jun22-742Bel 6 f 1:11⅗ft 2½ ▲115 57½ 44 2½ 11¼ HoleM6 Mdn 85 D'kEnc't'r115 J't toN'wOrl'ns C'n'gl'd 9
Apr30-745Aqu 6 f 1:10⅖ft 2¼ ▲113 31½ 42½ 44½ 47½ VasquezJ7 Mdn 83 Ha[illegible]24 Sai[illegible]tch Ne[illegible]ative 9
Apr22-743Aqu 6 f 1:10⅗ft 5¾ 108* 78½ 43½ 44 32¾ MoonL9 Mdn 87 P[illegible]N'tive11[illegible]gst'r D[illegible]t'r 9
Dec14-734Aqu 6½ f 1:17⅕sm 3 ▲115‡ 87¾ 913 714 713 MoonL9 Mdn 77 W[illegible]122 RedStre'k DestinyBen've 10
Dec 8-732Aqu 6 f 1:10⅘ft 2e▲115‡ 911 86¼ 511 43¾ MoonL8 Mdn 85 Erwin Boy 122 Mr. Beck Surf Catcher 13
Aug 4 Sar 5f ft 1:00⅖h Aug 2 Sar 3f ft :35h July 29 Sar 5f ft 1:03b

Pokers Brush **116** B. c (1971), by Poker—Brushwork II., by Botticelli.
Breeder, Mrs. Marcia W. Schott (Fla.). 1974 12 1 2 2 $16,040
Owner, Marcia W. Schott. Trainer, J. E. Picou. 1973 5 1 0 0 $3,820
Jly 29-743Sar 1 1-8 1:49⅘ft 4¾ 102‡ 31½ 32½ 33½ 2¾ LongJS4 Alw 91 Peleus 113 Pokers Brush War Reason 8
Jly 23-745Aqu Ⓣ1 1/16 1:43 fm 9-5 ▲114 36 44½ 2½ 21½ Riv'aMA3 37500 88 M't'naN'tive114 P'k'rsBr'sh M'l'tsB'y 7
Jly 9-745Aqu Ⓣ1 1/16 1:41⅕hd 20 114 56½ 46 35 35¼ RiveraMA3 Alw 94 WildLand 115 Camelford PokersBrush 9
Jly 4-747Aqu 6 f 1:10⅕ft 7½ 117 76½ 76¼ 75½ 66¼ W'dh'seR5 Alw 86 Ni[illegible]114 Big Moses Bitache 8
Jun24-743Aqu 6 f 1:10 ft 18 116 44¼ 31 2½ 11 Vasq'zJ1 27500 93 P[illegible]h116 Mag'll'nes Pilot'sSon 8
Jun11-744Bel 6 f 1:11⅕ft 21 115 512 58 46 36¾ RiveraMA1 Alw 80 F'milyPhysic'n115 R'dStr'k P'k'rsB'sh 7
May 3-749Aqu 1 1:37⅗ft 2¼ ▲113 54 67½ 68½ 66½ Turc'teR6 25000 72 Flashing Sword 113 Dicey Dreidel 9
Apr20-744Aqu 1 1:35⅘ft 13 118 45½ 53 46 47 Cord'oAJr1 Alw 81 Bold a'dF'cy121 Turn toBo E'st'nP'g't 7
Aug 6 Sar 4f ft :46⅕h July 17 Bel 4f ft :49b July 2 Bel 3f ft :35⅕h

Toy King **116** B. c (1971), by Prince John—Justakiss, by Irish Lancer.
Breeder, Mereworth Farm (Ky.). 1974 6 1 1 1 $9,960
Owner, Poverty Hollow Farm. Trainer, V. J. Nickerson.
Jly 20-747Aqu 6 f 1:10⅗ft 7¾ 114 75 65½ 57 44¼ MapleE9 Alw 86 H'ppyDeleg'te117 RisingCr'st Aquin's 10
Jly 9-747Aqu Ⓣ1 1/16 1:41⅕hd 8 112 14 11½ 23 37½ MapleE1 Alw 91 La[illegible]gton 113 Haraka Toy King 8
Jun29-746Aqu 1 1:34⅖ft 5½ 111 1½ 3½ 33 49¾ RuaneJ5 Alw 85 G'[illegible]sW'd117 L's'gto[illegible]chona 7
Jun 1-744Bel 7 f 1:23⅘sy 4¼ 115 32 3½ 1½ 11 MapleE5 Mdn 83 Toy King 115 Tuxedo B[illegible]nell 11
May15-742Bel 6 f 1:11 ft 2¼ ▲113 78 66½ 59½ 610 MapleE5 Mdn 78 Debroumard113 Aquinas HatchetM'n 11
Apr30-742Aqu 6 f 1:11⅘ft 2 113 2h 2h 1h 2½ MapleE1 Mdn 83 BobbyM'rcer113 ToyKing Gr'ndgyTw'p 6
Aug 7 Sar 4f ft :49h Aug 2 Sar 3f ft :38b July 17 Aqu 4f ft :47⅗h

King's Day * **116** Blk. c (1971), by King of the Tudors—Day Line, by Day Court.
Breeder, Elmendorf Farm (Ky.). 1974 4 0 0 0 (——)
Owner, Elmendorf. Trainer, J. P. Campo. 1973 7 1 0 0 $5,940
Aug 3-742Sar 6 f 1:11⅕ft 18 119 810 712 99 84¼ SantiagoA5 Alw 80 Lothario 119 Aquinas Hudsonian 9
May 4-749Aqu 1 1:37⅖ft 28 111 85¼ 911 920 929 VeneziaM8 Alw 51 SportsEditor111 ForeignAffair PiaKid 9
Apr24-747Aqu 6½ f 1:18⅕ft 18 113 119 107¼1011 813 SantiagoA3 Alw 72 Pl'se[illegible] ThirdC'lv'ry Sp'rtsEdit'r 12
Apr13-741Aqu 6 f 1:10⅗ft 7 119 72¾ 64¾ 65¾ 66 Santi'goA6 Alw 84 JoMos[illegible] Gav[illegible] EmpireMan 8
Oct23-733Aqu Ⓣ1 1:36⅗fm 16 113 56¼ 76 810 810 SantiagoA1 Alw 82 I'mO[illegible]13 GreenCaribado[illegible] 8
Sep27-733Bel 1 1:37⅕ft 8¾ 121 1½ 66½ 67 69¾ SantiagoA1 Alw 72 Cannonade121 L'AmourRullah Throne 7
Sep18-733Bel 7 f 1:24⅗sy 10e 121 1111 89½ 33½ 15 Sant'goA4 Mdn 79 King'sDay121 Accipiter BuckHill 14
Aug15-733Sar 6 f 1:10⅘ft 14 119 66 67½ 67½ 58¾ SantiagoA1 Mdn 77 Dr.Zegarelli 119 Lea'sPass BuckHill 8
July 31 Sar 5f ft 1:00h July 27 Bel 5f ft :59⅗hg July 24 Bel trt 4f ft :48h

Plantagenet 119 B. g (1971), by First Landing—Royal House II., by Crepello.
Breeder, H. O. H. Frelinghuysen (Fla.). 1974 . 1 1 0 0 $9,000
Owner, Wilrun Farm. Trainer, E. Yowell. 1973 . 3 1 0 1 $5,880
Jly 17-745Aqu 6 f 1:09⅘ft 25 109 11 1½ 2h 1no Ve'ziaM2 31500 94 Plantagenet109 Joe Iz Long Hunt 7
Oct26-733Aqu 6 f 1:12⅕ft 5¼ 121 1½ 2h 11½ 1nk Vas'zJ2 M35000 82 Plantagenet121 BlessedN'te PlayH'se 12
Oct18-732Aqu 6 f 1:11 ft 7¾ 121 32½ 78 712 710 VasquezJ8 Mdn 78 Ridge121 Peleus Nile Delta 14
Sep26-734Bel 6 f 1:11⅘ft 38 121 26 22 1½ 31¼ VasquezJ4 Mdn 83 R'ghM'ch121 S'wOn t'eR'd Pl'nt'g'n't 12
Aug 9 Sar 3f ft :35b Aug 5 Sar 5f ft 1:00h July 24 Aqu 3f ft :37b

Hudsonian 116 B. c (1971), by Swoon's Son—Bethlehem, by Princequillo.
Br., Tilly Foster Stock Farm (N. Y.). 1974 . 2 0 0 1 $1,140
Owner, Kenyon Farm. Trainer, R. N. Blackburn. 1973 . 8 1 3 3 $17,830
Aug 3-742Sar 6 f 1:11⅕ft 6½ 119 56 56½ 42½ 3½ BaezaB1 Alw 83 Lothario 119 Aquinas Hudsonian 9
Jly 13-743Aqu 6½ f 1:16⅖ft 2 ▲117 64¾ 44½ 612 716 TurcotteR6 Alw 77 Quebec124 Knight ofHonor SharpDig 7
Dec18-734Aqu 1 1:37⅖ft 4-5 ▲120 2½ 2h 2h 23 TurcotteR4 Alw 77 Christoforo120 Hudson'n BuyAm'ric'n 7
Dec 6-738Aqu 6 f 1:11⅕gd 9-5e 120 3nk 1h 2h 2nk BaezaB5 HcpO 87 FrankAdams123 Hudson'n CacD'nc'r 9
Nov27-737Aqu 1 1:36⅘gd 3 122 21½ 1h 2½ 21 TurcotteR6 Alw 82 Glossary 122 Hudsonian Beau Legend 8
Nov17-736Aqu 6½ f 1:17⅘ft 6½ 122 31 32 34 36¾ SantiagoA7 Alw 80 R'kSupreme122 ...l'mb Hudson'n 7
Nov 9-735Aqu 7 f 1:25⅖ft 20 122 74 62½ 41 34¼ SantiagoA9 Alw 70 HeavyMayonn'se119 PiaKid Hudson'n 12
Oct29-732Aqu 6 f 1:12⅕sy 8 121 64½ 56 23 11 Sant'goA8 Mdn 82 Hudsonian121 WhoaBoy Pass theGlass 14
Oct 8-733Bel 6 f 1:11⅗ft 10 121 38 47½ 52 33½ Sant'goA7 Mdn 81 Camangie 111 Criterion Hudsonian 12
Aug 8 Sar 4f ft :49b July 28 Sar 5f ft 1:02b July 22 Bel tc 7f fm 1:30b

Aquinas 116 B. c (1971), by Never Bend—Copper Canyon, by Bryan G.
Breeder, Cragwood Estates, Inc. (Ky.). 1974 . 9 1 2 1 $10,250
Owner, Cragwood Stable. Trainer, M. Miller. 1973 3 M 0 1 $1,650
Aug 3-742Sar 6 f 1:11⅕ft 5 109♣1½ 11 11 2h DeM'oCJr6 Alw 84 Lothario 119 Aquinas Hudsonian 9
Jly 20-747Aqu 6 f 1:10⅗ft 15 104♣41½ 2½ 23 32¼ DeM'oCJr4 Alw 88 H'ppyDeleg'te117 RisingCr'st Aquin's 10
Jun27-747Aqu 7 f 1:23 ft 8½ 115 65 67 55½ 47 NemetiW5 Alw 79 Menocal 115 Pia Kid Bitache 8
Jun19-742Mth 6 f 1:09⅗ft 3 115 32 3½ 1½ 14 NemetiW7 Mdn 92 Aquinas 115 Syrian Star Last John 12
Jun 6-742Bel 6 f 1:11 ft 2¼e▲105♣1h 13 2h 46½ DeM'rcoC4 Mdn 82 Pi... ...ai J. Sprat 11
May25-742Bel 6 f 1:10⅖sy 2¼e▲108* 43 42½ 43½ 56¼ MontoyaD6 Mdn 85 Bl... 113 T... Search...tion 11
May15-742Bel 6 f 1:11 ft 11 103♣32 1½ 1½ 2½ DeM'coC10 Mdn 87 Debrouillard113 Aquinas HatchetM'n 11
Apr22-742Aqu 6 f 1:10⅗ft 6½ 113 31½ 32 32 47¾ Velasq'zJ4 Mdn 82 Storm 113 Lassington Blue Devil 8
Apr 8-742Aqu 6 f 1:11⅗ft 9¾e 113 21 2h 1h 52¼ Velasq'zJ4 Mdn 83 Sh'tUp andD'l 114 Tuxedo Tr'pic'lB'y 14
Nov24-732Aqu 6 f 1:11 ft 6½ 122 11 12 12 15 612 59¼†Velasq'zJ7 Mdn 79 NileDelta122 LittleCurrent WhoaBoy 14
†Placed fourth through disqualification.
Aug 9 Sar 3f ft :39⅘b July 31 Sar trt 4f ft :54b July 17 Bel 4f ft :49⅖b

Group Plan 121 B. g (1970), by Intentionally—Nanticious, by Nantallah.
Breeder, Eaton Farms, Red Bull Stable 1974 . 1 0 0 0 $570
& Mrs. G. Proskauer (Ky.).
Owner, Hobea Farm. Trainer, H. A. Jerkens. 1973 . 6 1 1 1 $9,420
Aug 3-742Sar 6 f 1:11⅕ft 19 124 68 68 55½ 4½ Cast'daM9 Alw 83 Lothario 119 Aquinas Hudsonian 9
Dec 8-733Aqu 6 f 1:10 ft 6¼ 122 1h 31½ 35 48 Vel'quezJ1 Alw 85 SpikedApple124 St'ryKnight Schroon 6
Nov29-733Aqu 6 f 1:11⅘m 7 122 76¾ 611 66½ 12 BaezaB8 Mdn 84 Gr'pPlan122 M'j'sticN'tive Inv'stig't'n 8
Nov16-734Aqu 6½ f 1:19⅕ft 6 122 76½ 65 42½ 33½ Vel'q'zJ10 Mdn 76 DreamWithMe122 Inv'tig't'n Gr'pPl'n 10
Nov 5-732Aqu 6 f 1:13 ft 5¼ 122 78 67 55½ 55¾ Velasq'zJ8 Mdn 72 SpanishDew112 Investigat'n JewelBag 8
Oct 9-731Bel 6½ f 1:17⅖ft 7-5 ▲121 63¼ 85¼ 87½ 812 Velasq'zJ9 Mdn 77 G'tl'm'sW'd121 Inv'tig't'n D'mW'hMe 10
Oct 1-733Bel 6 f 1:11 ft 6 120 53 1½ 11 2¾ VasquezJ7 Mdn 87 Downtown120 GroupPlan Investigation 7
Aug 8 Sar 3f ft :36⅘b Aug 1 Sar 4f ft :47h

Joy and Pleasure 119 Dk. b. or br. g (1971), by What a Pleasure—Faint for Joy, by Swoon's Son. Br., Waldemar Farms, Inc. (Fla.). 1974 . 4 1 0 1 $7,110
Owner, S. I. Joselson. Trainer, P. G. Johnson.
Jly 31-741Sar 6 f 1:11⅖ft 3 117 2h 1h 12 13½ Bel'nteE2 Mdn 73 J'yandPl're117 Hi'hC'n'r J't toN'wO's 14
Jly 24-741Aqu 6½ f 1:17⅖ft 3½ 117 2½ 2h 11 41¾ Bel'nteE8 Mdn 87 Face...117 F'm'l...m't ...t'n 12
Jly 17-741Aqu 6 f 1:11⅖ft 26 117 1½ 1½ 21½ 34½ Cas'daM10 Mdn 81 C'n... J't toN'wO'ns J...e 12
Jly 2-742Aqu 6 f 1:10⅘ft 16 117 31 31½ 45 78½ Cast'daM3 Mdn 80 H'yD'g'te117 C'n'gL'd J't toN'wO'ns 11
July 12 Bel trt 4f ft :50⅕h June 28 Bel 5f ft :59⅖h June 18 Bel 6f ft 1:14hg

(cont'd on next page)

Rough March **109** B. c (1971), by Go Marching—Deb Dance, by Rough'n Tumble.
Breeder, H. Massey (Ky.). 1974 3 0 0 0 (——)
Owner, Grandview Stable. Trainer, J. S. Nash. 1973 11 1 1 2 $10,830
Aug 3-74^{2}Sar 6 f 1:11⅕ft 23 119 7^{10} 8^{13} 8^8 $6^{3¾}$ HoleM^3 Alw 80 Lothario 119 Aquinas Hudsonian 9
Mar 6-74^{7}Hia 6 f 1:10⅖ft 4¼ 117 6^9 $6^{5½}$ 5^7 $6^{5¼}$ W'dh'seR^8 Alw 86 StarLance 122 JoJoTex Knowernever 12
Jan17-74^{9}GP 6 f 1:09⅕ft 108 110 $9^{8¾}$ 9^{12} 8^{15} $7^{9¾}$ W'dh'seR^8 AlwS 83 RealS'preme110 Eric'sCh'mp L'dReb'u 11
Nov10-73^{8}Atl 1$\frac{1}{16}$ 1:46⅖sl 8¾ 113 3^4 3^8 $6^{9½}$ 6^{20} BarreraC^5 AlwS 55 Hegem'y114 Mark thePr'ce HinkyDee 7
Oct30-73^{6}Aqu 1 1:36⅖ft 4¼ 119 5^3 6^{11} $5^{8¼}$ $4^{1¾}$ PincayLJr^4 Alw 83 S'r't'gaPr'ce121 LordF'r'stn'r Fl'gS'd 7
Oct23-73^{3}Aqu Ⓣ 1 1:36⅗fm 12 113 $6^{6¾}$ $8^{7½}$ $6^{9½}$ $6^{8¾}$ Cord'oAJr^5 Alw 83 I'mOnTop113 GreenGambados Relent 8
Oct 6-73^{4}Bel 6 f 1:10⅗ft 8½ 121 $7^{8¼}$ 7^9 6^5 $4^{3¾}$ PincayLJr^1 Alw 86 FlipSal 121 FrankieAdams W'dMcAl'r 9
Sep26-73^{4}Bel 6 f 1:11⅘ft 8-5 121 5^8 $5^{5½}$ $3^{1½}$ $1^{½}$ Pinc'yLJr^8 Mdn 84 R'ghM'ch121 S'wOn t'eR'd Pl'nt'g'n't 12
Aug 9 Sar 3f ft :36h July 17 Bel 5f ft 1:02h July 13 Bel 3f ft :34⅕h

Face Mask **119** B. g (1971), by Forward Pass—Bemuse, by Princequillo.
Breeder, King Ranch, Inc. (Ky.). 1974 1 1 0 0 $5,700
Owner, King Ranch. Trainer, W. J. Hirsch.
Jly 24-74^{1}Aqu 6½ f 1:17⅖ft 17 117 $7^{9½}$ 7^9 $6^{6½}$ $1^{¾}$ Sant'goA^3 Mdn 89 FaceMask117 F'r'm'tDip'm't Prom't'n 12
Aug 8 Sar 3f ft :37b Aug 3 Sar 5f ft 1:00h Aug 1 Sar 4f ft :52b

Cunning Lad **119** Ch. g (1971), by Bold Lad—Treacherous, by Ambehaving.
Breeder, Lazy F Ranch (Ky.). 1974 3 1 1 1 $8,930
Owner, Lazy F Ranch. Trainer, S. W. Ward. 1973 1 M 0 0 (——)
Jly 17-74^{1}Aqu 6 f 1:11⅖ft 4¼ 117 $2^{½}$ $3^{1½}$ $1^{1½}$ $1^{3½}$ Gustin'sH^9 Mdn 86 C'n'gL'd117 J't'aN'wO'ns J'y'dPl'e 12
Jly 2-74^{2}Aqu 6 f 1:10⅘ft 5 117 2^h $2^{½}$ 2^3 $2^{3½}$ GustinesH^5 Mdn 85 H'y'g'te117 C'n'gL'd J't'aN'wOr'ns 11
Jun22-74^{2}Bel 6 f 1:11⅗ft 10 115 $1^{½}$ 1^h $1^{½}$ $3^{1¾}$ GustinesH^2 Mdn 83 D'l'c'c'r115 J'toN'wOrl'ns C'n'gL'd 9
Sep26-73^{3}Bel 6 f 1:11⅕ft 17 121 10^{10} $9^{9¼}$ 9^{16} 10^{28} G'stinesH^7 Mdn 69 W'dMcAl'r121 S'v'rB'dge Q'nC'yL'd 12
Aug 7 Sar 6f ft 1:15⅗b Aug 3 Sar 4f ft :47⅖h July 29 Sar 5f ft 1:00⅘b

A handicapper who evaluates horses according to their class might well be baffled by this allowance race. Four horses were beaten by less than a length against similar allowance company in their last starts. Three other members of the field won maiden races recently. And another won a high-priced claiming event.

But a man armed with speed figures would know that the claiming horse, Plantagenet, is toweringly superior. He ran six furlongs in 1:09⅘, over a track with a variant of −17, to earn an impressive figure of 109. That was Plantagenet's first start of the year; with the race and subsequent good workouts under his belt, he should be able to duplicate or improve upon that performance. If he does, none of his rivals should be able to touch him.

Pokers Brush, whose figure of 100 is the second-best in the field, is four lengths slower than Plantagenet. The lightly raced horses who seem eligible to improve — Face Mask, Group Plan, and Cunning Lad — would have to improve by about 20 points (or eight lengths) in order to win.

Despite Plantagenet's obvious merits the bettors at Saratoga didn't know quite what to do with this race. Because Plantagenet had beaten only claiming horses, they doubted his class and made him a very tepid favorite at 3 to 1. He won and paid $8.80, with Face Mask second and Pokers Brush third.

Speed figures not only help a horseplayer pick winners, but they give him an understanding of the sport that even many supposed experts lack. Because I am a speed handicapper, I felt that I could comprehend and appreciate the career of Secretariat more fully than almost any racing fan — and perhaps as much as his owner, trainer, and jockey.

Long before the world was hailing Secretariat as a superhorse, I knew — as did my fellow figure men — that the colt was something special. In the third race of his career, a routine allowance event at Saratoga, he had run a figure of 120. It was by far the biggest figure I had ever made for a two-year-old, and it was not far from the biggest figure I had ever made for any horse, 129. Secretariat lived up to his initial promise, running in the 115-to-120 range for the rest of the year, winning ten races in a row.

When his winning streak was broken in his final prep race for the Kentucky Derby, the Wood Memorial Stakes at Aqueduct, it was obvious that something was wrong with Secretariat. His figure was a dismal 108, the worst he had run since the first race of his career. But he rebounded in the Derby and the Preakness to run figures of 129, and this would be his usual level of performance for the rest of his career, with one glorious exception — the Belmont Stakes.

Any sports fan could appreciate Secretariat's 31-length victory, but only a speed handicapper could measure just how extraordinary it was. Secretariat earned a figure of 148 that day — so much higher than any race I had ever seen that the horse had seemed to step into a different dimension. As so often happens with horses, even cheap ones, who run one extraordinary race, Secretariat resumed running his usual figures in the high 120s. When he was upset by Prove Out in the Woodward Stakes at Belmont, his apologists made a thousand excuses for him and blamed the jockey, Ron Turcotte, but the figures disclosed what had happened. Secretariat ran a 128, his usual race, and had simply been beaten by a horse who was better on that day.

Romanticists could appreciate Secretariat for his strength, his grace, his exciting style of running. But for me the most awesome moment of his career came two days after the Belmont Stakes, when I sat down with paper, pencil, and the Belmont charts, calculated my track variant and wrote down the number 148 for the eighth race that day. For a true addict, speed figures are the most beautiful part of the game.

10

Class

IN THE FALL of 1973, I made a special trip to Belmont Park to bet a two-year-old named Stonewalk in the Cowdin Stakes. Although he had previously beaten only mediocre horses in a maiden and an allowance race, Stonewalk had earned speed figures worthy of a champion. I was unconcerned that he had not yet demonstrated his class by facing strong opposition. Because I am committed to the belief that time is the one way to measure a horse's ability, I consider class to be relatively unimportant.

Before the races that day I had lunch with Mannie Kalish, the well-known New York handicapper and a man who believes in class. I expressed my enthusiasm for Stonewalk and he replied, with a touch of condescension, "Oh, so you're another one of those speed guys." Kalish said he liked Protagonist in the Cowdin. The colt had recently raced in the Futurity Stakes, had been bumped and knocked off stride, but still managed to finish third. In Kalish's eyes, this performance in stakes competition verified Protagonist's class and his superiority over Stonewalk.

That was absurd, I argued. Stonewalk had run ten lengths faster than Protagonist, and this precise measurement of their capabilities was a lot more meaningful than some vague, elusive, undefinable thing called class. Kalish thought I was a naive kid who hadn't matured enough to understand the complexities of the game. I thought he was a doddering fool who, like most of the sport's traditionalists, are blinded to the importance of speed. There was no middle ground on which we could compromise. Speed handicappers and classifiers rarely have a meeting of the minds.

When Protagonist rallied to beat Stonewalk by two lengths, I could not explain the outcome of the race in any way that was consistent with my own philosophy. Although most races can be best handicapped and understood with speed figures, there are many exceptions like the Cowdin when class prevails and speed proves to be meaningless. To me, this is the greatest mystery of the game. If I could some day discover and define the interrelationship between the two factors, I would consider it an intellectual breakthrough of the first magnitude.

I do not have the complete answer. But I have learned some applications of the class factor that will provide indications of a horse's ability when speed figures will not. In situations where speed figures are useless — in grass races and at tracks that do not have an electric timer — they are indispensable.

The class level at which a horse is entered will often provide clues about his trainer's intentions. The opinion of a trainer about his animal can be self-fulfilling. If he thinks the horse is entered in a spot where he can win, the trainer will probably do everything possible to get him into razor-sharp condition. If he believes the horse is overmatched, the trainer may not bother to prepare him for his optimum performance and may tell his jockey not to abuse the horse. Such manipulations seem to explain, as speed figures could not, the in-and-out past performances of Covered Hoop.

Covered Hoop **114** B. g (1971), by Gyro—Miss Lawdy, by Hoop, Jr.
Breeder, L. & E. Jackson (Ky.). 1974 11 3 0 0 $12,755
Owner, N. A. Martini. Trainer, J. G. Moos. $13,000

Apr24-743Aqu	1 1-8	1:54⅕ft	6½	118	1½	11½	12	13½	VeneziaM2	9000	64	CoveredHoop118	St'lArch	Hitch'gPost	7
Apr10-741Aqu	7 f	1:25⅘sy	7	116	64½	89¼	813	715	Ve'ziaM5	12500	57	Manly One 116	Warbum	Pete Simon	8
Apr 5-745Aqu	1	1:39 sy	7	116	12	11½	13	12¾	VeneziaM7	9000	72	C'v'r'dH'p116	R'dyM'n'yK'te	R'n'gB'k	7
Mar14-744Aqu	1	1:40⅕ft	5	112	53½	611	616	617	V'n'ziaM4	13000	49	TimeTells107	NewsW'tch	D'rbyt'nM'n	6
Mar11-746Aqu	6½ f	1:19⅕ft	13	116	54	65½	68	57¼	Ve'ziaM5	16000	73	PurchaseStreet	Bavaria	Anecdote	6
Feb22-747GP	Ⓣa1 1/16	1:47 fm	16	116	89½	53½	46	45¼	MiceliM1	16000	74	Onaduel 116	Talk Less	Lt. Ted	10
Feb11-7410GP	Ⓣa1 1/16	1:47⅖fm	8	112	23	24	2h	32	KellyJ3	10500	75	Mr.Art116	Thr'st ofCour'ge	H'rtHouse	10
Feb 4-745GP	1 1/16	1:46 gd	7½	105*	31½	13	14	1nk	GarridoJ5	9000	71	CoveredH'p105	Hitch'gPost	PatHand	10
Jan29-746GP	Ⓣ 1 1/16	1:46⅕syl	25	113	920	916	814	811	BoveT1	13000	62	Assagal 112	CosyMan	ArmsAndArmor	9

May 16 Bel tc 6f fm 1:15⅖h May 7 Bel 6f ft 1:14⅘h May 4 Bel 4f sy :47⅘h

Covered Hoop won a $9000 race early in 1974, lost four times in higher-class company, then dropped to $9000 and won again. Trainer J. G. Moos was presumably convinced by this time that $9000 was his horse's precise value. When he entered him for $12,500 on April 10, he was probably not making a serious attempt to win. In fact, a bad defeat might benefit Moos when he entered Covered Hoop at his proper level. The horse's odds would be better and, more important, other trainers might be discouraged from claiming him. After Covered Hoop lost by 15 lengths and then was entered for $9000 on April 24, literal-minded speed handicappers might have dismissed him because his most recent race had been so bad. But they should disregard that dismal performance and figure that Covered Hoop will improve dramatically because of his drop in class. A drop from $12,500 to $9000 won't make a horse improve by 15 lengths, but a change in the trainer's intentions will.

If Covered Hoop had been dropped instead to $6500, the situation would be much different. The betting public would undoubtedly make him a heavy favorite, reasoning that an established $9000 horse figures to demolish such cheap opposition. But an astute handicapper would be skeptical, realizing that no trainer would be willing to lose a $9000 animal for $6500 unless something was seriously wrong with him. Whenever a horse's record suggests that he can win at a certain claiming level, and he is entered for a lower price, the drop in class is a negative sign. These dropdowns are the worst bets in racing. They seldom win, and when they do their odds are unappetizingly low. No matter how superior his figures may be, I will not bet a horse who is entered for a suspiciously low claiming price. And if he does not have superior figures, I will bet against him with enthusiasm.

The distinction between a negative drop in class and a useful one can be very subtle. A handicapper trying to pick the winner of the ninth race at Aqueduct on November 22, 1973, practically had to read the minds of the trainers in order to evaluate three horses that were dropping sharply in class — Steal a Dance, He's a Card, and Dealer.

Steal a Dance won his last start for $10,000, and previously performed well for $13,000 and $15,000. In view of his sharp form, he is worth at least $10,000 and should be running at that level. But trainer Johnny Campo has entered him for an $8000 price tag. One should always be suspicious when a horse drops in class after a victory. Campo must know that Steal a Dance is not as good as he looks on paper.

Steal a Dance * **112** Dk. b. or br. g (1968), by No Robbery—Witch's Dance, by Bolero.
Breeder, Jonabell Farm (Ky.). 1973 15 1 1 1 $9,700
Owner, Arlene Schwartz. Trainer, J. P. Campo. $8,000 1971 18 3 4 0 $66,759
Oct31-731Aqu 6 f 1:11⅕sy 3 ▲116 87¼ 67 54 11 Pin'yLJr4 10000 87 Steal aDance116 StansStory Chili II. 13
Oct20-731Aqu 6½ f 1:16⅘ft 53 116 72¾ 911 916 920 And'onP9 15000 72 DeltaTr'ffic116 B'ldM'rit Ch'fC'chise 9
Oct13-732Bel 6 f 1:10⅕ft 5¼ 116 87 63½ 22 22 Pin'yLJr2 13000 90 CountCasp'r116 St'l aD'ce ThreeOn'ns 9
Oct 5-732Bel 6½ f 1:17⅖ft 2½e▲116 65½ 74¼ 42½ 41¾ C'd'oAJr3 15000 87 IrishMate116 Cerril SilentRoamer 10
Sep29-732Bel 7 f 1:23⅗sy 14 112 1½ 21½ 47½ 813 Vel'q'zJ3 18000 71 Overide114 NeverConfuse RoyalQ'ster 10
Sep11-732Bel 6½ f 1:16⅘ft 10 116 52½ 74¼ 73 55 C'd'oAJr3 20000 87 He's aC'd114 Prez'sSon B'k theSyst'm 10
Aug11-738Sar 7 f 1:24⅖sy 25 113 67 810111911120 Balta'rC7 35000 65 Y'ungEd107 Cl'seC'mb't Inv'st'dPower 11
Aug 8-738Sar Ⓣ 1⅛ 1:47⅖fm 5 112 57½ 66¼ 88¾ 813 Tur'tteR3 40000 81 InCamera118 Avant DonQuixote II. 8
Jly 6-739Aqu 🅃 1 1/16 1:44 gd 6¾ 112 11½ 1½ 1h 3¾ Turc'teR6 35000 85 Sh'lt'rB'y116 St'n'yB't'ry St'l a D'nce 9
Nov 14 Bel trt 4f ft :50⅘b Nov 10 Bel trt 4f ft :51b Sept 25 Bel trt 4f ft :51b

He's a Card * **116** Gr. g (1969), by Bold Lad—Flash Card, by Count Fleet.
Breeder. G. M. Humphrey (Ky.). 1973 10 2 0 0 $10,620
Owner, J. Taub. Trainer, J. Parisella. $8 5[illegible] 1972 11 1 0 1 $3,820
Nov15-739Aqu 6½ f 1:17 ft 9-5 ▲116 85½ 85¾ 96¼ 65 Pin'yLJr8 15000 86 Gay Gallant 116 Bostons Boy Brumidi 12
Sep26-732Bel 6 f 1:10⅖ft 8¼ 124 98¼ 86¾ 85¾ 54¾ PincayLJr8 Alw 86 SirArctic121 Maskos Jim theB'rt'nd'r 9
Sep11-732Bel 6½ f 1:16⅘ft 5½ 114 62¾ 51¾ 1h 1nk Turc'teR2 19000 92 He's aC'd114 Prez'sSon B'k theSyst'm 10
Sep 3-731Bel 6 f 1:09⅘ft 13 115 65½ 54½ 54 42 Turc'eR10 18000 92 Corporation112 W'eOldOwl II. B'ldP'p 11
Jly 4-734Mth 6 f 1:10⅕ft 21 114 65½ 67½ 66 42 C'pedesR9 19000 89 SocialEnd'v'r113 Dot'sImp Ni'tDr'gn't 9
Jun20-736Mth 6 f 1:09⅘ft 2½ ▲117 912 911 98 97¼ Mic'liM6 c15000 86 DoctorArt119 FlyingAh'd Jessie'sJest 10
Jun14-737Mth 6 f 1:10⅖ft 5½ 118 99¾ 915 814 712 BlumW11 Alw 78 Kinzua111 SpearCarrier StudentL'mp 12
Oct 25 Bel trt 4f ft :50⅗b Oct 23 Bel trt 4f ft :49b

Dealer * **112** Dk. b. or br. c (1969). by Swaps—Prize Day. by Royal Charger.
Breeder. L. Combs II. & 1973 19 1 2 3 $21,690
Cambridge Stable (Ky.). 1972 17 5 1 1 $31,960
Owner, S. Sommer. Trainre, F. Martin. $8,000
Nov 9-732Aqu 6½ f 1:18 ft 8 116 22 2½ 2½ 67¼ Cas'daM6 13000 79 B'ddyFr'd'hs116 D'bl'yR'y'l BritishR's 10
Oct16-735Aqu 6 f 1:10⅘ft 6 116 1h 42½ 913 913 C'oAJr10 20000 76 Bold Pep 116 Sea Bird II. Wauwinet 10
Oct 1-735Bel 6½ f 1:17 ft 3 116 34 54 89½ 911 Vel'q'zJ4 30000 80 PrimePrince116 Corporation RibR's! 9
Sep21-735Bel 6 f 1:09⅖ft 4-5e▲116 3nk 42 44 47¾ Vel'q'zJ6 35000 88 WildcatC'try119 R'neD'p't D'dasPr'ce 8
Aug27-738Bel 7 f 1:21⅘ft 13 115 12 3½ 810 821 Pin'yLJr3 50000 72 Accohick120 Tunex GustavusAdolphus 8
Aug18-733Sar 6 f 1:10 ft 8-5e▲118 65 63¾ 64¾ 63½ S'tiagoA2 50000 86 EnglishDancer114 Accohick ScareTag 7
Jly 23-737Aqu 🅃 1 1:39 yl 3½ 116 13 23 411 417 Belm'nteE4 Alw 69 RockyM'nt116 StarEnvoy Straph'ng'r 4
Jly 13-738Aqu 1 1-8 1:49 ft 7¼ 108* 11½ 11 32 46½ WallisT6 50000 84 GustavusAd'lph's115 Cheriepe Trupan 7
Nov 5 Bel trt 4f ft :50b Oct 27 Bel trt 6f ft 1:14h Oct 10 Bel trt 4f ft :47⅕h

He's a Card won for $19,000, ran creditably in an allowance race against horses worth at least $30,000, then was entered on November 15 for $15,000. That was a negative drop, and He's a Card ran a dull race. Now he drops again, to $8500. Trainer John Parisella paid $15,000 for the gelding earlier in the season and has recouped only a fraction of his investment. Yet he has seemingly given up on He's a Card and is willing to lose him cheap.

Dealer couldn't win for $30,000; he couldn't win for $20,000; he couldn't win for $13,000. But he displayed some signs of life in his last start, showed speed to the stretch before he tired, and may have found his proper level at $8000. Trainer Frank Martin has not entered him here because he is trying to get rid of a cripple; he thinks this is a race that Dealer has a chance to win.

Martin was right. Dealer won by 4½ lengths, paying $15, as He's a Card ran third and Steal a Dance finished ninth.

Drops in class are most easily recognizable when a horse moves from one claiming level to another. But allowance races have step by step gradations just as claimers do. The lowest-grade allowance races are those for "nonwinners of a race other than maiden or claiming." The competition gets progressively tougher in races for "nonwinners of two . . ." "nonwinners of three . . ." up to the high-grade allowance races with conditions that even stakes-caliber horses can meet. When a horse is overmatched in allowance company and then entered in a race where he fits the conditions perfectly, the drop in class may be just as meaningful for him as for a claiming horse who is lowered in price.

There are many circumstances in which the relative class of horses cannot be measured so easily. If a solid $10,000 claimer is entered in an allowance race for "nonwinners of a race other than maiden or claiming," how does his class compare with that of horses who have been running regularly in allowance company? The only answer to the question can come from observation and experience. If the race is being run in Kentucky, the $10,000 claimer is probably superior. In New York, he would be overmatched. How does a New England handicapper evaluate a top-grade New York allowance horse running in a stake at Suffolk Downs? He learns from experience that the New York horse is usually superior. What does a handicapper at Dover Downs do when he encounters a maiden-special-weight horse from Liberty Bell running in a maiden-special-weight race at his home track? He learns that he should mortgage his house and bet it all on the Liberty Bell invader.

Even when their designated class levels don't reflect it, there are certain groups of horses that will regularly beat other groups of horses. When a handicapper can identify these hidden class advantages, he can find some of the best bets in racing. A studious horseplayer at Shenandoah Downs on September 9, 1972, could have found an excellent wagering opportunity by diagnosing that a maiden had a great edge in class over a field of allowance horses (see pages 166–167).

Only three horses in this field — Come On Rabbit, Deep Rang, and Bonus Money — have respectable records in allowance company, and they appear to be the class of this field. They have been running against each other for most of the season, taking turns beating each other; they all seem to be of roughly equal ability. Just how good are they? We can see that Deep Rang was unable to win against $7500 maiden claimers at Pimlico, but was immediately transformed into a star when he came to West Virginia — evidence that the Shenandoah allowance ranks are rather weak. We can get a further indication of the quality of these horses by doing homework in back issues of the *Racing Form*. In the edition of August 28, we can look up the past performances for the race in which Bonus Money beat Come On Rabbit. The horse who finished third behind them, Tumble Bug, had lost his previous start in a $4000 claiming race at Timonium that was run in the dismal time of $1{:}11\frac{2}{5}$ for $5\frac{3}{4}$ furlongs. Obviously, the so-called allowance horses in West Virginia are no better than cheap claimers in Maryland.

One of the horses in this field is coming from Maryland.

SHENANDOAH

6 FURLONGS — SHENANDOAH DOWNS — START — FINISH

6 FURLONGS. (1.10 4/5) ALLOWANCES. Purse $7,500. 2-year-olds. Weights, 120 lbs. Non-winners of a race other than maiden or claiming since August 10, allowed, 3 lbs. One race since July 10, 6 lbs. Winners of races other than maiden or claiming since August 10 to carry 2 lbs. extra for each such race won.

Coupled—Come On Rabbit and Bonus Money.

Smoked Salmon

Own.—Gray W L

Ch. c. 2, by Loom—Traffic Dream, by Traffic Judge
Br.—Fletcher W D (Va)
Tr.—Edwards W H Jr

114

	St.	1st	2nd	3rd	Amt.
1972	1	M	1	0	$760

2Sep72- 2Tim fst 5¾f .23⅕ .47⅘ 1.09⅘ Md Sp Wt 2 3 1½ 1^{1} 1½ 2^{2} Barnes T 118 5.60 89–12 Prince Wave 118^{2} Smoked Salmon 118^{nk} Piano Top 118^{5} Bore out 7

LATEST WORKOUTS Aug 8 Del 4f sl .49 b Aug 5 Del 3f fst .38 b Aug 2 Del 3f fst .38⅕ b

Come On Rabbit

Own.—Digiacomo A

Ch. g. 2, by Hedevar—Nimble Patty, by Alsab
Br.—Di Giacomo A (W.Va)
Tr.—Longerbeam M G

109^{5}

	St.	1st	2nd	3rd	Amt.
1972	10	1	2	2	$3,079

28Aug72- 8ShD fst 6f .23⅕ .47⅗ 1.14 Allowance 4 4 77½ 74¾ 5^{6} 2^{3} Romaine R^{7} b 112 *.70e 81–21 Bonus Money 119^{3} Come On Rabbit 112^{nk} Tumble Bug 116^{2} Gamely 8

22Aug72- 4ShD fst 5½f .23⅗ .47⅘ 1.08 Allowance 8 8 8^{15} 87½ 76¾ 66¾ Vasil A b 119 *3.10 79–17 Forgene 119^{2} Triptique 119^{nk} Nashville Champ 119^{1} Checked 8

21Jly72- 9ShD fst 5½f .24 .48⅕ 1.08⅖ Handicap 4 9 99¾ 95½ 73½ 63¾ Grove P b 114 *2.20e 81–15 Fathers Ace 116¾ ◻Deep Rang 114^{1} Lover s Lyre 112^{hd} No Threat 10

15Jly72- 7ShD fst 5½f .23⅘ .48⅘ 1.09⅗ Allowance 9 10 106¾10^{8} 96½ 31¾ Vasil A b 119 33.90 76–18 DeepRang 1161½ FthersAce 119^{nk} ComeOnRbbit 1191½ Rallied Gamely 10

15Jly72–Evening Program

6Jly72- 6CT fst 4½f .22⅗ .46⅘ .53⅖ Allowance 6 10 9^{11} 8^{9} 49½ Vasil A b 119 16.50 83–10 Save The Eagle 116^{3} Lover s Lyre 116^{6} Cupid s Boy 119^{nk} Mild bid 10

21Jun72- 1CT sly 4½f .23⅖ .48⅗ .55 Md Sp Wt 2 6 2^{3} 2^{2} 12½ Vasil A b 119 3.60 84–12 Come On Rabbit 1192½ He s Myrullah 1192½ Sailor Max 1191½ Driving 7

6Jun72- 2CT fst 6½f .24⅗ .49⅕ 1.22⅘ Md Sp Wt 6 3 43½ 4^{4} 56½ 4^{8} Vasil A 118 4.90 67–19 Deep Rang 115^{4} Glint Of Gold 115^{4} Speonk 118^{hd} Weakened 8

LATEST WORKOUTS Jly 20 ShD 3f fst .39 b

Deep Rang *

Own.—Mihalick G

Dk. b. or br. f. 2, by Terrang—Deep Love, by Our Love II
Br.—Mihalick G (Va)
Tr.—Palmer J R

114

	St.	1st	2nd	3rd	Amt.
1972	11	2	3	1	$5,710

2Sep72- 4ShD fst 6f .23⅘ .47⅘ 1.14⅕ Allowance 2 1 21½ 21½ 2^{2} 21½ Lewis W R Jr 116 *.90 81–17 Forgene 1191½ Deep Rang 116^{2} Dream Pro 119^{8} Gamely 6

18Aug72- 9ShD fst 6f .22⅘ .47 1.14⅖ Handicap 1 1 2^{3} 3^{2} 32½ 21¾ Sam J 116 3.90 80–16 Fathers Ace 1191¾ Deep Rang 116^{1} Bonus Money 114^{4} Gamely 6

21Jly72- 9ShD fst 5½f .24 .48⅕ 1.08⅖ Handicap 2 1 2½ 4^{2} 3^{1} 2¾ Sam J 114 3.40◻ 83–15 Fathers Ace 116¾ ◻Deep Rang 114^{1} Lover s Lyre 112^{hd} Bore Out 10

21Jly72–Disqualified and placed third

15Jly72- 7ShD fst 5½f .23⅘ .48⅘ 1.09⅗ Allowance 5 1 2½ 31½ 2^{hd} 11½ Sam J 116 3.40 78–18 Deep Rang 1161½ Fathers Ace 119^{nk} Come On Rabbit 1191½ Driving 10

15Jly72–Evening Program

15Jun72- 4CT fst 4½f .23⅕ .47⅘ .54 Allowance 7 2 3^{2} 33½ 2^{3} Detiege C 117 6.50e 86–14 Dream Pro 120^{3} Deep Rang 117^{hd} Lover s Lyre 117^{5} Gamely 8

6Jun72- 2CT fst 6½f .24⅗ .49⅕ 1.22⅘ Md Sp Wt 4 1 11½ 1^{2} 1^{2} 1^{4} Detiege C 115 *1.10 75–19 Deep Rang 115^{4} Glint Of Gold 115^{4} Speonk 118^{hd} Handily 8

23May72- 4Pim fst 5f .23⅕ .47⅕ 1.00⅖ Md 10500 5 1 3^{4} 6^{13} 6^{13} 44¾ Hinojosa H 117 7.90 78–19 Strong Side 1201½ Lady Ara 117½ Royal Carle 117^{3} Late foot 8

17May72- 3Pim fst 5f .22⅘ .48 1.01 Md 7500 8 7 67½12^{10} 76¾ 54½ Moreno O 117 9.40e 75–16 With Pluck 116^{2} Stewart Little 120¾ I m Gonna Fly 108^{1} Late foot 12

LATEST WORKOUTS Aug 10 CT 3f fst .37 b

Philbrook

Own.—Mims T B

Dk. b. or br. c. 2, by One Sub—Sea Muffin, by Battlefield
Br.—Mims T B (Va)
Tr.—Windle G B Jr

114

	St.	1st	2nd	3rd	Amt.
1972	2	M	0	1	$299

29Aug72- 1ShD fst 6f .23⅘ .48⅖ 1.15⅖ Md Sp Wt 6 5 5^{4} 45½ 3^{2} 31½ Kloss G 118 4.30 75–17 Merry Flirt 115¾ Weird Harrold 118¾ Philbrook 118^{4} No Mishap 10

22Aug72- 1ShD fst 5½f .23⅘ .48⅗ 1.09 Md Sp Wt 9 9 75½ 75¾ 5^{3} 5^{3} Kloss G 119 4.90 78–17 Double Flash 116no Fine Delite 119no Weird Harrold 119½ Late bid 9

LATEST WORKOUTS ●Aug 4 ShD 5f fst 1.02⅗ hg Jly 25 ShD 3f fst .36⅗ hg

Merry Flirt *
Own.—Miller P J

B. f. 2, by Li'l Fella—Mary McCann, by British Buddy
Br.—Miller P J (W.Va)
Tr.—Smith F Jr

111

St. 1st 2nd 3rd Amt.
1972 6 1 1 1 $2,806

29Aug72- 1ShD fst 6f .23⅘ .48⅖ 1.15⅖ Md Sp Wt 1 1 22 22 2hd 1¾ Sam J 115 5.30 77-17 Merry Flirt 115¾ Weird Harrold 118¾ Philbrook 1184 Driving 10
16Aug72- 5Tim fst 5¾f.24 .48⅘ 1.11⅖ ⒻMd Sp Wt 1 4 3nk 3nk 3nk 43½ Grove P 118 6.90 79-15 Misty Eyes 118no Arizona Witch 1181 Solindra 1182½ Speed, tired 8
21Jly72- 6Del fst 5½f .22⅕ .47 1.06 Md 10500 1 5 31½ 45 38 313 Jimenez C 117 4.10 75-17 Take Charge 120¾ Tall Award 12012 Merry Flirt 117no Evenly 8
13Jly72- 1Del sly 5½f .22⅖ .47⅕ 1.07⅕ Md 7500 4 9 913 814 89½ 22½ Hinojosa H 117 7.70 79-14 April Treat 1172½ Merry Flirt 117no Tuscarawas 1203 Closed fast 10
29Jun72- 3Del sly 5½f .22⅗ .48⅗ 1.08⅖ Md 7500 2 5 21½ 55½ 46½ 56 Jimenez C 117 3.00 70-18 Popeyes Proof 1173 Primpies Cutie 118¾ Tiger Magic 120¾ Brief speed 10
8Jun72- 2Del fst 5f .22⅕ .46⅗ .59 ⒻMd Sp Wt 3 4 53½ 46 711 714 Black A N 119 54.20 80-14 Honorable Miss 1191½ Tuerta 1198 Curupi 1192 Early speed 12
LATEST WORKOUTS Aug 12 ShD 4f fst .49 b

Hug Bug
Own.—Skinner J L

Dk. b. or br. f. 2, by Rash Prince—Accepted Dare, by Prince Dare
Br.—Skinner J L (Md)
Tr.—Skinner J L

111

St. 1st 2nd 3rd Amt.
1972 2 M 0 0

11Jly72- 3Lib fst 5½f .22⅖ .48⅕ 1.09 Md 6500 6 3 2hd 21½ 44½107½ Rowland J5 110 62.70 67-23 Morning Shower 1182½ Tucson Twist 1151 Ray s Pet 118½ Tired 12
16Jun72- 5Lib fst 5f .23⅖ .49 1.01⅗ ⒻClm 8000 4 6 76½ 79½ 714 729 Rowland J5 111 31.50 55-21 Poppy Jackie 1204½ Western K. 118½ Tight Fight 1143 Trailed 7

Easter Psalm
Own.—Torreyson L E

Dk. b. or br. f. 2, by War Tune—Happy Hobby, by Piet
Br.—Torreyson L E (Md)
Tr.—Torreyson L E

114

St. 1st 2nd 3rd Amt.
1972 8 1 2 1 $2,940

24Aug72- 4ShD fst 5½f .23⅘ .48⅕ 1.08⅘ Clm 5000 7 7 55½ 53 31 21 Addesa E b 119 *2.20 81-18 Cupid s Boy 1191 Easter Psalm 119hd Transplant 116½ Blocked, missed 7
10Aug72- 4ShD fst 5½f .23⅗ .48 1.08⅗ Clm 5000 1 5 64 64½ 32 3¾ Addesa E b 118 2.30 82-15 Till Best 116½ Lady Ski 116nk Easter Psalm 1184 Rallied 6
3Aug72- 6ShD my 6f .23⅕ .48 1.15 Clm 5000 1 3 66 42½ 31½ 43 Addesa E b 119 3.70 76-15 Chanook 1151 Till Best 1152 Mountain Mamma 115no Good try 9
20Jly72- 1ShD fst 5½f .24⅘ .49⅖ 1.09⅗ Md 5000 2 3 31½ 2hd 13 16 Addesa E b 118 2.10 78-18 Easter Psalm 1186 Sailor Max 1185 Caralette 1152 Driving 9
6Jly72- 2CT fst 4½f .23 .47⅖ .54 Md Sp Wt 3 7 66 44 43½ Addesa E b 118 4.80 85-10 Fathers Ace 1192½ Gama Queen 1161 Bonus Money 119hd No rally 10
19Jun72- 1CT fst 4½f .23⅖ .47⅘ .54⅗ ⒻMd Sp Wt 1 7 79½ 66½ 49 Addesa E 119 5.00 77-11 Save The Eagle 1197 Moby Doll 1191 Lady Wakefield 1141 Late foot 9
8Jun72- 1CT fst 4½f .23 .48⅖ .55⅕ Md 5000 7 7 67½ 47 41½ Addesa E 119 *2.30 81-12 Lady Ski 1161½ Sailor Max 119no Cagey Baby 119no No rally 10
1Jun72- 1CT fst 4½f .23⅗ .48⅕ .54⅘ Md 5000 5 7 46½ 37 28 Addesa E 119 *2.20 77-12 Lover s Lyre 1198 Easter Psalm 1191½ Minnie Sue 119½ Gamely 8

Bonus Money
Own.—Longerbeam Betty

Dk. b. or br. g. 2, by Idyll Money—Monte's Pette, by Monte Cristo
Br.—Longerbeam Mr-Mrs M G (W. Va)
Tr.—Longerbeam M G

122

St. 1st 2nd 3rd Amt.
1972 7 2 1 2 $4,000

28Aug72- 8ShD fst 6f .23⅕ .47⅗ 1.14 Allowance 6 5 32 12 13 13 Vasil A b 119 *.70e 84-21 Bonus Money 1193 Come On Rabbit 112nk Tumble Bug 1162 Driving 8
18Aug72- 9ShD fst 6f .22⅘ .47 1.14⅖ Handicap 6 5 13 1hd 2½ 32¾ Vasil A b 114 3.60 79-16 Fathers Ace 1191¾ Deep Rang 1161 Bonus Money 1144 Weakened 6
9Aug72- 4ShD fst 3½f .22⅖ .34⅗ .41 Allowance 3 6 43½ 1½ Vasil A b 120 *1.40[D] 90-10 [D]Bonus Money 120½ Lind 1172 Black Go 120nk Swerved start 6
9Aug72-Disqualified and placed sixth
29Jly72- 6ShD fst 6f .23⅕ .47⅗ 1.14⅖ Allowance 3 3 68½ 35 33½ 22½ Vasil A 119 4.10 79-17 Chatsrullah 1192½ Bonus Money 1194 Juss Fishing 1162½ Gamely 9
29Jly72-Evening Program
21Jly72- 9ShD fst 5½f .24 .48⅕ 1.08⅖ Handicap 3 4 88½ 85½ 86½ 88¾ Fitzgerald R 115 *2.20e 75-15 Fathers Ace 116¾ [D]Deep Rang 1141 Lover s Lyre 112hd No Factor 10
12Jly72- 1ShD fst 3½f .22⅗ .34 .40⅖ Md Sp Wt 5 5 1hd 16½ Vasil A 119 *.70 93-05 Bonus Money 1196½ Sailor Max 1193½ Gin Stone 1091½ Mild drive 10
6Jly72- 2CT fst 4½f .23 .47⅖ .54 Md Sp Wt 2 1 43 33½ 33½ Vasil A 119 *1.80 85-10 Fathers Ace 1192½ Gama Queen 1161 Bonus Money 119hd Mild bid 10
LATEST WORKOUTS Aug 3 CT 3f my .38⅘ b Jly 20 ShD 3f fst .39 b

Rob-O-Let
Own.—Houston R B

Dk. b. or br. c. 2, by Restless Cloud—Betaway, by Bossuet
Br.—Houston R B Jr (Va)
Tr.—Thomas M

114

St. 1st 2nd 3rd Amt.
1972 3 1 0 1 $1,600

28Aug72- 8ShD fst 6f .23⅕ .47⅗ 1.14 Allowance 8 3 2½ 64½ 78 716 Grove P 119 5.70 68-21 Bonus Money 1193 Come On Rabbit 112nk Tumble Bug 1162 Stopped 8
15Aug72- 1ShD fst 6f .23 .48⅗ 1.15⅖ Md Sp Wt 4 1 13 12 13 12 Fitzgerald R 119 2.20 77-19 Rob-O-Let 1192 Fine Delite 1193 Chaptico Challenge 1191½ Mild Drive 7
10Jly72- 1ShD fst 3½f .22⅖ .34⅗ .40⅘ Md Sp Wt 8 1 24 32½ Fitzgerald R 119 5.40 88-08 Cagey Baby 1192½ He s Myrullah 119no Rob-O-Let 1192½ No mishap 10
LATEST WORKOUTS ●Aug 10 CT 3f fst .36⅗ b

Smoked Salmon raced once at Timonium, finishing second in a maiden-special-weight event that was run in the good time of 1:09⅘. He was beaten by Prince Wave. With a little further research, we can find Prince Wave's record and see that he had come to Timonium from the big leagues, Monmouth Park, where he had finished second in a maiden-$14,000-claiming race. Smoked Salmon's performance against this rival suggests that he is much superior to the West Virginia allowance horses, who probably aren't worth more than $5000 or so.

After reaching this conclusion on that day in 1972, I was congratulating myself for my own brilliance. I went to Shenandoah to bet Smoked Salmon, knowing his odds had to be excellent since his superiority could be detected only by the most sophisticated handicapping. After Smoked Salmon won, I collected the princely payoff of $4.40. Horseplayers aren't so dumb.

There is another type of class advantage that is so subtle that the betting public rarely detects it and that provides some of the most solid and lucrative opportunities in racing. Even races with a precise class designation—$10,000 claiming company, for instance—come in great variety. There are weak fields of $10,000 claimers and highly competitive fields of $10,000 claimers. A horse moving from an unusually strong field into an average one would be taking what amounts to a drop in class. Steve Davidowitz discovered a way to identify these strong fields, which he christened the Key-Race Method.

On August 5, 1972, Steve and I watched Scrimshaw defeat Gay Gambler by four lengths in an allowance race on the grass at Saratoga. There seemed to be nothing exceptional about the race. Its time was not particularly fast. The horses in the field did not have dazzling credentials.

A week later the Bernard Baruch Handicap was run at Saratoga and drew so many of the nation's star turf runners that it was split into two divisions. Scrimshaw won the first division impressively. The second division was captured in track-record time by Chrisaway, a 50-to-1 shot who had finished ninth behind Scrimshaw in that allowance race. The performance of these two horses suggested that the field on August 5 had been very strong — of stakes caliber, in fact. When Gay Gambler was entered in an average allowance race a few days later, we knew that we could view him as if he were a stakes horse dropping sharply in class. He won and paid $5. Chartered Course, who had finished a distant last on August 5, won his next start and paid $25. Mongo's Image, another of the also-rans in that field, came back to win and returned $17.

To detect these key races, I keep a set of all the result charts at the track I am following. Whenever a horse wins, I note on the chart of his previous start his victory and the class in which he accomplished it. When two horses come out of the same field and win, I will pay careful attention to any horse in that field when he makes his next start. During the winter of 1973, I was looking for key races at Shenandoah Downs and found one in the first race on November 15.

The winner, Wild Journalist, had come back to finish second in an allowance race. Meadow Lady subsequently won in maiden-special-weight company. Lee Bee won for $5000. Bien Chica and Rough Powder, the seventh- and eighth-place finishers, won their next starts in maiden-claiming company. Then the sixth-place finisher, Godie's Lady, was entered in a $2500 maiden-claiming event. Her past performances couldn't have been more dismal.

Godie's Lady was such a hapless creature that she had never finished in the money during her ten-race career. But

FIRST RACE **3 ½ FURLONGS. (.39) MAIDEN SPECIAL WEIGHTS. Purse $2,100. 2-year-olds. Weight, 118 lbs.**

Shenand'h

NOVEMBER 15, 1973

Value of race $2,100, value to winner $1,260, second $420, third $210, fourth $105, fifth $63, sixth $42. Mutuel pool $10,179.

Last Raced	Horse	Eqt.A.Wt	PP	St	¼	Str	Fin	Jockey	Odds $1
8Nov73 ^{1}ShD^{3}	Wild Journalist	b 2 115	5	1	1^{3}	1^{4}	$1^{3\frac{1}{2}}$	Sanders M L	1.30
3Nov73 ^{9}ShD^{8}	Meadow Lady	b 2 115	10	3	$2^{\frac{1}{2}}$	2^{3}	2[illegible]	Kirk D	3.10
30Oct73 ^{1}ShD^{2}	Lee Bee	2 111	8	5	5^{1}	5^{2}	3^{1}	Shelton P^{7}	2.40
31Oct73 ^{3}ShD	Berk Motley	b 2 118	4	2	3^{4}	3^{3}	$4^{\frac{1}{2}}$	Dalgo M J	11.00
	Captain America	2 118	1	9	7^{1}	7^{2}	5^{2}	Detiege C†	19.50
24Oct73 ^{3}ShD^{7}	Godie's Lady	2 117	9	4	6^{3}	$6^{\frac{1}{2}}$	6^{nk}	Reynolds L	75.30
1Nov73 ^{1}ShD^{9}	Bien Chica	2 115	7	6	4^{hd}	$4^{\frac{1}{2}}$	7^{2}	Canizo V	77.60
	Rough Powder	2 118	6	8	9^{10}	8^{hd}	8^{1}	Castaneda O	51.60
24Aug73 ^{2}CT^{10}	Trail Fire	2 115	3	7	$8^{\frac{1}{2}}$	9^{10}	9^{8}	Smith D D	28.20
18Oct73 ^{1}ShD^{10}	Robin Diane K.	2 115	2	10	10	10	10	Grove P	72.10

Time, :22⅘, :34⅖, :40⅘ Track fast.

Official Program Numbers

$2 Mutuel Prices:				
	5-WILD JOURNALIST	4.60	3.00	2.40
	10-MEADOW LADY		3.40	2.80
	8-LEE BEE			2.60

dk b or br. f, by Journalist—Wild Harp, by Royal Lover. Trainer Adams J P. Bred by Soule C I Jr (Md).
IN GATE AT 7:20 OFF AT 7:20 EST Start Good Won Easily

Owners— 1, Adams Jr & Stokely; 2, Wood R W; 3, O'Neill W D Jr; 4, Letourneau B; 5, Wood H G; 6, McCanns R L. 7, Armstrong R; 8, Michael C W; 9, Reid G W; 10, Krebs V.

† Apprentice allowance waived: Captain America 7 pounds.
Overweight: Godie's Lady 2 pounds.
Scratched—Distaff Dilly; Old Man Even Up; Capitol Love; Len Hauss (3Nov73 ^{1}ShD^{9}).

in the November 15 key race she had beaten two horses who subsequently won for $3000 and $3500. In a $2500 race, Godie's Lady was theoretically a standout on the basis of class. A handicapper with the courage of his convictions would have collected a $16.20 payoff.

The various applications of class that I use in handicapping are extremely valuable, but they do not explain all the situations in which class will determine the outcome of a race. I am sure there are many other facets of the class factor that I have not yet dreamed of. No matter how smart a horseplayer would like to think he is, there are always new things to learn, new areas to explore.

11

Money Management

I WAS BUBBLING with optimism and self-confidence when I went to Laurel Race Course on opening day of the 1973 season. There were two horses on the program — Samoht in the fifth race and Amorio in the ninth — who looked like superb bets. If one of them was successful, I would have a good day. If both of them won, it would be a spectacular afternoon.

Samoht lost and Amorio won at 3-to-2 odds, so I should have made a modest profit. I didn't. Instead, I managed to lose $700. Arranging this debacle did not require any unusually aberrant behavior — just the sort of erratic money management that is a common racetrack disease and prevents many sound handicappers from beating the races.

I wanted to make a strong bet on Samoht in the fifth and thought it would be nice to make a modest score early in the day so that I could be betting the track's money by that time. I took a few chances, therefore, on the daily double and the third-race exacta, and by the fifth race I was losing $100. I briefly considered cutting down my wager on Samoht but when he went off at 11 to 1, I decided that any such restraint would be an act of cowardice. I bet $300, and when he finished out of the money I was beginning to worry. I didn't want to go into the Amorio race in a position where I would have to make a big bet just to get even. So I tried to recoup quickly. I took a shot at the seventh-race exacta and when that failed I convinced myself I had found a promising horse in the eighth race. I bet $100 on Return to Reality, and when he finished second I was minus $550 going into the Amorio race. My horse's odds were 3 to 2 — a generous price considering his credentials — but even a maximum bet of $300 wouldn't get me even. And I was feeling so shaky by this time that I didn't want to risk so much. So I compromised. The ninth race was another exacta event, and I decided to play three exactas for $50 apiece, combining Amorio with the horses I considered likely to finish second. Amorio won easily, but an impossible longshot ran second and wiped me out. It was the worst day of my life at a racetrack, not only in terms of money but in terms of stupidity. If I had just done roughly what I had intended to do at the start of the day — bet $300 to win on each of the two horses I liked — I would have shown a $150 profit for the afternoon.

Every horseplayer has had similar experiences, probably more often than he would care to remember. He may plan his course of action meticulously before he goes to the track, but when he is there he will be subjected to such an onslaught of emotions — overconfidence, lack of confidence, greed, conservatism, complacency, desperation, panic — that he will not be able to function like a machine. But he must try. Even when a man has mastered the art of handicapping, he has not learned how to beat the races. Money management is, with no exaggeration, 50 percent of the game. I know many excellent handicappers who seldom show a profit because they cannot properly discipline their betting and control their emotions. And I know people with seemingly inferior handicapping skills who manage to win because they know how to bet intelligently.

Most handicapping books suggest, and many horseplayers share the belief, that the one secret of successful betting is extreme patience. The stereotype of the professional gambler is a man who makes only a few bets a week. He sits immobile, race after race and day after day, waiting for the occasional spot that offers a golden opportunity. With all the discipline of a Calvinist spurning the temptations of the flesh, he resists the siren call of daily doubles, exactas, trifectas, 50-to-1 shots, and any race in which his convictions are less than total. Then the moment comes: he finds a solid 8-to-5 shot who meets all his requirements; he walks to the window and bets his bankroll. Whether he wins or loses, his equanimity is unaffected. He returns to his seat to wait, wait, wait for the next solid situation.

Many of the people who believe that this is the way to beat the races are losers who are deceiving themselves about their own abilities and ignoring the psychological realities of the racetrack. A horseplayer may go to the track, bet a succession of losers, and then cash one solid winner that gets him even for the day. Afterward he rationalizes, "That winner was a real standout. If I could just wait for horses like that and sit out all the other races, I'd be a winner."

But this is easier said than done, as one of my racetrack

acquaintances learned not long ago. Ray Fritz was a waiter in a Georgetown restaurant who went to the races on his days off. He was too eager for action, too prone to bet every race, but he believed that if he ever became a full-time gambler he would be motivated to exercise the necessary restraint. One day at Bowie he parlayed a borrowed $200 into $2000 and decided to fulfill every casual horseplayer's dream. He quit his job and became a professional gambler. His calling came naturally enough. Ray's father was a big bettor and his whole family loved to gamble. A year before, he had made a junket to Las Vegas with his grandmother, his father, two aunts, and two uncles. Having had so much exposure to betting, Ray knew the secret of success: self-discipline. If he was going to beat the horses, he had to pick his spots carefully. He couldn't bet nine races a day with gusto and hope to survive.

Ray started his new career by wagering $200 on solid, conservative selections; he passed many races and made only token bets on most of the others. The strategy worked beautifully. After two weeks he was more than $4000 ahead.

But difficulties were arising. When a horseplayer is trying to operate with extreme patience and caution, what does he do when he finds a 10-to-1 shot who looks very promising but does not quite meet all his requirements for a strong wager? If he doesn't bet and the horse wins, he is going to be haunted by the missed opportunity and start cursing his own conservatism. After his initial flurry of success, Ray became so confident about his own handicapping ability that he started playing these marginal horses. If an animal didn't quite qualify for his maximum $200 bet, he might venture $100 or $150.

As he began to deviate from his original policy of restraint, Ray began to lose. He knew he should retrench and renew his determination to wait for the solid opportunities. But it is painfully difficult for any gambler suffering through a losing streak to resist trying to recoup immediately. Ray was betting more than ever in an effort to recover his losses. As these losses continued to mount, he was shooting for the moon every day. Instead of hoping to cash one $200 bet on a 2-to-1 shot, he was thinking, "If I hit this horse I'll parlay it onto the next race, and then if I hit the exacta I'll win ten grand."

Betting wildly, desperately, Ray was losing $500 a day but kept going back to the track, figuring his lucky day might be imminent. It never came, and Ray was wiped out. He now has a job as a salesman and goes to the track on his days off.

The "professional" approach of playing very few races rarely works in actual practice for anyone who lacks the self-control of a Hindu holy man. But the concept behind this approach is undeniably sound. Any horseplayer who hopes to win consistently must do it on the few races that he can decipher clearly and bet with confidence. After my $700 fiasco at Laurel, I was convinced for the last time that I needed some system of betting that would force me to take maximum advantages of the races I knew offered good opportunities. At the same time I needed a method that would permit me to be a human being who likes action, who likes to take stabs on 50-to-1 shots and shoot for a fortune in exacta races. I finally developed a realistic set of guidelines that simultaneously disciplines me and allows me the latitude for some self-indulgence.

I divide all possible wagers into two categories: prime bets and action bets. Primes are the crème de la crème. They are the horses who meet all my important handicapping requirements, who I realistically think have a better than 50 percent chance of winning, and who are going to the post at odds of 7 to 5 or higher.

Many horseplayers would disdain such low odds. When I was a $2 bettor, I thought anyone who played favorites was revealing a lack of imagination in his handicapping or a weakness in his character. And I was right not to wager on favorites then, because I lacked the skill to pick the high percentage of winners that is necessary to make them worthwhile.

Nobody can pick even short-priced winners with unfailing success, of course, because certainties do not exist in racing. A horse who looks unbeatable on paper often loses because of bad racing luck, larceny, or imperceptible changes in his condition. But a handicapper equipped with good figures and good judgment should be able to hit at least 50 percent of his most solid selections. If he wins with half of the 7-to-5 shots he bets, he will make a profit of 20 percent on his investments. That is a healthy rate of return.

Any nonprime bet is an action bet. It may be a 50-to-1 flyer. It may be an exacta in which I hook up three or four horses. It may be a solid horse who narrowly misses qualifying as a prime. It may be a virtual sure thing whose odds are inadequate.

The starting point in my betting system is to set a fixed amount for prime bets. This amount should equal somewhere between 5 and 10 percent of a horseplayer's total betting capital. If he has $3000 earmarked for gambling, he might make $150 prime bets. This amount should be high enough to make losing hurt just a little and restrain a horseplayer from making a prime bet unless he is very confident. It should be high enough so that a man who hits one 7-to-5 shot will consider his profits a very adequate day's pay. But the amount should not be so high that it will make a horseplayer too conservative or uncomfortable and wreck his equilibrium if he loses two or three bets in a row.

Having set the amount of a prime bet, I permit myself to lose no more than two-thirds of this sum on all my action bets during the course of a day. And I may bet no more than one-third of a prime on any race. If a horseplayer making $150 prime bets goes to the track on a day when he can find no outstanding wagers, he may bet no more than $50 on any race and lose no more than $100 during the course of a day. If he does make a prime bet, he still may lose $100 in action bets in addition to his $150.

I think these guidelines are sane and realistic. The prime bets insure that a horseplayer will be putting his big money where it belongs. The action bets give him an outlet for his gambling instincts and give him the chance to make a substantial profit even if he happens to be wrong on the one race where he has a strong conviction.

The chief difficulty of this method is making the fine-line decision whether a very promising horse should be a prime or merely an action bet. This is never easy. When I handicap the races before going to the track, I look for horses who may deserve a prime bet, but I never make a final decision until the race itself. Sometimes the track condition, the appearance of the horse, the odds, or other factors will sway me. Sometimes I will be agonizing until five minutes before post time and be guided by my instincts.

But no matter how excruciating the decision may be, a horseplayer must make it one way or another. If he is operating with $150 prime bets and $50 maximum action bets, he will invariably be tempted to compromise and wager $100 or so when he can't make up his mind how much he likes a horse. This is the surest road to ruin at the racetrack: betting fairly large sums of money on horses who are fairly good. When he starts blurring the distinction between prime and nonprime bets, a horseplayer is taking a step that will inevitably lead toward helter-skelter betting with no proper balance between his strong and weak selections. And eventually he is going to have days when he comes home depressed and wondering, "How did I lose five hundred dollars today? There wasn't a single horse I really liked."

Horseplayers ought to get into the habit of betting to win only, and avoiding the false security of place and show wagers. The mathematics of betting is such that the tracks and the state extract a slightly higher percentage from the place and show pools. This adds up in the long run. If a gambler maintains a list of all his prime bets during the course of a year, he will almost surely find that betting to win only will produce the greatest return.

Betting horses both to win and place offers one psychological advantage. When his selection finishes second, a horseplayer will get his money back and perhaps make a small profit. Some horseplayers become so distressed when they lose by a nose that their confidence is undermined and their subsequent judgment is warped. Win and place betting makes them feel more comfortable. But ideally a horseplayer should be willing to take the consequences when he makes a serious bet. He should recognize that in the long run the good and bad breaks will even out and he will make more money if he has the courage to stick to win betting only.

The stick-in-the-mud purists who write most handicapping books usually counsel their readers to avoid not only place and show bets, but also the temptations of gimmicks like the exacta, in which the object is to pick the first two finishers in a race in correct order. Exactas have become very popular at American tracks during the last few years, and I personally find them irresistible. They offer a way to bet sound, logical horses and still make large profits with a fairly small investment. There is nothing sinful or unprofessional about that.

When I encounter a prime bet in an exacta race, my enthusiasm for the exacta usually depends on the odds of my horse. If he is 2 to 1 or better, I am inclined to bet most of my money to win. When I locate a solid horse at a good price, I want to be sure that I am going to make an ample profit if he wins, without having to worry about who will run second. If I have a conviction about the horse who is likely to run second, I may place a small portion of my prime bet on a single exacta combination.

But when a prime bet is going to the post at unappetizing odds — 7 to 5 or less — I may be inclined to gamble. If I can narrow down the other contenders, I may invest my whole prime bet in a few exacta combinations. If my horse wins and I lose money on the race, I am prepared to feel very stupid.

Exactas are most attractive in nonprime situations. There are many times an astute handicapper will not be able to isolate the likely winner of a race but can separate the contenders from the noncontenders. By combining three or four horses in the exacta, he can bet with some confidence. I know a horseplayer named André who developed this technique to the point of near perfection.

André is a racetrack jetsetter who spends his winters at Hialeah and Gulfstream, his summers at Longchamp in Paris, and his autumns at Belmont Park. When he is not gambling he does not deign to engage in gainful employment, though he does write a little avant-garde prose. (When he employed his ornate style on an examination at

Yale, the professor gave him an F with the notation, "If English is not your native language, please see me.") So André's friends, most of whom work for a living, have always viewed him as something of a wastrel. But two years ago they were forced to start treating him with more respect. After conceiving his system, André won more than $8000 in a single Florida season while betting almost exclusively at the $2 exacta window.

During his periodic stays in France, André followed with admiration the exploits of the legendary horse bettor known as Monsieur X. The tierce, a bet in which the object is to pick the first three finishers in a race, is a national mania in France, and Monsieur X won it so often that the country's racing authorities had to change the rules of the game to foil him. Monsieur X's technique was to study the tierce field, which would usually contain about twenty horses, and eliminate roughly half of the entrants, the ones he figured had no chance at all. Then he would play all the combinations involving the contenders. He had to invest a small fortune, but he won a large fortune.

André believed that he could adapt this method for use at the Florida tracks. He had observed that a powerful bias existed at Hialeah and Gulfstream: horses with early speed and inside post positions were dominant. And horses who had been competing during the first segment of the Florida season at Calder Race Course had an advantage over seemingly classier rivals that had been rested since the end of the New York season.

André would unhesitatingly eliminate stretch runners, horses in outside post positions, and horses who had not raced recently, and then combine four or five contenders in the exacta, investing about $50 a race. His purist friends were horrified. One of them scolded him: "Five horses in a race! You're betting like you're at the supermarket." But André collected so many astronomical exactas that he silenced all the skeptics.

When a horseplayer has developed a workable method of handicapping and adopted a rational system of money management, he may hope that he will now be able to live without the drastic, unsettling rises and falls of fortune that most gamblers must endure. But he won't. He will still experience the dizzying exhilaration of occasional winning streaks that make him think he is God, and, much more often, the excruciation of losing streaks that threaten to unhinge him completely.

Long winning or losing streaks can make or break a horseplayer's year. He must learn to understand and cope with them. Most so-called runs of luck at the racetrack are caused not by fate but by the bettor himself—by the astuteness of his handicapping and by his own mental attitude. Nongamblers may think that this sounds ridiculous: one individual's state of mind has no influence on the performance of a group of dumb animals. But an experienced horseplayer knows that when he goes to the track with a negative attitude, thinking, "I can't afford to lose more than one hundred dollars today," he is foredoomed to lose at least $100. And when he goes to the track with an air of quiet assurance, realizing that there are no certainties in racing but also feeling supremely confident of his own abilities as a handicapper, he is likely to be a winner.

This may sound as if it borders on the occult, but a horseplayer must try to develop a sense of when he is likely to lose and when he is likely to win. One season at Bowie I was suffering through a run of what seemed to be legitimate bad luck. My handicapping was sharp, but I had lost six straight photo finishes on horses I had bet seriously. Then, finally, I made a healthy wager on a 16-to-1 shot, sweated out an interminable three-horse photo, and won it. That night I celebrated by taking my girl friend to Duke Zeibert's Restaurant for lobster and told her excitedly, "This is just the beginning. I'm going to win a lot of money in the next few weeks." I recounted the tale of Sun in Action, when one winner so changed my mental attitude that a months-long losing streak was transformed overnight into a monumental winning streak. She was still doubtful. Two weeks later, after an unbroken string of successes for me at Bowie, we were celebrating over crab imperial at La Bagatelle and she asked me, "Did you really know you were going to win?" I did. A horseplayer can feel it, know it as well as he knows himself. When he is in command of the handicapping techniques that are working at a particular time and place, when he is brimming with confidence in his own skills, he knows. These great winning streaks usually do not last very long, but while they do they are the high points of a gambler's life. During the time they are running their course, a horseplayer must consciously try to capitalize on them. He should go to the track every day he can and be much more aggressive than usual in his betting, perhaps raising the scale of his wagers until the streak ends.

Losing streaks are much more difficult to recognize because nobody wants to recognize them. But a horseplayer who has the experience and honesty to sense when he is about to lose can save himself a lot of money.

A few years ago at Saratoga I watched a professional handicapper operate throughout the four-week season and witnessed a display of perception and discipline that was almost superhuman. The man's handicapping was consistently brilliant; during the first two weeks of the meeting he won more than $6000. Then he encountered a race in which he was torn between two horses. He had been leaning toward one but a few minutes before post time changed his mind and bet $400 on the other. The wrong horse won, and he left the track uncharacteristically shaken and depressed. The next day he told me, "That race really messed up my head. I'm going to take it easy betting for a while." For the next week he wagered on a piddling scale, rarely venturing more than $20 on a race. I was appalled. Here was a man riding on the crest of a winning streak that most horseplayers could only dream about, and he virtually stopped betting after just one tough loss. After a week of this restraint, my friend told me he had found the horse who was going to restore his confidence — a filly named Table Flirt who was a superior mudder and would be competing over a sloppy track. He bet $500 to win, and Table Flirt romped home by seven lengths at odds of 9 to 5. My friend immediately resumed betting with his usual gusto and finished the Saratoga meeting with a $9000 profit. Yet if he had not taken that week's breather, if he had allowed that one unsettling defeat to plunge him into a state of depression and a losing streak, Saratoga might have been a disaster for him.

Every horseplayer should learn to recognize the harbingers of a losing streak. I have detected three reliable signs that disaster is just around the next bend.

A few painful or unlucky losses — caused by photo finishes, disqualifications, or jockeys' errors — can wreck a bettor's mental attitude. He starts thinking, subconsciously, that he is fated to lose, so it doesn't matter what he does. In this frame of mind he will inevitably start handicapping sloppily and betting masochistically.

A horseplayer will often get into trouble when the conditions change abruptly at the track where he is operating. If he has been using a track bias to his advantage, he will have a great deal of trouble adjusting when the track returns to normal and the bias ceases to exist.

The most disastrous losing streaks usually come immediately after a horseplayer has enjoyed a great winning streak. His self-assurance gradually changes into cockiness and overconfidence. He begins to think that anything he does will turn out right, and without realizing it he becomes careless and undisciplined in his handicapping and betting. Danny Lavezzo, a bettor who owns the fashionable New York bar P. J. Clarke's, terms this phenomenon the "Messiah complex." Lavezzo had been spending a winter in Florida and had a phenomenal hot streak at Gulfstream and Hialeah. "It was one of those periods when speed on the rail was winning everything," he recalled, "and I was betting speed on the rail. I picked all the winners. Best bets at fifteen to one, things like that. After a while, I thought I was infallible. I was getting a Messiah complex. I should have realized that was the beginning of the end. I was lucky to break even for the season."

The turning point from a winning streak to a losing streak usually comes at approximately the moment when a horseplayer utters the words, "How long has this game been going on?" It happened to me in the fall of 1972 at Laurel. For six weeks I had been picking long-priced winners at a phenomenal rate. When I touted all my friends onto Dismas and watched him win easily and pay $39.40, I was overcome by the Messiah complex. Even with colleagues like Clem Florio, who had taught me much of what I know about horse racing, I was exuding an air of smug, obnoxious superiority. I was God's gift to the art of handicapping. Of my next twenty prime bets, nineteen lost. "This game," Clem reminded me, "will keep you humble."

Losing streaks, like many illnesses, can usually be cured if they are detected early. When a horseplayer recognizes the signs of a losing streak he may continue going to the track and cut his bets down drastically. If he succumbs to temptation too easily, he should stay away from the track for a few days, recycle his thinking, and return to action on a day when he sees a solid prime bet or at least finds the races generally promising. These periods of abstinence may save him hundreds or even thousands of dollars during the course of a year. And at the end of the year, when a horseplayer is totaling his net profits or losses, a thousand saved is as good as a thousand earned.

All horseplayers, even the monomaniacs like me, live a portion of our lives away from the racetrack, and sometimes external forces will adversely affect our performance as gamblers. One such factor is money. When a man is beset by financial pressures in his personal life, he cannot hope to function well at the track; it is an old gambling axiom that scared money never wins. Walter Haight, the late racing columnist of the Washington *Post*, gave me a piece of advice about money when I was a fledgling horseplayer, and I have never forgotten it. "When you're at the track," he said, "you've got to think of money as if it were chips or pebbles that are only used to keep score of how well you're doing. When you start thinking that you could be using your gambling money to pay the rent, or buy a new suit, you'll never be able to win." A horseplayer ought to maintain a betting fund completely separate from the money he lives on. This is especially important if he is married, so that his wife does not have to worry that every trip he makes to the track may be taking food out of the kiddies' mouths.

While horseplayers sometimes cannot control the financial pressures in their personal lives, they have no excuse for letting alcohol interfere with their gambling. Unfortunately, many racetrackers occasionally mix booze and betting. The results can be disastrous. A Washington horseplayer named Carlos Meyer holds what may be the all-time record for money not won because of drinking: $13,920.

A few years ago Carlos was working as a bartender in Georgetown. His boss, an inveterate horseplayer, had received some information from usually reliable sources about a three-year-old ready to win his next start at Hialeah. When the horse's name appeared in the overnight entries, he was listed at 20 to 1.

The boss's bookie had been arrested the week before and there was no way he could place a substantial wager in Washington. So he and his friends who wanted to bet the horse pooled their money and bought a ticket on a 10 A.M. flight to Miami the next day. They gave the ticket to Carlos, along with their betting money of $600. With $600 in his pocket, especially if it is somebody else's money, Carlos is likely to misbehave. Which he did that night. He hit most of the bars on M Street, celebrating as if the horse had already won, drinking rum and Cokes until four in the morning. He didn't know how he got home, but he did manage to set his alarm for 9 A.M. He woke up at two in the afternoon. The alarm clock was lying on the floor, where he had hurled it five hours earlier when its buzzing disturbed his slumber. Carlos called his boss and told him what had happened. His boss was mad. He was a little madder that evening after he learned that the horse had won and paid $46.20. Carlos did not come out of hiding for several days.

As harmful as money problems and alcohol may be, the most deleterious effects on a horseplayer's concentration are caused by women. When a gambler has had an exceptional day at the track, or is in the midst of a great winning streak, he may exude a sense of self-esteem and confidence to which women respond. If this occurs the horseplayer is dangerously apt to fall in love, and the distraction is sure to wreck him at the track. This has happened to me twice. Once I took a date to Bowie and picked five straight winners; the day was so marvelous that it started an immediate romance. I had losing days on my next twenty-one trips to the track. The other time it happened at Saratoga. I won $2000 on an exacta and a few hours later happened to meet a fascinating woman. The reaction was such that I promptly lost more than $2000 in the next week.

Pittsburgh Phil, the legendary gambler who won nearly $2 million in his racing career, had strong opinions about the opposite sex. "A man who wishes to be successful," he wrote, "cannot divide his attention between horses and women. A man who accepts the responsibility of escorting a woman to the race track and of seeing that she is comfortably placed and agreeably entertained cannot keep his mind on the work before him. A sensible woman understands this and cannot feel hurt at my words."

In my youth I once thought that the remedy for the inevitable problems that are posed by women would be to find a woman who was a full-fledged horseplayer herself. She would be sympathetic to my compulsion and might even be able to help me handicap. I was a junior at Harvard when I discovered her. I read a column in a Detroit newspaper about a girl at Michigan State University who had been playing the horses since she was twelve, betting with her hairdresser who also happened to be a bookmaker. I showed the story to my friends, who agreed that this was probably the woman of my dreams and took up a collection so that I could invite her to Boston for a weekend. I wrote her a letter that began:

> Dear Roberta,
> When I read the story that said you had been playing the horses since you were twelve, I knew I had found love . . .

Roberta accepted the invitation and I planned a big day of gambling for our blind date: Suffolk Downs in the afternoon, Lincoln Downs at night. Roberta proved to be a capable handicapper and we both won modestly at Suffolk. I started studying the evening card at Lincoln and was getting enthusiastic about a longshot named Kentucky Cousin in the fifth race. But Roberta folded her *Racing Form* emphatically and said, "I'd rather go to dinner." I could not understand how a person of sensitivity could pass up an hour and a half trip to see a bunch of battle-scarred $1500 claimers running at a dumpy Rhode Island track, but I capitulated and blew the afternoon's winnings on dinner. The next morning I checked the Lincoln results and saw that Kentucky Cousin had won and paid $103.60. I had learned my lesson about mixing women and horses.

12

Putting It All Together

EVEN AFTER A HORSEPLAYER has learned all the important principles of handicapping, he may feel lost and bewildered when he tries to put his knowledge to practical use. As he analyzes a race, he will be dealing with literally thousands of pieces of information in the *Racing Form*. Ideas about speed, class, consistency, and condition will be swirling through his head. Where does he begin? How does he proceed?

I begin by writing down the speed figures that each horse has earned in his last few starts. I focus my attention on the horse with superior figures who could win today's race if he were to only duplicate his most recent performance. Then I ask myself questions about the horse, trying to judge if he is likely to run well again.

Is he reliable? I hesitate to bet a horse seriously on the basis of just one good race or big figure. Ideally, a horse should consistently run figures that are good enough to win today. Regardless of his figures, I demand that a horse show some ability to win. If he displays sucker-horse tendencies, if he has previously been entered in races that he should have won but didn't, I will view him with skepticism.

Is he in condition? A horse's physical condition can vary greatly from race to race. Even if he ran sensationally fast in his last start, I need some positive evidence that he will do it again today. I will usually assume that a horse is fit if he is trained by an extremely competent, reliable man. Otherwise, his record should show a recent race — within the last week or so — or good workouts. The final measurement of a horse's condition is made when he comes onto the track. No matter how good he looks on paper, he must also look good in the flesh.

Is he entered under suitable conditions? A horse must be entered at an appropriate distance, or all his other handicapping virtues may be irrelevant. If he is running on a muddy track, he must not have shown a previous dislike for the mud. If he is racing on a track with a pronounced bias, that bias should be in his favor.

Even if a horse with superior figures fulfills all these criteria, he may still be a risky bet. A handicapper must evaluate the other entrants in the race, not only by looking at their figures, but by judging if any of them is likely to wake up and improve dramatically upon his recent performances. He should pay careful attention to certain types of horses whose bad figures may be irrelevant or misleading:

1. A horse who has just been acquired by a leading trainer or that has been prepared in a manner the trainer has used with success in the past.

2. A horse who has been manipulated for purposes of a betting coup and receives strong betting action.

3. A horse who has been running recently under inappropriate or disadvantageous conditions: at the wrong distance, in the wrong class, with a bad jockey, on the turf, on a muddy track.

4. A horse who was hindered by a track bias in his last start.

5. A horse with the change-of-pace pattern.

6. A horse coming out of a "key race."

The ideal betting situation is a race in which one horse possesses clearly superior figures, gives all the indications that he will reproduce his good form, and meets no opponents who seem likely to improve sharply. These clear-cut prime bets seldom materialize more than once a week.

Sometimes the horse with the top figure can be eliminated on fundamental handicapping grounds, and the horse with the second-best figure will be a solid bet. Other times all the horses with established form will be so weak that a wake-up horse can be played with confidence.

It is dangerous to generalize too much about what constitutes a good betting opportunity. The game offers infinite variety. Handicapping is not a test of a man's ability to apply the right formula to the right situation. It is a test of his creative intelligence.

To demonstrate how the handicapping process works, I have selected a few races that were run in Maryland and New York during 1973 and 1974. Some are complex and some are easy, but each of them involves several important principles. Of course, no set of illustrative races, however large, could raise all the questions that a handicapper must resolve in actual practice. Even horseplayers with decades of experience are constantly facing new problems and new intellectual challenges.

8th Bowie Race Course

MARCH 6, 1974

6 FURLONGS (chute). (1:08⅗). ALLOWANCES. Purse $7,000. 4-year-olds and upward which have never won a race other than maiden, claiming, starter or hunt meeting. Weight, 122 lbs. Non-winners of a race other than claiming in 1974 allowed 3 lbs.; such a race since Nov. 30, 5 lbs.; since Oct. 22, 7 lbs.; since Sept. 10, 10 lbs.

Cary Street **117** B. c (1970), by Ambernash—Bloomin Alibi, by Alibhai.
Br., Hilltop Stable & J. L. Reynolds (Md.). 1974 4 0 1 1 $2,380
Owner, J. L. Reynolds. Trainer, H. R. Fenwick. 1973 7 1 0 2 $5,124
Feb14-745Bow 6 f 1:12⅘ft 5¾ 114 32 32 4nk 2no Cusim'noG1 Alw 79 Impr'sive Imp112 C'ryStr't B'kSt'eT'k 7
Feb 6-748Bow 6 f 1:10⅖fr 7 115 54 42½ 32 32¾ GinoL1 Alw 88 KingHotTot112 B'leStr'tBoy C'ryStr't 9
Jan18-748Bow 6 f 1:12 ft 49 114 55 64¼ 73¾ 73½ CusimanoG2 Alw 79 Com[illegible]ur119 [illegible]n'rt [illegible] 8
Jan 2-746Bow 1 1/16 1:47⅗ft 12 119 12 2h 47½ 57¾ Cusim'noG1 Alw 62 Imp[illegible]ula[illegible]112 P[illegible]Scene [illegible] 7
Dec10-737Lrl 6 f 1:12⅕gd 37 120 821 88½ 87¼ 55¼ CannesaJ9 Alw 83 Vi[illegible]eld120 [illegible]F'l T[illegible]P'[illegible]r 12
Nov19-737Lrl Ⓣ 1 1:37⅗fm 4¾ 119 2½ 1½ 22 55¼ WalshE4 Alw 77 S'n'sB'th'rJim112 Gr'tR'lty Th't'sHim 12
Nov13-734Lrl Ⓣ 1 1:39⅘fm 5¼ 119 13 13½ 13 13¼ Cusim5oG7 Mdn 71 CaryStr't119 Princ'sFree West'nWilly 8
March 2 Pim 5f gd 1:04⅗h Feb 2 Pim 5f ft 1:02h Jan 26 Pim 5f sl 1:05b

77 72 83

Midnight Caller * **112** Gr c (1970), by Count Brook—Susie Gray, by Trojan Monarch.
Br., R. E. Vogelman, Jr. & R. R. Hunt (Md.1974 2 0 0 0 (——)
Owner, R. E. Vogelman, Jr. Trainer, R. E. Vogelman, Jr. 1973 11 4 1 1 $14,776
Feb26-748Bow 6 f 1:12⅖ft 12 112 1h 3½ 53½108¼ WrightDR4 Alw 73 KinwoldsD'ke122 H'dyHit T'ch ofP'p'r 10
Feb14-745Bow 6 f 1:12⅘ft 15 112 2h 2h 1h 67½ WrightDR5 Alw 71 Impr'sive Imp112 C'ryStr't B'kSt'eT'k 7
Jun30-736Del 6 f 1:11⅗ft 7¾ 112 62¾ 77 78 89½ W'ghtDR7 Alw 77 Kim[illegible] 112 Neve[illegible]ch Pay Pappa 8
Jun13-738Del 6 f 1:12⅕sl 5½ 114 74¼ 68½ 56½ 611 WrightDR3 Alw 73 Ki[illegible]12 [illegible]linch Hip High 8
Jun 3-734Del 6 f 1:12 ft 15 114 3½ 1h 1h 11¼ Wr'htDR6 16500 85 M[illegible]Caller11[illegible] Hostile Key Ring 7
May28-735Pim 1 1/16 1:48⅗sy 8½ 112 2½ 24½ 48 516 WrightDR7 Alw 46 KitchenG'sip112 That'sHim H'eJerome 7
May14-735Pim 6 f 1:12⅘ft 7½ 114 21½ 21 11 1nk W'htDR3 11500 82 Midn'tC'll'r114 M'sicCity St'rMon'rch 11
Apr26-732Pim 6 f 1:12⅖sy 4 114 11½ 13 16 18 Br'leVJr9 c6500 84 MidnightCall'r114 ValleyBoss ArchieJ. 9
Feb 24 Bow 4f ft :50⅖b Feb 23 Bow 4f ft :48h Feb 12 Bow 4f ft :49b

60 59

Thayer * **112** B. g (1968), by Tudorka—Simoom, by Level Lea.
Breeder, J. P. Thayer (Va.). 1974 4 1 1 0 $6,150
Owner, F. A. Greene, Jr. Trainer, H. Steward Mitchell. 1973 24 5 4 3 $22,102
Feb21-749Bow 1 1/16 1:44⅗ft 2½ 112 13 13 2½ 25 GinoL4 Alw 80 Sentimentalist 112 Thayer Brumidi 7
Jan29-744Bow 7 f 1:25⅗m 1 ▲112 1h 1h 54 58 GinoL1 Alw 69 Meformore115 Impsular FamousJim 7
Jan19-747Bow 1 1/16 1:45⅘ft 4¼ 114 12½ 12½ 14 19 GinoL3 13500 79 T[illegible]4 Pic[illegible]he Whi[illegible] 10
Jan 4-746Bow 1 1/16 1:47⅖m 2¼ ▲114 1h 13½ 1h 52¾ GinoL1 16500 68 Sa[illegible] 116 [illegible]ame [illegible] 7
Dec29-736Lrl 7 f 1:27⅘sl 4 112 2h 1h 16 17 GinoL7 13000 72 Tha[illegible]112 Ti[illegible] Landers[illegible] 8
Dec10-735Lrl 1 1:38⅖m 2½ 112 11½ 13 13 12 GinoL1 9000 81 Thayer 112 Arlo Man Dark Stone 9
Nov29-734Lrl 6 f 1:12 gd 5½ 120 32 21 1½ 13¾ GinoL6 8000 89 Thayer120 DonHernando KingElinol 9
March 2 Bow 5f ft :59⅘h Feb 18 Bow 5f ft 1:00h Feb 12 Bow 6f ft 1:13⅖h

92 84 103

Back Stage Talk **115** Ch. g (1970), by Stage Door Johnny—Patty's Song, by Spy Song.
Breeder, Walnut Hall Farm, Inc. (Ky.). 1974 7 1 0 2 $4,440
Owner, Spartan Stable. Trainer, A. J. Hemmerick. 1973 2 M 1 0 $1,040
Feb26-748Bow 6 f 1:12⅖ft 14 115‡109½1013 97 62 RhodesD9 Alw 79 KinwoldsD'ke122 H'dyHit T'ch ofP'p'r 10
Feb14-745Bow 6 f 1:12⅘ft 33 112‡ 44 53½ 52¼ 32½ RhodesD2 Alw 76 Impr'sive Imp112 C'ryStr't B'kSt'eT'k 7
Feb 6-748Bow 6 f 1:10⅖fr 31 112‡ 76 88½ 88½ 55½ RhodesD6 Alw 85 King[illegible]Tot112 B[illegible]tr'tBo[illegible] C'[illegible]tr't 9
Jan30-741Bow 6 f 1:13⅘gd 3 ▲110⁂88½ 84¼ 42 11 RhodesD8 Mdn 74 Bac[illegible] Talk 110 Ru[illegible]Elo[illegible]st 12
Jan23-745Bow 1 1/16 1:47⅕gd 16 110* 2h 56½ 8151020 RhodesD3 Alw 52 Sa[illegible]12 HipHigh Dream[illegible]Me 10
Jan16-741Bow 7 f 1:24⅘ft 85 110⁂75¾ 52 33½ 31½ RhodesD11 Mdn 79 T'l aLie120 Kinw'ldsD'ke B'kSt'geT'lk 12
Jan 4-745Bow 6 f 1:12 m 17 110⁂1120111910169 15 RhodesD8 Mdn 68 Mr. Q.120 TopThis KinwoldsDuke 12
Feb 23 Bow 4f ft :48⅗h Jan 29 3f my :38b Jan 11 Bow 4f sy :50⅗bg

76 71 65

Path o' Ray * **112** Dk. b. or br. g (1969), by Reneged—Le Muy by Education.
Br., P McLean & W. G. Robins (Ky.). 1974 4 1 0 1 $4,560
1973 9 0 1 1 $2 040
Owner, Beelu Farm. Trainer, Dean Gaudet.
Feb26-748Bow 6 f 1:12⅖ft 6¾ 113 61¾ 63¼ 74½ 41¾ Cusim'oG10 Alw 79 KinwoldsD'ke122 H'dyHit T'ch ofP'p'r 10
Feb14-746Bow 6 f 1:12 ft 2¼ ▲114 2h 1½ 14 13¼ WalshE1 c7500 83 PathO'Ray114 FastH'ry RoyalEmp'ror 7
Jan14-746Bow 1 1/16 1:42 ft 6 114 66½ 56¼ 613 614 Cusi'oG7 c10500 84 Hus[illegible]e119[illegible] Whisk[illegible] 8
Jan. 5-749Bow 1 1/16 1:48⅕sm 7¾ 114 43½ 42 31½ 32¼ KurtzJ2 11500 65 Cha[illegible]ie[illegible].119 [illegible]gade Pa[illegible]Ray 10
Dec26-733Lrl 1 1:42⅘sy 4½ 116 54 42½ 810 813 KurtzJ5 12500 46 Pi[illegible]ureFrame1[illegible] [illegible]tet D[illegible]rk[illegible]one 11
Nov30-736Lrl 1 1-8 1:52⅗ft 6-5 ▲116 13 12½ 12½ 21¼ KurtzJ1 12500 83 FirstColumn116 PathO'Ray BoldGent 6
Nov22-739Lrl 1 1:38⅕ft 19 116 55 2h 11 31¾ Fel'oBM7 12500 80 Compatriot120 TimothyO. PathO'Ray 8
Jan 11 Bow 3f sly :37b

Touch of Pepper **117** Gr. c (1970), by Idolater—Slacks, by Saggy.
Breeder, Fred Howard (Pa.). 1974 3 0 1 1 $2,380
1973 4 1 1 2 $5,345
Owner, G. W. Dalphon. Trainer, W. E. Hairfield.
Feb26-748Bow 6 f 1:12⅖ft 2¼ ▲119 51¾ 53 43½ 31 LeeT8 Alw 80 KinwoldsD'ke122 H'dyHit T'ch ofP'p'r 10
Jan23-745Bow 1 1/16 1:47⅕gd 2 ▲117 69 69½ 55 54½ Cusim'noG2 Alw 67 Samoht112 HipHigh DreamWithMe 10
Jan 7-748Bow 1 1/16 1:48⅗gd 2¼ ▲119 1½ 2h 2h 2h BlackAS2 Alw 65 Dar[illegible]y11[illegible]P'per [illegible]m 8
Dec29-737Lrl 6 f 1:14⅘sl 2¼ ▲120 86½ 85¼ 43 21¾ BlackAS8 Alw 73 Bi[illegible]l 111 [illegible]ep'r [illegible]on 10
Dec10-737Lrl 6 f 1:12⅕gd 3¼ 120 1225 1214 65¼ 31 BlackAS3 Alw 87 Vi[illegible]Ha[illegible]ield12[illegible]F'l [illegible]p'r 12
Nov22-735Lrl 6 f 1:12 ft 3¼ 120 1h 1h 1h 11 BlackAS6 Mdn 89 T'chOfP'p'r120 Kinw'dsDuke Aft'D'n'r 7
May23-734GS 6 f 1:13⅘sy 4½ 113 87 68½ 33½ 32¾ M'leyJW4 Mdn 72 BoldF'wn114 SturdyUn'n T'ch ofP'p'r 11
March 4 Bow 4f ft :48hg Feb 25 Bow 3f ft :36⅗b Feb 21 Bow 5f ft 1:01h

Handy Hit **112** B. g (1970), by John William—Handy Sandy, by Tuscany.
Breeder, E. Howell (Md.). 1974 5 0 2 1 $4,184
1973 9 1 1 1 $4,314
Owner, J. J. Carpenter. Trainer, R. E. Dutrow.
Feb26-748Bow 6 f 1:12⅖ft 2¾ 112 2h 1h 2½ 21 HawleyS5 Alw 80 KinwoldsD'ke122 H'dyHit T'ch ofP'p'r 10
Feb 9-744Bow 6 f 1:11⅖sy 12 114 34½ 24 22 22 W'htDR6 c10500 84 Little Seth 114 Handy Hit Swoonbeam 9
Jan31-747Bow 6 f 1:12⅖ft 9¼ 114 64½ 64½ 43 41¼ Wr'htDR9 10500 80 S[illegible]14 [illegible]h T[illegible]yBoss 11
Jan 8-747Bow 6 f 1:12 gd 16 112 1h 1h 12 82¼ Wr'htDR1 12500 81 Bea[illegible]104 [illegible]R[illegible]m'ce [illegible]n'eM'n 12
Jan 1-749Lrl 6 f 1:14 m 11 116 27 23 21 42† W'ghtDR4 12000 77 Lit[illegible]eSe[illegible]116 [illegible]chme[illegible]r.Titus 6
†Placed third through disqualification.
Dec 6-735Lrl 6 f 1:11⅘gd 7 116 1h 1h 21½ 26 Wri'tDR9 10000 84 NightTr'nL'ne116 H'ndyHit JimArthur 12
Nov19-735Lrl 6 f 1:11⅗ft 23 116 22½ 24 22 2½† WrightD5 10000 90 John deGreat120 HandyHit Jok'rsWild 12
†Disqualified and placed third.
Feb 7 Lrl 4f m :50b Jan 29 Lrl 4f m :49⅗b

Thayer's credentials appear impeccable. Not only has the horse won four of his last seven starts, but his speed figures are consistently superior. His worst performance of the season — a figure of 84 in his next to last race — looks good enough to beat this field. A duplication of his best performance would demolish it.

There are no questions about Thayer's current condition. He is trained by a very competent man, H. Steward Mitchell. He raced only twelve days ago. Since that effort he worked five furlongs in a torrid :59⅘.

Thayer has been running in route races recently, and if he were a slow-breaking plodder there might be questions about his suitability at today's six-furlong distance. But he is a speed horse and he should relish the distance. He was leading by three lengths at the six-furlong mark of his last race. His past performances show that he won two of his three previous starts at three-quarters of a mile.

The only horse in this field with a figure that might menace Thayer is Path o' Ray, who earned an 89 in his next to last start. Path o' Ray was trained by King T. Leatherbury, one of the best horsemen in Maryland, in that race. He was claimed by a lesser trainer, Dean Gaudet, and subsequently ran much worse. There is no reason to expect that he will revert to his best form today.

Thayer's most formidable rival is Handy Hit, not so much because of the qualifications of the horse, but because of the qualifications of his trainer. Dick Dutrow is the superstar of the Maryland circuit. His horses frequently come to life and win under more improbable circumstances than these. If Dutrow had claimed Handy Hit in his last race, a bettor might reasonably fear that the horse was capable of improving five or ten lengths. But Dutrow has already raced Handy Hit once and his performance was nothing extraordinary. There is no evidence to suggest that Handy Hit will wake up today.

Thayer's credentials qualify him as a classic prime bet. He is the best horse; he is in excellent condition; he is trained by a good man. If Dutrow's horse should improve greatly to beat him, we can assuage our grief by rationalizing that we are bound to win money in the long run on horses like Thayer.

Thayer got his competition from an unexpected source, the long shot Midnight Caller, but raced him into defeat after a head-and-head battle and won by 1¾ lengths. Handy Hit, untouched by Dutrow's customary magic, was nowhere. Thayer paid $5.80 to win, a price that probably wouldn't allow a handicapper to retire to Aruba but was extremely generous under the circumstances.

EIGHTH RACE Bow March 6, 1974 — **6 FURLONGS (chute). (1:08$\frac{3}{5}$). ALLOWANCES. Purse \$7,000. 4-year-olds and upward which have never won a race other than maiden, claiming, starter or hunt meeting. Weight, 122 lbs. Non-winners of a race other than claiming in 1974 allowed 3 lbs.; such a race since Nov. 30, 5 lbs.; since Oct. 22, 7 lbs.; since Sept. 10, 10 lbs.**
Value to winner \$4,200; second, \$1,540; third, \$840; fourth, \$420. Mutuel Pool, \$98,230.

Last Raced	Horse	EqtAWt	PP	St	¼	½	Str	Fin	Jockeys	Owners	Odds to \$1
2-21-74^{9} Bow^{2}	Thayer	b6 112	3	3	$2^{1\frac12}$	$2^{1\frac12}$	1^{h}	$1^{1\frac34}$	LGino	F A Greene Jr	1.90
2-26-74^{8} Bow^{10}	Midnight Caller	b4 112	2	4	1^{h}	$1^{\frac12}$	$2^{2\frac12}$	2no	DRWright	R E Vogelman Jr	33.70
2-26-74^{8} Bow^{4}	Path o'Ray	b5 112	5	5	$4^{1\frac12}$	3^{h}	$4^{2\frac12}$	3^{2}	EWalsh	Beelu Farm	7.80
2-26-74^{8} Bow^{3}	Touch of Pepper	b4 117	6	2	5^{2}	5^{5}	5^{5}	4^{h}	TLee	G W Dalphon	2.30
2-26-74^{8} Bow^{2}	Handy Hit	b4 112	7	1	3^{h}	$4^{2\frac12}$	3^{h}	$5^{4\frac14}$	SHawley	J J Carpenter	3.20
2-14-74^{5} Bow^{2}	Cary Street	b4 117	1	6	6^{2}	6^{2}	$6^{1\frac12}$	6^{1}	GCusimano	J L Reynolds	7.10
2-26-74^{8} Bow^{6}	Back Stage Talk	b4 115	4	7	7	7	7	7	DRhodes^{7}	Spartan Stable	28.70

OFF AT 4:19 EDT. Start good. Won driving. Time, :23$\frac15$, :46$\frac25$, 1:11$\frac25$. Track fast.

\$2 Mutuel Prices:			
3-THAYER	5.80	4.60	3.60
2-MIDNIGHT CALLER		18.20	8.80
5-PATH O'RAY			5.80

B. g, by Tudorka—Simoom, by Level Lea. Trainer, B. Steward Mitchell. Bred by J. P. Thayer (Va.).

THAYER vied for the lead from the outset, secured the lead approaching the eighth pole and drew clear under vigorous urging. MIDNIGHT CALLER took the early lead under a hustling ride and gave way grudgingly in the drive to narrowly hold for the place. PATH O'RAY, never far back, finished with good courage between horses. TOUCH OF PEPPER, hustled to remain within striking distance early, lacked a late response. HANDY HIT, prominently placed, weakened while lugging in through the drive. CARY STREET was outrun.

Scratched—Beale Street Boy.

9th Bowie Race Course

FEBRUARY 26, 1974

1$\frac{1}{16}$ MILES. (1:41$\frac35$). CLAIMING. Purse \$3,700. 4-year-olds and upward, registered Maryland-breds. Weight, 122 lbs. Non-winners of two races since Jan. 15 allowed 3 lbs.; a race, 6 lbs.; a race since Jan. 8, 9 lbs. Claiming price, \$3,000.

COUPLED: MARYLAND PRINCE and ROSARYVILLE.

Bar Tab * — 119

B. g (1964), by Trojan Monarch—Tabarina, by The Yuvaraj.
Breeder. J. L. Skinner (Md.). 1974 4 1 0 0 \$2,916
Owner, Bear Creek Farm. Trainer, J. N. Skinner. **\$3.000** 1973 16 3 2 1 \$12,276

Feb19-74^{9}Bow 1 1-8 1:55$\frac15$ft 12 119 $4^{2\frac12}$ 5^{5} $5^{5\frac12}$ $4^{7\frac12}$ Rowl'ndJ^{7} 4000 63 Potestas114 King ofFr'ce V'd'rbiltAve. 9
Feb12-74^{9}Bow 1$\frac{1}{16}$ 1:48$\frac25$ft 2½ ▴114 6^{11} $4^{3\frac14}$ 3^{nk} $1^{4\frac12}$ Rowl'ndJ^{3} 3000 66 BarTab114 PullNoP'nches Pr'tyLaura 12
Feb 1-74^{9}Bow 1$\frac{1}{16}$ 1:48$\frac45$ft 4½ 113 $6^{5\frac12}$ $6^{9\frac12}$ $5^{7\frac12}$ $4^{4\frac12}$ RowlandJ^{7} 3000 59 We[illegible]hampton10[illegible] R[illegible]saryvil[illegible] Mi[illegible]sen 9
Jan17-74^{9}Bow 1$\frac{1}{16}$ 1:48$\frac15$ft 14 113 6^{13} 4^{7} $4^{4\frac12}$ $4^{6\frac14}$ RowlandJ^{6} 3000 61 A[illegible]onis[illegible]13 S[illegible]ychelles [illegible]rook's [illegible]est 12
Dec13-73^{9}Lrl 1 1-8 1:55 sy 11 114 8^{7} 10^{17} 10^{25} 10^{26} Rowl'ndJ^{11} 3000 46 K[illegible] ofF[illegible]ance[illegible] C[illegible]Jude[illegible]R'ly 12
Sep14-73^{9}Bow 1$\frac{1}{16}$ 1:47$\frac15$sy 4½ 114 9^{21} 9^{21} 9^{15} 9^{20} RowlandJ^{8} 3000 52 Cut theDick113 StarBama TriplePride 9
Aug16-73^{7}Tim 1 1:39$\frac25$ft 19 119 7^{14} 6^{16} 6^{17} 5^{15} Rowl'dJ^{4} A2500 65 Last Hill 119 Timmy Willie Gun Gold 7
Aug 5-73^{3}Del 1-70 1:43$\frac25$ft 4 117 7^{13} 8^{13} 8^{14} 7^{15} RowlandJ^{4} 5000 65 FearABit117 Aboriginal ColonelJerry 8

Jan 15 Lrl 6f fr 1:17b Jan 5 Lrl 6f sl 1:22b Dec 29 Lrl 6f hy 1:21b

Dean's Sister — 101

Dk. b. or br. f (1970), by Telekinesis—Wayward, by Double Brandy.
Breeder, Dr. D. L. Price (Md.). 1974 4 2 1 0 \$2,914
Owner, J. Eshelman. Trainer, H. Ravich. **\$3.000** 1973 19 1 2 0 \$3,660

Feb14-74^{9}Bow 1$\frac{1}{16}$ 1:49$\frac45$ft 3¼ 107** $2^{1\frac12}$ 2^{2} 2^{2} 2^{1} McC'onCJ^{3} 3000 58 Therapist114 Dean'sSister DizzySag 9
Feb 7-74^{9}Bow 1$\frac{1}{16}$ 1:48$\frac35$gd 9 122 1^{3} 2^{h} $3^{3\frac12}$ 8^{8} WrightDR^{2} 3000 57 ⒻTi'e f'rAd't're M'sPr'v'ra M'b'lM'b'l 12
Jan12-74^{8}Dov 1$\frac{1}{16}$ 1:48 ft 9-5 ▴113 1^{3} 1^{8} 1^{10} 1^{20} Thornt'nJ^{1} 2500 96 Dean'sSist'r113 Eclipsed Doll ofSatin 7
Jan 6-74^{8}Pen 5½ f 1:08 m 14 112 $7^{4\frac12}$ 4^{3} 2^{1} 2no†HinojosaH^{5} 2500 83 Ⓕ[illegible]pril[illegible]115 [illegible]ean'sSister Sampere 12
†Placed first through disqualification.
Dec12-73^{1}Lrl 6 f 1:12 ft 20 109 5^{4} $5^{3\frac12}$ $9^{7\frac34}$ $9^{9\frac12}$ Felic'noP^{1} 3000 79 T[illegible]H'rn112 P[illegible]m'c Ike Mys'lM's 12
Dec 1-73^{9}Pen 5½ f 1:06 ft 3¾ 112 $10^{6\frac12}$ $9^{9\frac12}$ $7^{9\frac12}$ $7^{7\frac34}$ DennieD^{9} 3200 87 ⒻP'ssTime118 Cr'kpotL'dy B'shf'lSue 11
May16-73^{7}Pim 6 f 1:12 ft 27 111 $6^{4\frac12}$ 8^{8} 10^{15} 10^{12} HowardR^{1} Alw 74 ⒻShunned111 PennyFlight Solindra 10
May 1-73^{1}Pim 6 f 1:14 ft 12 110 1^{h} 1^{h} 1^{3} $1^{1\frac14}$ McC'nG^{2} M5000 76 Dean'sSister110 S'plyTouch KeepPete 12

Feb 24 Bow 4f ft :51$\frac35$b Dec 28 Lrl 5f hy 1:07b

(cont'd on next page)

Quill Pen **108** B. m (1969), by Victorian Era—Gold Quill, by Sunny Boy.
Breeder, E. P. Taylor (Md.). 1974 3 0 0 0 (—)
Owner, Vin Lo Stable. Trainer, A. Bertando. $3.000 1973 25 2 0 3 $7,714
Feb21-74 2Bow 7 f 1:26 3/5 ft 28 113 12 9 10 8/12 9 11 9 7/14 Cusim'oG 9 4000 65 FearABit112 RoadToRock Peachey 12
Feb 5-74 3Bow 1 1/16 1:46 4/5 fr 8 3/4 108 7 9/12 6 9/12 7 10 7 6/12 JimenezC 5 5000 67 Spice Ashore [illegible] 7
Jan21-74 4Bow 1 1/16 1:49 1/5 sy 2 3/4 e 116 7 9 3/4 7 6 7 13 7 16 WalshE 5 5000 46 Ⓕ [illegible] 7
Dec15-73 2Lrl 7 f 1:26 2/5 ft 7 1/2 116 6 8 6 6/12 2 2 1 1/2 KurtzJ 2 4000 79 Quill [illegible] Sea [illegible] 8
Dec 3-73 3Lrl 1 1:39 2/5 ft 15 113 6 13 6 3 3/4 3 1/12 5 2/14 KurtzJ 1 5000 74 Ⓕ [illegible]kAng'l 116 M'd'yPrize M'sL'dt'n 9
Nov19-73 9Lrl Ⓣ 1 1/16 1:45 3/5 fm 7 1/2 e 113 8 10 4 5/12 5 7 4 1 3/4 KurtzJ 2 5000 76 ⒻSlide f'rM'e111 T'oAnx's S'b'naL'ne 12
Nov12-73 1Lrl 6 f 1:13 3/5 ft 11 112 8 9 3/4 7 8 5 4 3/4 3 1/12 Fel'noBM 3 3000 79 ⒻAuntieJ'n105 Sum'rPl'n'g QuillPen 11
Feb 20 Bow 3f ft :38 2/5 b Jan 17 Bow 5f ft 1:02 2/5 b

Doc's Line **113** Dk. b. or br. g (1970), by Roman Line—Honey Doc, by Martins Rullah.
Br., Dr. & Mrs. G. G. Meredith (Md.). 1974 3 0 0 0 $96
Owner, C. A. Faulkner. Trainer, L. W. Donovan. $3.000 1973 24 3 3 2 $8,586
Feb14-74 9Bow 1 1/16 1:49 4/5 ft 17 113 9 19 9 14 9 13 7 8/12 MorenoO 8 3000 50 Therapist114 Dean'sSister DizzySag 9
Jan28-74 8Dov 1 1:44 2/5 sy 3-2 ▲115 5 5 5 7 5 8/12 4 9 Bradf'rdB 3 2500 63 Ca[illegible]7 DirectHit JackieJunior 7
Jan 4-74 7Dov 1 1:42 4/5 gd 9-5 ▲120 5 5/12 5 10 5 9/12 5 6 3/4 MorenoO 1 2500 73 B'[illegible]ay112 Nipigon DivotAsph'l 6
Dec 4-73 3Lrl 1 1:41 ft 15 117 12 17 12 18 11 18 8 12 MorenoO 1 3000 56 Wha[illegible]ker [illegible]20 Miessen Maxi Mini 12
Nov26-73 9Lrl 1 1-8 1:55 2/5 ft 4 1/4 119 5 3/12 5 3 5 2 3/4 5 7 MorenoO 2 3000 63 WingedC'rier112 BaronJet R'galBr'ze 7
Jan 27 Dov 4f sy :51 2/5 b Jan 16 Dov 6f ft 1:17h Jan 11 Dov 5f sy 1:06 2/5 b

Maryland Prince **119** B. c (1970), by Frankie's Nod—Tussy Bell, by Tuscany.
Br., W. T. Leatherbury & E. Wayson (Md.). 1974 3 1 1 0 $3,188
Owner, W. T. Leatherbury. Trainer, K. T. Leatherbury. $3.000 1973 16 1 0 2 $4,500
Feb 9-74 1Bow 7 f 1:26 4/5 sy 8-5 ▲113 10 7 10 9/14 4 4/12 1 1/12 WalshE 7 3000 71 M'ryl'dPr'ce113 S'rdSw'l'o'r H'ds'eG'k 12
Jan29-74 2Bow 6 f 1:13 4/5 m 3 1/4 114 4 7 3 5 5 2 2 1/12 WalshE 8 4000 72 L'[illegible]119 [illegible] 11
Jan 7-74 2Bow 6 f 1:14 gd 2 ▲112 9 5/12 9 6/12 4 2 4 1/12 WalshE 7 4750 71 L[illegible]Rul[illegible] 115 [illegible] 12
Nov 2-73 3Lrl 7 f 1:25 ft 4 3/4 112 5 3 3 4 3 3/12 3 1 WalshE 3 7000 85 Blu[illegible]k110 [illegible] 10
Oct 9-73 9Bow 1 1/16 1:48 2/5 ft 3 1/4 114 4 3 3 3/12 3 1 3 nk WalshE 4 7500 66 Red'dic'te119 M'rnTilNite M'rvl'dP'ce 7
Sep28-73 7Bow 7 f 1:26 ft 5 3/4 114 9 4 3/4 9 10 8 8/12 5 3 3/4 P'ss'reWJ 8 7500 71 NobleP'mise114 Jamb'lot S'oOutLoud 12
Jan 5 Bow 4f sl :50 2/5 b Jan 1 Bow 3f m :39 2/5 b

Ambi Hula * **113** Dk. b. or br. g (1969), by Ambiopoise—Hula Hop, by Hill Prince.
Br., Mr. & Mrs. H. J. O'Donovan (Md.). 1974 3 0 0 2 $1,236
Owner, F. J. De Francis. Trainer, J. S. Clark. $3.000 1973 26 1 3 5 $13,562
Jan26-74 9Bow 1 1-4 2:08 2/5 m 4 3/4 115 9 10 7 8/12 7 11 6 7 McC'nG 4 H5000 74 Mendelson113 RapidTreat MintCopy 9
Jan19-74 2Bow 1 1-8 1:55 2/5 ft 2 1/4 ▲119 12 22 10 8/14 3 1/2 3 1/2 Jimen'zC 6 c5000 69 SpringHop113 Save theMaxi AmbiH'la 12
Jan 2-74 9Bow 1 1/16 1:48 1/5 ft 9-5 ▲114 7 9/12 7 9 6 8/12 3 4/12 HawleyS 6 8500 62 [illegible]114 [illegible] 8
Dec15-73 9Lrl 1 1-8 1:53 4/5 ft 6-5 ▲116 7 11 7 7/14 4 2/12 1 2 HawleyS 7 6500 78 Amb[illegible]116 [illegible] 7
Dec 3-73 2Lrl 1 1:38 2/5 ft 14 116 7 8 9 6 3/4 6 7 5 3/14 McH'eDG 2 8000 78 Hu[illegible]Puppie116 [illegible] 10
Nov24-73 5Lrl 1 1:38 3/5 ft 4 3/4 107 6 4/12 6 4 3/4 6 9/12 6 11 Minerv'iF 4 7000 52 Octet 113 CharlieJr. UncAllan 12
Nov 5-73 5Lrl 1 1:39 3/5 sy 5 3/4 116 10 14 10 11 5 3/12 3 3/4 B'c'leVJr 1 8000 74 BoldLord114 SuperBuper AmbiHula 10
Feb 14 Pim 4f my :51h

Exclusive Helio **113** B. g (1970), by Exclusive Nashua—Hello Helio, by Helioscope.
Breeder, Buck Ridge Stable (Md.). 1974 5 0 0 0 $240
Owner, Buck Ridge Stable. Trainer, W. B. Hill. $3.000 1973 20 1 2 0 $4,836
Feb13-74 1Bow 6 f 1:12 3/5 ft 13 113 5 2 3/4 7 6/14 6 8 7 11 AlbertsB 4 3000 69 M'nsinger113 NightPrinc's Br'th'rLen 12
Feb 4-74 9Bow 1 1/16 1:48 1/5 ft 17e 114 6 5 3/4 9 8/12 12 19 12 20 AlbertsB 9 4000 47 PrinceJ'k'r113 Br'k'sBest K'g ofFr'nce 12
Jan29-74 2Bow 6 f 1:13 4/5 m 19 114 10 15 9 13 9 8/12 7 5/12 LeeT 6 4000 68 L'[illegible]119 [illegible]Prince [illegible]R'n 11
Jan11-74 2Bow 7 f 1:28 1/5 m 11 114 3 3 4 5/12 6 7/12 6 3/14 LeeT 10 4000 61 R[illegible] [illegible] 12
Jan 4-74 9Bow 1 1/16 1:50 m 16 114 1h 2 3 3 3/12 4 7 3/4 LeeT 3 4000 50 [illegible]114 [illegible]Joker [illegible]ate 7
Dec28-73 2Lrl 1 1:44 3/5 hy 4 3/4 112 1 2/12 2 1/12 4 7 7 11 StovallR 7 3000 39 BobH'rse110 Save theMaxi S'bleIsl'nd 12
Dec 6-73 9Lrl 1 1:40 2/5 ft 25 115 8 12 9 17 11 8 3/4 8 9 Bel'lleEM 6 5000 62 Bite theBul't112 Mend'lson VilliersL'd 12
Nov27-73 1Lrl 6 f 1:12 3/5 ft 33 116 9 7 3/4 9 12 8 9/14 7 4/12 Belv'leEM 4 4000 81 VilliersLad117 AClearDay VegasHope 12
Jan 26 Lrl 4f sl :50 3/5 b

Colonel Jerry * **116** Dk. b. or br. g (1967), by Martins Rullah—Sturdy Miss, by Unbreakable.
Breeder, Harford Stud, Inc. (Md.). 1974 2 1 1 0 $2,820
Owner, W. H. Wolfendale III. Trainer, W. H. Wolfendale III. $3,000 1973 34 5 5 7 $20,878
Jan17-74 9Bow 1 1/16 1:48 1/5ft 4 119 9 17 11 15 11 19 10 16 B'v'leEM 8 c3000 51 Adonis 113 Seychelles Brook's Best 12
Jan 9-74 9Bow 1 1/16 1:50 sy 7-5 ▲119 6 12 5 8 3/4 2h 1 2 1/2 Belv'leEM 2 3000 58 Col[illegible] No[illegible]D[illegible]id P'nc'yM'gin 12
Jan 5-74 7Pen 1 1:43 2/5m 5 3/4 116 4 6 1/4 4 6 5 2 1/2 2 3/4 HedgeD 6 Hcp0 66 Am[illegible]126 [illegible] Jerry Magoni 6
Dec 7-73 9Lrl 1 1:40 ft 8 3/4 116 4 3 3 6 1/2 7 11 7 10 CanessaJ 7 4000 61 Ri[illegible]d 116 [illegible]uine DoubleDay 11
Nov29-73 9Lrl 1 3/16 2:00 3/5ft 5 1/2 116 9 7 1/4 8 5 3/4 6 5 4 3 3/4 CanessaJ 5 4000 69 Mr. Janin 116 Big Vin Potestas 12
Dec14-73 9Lrl 1 1-8 1:55 1/5gd 4 114 1 4 1 2 2h 2 1 1/2 Hi'j'aH 12 c3000 80 ContentedCl'n116 ColonelJerry Adonis 12

Seven Never **113** B. g (1970), by Seven Corners—Prize Pet, by Little Reaper.
Breeder, M. E. Pellens (Md.). 1974 3 0 0 0 (——)
Owner, Mary E. Pellens. Trainer, W. G. Meyers. $3,000 1973 9 2 1 0 $7,125
Feb14-74 9Bow 1 1/16 1:49 4/5ft 2 1/2 ▲113 3 4 1/2 3 2 3 4 6 7 1/2 Rowl'ndJ 2 3000 51 Therapist114 Dean'sSister DizzySag 9
Feb 4-74 5Bow 7 f 1:25 ft 19 108 9 6 1/4 8 8 1/4 9 10 10 11 Cusim'oG 8 5000 69 L'ndR'l'r117 Sp'nishSt'm M'dis'nStr't 12
Jan25-74 5Bow 6 f 1:13 4/5m 11 108‡10 8 1/2 11 12 11 11 11 8 1/2 VillonA 8 5000 65 Hy [illegible]le 115 [illegible] Oto [illegible]rus [illegible] 11
Apr18-73 4Pim 6 f 1:12 ft 19 114 6 3 1/2 5 3 1/2 6 7 1/2 5 8 3/4 CookeC 6 13500 77 C[illegible]Jim [illegible] Party U[illegible] H[illegible]tile 6
Apr 6-73 6Pim 6 f 1:13 1/5gd 8 1/4 114 4 3 1/2 3 1/2 3 1/2 5 1 3/4†CookeC 7 13500 78 [illegible]'d[illegible]x114 S[illegible]s[illegible]'t A[illegible]'l 9
†Placed fourth through disqualification.
Mar17-73 3Pim 1 1/16 1:49 4/5m 18 114 3 4 1 2 2h 3h CookeC 3 1500 56 D'nnyAgain114 Bally forY'u S'v'nN'v'r 9
Feb23-73 7Bow 6 f 1:13 1/5ft 26 114 9 9 1/4 8 8 1/4 10 10 10 5 CookeC 11 11500 72 What aTr'sure Starkadder AngelSkin 12
Feb 9-73 7Bow 7 f 1:27 m 15 114 5 8 1/4 6 6 1/4 8 6 3/4 8 12 CookeC 6 13500 58 LandingGray114 Nepperham C'tPl'ck 8
Jan 30 Pim 5f my 1:04 2/5h Jan 19 Pim 6f ft 1:17 3/5b Jan 12 Pim 5f [illegible] 1:05b

Ambi Hula, like Thayer, has figures that are consistently superior to those of the horses he is facing today. He should be an easy winner if he duplicates any of the ten races in his past performances. But will he?

Ambi Hula was running in $8000 claiming company for most of the season and was slightly overmatched. When he was dropped to $6500, he won convincingly. He was a solid $6500 animal. Yet despite this record his trainer entered him in a $5000 claiming race. Something had to be wrong with the horse, for neither trainers nor any other businessmen give away $6500 merchandise for $5000. Ambi Hula couldn't even win that cheap race.

Henry Clark, an astute veteran horseman, claimed the supposed bargain for $5000 and ran him a week later. Ambi Hula confirmed that he did indeed have problems. He ran his worst race, and his worst figure, in months. So Clark wisely rested him for a month, trying to correct whatever ailed the animal.

If Clark had entered Ambi Hula for $5000 or thereabouts,

a handicapper might bet the horse because he respected the trainer's expertise and thought he may have revivified his new acquisition. But by entering Ambi Hula for $3000, Clark was practically announcing that the animal's problems were dire. Trainers do not give away $5000 merchandise for $3000. Dropdowns of this type do occasionally win — it is conceivable that Ambi Hula has enough left in him to be a decent $3000 horse — but generally they are the worst bets in racing.

Only three other horses in this field — Maryland Prince, Dean's Sister, and Bar Tab — have respectable credentials.

Maryland Prince, like Ambi Hula, is evidently a horse beset with problems. After running well for $7000 earlier in the season, he gradually descended to the bottom of the class ladder. He won his last start for $3000, which may suggest that he has found his proper level. But Maryland Prince won that race only because he was facing an extraordinarily weak field. His figure was 57, which will rarely win anything. Maryland Prince did rally strongly from tenth place in that seven-furlong event, a performance that might lead some handicappers to conclude that he will improve at today's distance of a mile and one-sixteenth. But his past performances seem to suggest that he prefers sprints. Like many fast-closing sprinters, he cannot sustain his rally at a longer distance.

Dean's Sister, a speed horse, earned a figure of 60 in her last start, over a track with a strong bias in favor of speed horses. In her previous race at Bowie on a more normal track, she tired badly.

Bar Tab won his next to last race in $3000 company, stepped up to $4000 where he was overmatched, and is dropped back to $3000 today. Whether winning or losing, he has displayed consistency of a sort, running figures in the

60s each time. He may not be an inspiring animal, but he is racing at the level where he properly belongs, and his usual figure should be good enough to win this race, assuming that Ambi Hula does not approximate his best form. Unless I were feeling very courageous, I would not make Bar Tab a prime bet. I prefer horses with stronger credentials and slightly sexier past performances. But Bar Tab does appear to have an edge in this field, and if his odds are reasonable he deserves a moderate bet.

NINTH RACE
Bow
February 26, 1974

1$\frac{1}{16}$ MILES. (1:41⅗). CLAIMING. Purse $3,700. 4-year-olds and upward, registered Maryland-breds. Weight, 122 lbs. Non-winners of two races since Jan. 15 allowed 3 lbs.; a race, 6 lbs.; a race since Jan. 8, 9 lbs. Claiming price, $3,000.
Value to winner $2,220; second, $814; third, $444; fourth, $222.
Mutuel Pool, $35,584. Exacta Pool, $73,870.

Last Raced	Horse	EqtAWt	PP	St	¼	½	¾	Str	Fin	Jockeys	Owners	Odds to $1
2-19-74^{9} Bow^{4}	Bar Tab	b10 119	1	2	6^{4}	6^{5}	6^{3}	$3^{1\frac{1}{2}}$	1^{1}	JRowland	Bear Creek Farm	5.20
2-14-74^{9} Bow^{2}	Dean's Sister	4 105	2	1	1^{3}	$1^{2\frac{1}{2}}$	$1^{1\frac{1}{2}}$	$1^{1\frac{1}{2}}$	$2^{1\frac{1}{4}}$	CJMcCar'n^{7}†	J Eshelman	7.10
2- 9-74^{1} Bow^{1}	Maryland Prince	b4 119	5	4	2^{h}	$3^{1\frac{1}{2}}$	2^{h}	2^{h}	$3^{\frac{1}{2}}$	EWalsh	W T Leatherbury	2.10
1-26-74^{9} Bow^{6}	Ambi Hula	b3 113	6	9	9	8^{2}	7^{2}	$6^{3\frac{1}{2}}$	$4^{2\frac{3}{4}}$	GMcCarron	F J DeFarncis	1.90
2-14-74^{9} Bow^{6}	Seven Never	b4 113	9	6	$5^{2\frac{1}{2}}$	$5^{2\frac{1}{2}}$	4^{1}	4^{1}	$5^{1\frac{1}{4}}$	GCusimano	Mary E Pellens	14.90
2-21-74^{2} Bow^{9}	Quill Pen	5 112	3	3	4^{h}	4^{h}	$5^{1\frac{1}{2}}$	$5^{1\frac{1}{2}}$	6^{8}	JKurtz	Vin Lo Stable	11.20
2-13-74^{1} Bow^{7}	Exclusive Helio	b4 113	7	5	$3^{1\frac{1}{2}}$	2^{h}	$3^{1\frac{1}{2}}$	7^{4}	7^{8}	GVasquez	Buck Ridge Stable	72.40
2-14-74^{9} Bow^{7}	Doc's Line	b4 113	4	8	7^{2}	$7^{2\frac{1}{2}}$	8^{8}	8^{12}	8^{15}	LGino	C A Faulkner	92.50
1-17-74^{9} Bow^{10}	Colonel Jerry	7 116	8	7	8^{1}	9	9	9	9	CCooke	W H Wolfendale III	12.10

†Three pounds apprentice allowance waived.

OFF AT 4:48 EDT. Start good. Won driving. Time, :24⅗, :49⅘, 1:15⅖, 1:42⅗, 1:49⅖. Track fast.

$2 Mutuel Prices:

1-BAR TAB	**12.40**	**5.80**	**3.20**
2-DEAN'S SISTER		**7.00**	**4.00**
5-MARYLAND PRINCE			**3.00**

$2 EXACTA (1-2) PAID $76.40.

B. g, by Trojan Monarch—Tabarina, by The Yuvaraj. Trainer, J. N. Skinner. Bred by J. L. Skinner (Md.).

BAR TAB, unhurried while saving ground early, brushed with EXCLUSIVE HELIO when lodging his bid between rivals entering the stretch and finished determinedly to secure the lead and draw clear in the closing yards. DEAN'S SISTER sprinted to a clear lead, continued willingly when called upon for the drive, then weakened in the final sixteenth. MARYLAND PRINCE, never far back, lacked a solid late response. AMBI HULA had a belated closing rally. SEVEN NEVER brushed EXCLUSIVE HELIO while making a mild bid into the stretch and hung. QUILL PEN saved ground to no avail. EXCLUSIVE HELIO raced forwardly placed, then was brushed between rivals when weakening into the stretch.

Overweight—Dean's Sister, 1 pound; Quill Pen, 4.

Maryland Prince claimed by J. L. Guthrie, trainer J. Gill. Ambi Hula cloimed by W. H. Hardesty, trainer E. D. Gaudet.

Claiming Prices—All $3000.

Scratched—Sergeant Major, Rosaryville.

The betting public loves to lose its money on horses with spurious "class." The crowd at Bowie made Ambi Hula the 9-to-5 favorite, with Maryland Prince 2 to 1. Ignoring the one solid $3000 animal in the field, they allowed Bar Tab to pay $12.40.

2nd Saratoga

AUGUST 18, 1973

6 FURLONGS. (1:08). MAIDENS. SPECIAL WEIGHTS. Purse $9,000. Colts and geldings. 2-year-olds. Weight, 119 lbs.

COUPLED: TRUMPETER SWAN and SHINING KNIGHT.

Office King 119 Ch. c (1971), by Vitriolic—Determine Gal, by Determine.
Breeder, Ocala Stud (Fla.). 1973 . 0 M 0 0 (——)
Owner, D. Sturgis. Trainer, J. B. Cantey.
Aug 14 Sar 4f ft :46⅖h Aug 10 Sar 6f ft 1:12⅖hg Aug 9 Sar 3f ft :37bg

Attaboy John 119 B. c (1971), by Wind Driven—Diva's Girl, by Royal Admiral.
Breeder, J. W. Warner (Va.). 1973 . 0 M 0 0 (——)
Owner, Mrs. C. MacLeod, Jr. Trainer, C. MacLeod, Jr.
Aug 11 Sar 5f ft 1:01hg Aug 8 Sar 6f ft 1:15⅗h Aug 4 Sar 3f gd :36⅗b

Bold and Fancy 119 B. c (1971), by Bold Hour—Khal Me Fancy, by Khaled.
Br., Mr. & Mrs. G. Grieger, Jr. (Cal.). 1973 . . 1 M 0 0 (——)
Owner, M. Vogil. Trainer, L. S. Barrera.
Aug11-73^{2}Sar 6 f 1:11 ft 64 114* 8^3 8$^{9\frac{3}{4}}$11^{15}11^{16} AmyJ^{12} Mdn 69 Tak[illegible]St[illegible]m 119 Hilo TheScotsman 12
Aug 6 Sar trt 3f ft :37b July 25 Bel trt 4f ft :48⅖h [illegible] 8 Sar 4f ft :49⅕bg
55

Royal Approval 119 B. c (1971), by Prince John—Recommendation, by Dark Star.
Breeder, C. E. Mather II. (Ky.). 1973 . 3 M 0 0 (——)
Owner, Avonwood Stable. Trainer, G. P. Odom.
Jly 18-73^{3}Aqu 5½ f 1:05⅖sft 16e 118 6^6 7$^{6\frac{3}{4}}$ 7$^{8\frac{1}{4}}$ 7$^{7\frac{1}{4}}$ Bal'zarC^{11} Mdn 79 Pia'[illegible] Sh't[illegible]D'l L'[illegible] 11
Jly 9-73^{3}Aqu 5½ f 1:04⅘sft 12e 118 8^6 7^{10} 7^{12} 7^{14} VeneziaM^8 Mdn 75 La[illegible]evil[illegible]18 Lor[illegible]For[illegible]'r Fl'[illegible] 11
Jun27-73^{4}Aqu 5½ f 1:04 ft 18 117 10^{23}10^{26}10^{28}10^{24} VeneziaM^4 Mdn 69 C[illegible]112 Th[illegible]Groush Firs[illegible]eau 10
Aug 17 Sar 3f ft :35⅖h Aug 14 Sar 4f ft :50b July 16 Bel 3[illegible] :37⅕[illegible]
68 52 32

Trumpeter Swan 119 Ch. c (1971), by Sea-Bird—Trumpery, by Tudor Minstrel.
Breeder, Greentree Stable (Ky.). 1973 5 M 1 1 $ 3,000
Owner, Greentree Stable. Trainer, J. M. Gaver.
Aug 8-73^{2}Sar 5½ f 1:06⅕sft 5¼ 119 6^5 6$^{7\frac{3}{4}}$ 6^9 7$^{5\frac{1}{2}}$ VasquezJ^9 Mdn 80 DingD'ngBell 119 Lea'sPass [illegible]uckHill 9
May26-73^{3}Bel 5½ f 1:06 m 9-5 ▲117 8$^{8\frac{1}{4}}$ 7^7 5^6 5$^{5\frac{1}{2}}$ TurcotteR^5 Mdn 88 G[illegible]nd Bo[illegible] [illegible]d Jay [illegible]ss 9
May16-73^{3}Bel 5½ f 1:05 ft 3¾ 117 5$^{2\frac{1}{4}}$ 4$^{1\frac{1}{2}}$ 1½ 2^h TurcotteR^5 Mdn 94 [illegible]S'cc'ss[illegible] T[illegible]p't'rSw[illegible] E'r[illegible]'d 9
May 7-73^{3}Aqu 5 f :58⅗sft 2 ▲117 6$^{8\frac{1}{2}}$ 6$^{7\frac{1}{2}}$ 4^8 4$^{9\frac{1}{2}}$ TurcotteR^4 Mdn 82 [illegible]Cup11[illegible] [illegible]ffezheim [illegible]Boy 9
Apr23-73^{3}Aqu 5 f :59⅗sft 6-5 ▲117 5$^{2\frac{1}{2}}$ 5^5 4$^{4\frac{1}{2}}$ 3$^{6\frac{1}{4}}$ TurcotteR^7 Mdn 81 WhoD'zit117 Jov'lJudge T'mp't'rSw'n 7
Aug 14 Sar 4f ft :46⅗h Aug 6 Sar 3f ft :34⅘hg July 31 Sar 4f ft :50⅖b
66 63 90

Right Pitch 119 Ch. c (1971), by Jaipur—Centrifuge, by Middleground.
Breeder, King Ranch, Inc. (Ky.). 1973 . 0 M 0 0 (——)
Owner, King Ranch. Trainer, W. J. Hirsch.
Aug 11 Sar 4f ft :49hg Aug 7 Sar 5f ft 1:03⅘b

Criterion 119 B. c (1971), by Sir Gaylord—Nature, by Nashua.
Breeder, R. N. Webster (Ky.). 1973 . . 2 M 0 0 $540
Owner, R. N. Webster. Trainer, L. Laurin.
Aug 8-73^{2}Sar 5½ f 1:06⅕sft 9½ 119 7^8 5$^{6\frac{1}{4}}$ 5^5 4$^{1\frac{3}{4}}$ Turc'tteR^3 Mdn 84 Di[illegible]'ngBell [illegible] [illegible]a'sPass BuckHill 9
Jly 31-73^{1}Sar 6 f 1:11⅗sft 8½ 119 4$^{1\frac{3}{4}}$ 5^5 8^9 7$^{9\frac{1}{4}}$ TurcotteR^5 Mdn 73 P[illegible]R'son119[illegible]BySt'm Lea'sP's 11
Aug 14 Sar 3f ft :37⅕b Aug 6 Sar 3f ft :37b July 29 Sar 3f ft :36⅖b
76 58

Bronze Express 119 Ch. c (1971), by Tobin Bronze—Nosey Body, by Tom Fool.
Breeder, D. A. Headley (Ky.). 1973 . . 2 M 0 0 (——)
Owner, Pastorale Stable. Trainer, G. T. Poole.
Aug 4-73^{4}Sar 6 f 1:12⅕sft 48 119 7^{13} 7^{15} 7^{13} 7^{14} P'leGTIII^1 Mdn 65 Th[illegible]n119 [illegible]r.Z[illegible]r'lli G'der'sGold 7
May16-73^{3}Bel 5½ f 1:05 ft 35 117 9^{11} 9^{12} 9^{14} 9^{17} CardoneE^9 Mdn 77 [illegible]f[illegible]cc's[illegible] T[illegible]t'rSw'n E'rF'd 9
Aug 13 Sar 5f gd 1:02⅕h Aug 9 Sar 4f ft :51b July 31 Sa[illegible] ft 1:03⅘h
47 43

Determined King **119** Blk. c (1971), by Determined Man—New Love, by Pardal.
Breeder, Herbert Allen (Ky.). 1973 3 M 3 0 $2,680
Owner, H. Allen. Trainer, E. Jacobs.
Jun14-73^{3}Bel 5½ f 1:05 ft 2½ 117 1½ 2^{1} 3^{1½} 2^{3½} BaezaB^{3} Mdn 90 Ev[illegible]117 Det'm'dK'g TakeBySt'm 9
Mar20-73^{3}GP 5 f :58⅕ft 4-5 ▲118 1½ 1^{h} 1^{h} 2^{3½} RotzJL^{2} Mdn 91 J.R.[illegible]118 DeterminedK'g Im'd'r'te 12
Feb13-73^{3}Hia 3 f :33⅗ft 8-5 ▲120 2 2^{1} 2½ RotzJL^{14} Mdn 93 Vi[illegible]120 DeterminedK'g Ohmyl've 14
Aug 17 Sar 3f ft :35⅖h Aug 13 Sar 5f gd 1:01h Aug 8 Sar 4f ft :49⅘b
72

Regal Rolfe **119** Ch. c (1971), by Tom Rolfe—Princess Cloud, by Prince John.
Breeder, W. L. Jones, Jr. & Claiborne Farm, Inc. (Ky.). 1973 0 M 0 0 (——)
Owner, Saron Stable. Trainer, S. E. Veitch.
Aug 10 Sar 5f ft 1:04⅗h Aug 6 Sar 5f ft 1:04⅖b

Shining Knight **119** Dk. b. or br. c (1971), by Round Table—Trophy Room, by Bold Ruler.
Breeder, Greentree Stud, Inc. (Ky.). 1973 5 M 1 1 $2,550
Owner, Greentree Stable. Trainer, J. M. Gaver.
Aug 8-73^{4}Sar 5½ f 1:06 ft 9 119 8^{13} 7^{10} 7^{9½} 6^{5¾} VasquezJ^{9} Mdn 81 SeaDee119 RedStr'k SparklingPl's're 9
Jly 18-73^{3}Aqu 5½ f 1:05⅖ft 6-5 ▲118 7^{6} 6^{5¾} 5^{6¼} 5^{4} MapleE^{4} Mdn 82 Pia'[illegible]8 Sh[illegible]D'l L[illegible] 11
May14-73^{3}Bel 5½ f 1:04⅖ft 6¾ 117 3^{nk} 1½ 2½ 2^{5½} VasquezJ^{4} Mdn 91 B.[illegible]Boy117 Shi[illegible]Knight B[illegible] 8
Apr30-73^{3}Aqu 5 f :59 ft 17 117 2^{1} 2^{h} 2½ 3^{5} VasquezJ^{7} Mdn 85 K'[illegible]'tive117 B[illegible]Hill S[illegible] 7
Apr16-73^{3}Aqu 5 f :59⅕ft 2½ 117 6^{5} 7^{8¼} 7^{10} 6^{9½} Velasq'zJ^{2} Mdn 79 L'v'rJohn117 K't theN'tive R'seA Cup 7
Aug 16 Sar 3f ft :34⅗h Aug 6 Sar 3f ft :34⅘hg July 30 Sar 6f ft 1:14⅘h
69 76 83

Two-year-old maiden races can be baffling because a handicapper must compare two types of horses that almost defy comparison: those who have shown promise in their brief racing careers and first-time starters who have shown promise in their workouts. As a general rule, the best bets in these events are horses who have raced only once or twice and have demonstrated some ability. First-time starters are at a disadvantage because of their inexperience. Horses who have raced several times have already proved themselves as losers.

In this race at Saratoga, four horses have shown signs of ability in actual competition. Trumpeter Swan ran very well on May 16 and finished second, but his only recent race was mediocre. He worked a half mile in a swift 46⅗ seconds since his last start, but he has worked well on previous occasions, and still has not been able to win in five tries.

Criterion has raced only twice, running poorly in his debut and then improving on August 8. Winners of two-year-old maiden races often have records like this, but there is one thing wrong with Criterion. His figure in his most recent start was a 75, which is not very good in New York maiden-special-weight company where the average winning figure is 93. Unless today's field is another unusually weak one, he must improve a great deal in order to win.

Determined King is already beginning to look like a sucker horse, finishing second in each of his three career starts. His figures are poor. He weakened at five and five and a half furlongs and is now running a longer distance. He has been laid off for two months, and his workouts are unimpressive. (A three-furlong work in $35\frac{2}{5}$ seconds is not particularly meaningful for a horse whose record shows he possesses plenty of early speed. If Determined King had a strong workout at six furlongs, that would be significant.)

Shining Knight is a five-time loser whose most recent race is a poor one.

Because none of the horses with established form has convincing credentials, a first-time starter may win this race. There are four colts in the field who are making their debuts, but only one of them has ever worked fast. Office King's workout line shows a half mile in $46\frac{2}{5}$ seconds and a six-furlong move in $1{:}12\frac{3}{5}$. Seeing these signs of ability, a thorough handicapper should plow through the daily workout listings in previous issues of the *Racing Form* to get a more complete picture of the horse's preparation. This was Office King's training schedule:

July 27: four furlongs in 47 seconds.
Aug. 1: five furlongs in $1{:}04\frac{3}{5}$.
Aug. 6: five furlongs in 1:02.
Aug. 9: three furlongs in :37.
Aug. 10: six furlongs in $1{:}12\frac{2}{5}$. (The clocker's footnotes said, "Office King acts sharp.")
Aug. 14: four furlongs in $:46\frac{2}{5}$.
Aug. 17: three furlongs in :37.

Office King had shown almost everything one could ask of a horse who had never raced. He was obviously fit, having worked seven times in three weeks. He had shown speed in his half-mile workout. He had covered today's distance in excellent time. He had a workout on the day before his debut (which the *Racing Form*'s past performances erroneously omitted), suggesting that the stable was trying to sharpen him for a winning effort at first crack.

Office King is the only horse in this field who has shown exceptional promise. There are not many times when a handicapper can bet seriously and confidently on a first-time starter, but this is an exceptional case.

SECOND RACE
Sar
August 18, 1973

6 FURLONGS. (1:08). MAIDENS. SPECIAL WEIGHTS. Purse $9,000. Colts and geldings. 2-year-olds. Weight, 119 lbs.
Value to winner $5,400; second, $1,980; third, $1,080; fourth, $540.
Mutuel Pool, $150,724. Off-track betting, $49,557.

Last Raced	Horse	EqtAWt	PP	St	¼	½	Str	Fin	Jockeys	Owners	Odds to $1
	Office King	2 119	1	11	$1^{1\frac{1}{2}}$	1^{4}	1^{3}	$1^{1\frac{1}{2}}$	EMaple	D Sturgis	1.90
6-14-73^{3} Bel^{2}	Determined King	b2 119	9	2	2^{1}	2^{3}	2^{3}	2^{2}	BBaeza	H Allen	3.60
8- 8-73^{2} Sar^{4}	Criterion	b2 119	7	5	6^{3}	3^{4}	3^{5}	3^{h}	RTurcotte	R N Webster	2.60
8- 8-73^{2} Sar^{7}	Trumpeter Swan	b2 119	5	6	9^{3}	9^{2}	4^{1}	4^{4}	RCSmith	Greentree Stable	a-4.90
8-11-73^{2} Sar^{11}	Bold and Fancy	2 119	3	3	4^{h}	4^{1}	$5^{1\frac{1}{2}}$	$5^{1\frac{1}{2}}$	MCastaneda	M Vogel	35.60
	Regal Rolfe	2 119	10	10	11	11	$7^{\frac{1}{2}}$	$6^{\frac{3}{4}}$	TWallis	Saron Stable	48.20
8- 8-73^{4} Sar^{6}	Shining Knight	2 119	11	9	$7^{\frac{1}{2}}$	$5^{1\frac{1}{2}}$	$6^{1\frac{1}{2}}$	$7^{1\frac{1}{2}}$	HGustines	Greentree Stable	a-4.90
7-18-73^{3} Aqu^{7}	Royal Approval	b2 119	4	8	8^{3}	7^{1}	8^{3}	8^{3}	EBelmonte	Avonwood Stable	20.40
8- 4-73^{4} Sar^{7}	Bronze Express	2 119	8	7	10^{2}	10^{1}	9^{3}	9^{4}	CBaltazar	Pastorale Stable	55.80
	Right Pitch	2 119	6	4	$5^{\frac{1}{2}}$	$8^{\frac{1}{2}}$	10^{5}	10^{8}	RPineda	King Ranch	29.90
	Attaboy John	2 119	2	1	$3^{1\frac{1}{2}}$	$6^{\frac{1}{2}}$	11	11	JVasquez	Mrs C MacLecd Jr	13.60

a-Coupled, Trumpeter Swan and Shining Knight.

Time, :22⅗, :46, 1:11⅘ (no wind in backstretch). Track fast.

$2 Mutuel Prices:				
	2-OFFICE KING	5.80	4.20	2.80
	9-DETERMINED KING		4.20	2.80
	7-CRITERION			2.60

Ch. c, by Vitriolic—Determine Gal, by Determine. Trainer, J. V. Cantey. Bred by Ocala Stud (Fla.).
IN GATE—2:04. OFF AT 2:04½ EASTERN DAYLIGHT TIME. Start good. Won ridden out.
OFFICE KING, rushed to the front along the inside after breaking slowly, drew off around the turn and held DETERMINED KING safe under good handling. The latter, a forward factor throughout, finished gamely while trying to get in during the late stages. CRITERION was going well at the finish. TRUMPETER SWAN rallied belatedly from the outside. BOLD AND FANCY, steadied behind ATTABOY JOHN at the turn, failed to seriously menace. SHINING KNIGHT was always outrun. RIGHT PITCH was through early. ATTABOY JOHN had brief speed.
Scratched—Covered Portage.

The virtues of Office King were not a well-kept secret. He received strong betting action, closing as the 9-to-5 favorite. Showing the early speed that he had displayed in his workouts, he raced to a four-length lead and won handily.

9th Saratoga

AUGUST 13, 1974

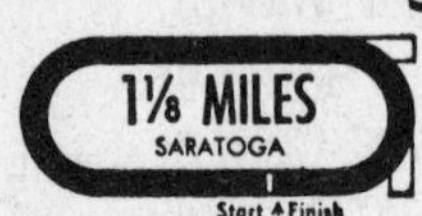

1⅛ MILES. (1:47). ALLOWANCES. Purse $10,000. 3-year-olds and upward which have not won a race other than maiden, claiming or starter. 3-year-olds, 116 lbs.; older, 122 lbs. Non-winners of $5,400 at a mile or over since July 15 allowed 2 lbs.; $5,700 at a mile or over since June 15, 4 lbs.; maidens, 6 lbs. 3-year-olds which have never won at a mile or over allowed 3 lbs.; older, 5 lbs. (Winners preferred.)

COUPLED: GRAND SALUTE and CHINCHONA.

Clarion Sky 114

B. g (1971), by Proud Clarion—Gibellina, by Ribot.
Breeder, J. W. Galbreath (Ky.). 1974 9 1 0 3 $4,900
Owner, Darby Dan Farm. Trainer, T. L. Rondinello. 1973 4 M 0 1 $1,080

Aug 5-749Sar Ⓣ 1⅛ 1:48⅖fm 39 114 1227122511171016 Riv'aMA10 Alw 69 Whatawip 117 Haraka RoyalBounder 12
May18-746Bel 🅃 1¼ 2:03⅕fm 7½ 113 814 812 711 710 HoleM2 Alw 78 Consigl'ri112 J'ntAgreem't Br'zeExp's 7
Apr13-748Kee 1 1/16 1:44 ft 6-5 ▲117 724 612 512 611 UsseryR4 Alw 75 TheGeneral 119 Trephine Alexander 8
Mar30-749Hia 1 1-8 1:49 ft 6¼e 122 10201018 918 816 Riv'aMA1 ScwS 71 Bushongo 122 Hasty Flyer Judger 10
Mar22-749Hia Ⓣa1 1/16 1:42⅕shd 4¾ 122 1020 919 813 74 RiveraMA5 Alw 95 LittleEcho115 Rule ofS'c's NewN'dle 10
Mar 7-746Hia 1 1-8 1:51⅗ft 1e▲122 1220 915 42½ 11 Riv'aMA11 Mdn 74 Clarion Sky 122 Advisedly Wise Rice 12
Feb13-744GP 1 1/16 1:43⅗ft 6 120 610 65½ 46 32¾ Cast'daM1 Mdn 80 EmperorRex120 R'se theAxe Clar'nSky 12
Jan30-744GP 1 1/16 1:46⅖ft 3¾ 120 12161013 610 34 HoleM11 Mdn 65 Maharajo120 BlueWonder ClarionSky 12
Jan23-743GP Ⓣa1 1/16 1:51⅘fm 15 120 11151115 64½ 31¾ HoleM12 Mdn 53 Alexander120 SandyHill ClarionSky 12
Dec15-731Aqu 1 1:37⅖ft 15 122 1414129 12121010 Casta'aM3 Mdn 70 Roger'sD'ndy122 Crit'rion Sp'nishL'rd 14
Aug 12 Sar 3f ft :39b Aug 4 Sar 3f ft :37⅖b July 31 Sar 6f ft 1:19⅘b

*El Carrerito 120

Ch. c (1970), by Aristophanes—La Chiflada, by Right of Way.
Breeder, Haras Ojo de Aqua (Arg.). 1974 17 1 2 3 $17,020
Owner, Camijo Stable. Trainer, J. Martin. 1973 6 1 0 1 $1,865

Aug 2-749Sar Ⓣ 1⅛ 1:48⅖fm 6 112 612 46 23 21¼ SmithRC2 25500 84 G'dHorse116 ElCarrerito AmericanW'y 9
Jly 24-747Aqu 1 1-8 1:51 ft 7¼ 115 510 46 3nk 41½†Riv'aMA7 22500 78 Stick toReason113 BoldCrusader Gano 7
†Placed third through disqualification.
Jly 8-747Aqu 🅃1 1/16 1:42⅖fm 20 112 58 55 76¾ 43 SmithRC1 24500 90 BoHatch 118 Volatil II. BlackSprings 10
Jly 2-744Aqu Ⓣ1 3/16 1:57⅖fm 32 111 24 1½ 1½ 1½ Sm'hRC6 17000 83 ElC'r'rito111 B'ldC's'd'r B'rkingSt'ple 8
Jun24-745Aqu 1 1:36⅕ft 19 113 57 42 65 57 Her'd'zS6 18000 79 St'k toR'son116 B'dCr's'd'r E'lySt'rll. 6
Jun17-747Bel Ⓣ 1 1:36⅕fm 28 115 54½ 814 919 915 Hern'ezS10 Alw 75 Jovial Judge 105 Camelford Prod 10
Jun 4-744Bel 🅃 1¼ 2:03⅖fm 14 112 31½ 21½ 23 33¾ Her'd'zS1 27500 83 RoughPlace116 Volatil II. ElCarrerito 6
July 22 Bel trt 4f ft :50⅖b

Group Plan 113

B. g (1970), by Intentionally—Nanticious, by Nantallah.
Breeder, Eaton Farms, Red Bull Stable 1974 2 0 0 0 $570
& Mrs. G. Proskauer (Ky.). 1973 6 1 1 1 $9,420
Owner, Hobea Farm. Trainer, H. A. Jerkens.

Aug10-749Sar 6½ f 1:17 ft 4½ 121 85¼ 77 85¾ 66½ MapleE8 Alw 84 Plantagen't119 FaceM'k PokersBrush 12
Aug 3-742Sar 6 f 1:11⅕ft 19 124 68 68 55½ 4½ Cast'daM9 Alw 83 Lothario 119 Aquinas Hudsonian
Dec 8-733Aqu 6 f 1:10 ft 6¼ 122 1h 31½ 35 48 Vel'quezJ1 Alw 85 Spi[illegible]ple124 [illegible]Knight Schroon 6
Nov29-733Aqu 6 f 1:11⅘sm 7 122 76¾ 611 66½ 12 BaezaB8 Mdn 84 Gr[illegible]122 M[illegible]stic[illegible]'tive Inv'stig't'n 8
Nov16-734Aqu 6½ f 1:19⅕ft 6 122 76½ 65 42½ 33½ Vel'q'zJ10 Mdn 76 D[illegible]W[illegible]hM[illegible] [illegible]v'tig't'n Gr'pPl'n 10
Nov 5-732Aqu 6 f 1:13 ft 5¼ 122 78 67 55½ 55¾ Velasq'zJ8 Mdn 72 SpanishDew112 Investigat'n JewelBag 8
Oct 9-731Bel 6½ f 1:17⅖ft 7-5 ▲121 63¼ 85¼ 87½ 812 Velasq'zJ9 Mdn 77 G'tl'm'sW'd121 Inv'tig't'n D'mW'hMe 10
Oct 1-733Bel 6 f 1:11 ft 6 120 53 1½ 11 2¾ VasquezJ7 Mdn 87 Downtown120 GroupPlan Investigation 7
Aug 8 Sar 3f ft :36⅘b Aug 1 Sar 4f ft :47h

The Scotsman 112

Dk. b. or br. c (1971), by Buckpasser—Fast Cookie, by Beau Gar.
Breeder, J. H. Adger & A. G. Clay (Ky.). 1974 14 1 2 3 $13,260
Owner, Saron Stable. Trainer, S. E. Veitch. 1973 6 M 0 3 $13,160

Aug 8-749Sar Ⓣ1 3/16 1:55⅕fm 9½ 112 Lost rider. TurcotteR3 Alw Camelford 118 Prod BigBrownBear 11
Jly 29-743Sar 1 1-8 1:49⅘ft 2½ ▲113 45½ 43 66 55¼ Turc'tteR6 Alw 87 Peleus 113 Pokers Brush War Reason 8
Jly 7-748Del 1 1/16 1:42⅘ft 29 110 56 64¾ 56 55¼ McC'onG3 HcpS 90 Gold andMyrrh110 ParkGuard Sherby 10
Jun30-748Suf 1 1/16 1:44⅗ft 4 116 45 45 53 34¾ Ander'nP2 HcpS 81 Sp'r inMyW'b116 KinR'n TheSc'tsman 6
Jun22-745Bel 1 1/16 1:43⅖ft 5½ 113 3nk 1h 2½ 23 HoleM3 Alw 82 D'mWithMe11[illegible] [illegible]m'n TheBigSw'g 8
Jun 5-746Mth Ⓣ1 1/16 1:44⅘fm 3¼ 120 109 89 59 52 AndersonP3 Alw 83 Assag'l 115 JovialJudge Br'zeExpr'ss 10
May25-748Bel 1 1:35⅗ft 58 126 98¼12101013 914 W'dheR1 ScwS 75 Accipiter 126 [illegible] of It Hosiery 12
May18-749Bel 6 f 1:10⅗ft 12 122 912 813 89¼ 612 MapleE4 Alw 78 Q'nCityLad122 F'lyPhys'n Silv'rD'bl'n 11
Apr17-747Kee 6½ f 1:17⅗ft 3¼ 117 85½ 87½ 44½ 21 UsseryR5 Alw 89 T.V.S'tan114 TheSc'tsm'n F'rB'seHit 9
Mar14-748SA 1 1-8 1:48⅖ft 20 120 55½ 79¾ 612 621 GrantH8 SpwS 69 Agitate 118 Ja Aglo Littlefly 8
Feb17-745SA 1 1/16 1:43 ft 12 118 52½ 31½ 32 36½ VasquezJ7 Alw 80 Agitate 116 BoldTalent TheScotsman 8
Feb 3-744SA 1 1/16 1:44⅘ft 3¾ 118 53½ 21½ 1h 11 VasquezJ8 Mdn 78 TheSc'tsm'n118 Rudy'sPro'se ElSeetu 11
Aug 12 Sar 3f ft :37⅘b Aug 6 Sar 4f ft :48b Aug 3 Sar 3f ft :36b

War Reason 112 Gr. g (1971), by Warfare—Morning Calm, by Hail to Reason.
Breeder, M. Church III. (Va.). 1974 7 1 0 1 $4,332
Owner, Beverly R. Steinman. Trainer, P. R. Fout. 1973 4 M 0 0 (——)
Aug 5-749Sar Ⓣ 1⅛ 1:48⅖fm 17 113 10 8¾ 6 8½ 5 8 6 7¾ Fel'anoBM5 Alw 73 Whatawip 117 Haraka RoyalBounder 12
Jly 29-743Sar 1 1-8 1:49⅘ft 31 114 6 11 6 10 4 5 3 2 RiveraMA1 Alw 90 Peleus 113 PokersBrush War Reason 8
Jly 21-748Del Ⓣ 1⅜ 2:14⅘fm 64 105 9 7¾ 9 12 7 12 6 12 Ber'diW9 HcpS 81 Scrims'w110 Cr'dRoses At theD'ce 9
Jly 7-747Del 1-70 1:42⅗ft 8¼ 120 4 2½ 4 3½ 4 5½ 4 6¾ PilarH4 Alw 77 Mr. Nace 115 OurHermis Mr. B. P. 8
Jun27-748Del Ⓣ 1 1:37⅘fm 5½ 117 5 3½ 5 3¾ 5 8 7 9¼ PilarH11 Alw 77 OurHermis112 Mr.Nace SirVivalAr'v'l 12
Jun18-743Del 1-70 1:44⅕ft 4 115 4 4½ 2 h 1 1½ 1 3 PilarH7 Mdn 75 WarReason115 IdleGossip Mich'lsMad 10
Aug 11 Sar 3f ft :37⅕b Aug 4 Sar 3f ft :36⅖h

Bold and Gallant 112 B. c (1971), by Gallant Man—Proved Bold, by Bold Ruler.
Breeder, E. P. Evans (Va.). 1974 9 1 2 1 $10,637
Owner, Buckland Farm. Trainer, J. P. Campo. 1973 2 M 0 0 (——)
Jly 22-744Aqu Ⓣ 1⅛ 1:51⅕ft 24 115 5 9 8 5¾ 9 17 9 19 W'dh'seR5 Alw 60 Prod 115 Royal Bounder Haraka 9
Jly 15-747Aqu 1 1-8 1:50 ft 12 113 7 14 8 17 8 25 7 24 Velasq'zJ1 Alw 61 J'ckSp't115 M'n't'ryPr'ciple J'geP'w'r 8
Jun30-748Suf 1 1/16 1:44⅗ft 10 113 5 11 6 16 6 11 6 18 RieraRJr4 HcpS 68 Spid'r inMyW'b116 KinR'n TheSc'ts'n 6
Apr20-742Aqu 1 1-8 1:51⅗ft 2½ ▲114 8 14 5 7½ 2 3 1 2¼ Velasq'zJ8 Mdn 79 B'ld a'dG'l'nt114 Tr'pic'lB'y M'j'tyR'r 8
Apr12-742Aqu 1 1:36⅘ft 3¼e 114 10 6 10 6 8 6¼ 5 5¼ McCar'nG2 Mdn 78 JohnBarl'yc'n122 Perf'ctDear H.Hour 13
Mar20-744Aqu 1 1-8 1:51⅗ft 3 114 5 6 6 6 3 3 2 nk Velasq'zJ3 Mdn 77 UpLikeT'der114 B'ld a'dG'nt P'nMyL'e 6
Mar12-743Aqu 1 1:39⅕ft 3¾ 122 3 2 3 5 3 6½ 2 6 Velasq'zJ3 Mdn 65 FirstSlice122 B'ld a'dG'l't Par'nMyL'e 6
Mar 2-742Aqu 6 f 1:11⅘ft 9½ 121 7 10 8 14 7 13 5 10 DitmoreA3 Mdn 74 Grandman121 Ned'sNative Criterion 8
Jan11-743Lib 1 1/16 1:50⅕sm 10 118 4 11 4 6 3 8 3 14 PinedaR3 Mdn 41 Spr'gF'w'd118 Gr't'nMate B'ld a'dG't 4
Aug 10 Sar trt 4f ft :50⅕b Aug 3 Sar trt 4f ft :50⅕h July 13 Bel trt 4f ft :50b

Dark Encounter 112 Dk. b. or br. c (1971), by Cornish Prince—Karate Skill, by Cohoes.
Breeder, Tricorn Farms, Inc. (Ky.). 1974 5 1 0 1 $7,320
Owner, F. G. Allen. Trainer, S. Watters, Jr. 1973 2 M 0 0 $600
Aug10-749Sar 6½ f 1:17 ft 24 116 12 14 12 11 10 9¾ 9 10 HoleM1 Alw 81 Plantagen't119 FaceM'k PokersBrush 12
Jly 4-747Aqu 6 f 1:10⅕ft 3¾ 117 5 3 5 2¾ 6 5½ 8 7¾ HoleM6 Alw 84 Nile Delta 114 Big Moses Bitache 8
Jun22-742Bel 6 f 1:11⅗ft 2½ ▲115 5 7½ 4 4 2 ½ 1 1¼ HoleM6 Mdn 85 D'kEnc't'r115 Jet'sN'wOrl'ns C'ng'L'd 9
Apr30-745Aqu 6 f 1:10⅖ft 2¼ ▲113 3 1½ 4 2½ 4 4½ 4 7½ VasquezJ7 Mdn 83 Haraka 113 SailorsWatch Ned'sNative 9
Apr22-743Aqu 6 f 1:10⅗ft 5¾ 108* 7 8½ 4 3½ 4 4 3 2¾ MoonL9 Mdn 87 Pr'dlyN'tive113 SeaS'gst'r D'kEnc't'r 9
Dec14-734Aqu 6½ f 1:17⅕sm 3 ▲115‡ 8 7¾ 9 13 7 14 7 13 MoonL9 Mdn 77 WhoaBoy122 RedStre'k DestinyBeh've 10
Dec 8-732Aqu 6 f 1:10⅘ft 2e▲115‡ 9 11 6 6¼ 5 1¼ 4 3¾ MoonL8 Mdn 85 Erwin Boy 122 Mr. Beck Surf Catcher 13
Aug 4 Sar 5f ft 1:00⅖h Aug 2 Sar 3f ft :35h July 29 Sar 5f ft 1:03b

Big Moses * 99 B. g (1971), by Raspberry Ice—Jane S., by High Lea.
Br., Mrs. J. Ellis & R. L. Dotter (S. C.). 1974 7 0 3 0 $7,500
Owner, Mrs. J. Ellis. Trainer, R. L. Dotter. 1973 4 2 0 1 $10,260
Jly 29-743Sar 1 1-8 1:49⅘ft 8¾ 109 2 ½ 2 ½ 2 3 6 6¾ RuaneJ5 Alw 85 Peleus 113 Pokers Brush War Reason 8
Jly 20-747Aqu 6 f 1:10⅗ft 2½ ▲114 5 3½ 5 4½ 6 9 8 11 VasquezJ8 Alw 79 H'ppyDeleg'te117 RisingCr'st Aquin's 10
Jly 4-747Aqu 6 f 1:10⅕ft 7 114 1 ½ 2 h 1 ½ 2 1 BaltazarC3 Alw 91 Nile Delta 114 Big Moses Bitache 8
Jun19-745Bel 6 f 1:10⅘ft 1 ▲113 2 2½ 3 3 4 4 5 7½ VasquezJ1 Alw 81 WeeMoe113 Bitache NileDelta 6
Jun 4-747Bel 6 f 1:10⅗ft 10 113 1 h 2 ½ 1 1½ 2 h VasquezJ5 Alw 90 MidnightMystic112 BigMoses Cerrito 9
May25-743Bel 6½ f 1:16⅘ft 6¼ 104‡ 2 ½ 2 h 2 1½ 4 4½ DotterMA7 Alw 88 C'm'sSunny110 F'tyPhy'n Mid'eM'tic 7
May14-741Bel 6½ f 1:17⅕ft 5½ 116 2 h 2 1½ 1 ½ 2 ½ Vasq'zJ7 37500 89 Magallanes113 BigMoses OurReward 9
Jly 19-733Aqu 6 f 1:12 ft 3-2 ▲119 4 2 3 2 2 2 3 2½ Vasq'zJ6 25000 80 ElEspanoleto119 Homeric BigMoses 6
Jly 10-735Aqu 5½ f 1:05⅘ft 12 118 1 1 1 1 1 2 1 1½ Vasq'zJ1 27500 84 BigMoses118 Sm'thO'Neil R'y'lD'nc'r 6
May24-733Bel 5½ f 1:06⅖sy 31 115 4 2½ 2 1 1 h 1 ½ Va'zJ10 M20000 87 BigMoses115 EarlyChief M'xic'nOnion 10
Aug 11 Sar 4f ft :49⅖b Aug 4 Sar 4f ft :50⅖b July 28 Sar 3f ft :38b

Zero Hour 109 Ch. c (1971), by Vertex—Desert Trail, by Moslem Chief.
Breeder, Mrs. V. Adams (Fla.). 1974 11 1 0 1 $5,950
Owner, H. T. Mangurian, Jr. Trainer, T. F. Root, Sr.
Aug 5-749Sar Ⓣ 1⅛ 1:48⅖fm 19 106‡ 8 5¾ 7 12 8 13 8 14 LongJS8 Alw 71 Whatawip 117 Haraka RoyalBounder 12
Jly 30-741Sar 1 1-8 1:51⅗ft 5¾ 108‡ 2 ½ 1 1½ 1 5 1 5½ LongJS1 Mdn 83 ZeroHour108 Pro andCon Ex'gger'ted 8
Jly 20-741Aqu Ⓣ 1⅛ 1:52 fm 27 105♣6 14 8 6 7 6½ 5 5 LongJS7 Mdn 70 DestinyBehave116 Gr'dSalute Yawohl 10
Jly 12-741Aqu 🅃 1 1/16 1:43⅗fm 25 105♣7 9½ 7 9 6 6½ 8 5¾ LongJS3 Mdn 81 R'y'lB'nder115 TheSw'g P'd'nMyL'e 10
Jly 2-742Aqu 6 f 1:10⅘ft 37 107♣10 11 11 12 11 12 10 10 LongJS9 Mdn 79 H'yD'g'te117 Chiel J't toN'wOr'ns 11
Jun22-742Bel 6 f 1:11⅗ft 26 105♣9 13 9 11 6 6 6 4¼ LongJS7 Mdn 81 D'kEnc't'r115 J't toN'wOrl'ns C'n'gL'd 9
Jun 1-744Bel 7 f 1:23⅘sy 7¼ 115 6 9 8 10 6 13 6 16 Velasq'zJ3 Mdn 67 Toy King 115 Tuxedo Brushnell 11
May24-743Bel 1 1:34⅘ft 10 114 8 14 8 14 7 16 7 19 Vel'quezJ8 Mdn 75 H'h'tM'n114 P's t'eGl's Sh'wOn t'eR'd 9
May18-742Bel 7 f 1:23 ft 2 ▲113 4 3 4 5½ 8 13 7 21 Vel'q'zJ11 Mdn 66 Lassington113 Yawohl E'st'rnP'geant 11
Aug 11 Sar trt 3f ft :37h Juily 27 Bel 4f ft :48⅘h July 8 Bel trt 4f ft :48⅕h

(cont'd on next page)

Chinchona **109** **Ro. c (1971), by Cyane—Chinchon, by Goya II.**
Breeder, Pine Brook Farm, Inc. (Ky.). **1974 9 0 0 3 $5,190**
Owner, Lillian F. O'Keefe. Trainer, M. Miller. **1973 6 1 2 0 $4,720**

Jly 29-743Sar 1 1-8 1:49⅘ft 8½ 113 813 815 814 711 Velasqu'zJ8 Alw 81 Peleus 113 Pokers Brush War Reason 8
Jly 15-747Aqu 1 1-8 1:50 ft 13 110 45½ 52¼ 55½ 44½ NemetiW5 Alw 80 J'ckSp't115 M'n't'ryPr'ciple J'geP'w'r 8
Jun29-746Aqu 1 1:34⅖ft 20 111 69 59½ 59 39¾ NemetiW4 Alw 85 G'ntlem'n'sW'd117 L's'gton Chinchona 7
Jun 8-743Bel T 1⅜ 2:15⅖fm 26 105 511 75¼ 64½ 42½ CardoneE4 Alw 94 BobbyMurcer112 Alexander [illegible] 8
May28-746Bel T 1¼ 2:02 fm 17 110 56 99 99½ 87 NemetiW9 Alw 87 Cr[illegible]110 [illegible]'ce [illegible]Obl'e 10
May 8-749Pim Ⓣ1 1/16 1:45⅗fm 3 112 2h 2½ 3nk 32½ McC'r'nG11 Alw 80 Cl[illegible]am115 [illegible]kpit [illegible]na 12
Apr29-747Pim 1 1/16 1:43⅖ft 6½ 112 55 31 33½ 36 McCar'nG7 Alw 82 B[illegible]re112 J.C.'sSh'd'w Ch'ch'na 10
Apr20-747Pim 6 f 1:12⅕ft 5½ 113 85¾108¼ 711 44¼ Pass'reWJ5 Alw 81 Ise' Wild 112 On to Glory Prash 12
Apr13-745Pim 6 f 1:12⅕sy 32 114 84¾ 87 64 42½ Pass'reWJ2 Alw 82 Millfleet113 On toGlory DeB'rry'sT'k't 10
Jly 20-735Del 5½ f 1:06⅕ft 1 ▲120 31 1h 2½ 1no WalshE4 Mdn 87 Chinchona120 Tex'sL'ger EarlC'rdig'n 8
Aug 12 Sar 3f ft :38b **July 25 Bel 6f sy 1:18b** **July 21 Bel 4f ft :50b**

Judge Power **111** **B. c (1970), by Traffic Judge—Just Fancy That, by Vertex.**
Breeder, Danada Farm (Ky.). **1974 14 4 2 1 $23,440**
Owner, Mrs. J. S. Nash. Trainer, J. S. Nash. **1973 13 2 4 1 $11,365**

Jly 29-743Sar 1 1-8 1:49⅘ft 4½ 119 59½ 57 55 45 Bracc'eVJr7 Alw 87 Peleus 113 Pokers Brush War Reason 8
Jly 15-747Aqu 1 1-8 1:50 ft 8¾ 120 34 42 32 33¼ Bra'leVJr3 Alw 82 J'ckSp't115 M'n't'ryPr'ciple J'geP'w'r 8
Jly 9-746Aqu 6½ f 1:16⅖ft 12 116 67 56¼ 55½ 46½ Br'leVJr4 32500 87 SpecialTex112 [illegible]senMood N'seWind 6
Jun22-745Bel 1 1/16 1:43⅖ft 3 120 5½ 53 69 614 W'dh'seR2 Alw 71 D'[illegible]11[illegible]m'n [illegible]gSw'g 8
Jun14-747Bel 1 1:36 ft 33 120 95½ 66½ 48¼ 49 Cast'daM6 Alw 79 H'[illegible]114 [illegible]L'd [illegible]P't'ge 10
May11-744GS 1 1-4 2:05⅕ft 8-5 ▲120 55 2h 13 18 BlumW6 H7500 74 Jud[illegible]wer 120 Algernon Thayer 7
Apr27-749Aqu 1 1-8 1:50 ft 6 119 64½ 31 2h 2½ Casta'daM3 Alw 84 Whickery 111 Judge Power Oilime 10
Mar23-745Hia Ⓣ1 1/16 1:41⅖hd 8 122 44 45 58½ 611 W'dh'seR2 Alw 80 St'ryKnight112 J'nGod'y P'p'r'dJabn'r 7
Mar13-746Hia 1 1-8 1:49 ft 1 ▲122 14 11½ 11 13 W'h'seR6 H7500 87 JudgePower122 G'l'ntExch'ge Olmedo 8
Aug 8 Sar 6f ft 1:15h **Aug 3 Sar 6f ft 1:14⅖h** **July 27 Bel 4f ft :49b**

Hy Button Shoes **112** **B. g (1971), by Misty Flight—Button My Shoe, by One Count.**
Breeder, Hymill Stables (Va.). **1974 11 1 1 2 $10,200**
Owner, Hymill Stable. Trainer, F. S. Schulhofer.

Aug 5-749Sar Ⓣ 1⅛ 1:48⅖fm 28 113 65 58 610 712 MontoyaD3 Alw 73 Whatawip 117 Haraka RoyalBounder 12
Jly 22-744Aqu Ⓣ 1⅛ 1:51⅕fm 40 115 24 32 55½ 56 MontoyaD1 Alw 73 Prod 115 Royal Bounder Haraka 9
Jly 13-743Aqu 6½ f 1:16⅖ft 13 117 43½ 66¾ 712 615 Cast'daM7 Alw 78 Quebec124 Knight ofHonor SharpDig 7
Jun 5-749Bel 1 1:35⅗ft 25 114 66 76½ 716 721 VeneziaM6 Alw 69 HatchetMan114 G'tlem'n's[illegible]aka 8
May27-747Bel 6 f 1:09⅘ft 27 121 912 914 811 610 VeneziaM7 Alw 84 Pr'c'lyN'tive121 NileD'lt[illegible]T'ke[illegible]St'm 10
Apr20-743Aqu 1 1:37 ft 12 116* 2h 44½ 38 36 MontoyaD1 Alw 76 Rule ofSuccess118 Capit[illegible]'nSh's 7
Apr 5-748Aqu 1 1:37⅘sy 5 116* 45 48½ 59½ 59¾ MontoyaD3 Alw 68 FirstSlice121 EmpireM'n B'ld a'dF'cy 6
Mar28-744Aqu 1 1:38⅕ft 1 ▲109* 66¼ 35 34½ 1h MontoyaD2 Mdn 76 HyB't'nSh's109 Tr'pic'lB'y M'nt'naH'r 6
Mar16-745Aqu 6 f 1:11⅕ft 2½ 117* 51¼ 3½ 3nk 2nk Mont'yaD8 Mdn 87 FreeAssociat'n122 HyB't'nSh's Mr.B'k 9
Aug 11 Sar 3f ft :36h **July 29 Sar tc 4f fm :48⅖h** **July 20 Bel 4f ft :47⅗h**

War Reason has the best figure in this nondescript allowance race. He earned a rating of 98 on July 29 while he was beating several of the contenders in today's field — The Scotsman, Judge Power, and Big Moses.

On that day practically every race at Saratoga was won by

a speed horse with an inside post position. War Reason managed to come from far behind, circle the field, and finish a close third. It was an impressive performance. His subsequent defeat on August 5 can be ignored. That race was run on the grass, and War Reason's record shows clearly that he is not a grass horse. Back on the main track today, he should be ready for a top effort.

Most of his competition appears very weak. El Carrerito is a turf horse. Dark Encounter is a sprinter. Zero Hour's figure in his recent 5½-length victory was atrocious. Clarion Sky and Bold and Gallant are off form. But there is one horse in this field likely to improve dramatically.

Group Plan made a promising debut for the year on August 3, when he finished fast and lost a six-furlong race by half a length. After that race, trainer Boo Gentry sold him to Allen Jerkens. Wasting no time, Jerkens entered him in another sprint on August 10. Group Plan finished a lackluster sixth, 6½ lengths behind the winner, earning a figure of 85 that would not menace the horses he is facing today. Yet many indications are present that this is going to be another Jerkens training miracle.

Jerkens always does well with horses he acquires privately. In 1973 he bought Prove Out and within nine days transformed him from a nonentity into a star.

Jerkens wins often when he enters a horse within three or four days of his last start. In 1973 he brought Onion back after three days' rest and upset Secretariat at Saratoga.

Jerkens' greatest strength is his ability to convert sprinters into routers. He made his reputation in the early sixties when his sprinter Beau Purple beat the great Kelso three times.

A horseplayer could logically bet Group Plan on the basis of faith in Jerkens. Or he could logically bet War Reason because of his superior figures and established handicapping merits. There are no rules that govern the situation. This is one of the close, agonizing decisions that separate the winners from the losers.

NINTH RACE Sar August 13, 1974 1⅛ MILES. (1:47). ALLOWANCES. Purse $10,000. 3-year-olds and upward which have not won a race other than maiden, claiming or starter. 3-year-olds, 116 lbs.; older, 122 lbs. Non-winners of $5,400 at a mile or over since July 15 allowed 2 lbs. $5,700 at a mile or over since June 15, 4 lbs.; maidens, 6 lbs. 3-year-olds which have never won at a mile or over allowed 3 lbs.; older, 5 lbs. (Winners preferred.)

Value to winner $6,000; second, $2,200; third, $1,200; fourth, $600. Mutuel Pool, $89,914. Off-track betting, $110,144. Triple Pool, $102,090. Off-track betting Triple Pool, $219,582.

Last Raced	Horse	EqtAWt	PP	St	¼	½	¾	Str	Fin	Jockeys	Owners	Odds to $1
8-10-74^{9} Sar^{6}	Group Plan	b4 113	3	4	$2^{1\frac{1}{2}}$	1^{h}	1^{h}	1^{6}	$1^{8\frac{1}{2}}$	EMaple	Hobeau Farm	2.50
8- 8-74^{9} Sar	The Scotsman	b3 113	4	10	$7^{\frac{1}{2}}$	5^{h}	$5^{1\frac{1}{2}}$	4^{2}	2^{h}	RTurcotte	Saron Stable	3.50
7-29-74^{3} Sar^{4}	Judge Power	b4 118	12	8	9^{1}	8^{2}	6^{4}	$3^{\frac{1}{2}}$	$3^{2\frac{1}{2}}$	MCastaneda	Mrs J S Nash	7.30
8- 5-74^{9} Sar^{10}	Clarion Sky	3 114	1	12	12	$11^{\frac{1}{2}}$	10^{2}	5^{h}	$4^{3\frac{3}{4}}$	MARivera	Darby Dan Farm	20.30
7-29-74^{3} Sar^{6}	Big Moses	3 103	8	1	1^{h}	2^{3}	2^{3}	2^{2}	$5^{\frac{3}{4}}$	MADotter^{10}	Mrs J Ellis	11.30
7-29-74^{3} Sar^{7}	Chinchona	b3 109	10	6	$8^{\frac{1}{2}}$	$7^{\frac{1}{2}}$	9^{2}	9^{2}	6no	ECardone	Lillian F O'Keefe	26.40
8- 5-74^{9} Sar^{6}	War Reason	b3 112	5	9	10^{8}	10^{6}	8^{h}	$8^{1\frac{1}{2}}$	7^{nk}	BMFeliciano	Beverly R Steinman	6.20
7-22-74^{4} Aqu^{9}	Bold and Gallant	b3 112	6	11	11^{2}	12	11^{5}	$10^{1\frac{1}{2}}$	8^{2}	VBraccialeJr	Buckland Farm	14.40
8- 2-74^{9} Sar^{2}	El Carrerito	4 120	2	3	$4^{1\frac{1}{2}}$	4^{4}	4^{h}	$6^{1\frac{1}{2}}$	9no	RCSmith	Camijo Stable	8.80
8-10-74^{9} Sar^{1}	Dark Encounter	3 113	7	2	3^{1}	3^{1}	3^{4}	$7^{\frac{1}{2}}$	10^{2}	MHole	F G Allen	20.80
8- 5-74^{9} Sar^{8}	Zero Hour	3 109	9	5	5^{h}	6^{1}	7^{h}	11^{1}	11^{13}	JSLong^{7}	H T Mangurian Jr	20.30
8- 5-74^{9} Sar^{7}	Hy Button Shoes	b3 112	11	7	$6^{1\frac{1}{2}}$	9^{1}	12	12	12	DMontoya	Hymill Stable	47.40

OFF AT 5:59 EDT. Start good. Won driving. Time, $:23\frac{3}{5}$, :47, $1:10\frac{4}{5}$, $1:35\frac{4}{5}$, $1:48\frac{4}{5}$. Track fast.

$2 Mutuel Prices:			
3-GROUP PLAN	7.00	4.20	3.80
4-THE SCOTSMAN		4.40	3.60
12-JUDGE POWER			3.80

$2 TRIPLE (3-4-12) PAID $256.00.

B. g, by Intentionally—Nanticious, by Nantallah. Trainer, H. A. Jerkens. Bred by Eaton Farm, Red Bull Stable and Mrs. Proskauer.

GROUP PLAN saved ground while vying for the lead with BIG MOSES, put that one away approaching the stretch and increased his advantage under pressure. THE SCOTSMAN rallied from the outside leaving the far turn and continued on with good courage. JUDGE POWER split horses after entering the stretch and finished well. CLARION SKY, void of early foot, rallied entering the stretch but failed to sustain his bid. BIG MOSES was used up dueling for the lead. WAR REASON was always outrun. ELCARRERITO was through after going three quarters. DARK ENCOUNTER, a factor to the stretch, had nothing left. ZERO HOUR was through early. HY BUTTON SHOES had brief speed.

Overweight—The Scotsman, 1 pound; Dark Encounter, 1; Big Moses, 4.

Scratched—To The Tune, Grand Salute, Crag's Corner.

Group Plan supported the judgment of the many New York horseplayers who think Allen Jerkens is God. He won by 8½ lengths, earning a figure of 106, and went on to establish himself as one of the better horses in the country. War Reason was never close.

7th Pimlico Race Course

MARCH 20, 1974

6 FURLONGS. (1:09⅕). CLAIMING. Purse $5,500. Fillies. 3-year-olds. Weight, 122 lbs. Non-winners of two races since Feb. 7 allowed 3 lbs.; a race, 5 lbs.; a race since Jan. 30, 8 lbs. Claiming price, $7,500; for each $250 to $7,000, allowed 1 lb. (Races where entered for $6,000 or less not considered.)

COUPLED: GLITTERING GOLD and I'M DIANA.

Annie Oak — 107

B. f (1970), by Rambunctious—Activation, by Prove It.
Breeder, Mrs. F. Biere (Md.). 1974 5 0 2 0 $1,620
Owner, E. M. Casey. Trainer, G. W. Walters. $7,500 1973 4 1 1 0 $1,826

Mar11-747ShD 6 f 1:15⅕ft 10 114 2½ 2³ 3³ 4⁶ EspinosaV6 Alw 66 JetAppeal 118 WmRLewisJr Ch'sCh'r 7
Feb26-748ShD 5½ f 1:09⅘ft 4½ 115 5³¼ 4⁴½ 6⁶ 8⁸¾ EspinosaV6 Alw 70 H'rySt'p118 Ch'sCh'g'r En'gh'sEn'gh's 9
Feb14-747ShD 6 f 1:14⅗ft 6¾ 114 1³ 1⁵ 1⁴ 2¹½ EspinosaV8 Alw 79 JiggerMan118 AnnieOok En'gh'sEn's 8
Feb 1-749ShD 3½ f :41⅖ft 3¾ 115 5 3¹½ 4³ 4² EspinosaV5 Alw 86 DimmitCh'rg'r120 AvidC'rt R'ghP'der 6
March 9 CT 3f ft :37b **Feb 24 CT 3f ft :36b**

Glittering Gold — 114

B. f (1971), by Hedevar—Bob's Princess, by Selinsgrove.
Breeder, F. D. Vechery (Md.). 1974 4 2 0 0 $3,924
Owner, F. D. Vechery. Trainer, K. T. Leatherbury. $7,500

Mar 8-743Bow 6 f 1:15⅗ft 5½ 119 2¹½ 1h 1¹½ 1²½ WalshE1 5500 65 ⒻGlit'rgGold119 S'c'ndS'a Sp'shC'f'e 7
Feb26-743Bow 6 f 1:14⅖ft 9 117 3½ 3²½ 3² 5²¾ WalshE3 6000 68 [illegible]14 Sp[illegible]e Dar'gD'nd 9
Feb13-744Pen 5½ f 1:05⅕ft 4½ 113 5⁴½ 4⁵½ 4¹¾ 5⁷¾ NobleJF2 Alw 89 N[illegible]21 Pri[illegible] CrackR'g'nt 6
Feb 7-741Pen 5½ f 1:06⅕ft 14 118 4¹¼ 5²¼ 4⁴½ 1h N'leJF12 M3500 92 G[illegible]gG'ld118 Ap'cheW'dge D'lBr'h's 12
Feb 23 Bow 3f ft :37⅗b **Jan 31 Pen 4f sl :52hg** **Jan 23 Pen 6f sl 1:19⅗bg**

Tree Lace — 114

B. f (1971), by Advocator—Rubber Game, by Reneged.
Breeder, K. C. Firestone (Ky.). 1974 6 0 3 2 $3,804
Owner, E. J. Wirth. Trainer, R. Cartwright. $7,500 1973 12 1 1 1 $3,588

Mar11-746Bow 6 f 1:14⅕ft 5½ 112 1³ 1² 1² 1²½ KurtzJ4 7000 70 ⒻBanana 114 Tree Lace Inky B. 7
Feb 9-742Bow 6 f 1:13⅕sy 5½ 114 3nk 2¹ 1h 2¹ GinoL3 c5500 76 ⒻDaringDiamond119 TreeL'ce Nad'te 12
Jan30-742Bow 7 f 1:28⅗gd 14 114 1½ 1½ 2³ 3⁶¼ GinoL2 5500 56 ⒻHelloKim112 Dar'gD'm'nd TreeL'ce 12
Jan22-742Bow 6 f 1:14⅘m 6¾ 114 4¾ 3nk 2h 3² GinoL3 5500 67 Ⓕ[illegible]14 [illegible]n'cki [illegible] 12
Jan10-746Pen 5½ f 1:08⅕sy 4½ 114 2h 2¹ 2² 2¹¾ Reynl'dsR2 5000 80 Ⓕ[illegible]tQ[illegible]estion [illegible] [illegible]reeLace [illegible] 7
Jan 3-745Bow 6 f 1:14⅘m 14 114 7⁶¼ 8⁹ 7¹⁰ 10⁶¾ Pass'eWJ6 7500 62 ⒻL[illegible]sDec'n114 Mary[illegible]dQ'n F'k[illegible]eBillie 12
Dec16-734Pen 6 f 1:14⅖gd 2½ 112 2² 3²½ 5¹¼ 4¹¼ DennieD4 5000 73 ArcticM'nd117 R'dheadD. CatfishJ'nh 10
Dec10-732Lrl 1 1:42 m 13 113 1½ 2¹½ 6⁷½ 7¹³ CookeC2 7500 50 LottaJack120 SolarCircle DabneyR'd 9
Nov22-732Lrl 7 f 1:27⅕ft 12 116 1½ 1½ 2½ 3² CookeC3 7500 73 BoldSq'w109 MissOverdrive TreeLace 8
March 3 Lrl 7f ft 1:30 ⅖b

Daring Diamond — 117

Ch. f (1971), by Choker—Lordy Me, by Our Babu.
Breeder, Fellowship Farm (Fla.). 1974 6 2 1 1 $7,410
Owner, J. R. Whorl. Trainer, T. C. Patterson. $7,000 1973 6 2 1 0 $6,320

Mar11-746Bow 6 f 1:14⅕ft 4 114 4⁴ 5⁶ 5⁶ 5⁸¾ ShukN5 7000 63 ⒻBanana 114 Tree Lace Inky B. 7
Feb26-743Bow 6 f 1:14⅖ft 3-5 ▲117 5³ 6⁵ 5²½ 3²½ Cus'noG5 c5500 68 ⒻLi'lBuy'r114 Sp'nishC'fee Dar'gD'nd 9
Feb 9-742Bow 6 f 1:13⅕sy 3-2 ▲119 7⁴¾ 5⁶ 3³ 1¹ Cusim'oG1 5500 77 ⒻDaringDiamond119 TreeL'ce Nad'te 12
Jan30-742Bow 7 f 1:28⅗gd 2¾ ▲119 5³½ 4³½ 3³ 2nk Cusim'oG3 5500 62 ⒻHelloKim112 Dar'gD'm'nd TreeL'ce 12
Jan15-745Bow 7 f 1:26⅖ft 8-5 ▲114 5⁴½ 4⁵½ 2½ 1¾ Cu'manoG1 8500 73 Ⓕ[illegible]aringDiam'd[illegible] InkyB. C[illegible]per[illegible]k 10
Jan 2-744Bow 7 f 1:27⅖ft 11 113 6⁷½ 7⁷ 6¹⁰ 6¹⁴ Cus'noG5 13500 54 G'laS[illegible]114 D[illegible]M'n [illegible]G 7
Dec 7-734Lrl 6 f 1:13⅖ft 2 ▲116 6³¼ 5⁴ 5⁴ 5² Cus'noG6 12500 80 Ⓕ[illegible]ooM'chTime1[illegible]8 B[illegible]dSq'w [illegible]dev'e 9
Nov20-736Lrl 6 f 1:11⅘ft 4½ 103♣6⁴½ 6⁷ 5¹¹ 5¹¹ Ber'diW6 15500 79 RedRamage115 Cheri'te M'ndat'ryC't 6
Sep24-736Bow 6 f 1:13⅘ft 3-2 ▲114 4⁴½ 3¹½ 2h 1¹¾ Haw'yS2 c12500 74 DaringD'm'nd114 JigTimeR'se DiB'ss 7
Aug27-734Mth 6 f 1:11⅘ft 9-5 ▲117 3³½ 3⁴½ 1½ 1¹½ Us'ryR5 M10000 83 ⒻDar'gDiam'd117 H'zyTr'th Pl'dLake 9
Aug17-734Mth 5½ f 1:07⅘gd 23 112* 6⁴¾ 5⁶½ 6⁵¾ 2¹ M'tinR5 M10000 77 ⒻM'l'caM'n'r117 D'r'gD'm'd O'sL'd'n 8

Sharp Nurse — 105

B. f (1971), by Piercer—Special Nurse, by New Moon.
Breeder, J. E. Hughes (Md.). 1974 5 1 0 0 $2,520
Owner, J. E. Hughes. Trainer, G. L. Ballenger. $7,000 1973 10 M 2 1 $2,344

Feb27-745Bow 6 f 1:13⅗ft 26 110 5²¾ 4⁴½ 3⁵½ 5¹² Jamtg'dW4 6000 63 B'c'pGary119 Br'veTonto F'rM'reY'rs 7
Feb 9-742Bow 6 f 1:13⅕sy 8½ 110‡ 8⁵ 10⁹½ 10¹¹ 8⁸ Miner'niF2 5000 69 ⒻDaringDiamond119 TreeL'ce Nad'te 12
Feb 4-743Bow 6 f 1:13⅖ft 18 110‡ 7⁸½ 7⁷ 7⁹ 5⁶¼ Min'viniF2 7000 70 ⒻM[illegible]Qu'n[illegible]14 In[illegible]B. C[illegible]p'rM[illegible]k't 10
Jan22-744Bow 6 f 1:12⅘m 21 108* 6⁹½ 6¹⁵ 6¹⁴ 6¹⁸ Min'niF5 12500 61 M[illegible]13 N[illegible]ght [illegible]k'r 6
Jan11-741Bow 6 f 1:16⅕m 6½ 112‡ 6⁶¾ 6⁷½ 5⁵½ 1nk Min'niF6 M7500 62 ⒻSh[illegible]rpNurse1[illegible] [illegible]sNadia A[illegible]ulon 12
Dec20-731Lrl 7 f 1:29⅕sl 7½ 112‡ 6⁴ 5⁹ 5¹⁰ 5⁶¼ M'niF12 M5000 59 Ⓕ[illegible]ceWh'l 119 S't'n'sSq'w E[illegible]ma'sL'y 12
Dec 7-732Lrl 1 1:40⅕ft 21 108‡ 8⁶½ 9¹⁰ 10¹⁴ 11²⁰ Min'niF1 M9500 52 Sam 'N H'bie120 V't'r'sD'cer B'c'pG'y 12
Nov29-731Lrl 7 f 1:28⅕gd 4 110‡ 6⁹½ 4⁴½ 2³ 2³½ Min'niF4 M5000 67 C'zinsJimAndy120 Sh'pN'se L'stS'nd'l 12
Oct31-731Lrl 7 f 1:28⅖gd 7½ 110‡ 7⁵¾ 5⁷½ 4⁵½ 2¹½ M'iniF11 M5000 67 F'rM'reY'rs120 Sh'pN'rse D'ntotheS'a 12
March 16 Bow 4f ft :50bg **March 12 Bow 4f ft :51⅖b** **March 5 Bow 3f ft :37⅗b**

(cont'd on next page)

I'm Diana 114 Ch. f (1971), by I'm Nashville—Brutessa, by Dear Brutus.
Breeder, R. R. Bailey (Va.). 1974 5 0 0 0 $672
Owner, C S W Stable. Trainer, K. T. Leatherbury. $7,500 1973 6 1 0 0 $2,32[illegible]

Mar 7-746Bow 1 1/16 1:48⅕sft 6½ 109 31½ 2½ 45½ 57½ WalshE4 7500 59 ArloFleet112 PrinceSwept NoNoAlvin 10
Feb26-744Bow 1 1/16 1:50⅖sft 7¾ 109 43 3nk 21 41 WalshE4 7500 55 PrinceSwept114 Br'kmoore CafeNoir 7
Feb14-747Bow 1 1/16 1:49⅕sft 12 109 912 88½ 67 68¾ WalshE5 11500 53 I'm InNeed113 DabneyRoad NineP'nts 9
Feb 1-743Bow 6 f 1:13⅘sft 7 112 813 812 711 73½ WalshE7 9500 70 ⒻS'[illegible] FriskieBillie 8
Jan15-745Bow 7 f 1:26⅖sft 17 114 43½ 56½ 64½ 44¾ LeeT6 c7500 68 ⒻDaringDiam'd114 InkyB. C'perM'k't 10
Dec 5-731Lrl 6 f 1:14 sy 3½ 119 54¼ 42 12 13 C'm'oG4 M5000 79 ⒻI'mDiana119 PalaceWhirl Sec'dSea 12
Nov 5-734Lrl 6 f 1:14⅗sy 16 112 66½ 69½ 68½ 65¼ Fel'noBM7 5000 71 ⒻEvNCh't108 Reb'lM'l Q'nOfTheBB's 7
Oct17-733Bow 7 f 1:26 ft 33 117 86 79½ 79¾ 78¼ McC'nG5 M5500 64 Whispinder115 Alson TighmansIsle 11
Oct 4-731Bow 6 f 1:14⅕sft 30 119 87 87¾ 66½ 66¼ McC'nG6 M5000 66 ⒻNadeete 119 Tree Lace Silver Jay 12

53 52 53

Gala Image 114 B. f (1971), by Dancer's Image—Brow Brook, by Lurullah.
Breeder, Glade Valley Farms, Inc. (Md.). 1974 4 0 0 0 (—)
Owner, Gert Leviton. Trainer, B. P. Bond. $7,500 1973 9 1 1 1 $4,910

Mar 5-748Bow 7 f 1:25⅖sft 41 112 37½ 412 814 818 Felic'oBM8 Alw 60 ⒻEngag'd120 C'tiousMill St'tingVix'n 9
Feb 5-748Bow 7 f 1:23⅗fr 4¾ 112 87½ 910 1016 1019 HawleyS3 Alw 68 ⒻEsth'rDin'h112 B'ldSq'w L'dyM'rine 10
Jan29-747Bow 6 f 1:14⅕sm 27 115 88½ 98½ 75¼ 53½ McH'ueDG5 Alw 68 ⒻD'cePrize120 M'sOverdrive Eth'rD'h 10
Jan 7-747Bow 6 f 1:13 gd 48 116 97 75½ 54 57 McCarr'nG6 Alw 71 ⒻRe[illegible] M'Ov'r'e 12
Dec 5-737Lrl 6 f 1:12⅖sy 8¾ 115 1113 1020 1014 107¼ HawleyS11 Alw 80 ⒻK[illegible] Advis[illegible] Qu'n 11
Nov 3-735Lrl 7 f 1:26⅕sft 2¼ 114 31 42 56 510 Feli'noBM7 Alw 70 ⒻNoiseD 114 B[illegible] 7
Oct26-737Lrl 6 f 1:11⅗sft 14 115 84 73½ 66½ 65¼ Felic'oBM6 Alw 86 ⒻNevsari 112 Maid At Sea Brash 10
Oct15-734Bow 7 f 1:25 ft 2¾ 119 52¼ 42 33½ 32¾ Bra'leVJr4 Alw 77 ⒻGroan 119 PleasureChest GalaImage 7

March 14 Bow 5f ft 1:04b March 2 Bow 3f ft :37⅗b Feb 25 Bow 6f ft 1:15⅘b

40 30 66

Copper Market 107 Ch. f (1971), by Hurry to Market—Azurita, by Rico Monte.
Breeder, W. H. Morgan (Ky.). 1974 8 0 0 2 $2,238
Owner, Larking Hill Farm. Trainer, E. D. Gaudet. $7,500 1973 10 1 1 0 $2,972

Mar 4-745Bow 6 f 1:12⅖sft 50 112 813 818 713 710 BlackAS5 9500 69 ⒻFriskieBillie114 M'sTid'lW've Ch'te 8
Feb20-747Bow 7 f 1:27⅘sft 23 112 68½ 66¾ 67 75 WrightDR1 9500 61 ⒻLibertine 117 FriskieBillie HiDottie 9
Feb13-743Bow 7 f 1:27⅘sft 4 113 910 85½ 64½ 51¾ Br'leVJr2 c7000 64 ⒻChesapeakeBay1[illegible] HelloKi 10
Feb 4-743Bow 6 f 1:13⅖sft 3¼ 112 1012 97½ 46 32½ Br'aleVJr6 7000 73 ⒻM[illegible]'n114 C'p[illegible]'t 10
Jan25-744Bow 6 f 1:14⅗sm 3¾ 112 711 710 58 42¼ Bra'leVJr1 7000 68 ⒻRebelMill114 [illegible]lW've InkyB. 7
Jan15-745Bow 7 f 1:26⅖sft 2¾ 114 75¼ 67 43½ 34 Br'c'leVJr4 7000 69 ⒻDaringDiam'd114 InkyB. C'perM'k't 10
Jan 8-744Bow 1 1/16 1:49 gd 2¼ ▲114 1h 41¾ 34½ 45½ BlackAS3 7500 58 DabneyR'd114 Bundy'sBoy Brookm're 6
Jan 3-745Bow 6 f 1:14⅘sm 3-2e▲114 97¾ 77½ 56 42 BlackAS8 7500 67 ⒻLy'sDec'n114 Maryl'dQ'n F'kieBillie 12

March 14 Bow 5f ft 1:06⅖b Feb 28 Bow 5f ft 1:06⅖b Feb 1 Bow 4f ft :50⅘b

49 56 51

Better Reason 114 Gr. f (1971), by Turn To Reason—Mabe Trader, by War Admiral.
Br., Mr. & Mrs. C. O. Goldsmith (Md.). 1974 3 M 0 0 $642
Owner, C. O. Goldsmith. Trainer, J. P. Considine. $7,500 1973 3 M 0 0 (—)

Mar 1-745Bow 6 f 1:12⅖sft 29 112 46 65¼ 1013 1016 StovallR7 7500 65 HelloKim109 Ch's'p'keB'g'ye D'lHimln 10
Feb 4-743Bow 6 f 1:13⅖sft 5 107* 32½ 42 35 45 Lindb'gG7 7500 71 ⒻM'ryl'ndQu'n114 InkyB. C'p[illegible] 10
Jan21-747Bow 6 f 1:13⅖sm 55 104* 53½ 43¼ 53¾ 44¼ Lindb'gG10 7500 72 Noth[illegible]es 11[illegible] F[illegible]e 10
Dec29-732Lrl 6 f 1:17 sl 23 111* 85½ 66¼ 1014 1013 L'b'gG3 M10500 51 Starb[illegible] TopO[illegible]ome[illegible]it 12
Dec 6-734Lrl 6 f 1:13 gd 8e 119 76½ 69½ 710 917 StovallR6 Mdn 67 ⒻDance Prize 119 Sailingon Nalgana 9
Nov14-733Lrl 6 f 1:13 ft 31 116 44 56½ 56½ 710 StovallR6 8000 74 ⒻRus'eChris118 C'nt'rb'ry E'ma'sL'dy 12

March 16 Pim 4f ft :50⅘b Feb 24 Bow 6f ft 1:16⅖b Feb 16 Bow 4f ft :50b

33 45 62

Scuttled 107 B. f (1971), by Salerno—Surfboard Betty, by Bold Commander.
Breeder, C. N. K. Church (Va.). 1974 4 M 0 0 $600
Owner, Mrs. R. Hutchinson. Trainer, C. R. Lewis. $7,500 1973 2 M 0 0 (—)

Mar 2-745Bow 6 f 1:11⅗sft 10 119 99¼ 912 819 922 Hinoj'aH12 Mdn 63 ⒻMamaloi119 SallyLov SirloinTip 12
Feb23-743Bow 7 f 1:27⅗sft 14 119 51¾ 3½ 52¾ 42¼ Hino'osaH9 Mdn 65 ⒻEn[illegible]'d119 High[illegible] Top o[illegible] 12
Feb 6-745Bow 7 f 1:24⅗fr 15 119 4nk 52¾ 42 46¼ Hinoj'saH2 Mdn 76 ⒻH'[illegible] T'p o[illegible] Fr[illegible]Wit 12
Jan 7-743Bow 6 f 1:12⅕sgd 11 119 75 811 814 819 Hino'saH3 Mdn 63 ⒻHea[illegible]ful119 [illegible] Heylaira 11
Dec28-734Lrl 7 f 1:31⅖shy 7¼ 119 1h 31 47 716 Hino'aH12 Mdn 38 ⒻBrightB'ndary119 Donetta Levanna 12
Dec 5-734Lrl 6 f 1:12⅘sy 37 119 31½ 1h 1h 55 Hin'j'saH2 Mdn 81 ⒻCauti'sMill 119 D'n'ta Castil'nRose 12

Feb 21 Lrl 3f ft :37b Jan 30 Lrl 5f m 1:06b

33 52 47

Jorak **112** **B. f (1971), by Bold Ambition—Divali, by Royal Note.**
Breeder, J. Krupnik (Md.). **1974 4 1 0 0 $2,652**
Owner, J. Krupnik. Trainer, J. J. Lenzini, Sr. $7,000 **1973 1 M 0 0 (——)**

Mar 7-74 2Bow	6 f 1:13⅕ft	4	115	$1^{1\frac{1}{2}}$	1^{3}	$1^{1\frac{1}{2}}$	1^{2}	KurtzJ4	M5000	77	Jorak 115 Black Mo A Poppy Formal	12
Feb13-74 3Bow	7 f 1:27⅘ft	39	105**	$8^{8\frac{3}{4}}$	$9^{6\frac{1}{2}}$	$7^{6\frac{1}{2}}$	7^{6}	McC'onCJ7	7500	60	Ⓕ Ch[illegible]akeB[illegible]y114[illegible]kyB. [illegible]	10
Feb 4-74 3Bow	6 f 1:13⅖ft	6¼	112	5^{3}	$5^{3\frac{1}{2}}$	6^{8}	$6^{7\frac{1}{2}}$	KurtzJ9	7000	68	Ⓕ M[illegible]ryl'[illegible]dQu'n[illegible]B. C'pp[illegible]M[illegible]t	10
Jan11-74 1Bow	6 f 1:16⅕sm	5	119	$4^{2\frac{1}{2}}$	2^{1}	2^{1}	$4^{2\frac{1}{4}}$	KurtzJ11	M7500	60	Ⓕ S[illegible]Nurse11[illegible]Nadia[illegible]mulon	12
Dec19-73 2Lrl	6 f 1:12⅖gd	24	119	8^{6}	8^{8}	9^{14}	9^{16}	KurtzJ5	Mdn	71	Ⓕ R'd'sL'nd'g119 Cl'rM'd'te Ma!'yM'd	11

March 16 Lrl 5f gd 1:03b **March 4 Bow 5f ft 1:02⅖b** **Feb 27 Bow 5f ft 1:02b**

Since the meeting began on March 18, almost every race at Pimlico was won by a speed horse who was able to get to the inside part of the track. The bias was so powerful that horses who did not have early speed or inside post positions could be eliminated almost automatically.

The fillies who drew the three inside post positions in this six-furlong race all have early speed and thus merit consideration. Annie Oak has been racing against males in allowance company at Charles Town, but the allowance tag is a bit deceptive. The horses in those fields probably weren't worth much more than $5000, and Annie Oak hasn't been able to win against them.

Glittering Gold has not run any glittering figures; her best effort is a 58. But she is lightly raced and is trained by the astute King T. Leatherbury, so she seems eligible for improvement.

Tree Lace has the best figure in this field, a 67, but her overall record is less than inspiring. She ran this good figure when she was able to break loose to a clear early lead, but there is no guarantee she will be able to do so again today, with two speed horses inside her. Tree Lace also seems to be developing sucker-horse tendencies, having finished second or third five times in a row without being able to win, even in $5000 company.

Since none of the horses favored by the track bias has awesome credentials, we must consider the other possible contenders in the field. Gala Image displayed some promise early in her career, but her form has deteriorated badly and she lost her last two starts by margins of 18 and 19 lengths. A drop in class from allowance company doesn't figure to help her enough to win today.

I'm Diana, the other half of Leatherbury's entry, has shown early speed in route races. But her figures are poor and her previous form in sprints suggests that she will be trying to rally from far behind — a nearly impossible task on this speed-favoring track.

Jorak has speed and opened a clear early lead to beat cheap maidens in her last start. But she will be severely

SEVENTH RACE Pim March 20, 1974 **6 FURLONGS. (1:09⅕). CLAIMING. Purse $5,500. Fillies. 3-year-olds. Weight, 122 lbs. Non-winners of two races since Feb. 7 allowed 3 lbs.; a race, 5 lbs.; a race since Jan. 30, 8 lbs. Claiming price, $7,500; for each $250 to $7,000, allowed 1 lb. (Races where entered for $6,000 or less not considered.)**
Value to winner $3,300; second, $1,210; third, $660; fourth, $330. Mutuel Pool, $49,373. Exacta Pool, $83,671.

Last Raced	Horse	EqtAWt	PP	St	¼	½	Str	Fin	Jockeys	Owners	Odds to $1
3-11-74^7 ShD^4	Annie Oak	3 114	1	4	1^1	1^2	1^3	1^4	GMcCarron†	Eleanor M Casey	29.30
3-11-74^6 Bow^2	Tree Lace	b3 114	3	3	$2\frac{1}{2}$	2^h	2^1	2no	GCusimano	E J Wirth	2.[illegible]0
3- 7-74^6 Bow^5	I'm Diana	b3 114	6	9	11	$7\frac{1}{2}$	$4^{1\frac{1}{2}}$	3^1	AAgnello	C S W Stable	a-3.90
3- 7-74^2 Bow^1	Jorak	b3 112	11	5	3^1	3^4	3^3	$4^{1\frac{3}{4}}$	JKurtz	J Krupnik	4.50
3-11-74^6 Bow^5	Daring Diamond	3 115	4	11	9^h	$10^{1\frac{1}{2}}$	$6^{1\frac{1}{2}}$	$5^{1\frac{3}{4}}$	JDavidson	J R Whorl	6.00
3- 4-74^5 Bow^7	Copper Market	b3 107	8	7	$10^{2\frac{1}{2}}$	8^1	$7\frac{1}{2}$	$6\frac{3}{4}$	CJMcCarron^7	Larking Hill Farm	12.30
2-27-74^5 Bow^5	Sharp Nurse	b3 105	5	10	7^h	9^h	$8^{1\frac{1}{2}}$	7^3	SGraham^7	J E Hughes	54.20
3- 2-74^5 Bow^9	Scuttled	3 114	10	1	$4\frac{1}{2}$	$6\frac{1}{2}$	$9^{1\frac{1}{2}}$	8^{nk}	HHinojosa†	Mrs R Hutchinson	11.30
3- 1-74^5 Bow^{10}	Better Reason	3 114	9	2	$6^{1\frac{1}{2}}$	4^1	$5\frac{1}{2}$	$9^{2\frac{3}{4}}$	WJPassmore	C O Goldsmith	50.40
3- 5-74^8 Bow^8	Gala Image	b3 114	7	8	8^h	11	11	10^1	BMFeliciano	Gert Leviton	6.50
3- 8-74^3 Bow^1	Glittering Gold	3 114	2	6	$5^{1\frac{1}{2}}$	5^h	10^1	11	EWalsh	F D Vechery	a-3.90

Coupled: a-I'm Diana and Glittering Gold. †Seven pounds apprentice allowance waived.
OFF AT 3:56 EDT. Start good. Won driving. Time, :24, :48⅕, 1:01, 1:14⅖. Track fast.

$2 Mutuel Prices:			
2-ANNIE OAK	**60.60**	**15.80**	**6.80**
3-TREE LACE		**4.40**	**3.00**
1A-I'M DIANA (a-Entry)			**3.20**

$2 EXACTA (2-3) PAID $152.00

B. f, by Rambunctious—Activation, by Prove It. Trainer, Marlene M. Croy. Bred by Mrs. F. Bierer (Md.).

ANNIE OAK sprinted to a clear lead leaving the backstretch and gradually extended her advantage thereafter under vigorous handling. TREE LACE raced in closest attendance under a hustling ride and continued gamely to hold on for the place. I'M DIANA lodged her bid from the outside entering the stretch and finished with good courage. JORAK gradually weakened. DARING DIAMOND passed tired horses. SCUTTLED had only brief early foot. GALA IMAGE was through early, as was GLITTERING GOLD.

Overweight—Daring Diamond, 3 pounds.
Corrected weight—Daring Diamond, 112.
Scuttled claimed by Spartan Stable, trainer A. J. Hemmerick.
Claiming Prices (in order of finish)—$7500, 7500, 7500, 7000, 7000, 7500, 7000, 7500, 7500, 7500, 7500.

handicapped by her outside post today. With several speed horses inside her, it seems unlikely that she could break on top and get to the rail.

This race, like the majority of races, is one in which no horse seems clearly superior. If it were run five times, it might produce five different winners. But it is being run today over a track with a powerful bias, and since none of the horses has any great edge in ability over his rivals, the bias is likely to determine the outcome. The speed horses breaking from the three inside posts — Annie Oak, Glittering Gold, and Tree Lace — are the ones who will be helped by the bias. A logical way to play this race would be to combine these three horses in the exacta and hope for the best.

Annie Oak stayed on the lightning-fast rail from start to finish and won easily at 29-to-1 odds. Tree Lace, true to her sucker-horse tendencies, ran second all the way and completed a $152 exacta. The surprise of the race was I'm Diana, who managed to rally in the middle of the track and finish third. This strong performance against the track bias indicated that she was in sharp form; I'm Diana went on to win her next start and paid $8.40. When Annie Oak ran again, without a track bias to help her, she tired as usual and finished far out of the money.

7th Saratoga

AUGUST 25, 1973

6½ FURLONGS (chute). (1:15⅕). Sixty-ninth running HOPEFUL. SCALE WEIGHTS. $75,000 added: 2-year-olds. By subscription of $150 each, which shall accompany the nomination; $375 to pass the entry box; $375 to start, with $75,000 added. The added money and all fees to be divided: 60% to the winner, 22% to second, 12% to third and 6% to fourth. Weight, 121 lbs. Trophies will be presented to the winning owner, trainer and jockey. Closed with 25 nominations.

Take By Storm **121** **B. c (1971), by Pronto—Great Achievement, by Bold Ruler.**
Breeder, O. M. Phipps (Ky.). **1973 . . 5 1 1 1 $10,080**
Owner, O. M. Phipps. Trainer, R. Laurin.

Date/Race	Dist.	Time	Cond.	PP	Wt.	1st call	2nd call	Str.	Fin.	Jockey	Class	Speed	Finishers	Field
Aug11-73^{2}Sar	6 f	1:11	ft	3	119	1^{h}	2^{h}	1^{3}	$16\frac{1}{2}$	TurcotteR^{1}	Mdn	85	TakeByStorm 119 Hilo TheScotsman	12
Jly 31-73^{1}Sar	6 f	1:11⅗	ft	$5\frac{3}{4}$	119	$5^{2\frac{3}{4}}$	4^{3}	4^{2}	2^{nk}	Pin'yLJr^{10}	Mdn	82	P[illegible]son119 [illegible]t'm [illegible]'sP[illegible]	11
Jly 4-73^{3}Aqu	5½ f	1:04⅗	ft	5	118	3^{2}	$3^{1\frac{1}{2}}$	3^{2}	$3^{3\frac{1}{2}}$	MapleE^{6}	Mdn	86	M[illegible] Lea[illegible]as[illegible] TakeB[illegible]t[illegible]rm	8
Jun14-73^{3}Bel	5½ f	1:05	ft	7	117	3^{2}	3^{1}	$2^{1\frac{1}{2}}$	3^{4}	VasquezJ^{9}	Mdn	90	Ev[illegible]d117 D[illegible]g Ta[illegible]	9
Jun 6-73^{4}Bel	5½ f	1:05⅖	ft	$3\frac{1}{4}$	117	3^{2}	2^{1}	2^{2}	$4^{7\frac{1}{2}}$	VasquezJ^{4}	Mdn	84	Gr'nGamb's117 DingD'gB'll OnHisOwn	9

95 88 80

Aug 21 Sar 4f ft :48b **Aug 17 Sar 4f ft :47⅖h** **July 26 Bel 4f ft :48⅖b**

(cont'd on next page)

Gusty O'Shay **121** Ch. g (1971), by Rose Argent—Stormy O'Shay, by Restless Wind.
Br., Mrs. G. T. Hopkins & Lola Peters (Md.1973.. 6 3 1 1 $ 13,292
Owner, Mrs. G. T. Hopkins. Trainer, H. E. Johnson.
Aug 6-737Sar 6 f 1:11 ft 20 117 14 14 1½ 2¾ Kot'koR7 AlwS 84 Az Igazi 117 Gusty O'Shay Lakeville 8
Jly 18-738Del 5½ f 1:05⅘ft 6¼ 119 13 1½ 15 16 Kot'koR8 15000 89 GustyO'Sh'y119 Anot'rEpis'de B'dF'ble 9
Jun13-737ShD 3½ f :41 ft 8-5 ▲118 5 11 12 15 EspinosaV8 Alw 90 GustyO'Sh'y118 Red'sBl'sing S'mC'rd 8
Jun 6-733Del 5 f 1:00⅖ft 42 120 13 13 13 13¼ Kot'oR11 M7500 87 GustyO'Sh'y120 B'dFable G'd Lit'leG'l 12
May24-734ShD 5½ f 1:10⅕sy 6¼ 118 611 612 613 318 Esp'saV5 M5000 57 SoftN't115 P'lh'm'sPride G'styO'Sh'y 6
Aug 22 Sar 4f ft :50b

100

Green Gambados **121** B. c (1971), by Swaps—Cargreen, by Turn-to.
Breeder, Harbor View Farm (Fla.). 1973.. 6 2 1 0 $14,558
Owner, Harbor View Farm. Trainer, J. W. Jacobs.
Aug15-737Sar 6 f 1:10⅗ft 4 121 21 22 43½ 47 Tur'tteR1 ScwS 80 AzIgazi121 Prince ofReason Totheend 6
Aug 7-735Sar 6 f 1:11⅖ft 7-5 ▲118 31 1h 1h 1h TurcotteR4 Alw 83 GreenG'mbados118 Totheend Pl'gAl'g 6
Jly 7-734Aqu 5½ f 1:04⅕ft 5½ 119 64¼ 45½ 46 24 BaezaB5 Alw 88 C'p'r'teH'dache119 GreenG'b's Ham 7
Jun30-734Aqu 5½ f 1:04 ft 2½ ▲119 87¾ 67½ 57½ 54 Cast'daM7 Alw 89 AzIgazi117 Pl'sC'dC'p'r'teH'che 9
Jun 6-734Bel 5½ f 1:05⅖ft 3½ 117 53½ 42½ 32 13 Cast'daM5 Mdn 92 GreenGamb's117 DingD'gB'll OnHisOwn 9
May16-733Bel 5½ f 1:05 ft 3½ 117 63¾ 64 65½ 65½ VasquezJ7 Mdn 88 R'le ofS'cc'ss117 Tr'p't'rSw'n E'rF'd 9
Aug 24 Sar 3f ft :36⅖b Aug 21 Sar 5f ft :59⅘h Aug 13 Sar 4f gd :48⅗h

83 93 86

Sea Dee **121** B. c (1971), by Crackpot—Acean Love, by Panacean.
Breeder, C. D. Morgan (Va.). 1973 4 2 1 0 $13,320
Owner, Mrs. C. D. Morgan. Trainer, L. S. Barrera.
Aug16-735Sar 6½ f 1:18⅘ft 3½e 119 11½ 11½ 13 1¾ Cast'daM7 Alw 86 Sea Dee 119 Mr. Sad Please Succeed 7
Aug 8-734Sar 5½ f 1:06 ft 5¾ 119 1½ 11½ 11 12½ Cast'daM8 Mdn 87 SeaDee119 RedSparkle Pl'sure 9
Jly 26-732Aqu 5½ f 1:04⅖ft 3½ 118 3½ 1h 2h 21½ Cast'daM8 Mdn 89 LordFo'st'r111 SeaDee SpinPl's'e 10
Jly 18-733Aqu 5½ f 1:05⅖ft 5 118 1½ 1h 1h 4½ Cast'daM6 Mdn 85 Pla'sAce118 ShutUp andD'l L'dFor't'r 11
Aug 23 Sar trt 4f ft :49b July 17 Bel trt 3f ft :36h July 6 Bel trt 4f m :50b

84 83 85

Az Igazi **121** Dk. b. or br. c (1971), by Time Tested—Fashionably, by Bald Eagle.
Breeder, B. P. Walden (Ky.). 1973.. 7 4 1 2 $52,165
Owner, J. R. Straus. Trainer, H. C. Pardue.
Aug15-737Sar 6 f 1:10⅗ft 3-5 ▲121 11 12 13 12 Ve'ziaM5 ScwS 87 AzIgazi121 Prince ofReason Totheend 6
Aug 6-737Sar 6 f 1:11 ft 6-5 ▲117 24 24 21½ 1¾ VenziaM5 AlwS 85 Az Igazi 117 Gusty O'Shay Lakeville 8
Jly 27-737Aqu 5½ f 1:03⅗ft 11 117 1½ 11 1h 2½ V'n'ziaM3 AlwS 94 RaiseA Cup120 AzIgazi Big Latch 8
Jun30-734Aqu 5½ f 1:04 ft 2½ 117 11½ 1½ 11½ 11½ VeneziaM1 Alw 93 AzIgazi117 Pl'sC'dC'p'r'teH'dch 9
Jun18-733Aqu 5½ f 1:04⅕ft 3¾ 117 11 1½ 12 15 V'ziaM1 M35000 92 AzIgazi117 MauiA. Lakeville 10
Jun 6-733Bel 5½ f 1:05⅕ft 4¼ 115 2h 2h 22 35 V'ziaM2 M35000 88 CorporateHeadache115 Ham AzIgazi 10
May10-733Aqu 5 f :59 sy 2½ 117 33 33 43½ 32 Uss'yR7 M27500 88 Flip Sal 117 Mexican Onion Az Igazi 10
Aug 21 Sar 5f ft 1:00b Aug 12 Sar 5f sy 1:01⅗h Aug 3 Sar 5f sy 1:03b

100 102 103

Prince of Reason **121** Dk. b. or br. c (1971), by Hail to Reason—Home by Dark, by Hill Prince.
Breeder, J. R. Gaines, J. J. Houlahan & 1973 6 1 1 3 $16,456
D. A. Headley (Ky.).
Owner, Saron Stable. Trainer, S. E. Veitch.
Aug15-737Sar 6 f 1:10⅗ft 4 121 53 54 23 22 C'd'oAJr3 ScwS 85 AzIgazi121 Prince ofReason Totheend 6
Aug 6-737Sar 6 f 1:11 ft 14 117 710 79 46½ 43½ Vel'q'zJ6 AlwS 81 Az Igazi 117 Gusty O'Shay Lakeville 8
Jly 31-731Sar 6 f 1:11⅗ft 2 ▲119 31½ 31½ 2½ 1nk C'deroAJr1 Mdn 82 PrinceofR'son119 ForeyStm Lord 11
Jly 14-732Aqu 6 f 1:11⅘ft 2e▲113* 63¾ 44½ 34½ 31¼ WallisT6 Mdn 83 WithApp118 Ch'rtoto Pr'ceofR'n 11
Jun20-733Aqu 5½ f 1:05⅖ft 2½ 117 87½ 77 66½ 33½ MapleE8 Mdn 82 Frozen117 Guider'sG ld Prince ofR'son 10
Jun14-734Bel 5½ f 1:04⅖ft 12 117 97¾ 55½ 53½ 32¼ MapleE7 Mdn 95 Ham 117 Cannonade Prince of Reason 10
Aug 24 Sar 3f ft :37⅕b Aug 20 Sar 5f ft :59⅘h Aug 14 Sar 3f ft :37b

95 93 89

Totheend **121** Dk. b. or br. c (1971), by Duel—Lady Patience, by Baybrook.
Breeder, Dr. Wallace S. Karutz (Fla.). 1973 8 1 2 1 $17,983
Owner, Mrs. M. Jolley. Trainer, L. Jolley.
Aug15-737Sar 6 f 1:10⅗ft 7¾ 121 31½ 32½ 33½ 37 Pin'yLJr2 ScwS 80 AzIgazi121 Prince ofReason Totheend 6
Aug 7-735Sar 6 f 1:11⅖ft 2¼ 118 2½ 2h 2h 2h PincayLJr3 Alw 83 GreenG'mbados118 Totheend Pl'gAl'g 6
Jly 27-737Aqu 5½ f 1:03⅗ft 17 114 74½ 86½ 711 710 MapleE1 AlwS 85 RaiseA Cup120 AzIgazi Big Latch 8
Jly 9-737Aqu 5½ f 1:05 ft 8½ 116 1h 1h 1h 2nk MapleE3 AlwS 88 WhoDuzzit 121 Totheend Sixsie 4
Jun13-738Mth 5½ f 1:05 ft 54 114 41 42¾ 41¾ 43 Barr'raC5 AlwS 89 WhoDuzzit116 IrishStudiant Pet Fox 7
May28-738Del 5½ f 1:04⅘sy 24 116 2½ 23 411 411 Impa'toJ7 AlwS 83 LoverJohn116 WhoDuzzit SharpVote 7
Apr19-733Aqu 5 f 1:00 ft 6 112* 23 22 22 1½ Cas'aK6 M30000 85 Totheend 112 Flip Sal Native Sea 7
Jan30-733Hia 3 f :33 ft 4 ▲120 12 131313 13¾ VasquezJ9 Mdn 87 NearGale120 H'ds'nC'ty Am'c'nMys'y 14
Aug 23 Sar 4f ft :48⅕h Aug 13 Sar 4f gd :49b July 24 Bel 3f ft :34⅗h

83 93 78

A handicapper studying the past performances for the Hopeful Stakes at Saratoga might conclude that Az Igazi was the logical favorite because of his consistently good figures. Gusty O'Shay was a contender, but he had weakened in his last start at six furlongs and now was running six and a half. Take By Storm and Prince of Reason had been improving steadily and would be helped by the longer distance of the Hopeful.

But any observant horseplayer would have to revise his analysis after he saw how the early races on the Saratoga program were run. The inside part of the track was like a paved highway; horses with speed on the rail were winning everything. In two races run before the Hopeful, horses who looked like cinches on paper couldn't even manage to finish in the money because they were breaking from the No. 6 post position.

The track bias would wreck Az Igazi's chances of winning America's most prestigious race for two-year-olds. Breaking from the No. 5 post position with several speed horses inside of him, he was not quite fast enough to get to the lead and get to the rail. He figured to be bogged down in the middle of the track for the whole race. Prince of Reason, a stretch runner in the No. 6 post, would be hurt even more by the condition of the track.

Take By Storm had the good fortune to draw the inside post position, but he doesn't have enough speed to get the lead. He will probably be on the rail, within striking distance, during the early stages of the Hopeful. But when he rallies, he may be forced to move to the outside for running room, and that will hurt his chances.

Gusty O'Shay, the Cinderella horse who started his career in $5000 maiden-claiming races, has blazing speed that none of his Hopeful rivals can match. He ran the first quarter of his most recent start in 21⅕ seconds. Gusty O'Shay should break quickly from the No. 2 post, hug the rail, and force the other horses to come outside him if they want to beat him.

Even if his credentials were modest, Gusty O'Shay might be a good longshot bet because of the track bias. But with a top figure along with the bias in his favor, he is clearly the horse to beat.

Gusty O'Shay went to the front, as expected, outrunning

SEVENTH RACE
Sar
August 25, 1973

6½ FURLONGS (chute). (1:15⅕). Sixty-ninth running HOPEFUL. SCALE WEIGHTS. $75,000 added. 2-year-olds. By subscription of $150 each, which shall accompany the nomination; $375 to pass the entry box; $375 to start, with $75,000 added. The added money and all fees to be divided: 60% to the winner, 22% to second, 12% to third and 6% to fourth. Weight, 121 lbs. Trophies will be presented to the winning owner, trainer and jockey. Closed with 25 nominations.

Value of race, $84,000. Value to winner $50,400; second, $18,480; third, $10,080; fourth, $5,040.
Mutuel Pool, $232,769. Off-track betting, $114,265.

Last Raced	Horse	EqtAWt	PP	St	¼	½	Str	Fin	Jockeys	Owners	Odds to $1
8- 6-73⁷ Sar²	Gusty O'Shay	b2 121	2	5	$1^{1\frac{1}{2}}$	$1^{\frac{1}{2}}$	$1^{1\frac{1}{2}}$	$1^{\frac{1}{2}}$	RKotenko	Mrs G T Hopkins	9.60
8-11-73² Sar¹	Take By Storm	2 121	1	7	4^{3}	3^{h}	$2^{\frac{1}{2}}$	$2^{2\frac{1}{2}}$	LPincayJr	O M Phipps	3.40
8-15-73⁷ Sar²	Prince of Reason	b2 121	6	1	6^{1}	6^{4}	$4^{\frac{1}{2}}$	$3^{2\frac{1}{2}}$	PAnderson	Saron Stable	4.30
8-16-73⁵ Sar¹	Sea Dee	2 121	4	3	2^{2}	2^{1}	3^{2}	$4^{2\frac{1}{4}}$	MCastaneda	Mrs C D Morgan	10.60
8-15-73⁷ Sar⁴	Green Gambados	b2 121	3	6	5^{1}	$5^{\frac{1}{2}}$	5^{1}	5^{3}	RTurcotte	Harbor View Farm	10.10
8-15-73⁷ Sar³	Totheend	b2 121	7	2	7	7	7	$6^{5\frac{1}{2}}$	JVelasquez	Mrs M Jolley	25.20
8-15-73⁷ Sar¹	Az Igazi	2 121	5	4	$3^{\frac{1}{2}}$	4^{3}	6^{3}	7	HGustines	J R Straus	1.00

Time, :22⅕, :45, 1:09⅘, 1:16⅖ (with wind in backstretch). Track fast.

$2 Mutuel Prices:			
2-GUSTY O'SHAY	21.20	7.00	4.80
1-TAKE BY STORM		5.60	4.20
6-PRINCE OF REASON			4.20

Ch. g, by Rose Argent—Stormy O'Shay, by Restless Wind. Trainer, H. E. Johnson. Bred by Mrs. G. T. Hopkins and Lola Peters (Md.).

IN GATE—4:48. OFF AT 4:48½ EASTERN DAYLIGHT TIME. Start good for all but AZ IGAZI. Won driving.

GUSTY O'SHAY, hustled to the front along the inside soon after the start, responded readily when challenged by SEA DEE midway of the turn, settled into the stretch with a clear lead while racing well out from the rail and was all out to turn back TAKE BY STORM. The latter, sent up along the rail after breaking slowly, was steadied along while continuing to save ground nearing the stretch, loomed boldly leaving the furlong grounds but wasn't good enough. PRINCE OF REASON, unhurried after breaking alertly, rallied leaving the turn and finished with good energy. SEA DEE prompted the pace, went after GUSTY O'SHAY approaching the stretch but gave way during the drive. GREEN GAMBADOS moved within striking distance after a half but lacked a further response. TOTHEEND was outrun after coming away in good order. AZ IGAZI stumbled following the start, recovered quickly to race forwardly to the stretch but had nothing left for the drive.

the other speed horses, Sea Dee and Az Igazi. But as he came into the stretch with a 1½-length lead, jockey Robert Kotenko unwisely allowed Gusty O'Shay to drift away from the rail. Laffit Pincay, Jr., saw the opening, drove Take By Storm along the inside, and got within a neck of the lead. Kotenko leaned to the left, trying to crowd and intimidate his rival, and Gusty O'Shay did the rest. He fought back gamely, held on to win by half a length, and paid a whopping $21.20.

9th Aqueduct

JULY 20, 1973

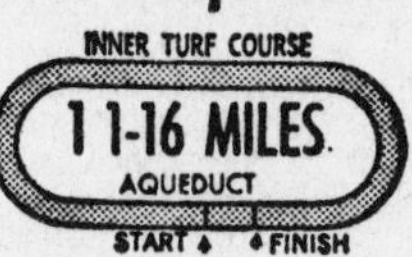

1$\frac{1}{16}$ MILES (inner turf). (1:41⅕). CLAIMING. Purse $9,000. Fillies and mares. 3-year-olds and upward. 3-year-olds, 114 lbs.; older, 122 lbs. Non-winners of two races at a mile or over since June 9 allowed 2 lbs.; two such races since May 14, 4 lbs.; one such race since July 2, 6 lbs. Claiming price, $12,500; 2 lbs. for each $1,000 to $10,500. (Races where entered for $9,000 or less not considered.) 3-year-olds which have never won at a mile or over allowed 3 lbs.; older, 5 lbs.

Pretty Butterfly — 100

B. f (1970), by Throne Room—Royal Lawn, by Royaumont.
Br., Clermont Farmsof New York (N. Y.). 1973 13 1 0 5 $6,960
Owner, Ges Stable. Trainer, J. Renick. $12,500

Jly 13-73^{4}Aqu	7 f 1:24⅘ft	21	114	7^6	7^6	6^9	$7^{7¼}$	G'tin'sH^{10}	15000	70	Ⓕ SelfDefense116 P'ficOc'n Gl'r'sA'f'r	11
Jly 3-73^{9}Aqu Ⓣ	1$\frac{1}{16}$ 1:46⅗fm	10	108*	3^3	$3^{1½}$	$5^{1½}$	3^2	Cast'daK^7	14000	71	Ⓕ M'sInt'n'ly105 D'pN'kline Pr'tyB'fly	8
Jun21-73^{1}Aqu Ⓣ	1 1:38⅕fm	10	108*	2^6	$3^{2½}$	$4^{3½}$	4^6	Cas'aK^{10}	15000	84	Ⓕ Tumb'gTo113 OurBestG'l MissN'b'y	10
Jun 4-73^{2}Bel Ⓣ	1$\frac{1}{16}$ 1:43⅗fm	6¼	113	5^5	4^3	$5^{8½}$	5^{11}	Turc'teR^6	16000	73	Ⓕ JustC'rious113 FirstPitch T'blingTo	10
May 8-73^{9}Aqu	1 1:38⅗ft	5½	114	$1^{½}$	2^h	$2^{1½}$	$3^{3½}$	Turc'teR^4	14000	70	Ⓕ M.S.Star118 Ov'dueM'gic Pr'tyB'fly	6
May 4-73^{2}Aqu	6 f 1:12⅘ft	6¼	116	7^{10}	7^9	$7^{4¾}$	$3^{½}$	C'd'oAJr^1	10000	78	Ⓕ G'aBeF't116 D'l'gTime Pr'tyB'terfly	7
Apr25-73^{1}Aqu	7 f 1:25 ft	12	114	4^2	5^4	$3^{6½}$	$3^{5¼}$	TurcotteR^2	9500	71	Ⓕ MissCoh'n111 M.S.St'r Pr'tyB't'rfly	9
Mar30-73^{8}Aqu	1 1:39⅕ft	7½	114	$1^{1½}$	2^h	$2^{½}$	$3^{2¼}$	TurcotteR^1	7500	69	Ⓕ SwiftSky116 AnneF. Pr'tyButterfly	7
Mar16-73^{2}Aqu	6 f 1:11⅗ft	6½	116	3^7	3^{11}	3^{12}	$5^{9¾}$†	TurcotteR^7	7000	75	Ⓕ K'pthetune116 St'b'ryR'y'l G'aBeF't	8
†Dead heat.												
Mar 7-73^{1}Aqu	6 f 1:13⅗gd	15	114	4^2	3^1	1^4	1^5	S't'goA^2	M5000	75	Pr'tyB't'rfly114 TieItUp Ab'sIrishR'se	13

June 19 Bel trt 4f ft :50⅗b May 29 Bel trt 4f sy :51b

Family Princess * — 103

Ch. f (1970), by First Family—Gala Girl, by Prince John.
Breeder, A. Rosoff (Fla.). 1973 11 1 2 1 $8,100
Owner, M. Gache. Trainer, J. T. Diangelo. $12,500 1972 17 1 3 6 $13,220

Jly 13-73^{4}Aqu	7 f 1:24⅘ft	30	116	11^{16}	11^{15}	10^{13}	$9^{8½}$	Bel'nteE^2	15000	68	Ⓕ SelfDefense116 P'ficOc'n Gl'r'sA'f'r	11
Jun12-73^{8}Bel	1$\frac{1}{16}$ 1:44⅕ft	12	118	9^{11}	$9^{9¼}$	$8^{8¾}$	$7^{7¼}$	Vel'q'zJ^1	16000	75	Ⓕ I'pieE'p'r'r113 R'y'l Gig O'rd'eM'gic	9
Jun 4-73^{2}Bel Ⓣ	1$\frac{1}{16}$ 1:43⅗fm	5½	111*	9^{11}	$9^{6½}$	9^{17}	9^{17}	WallisT^3	16000	67	Ⓕ JustC'rious113 FirstPitch T'blingTo	10
May11-73^{6}Aqu Ⓣ	1$\frac{1}{16}$ 1:48 yl	5¾	114	6^6	5^4	4^3	$8^{4¼}$	Arel'noJ^4	19000	62	Ⓕ Gr'nysD'l'g113 S'syC'ne Cr'meRh'da	9
Apr27-73^{5}Aqu	1 1:38⅘sy	9-5	▲118	$4^{4½}$	$1^{½}$	1^h	$2^{1½}$	C'd'oAJr^2	15000	71	Ⓕ M'tr'lC'se116 F'yPr'c's D'pN'ckl'ne	7
Apr21-73^{3}Aqu	6 f 1:12⅖ft	9-5	▲118	$5^{7½}$	$6^{7¾}$	$4^{7½}$	$3^{2¾}$	C'd'oAJr^4	17000	78	Ⓕ Cr'n ofSt'rs107 C'qu'r'gM's F'yPr's	7
Apr13-73^{6}Aqu	1 1:39 ft	7½	114	$7^{3¼}$	4^3	$5^{5½}$	$5^{5¼}$	Arell'noJ^7	22500	67	Ⓕ St'fC'p'tit'n115 M'gicSt'y S'syCy'ne	11
Apr 5-73^{6}Aqu	1 1:39⅕gd	9-5	▲116	$1^{½}$	2^h	$1^{½}$	$1^{¾}$	C'd'oAJr^9	16000	71	Ⓕ F'milyPr'n's116 D't'dL've D'pN'kl'e	9
Mar28-73^{4}Aqu	6 f 1:12 ft	3¾	116	6^5	5^5	3^3	2^3	C'd'oAJr^1	16000	80	Ⓕ P'cificOc'n116 F'milyPr'c's Adv'c're	8
Mar20-73^{6}Aqu	6½ f 1:20 ft	3¼	116	$7^{7½}$	$6^{5¾}$	6^{12}	$4^{5¼}$	C'd'oAJr^1	17500	72	Ⓕ M.S.St'r118 P'cificOc'n C'meRhoda	8

July 18 Bel 3f ft :35⅗hg July 6 Bel 3f ft :35⅕h May 29 Bel 7f sy 1:29b

(cont'd on next page)

Madmoiselle Alice * 111 Ch. f (1969), by Red Fox—Knuckles, by Hasty Road.
Breeder Mrs. W. C. Rigg & Brook Hill Farm (Va.). 1973 23 0 5 5 $13,160
1972 9 1 1 0 $3,116
Owner, L. Chang. Trainer, O. S. Barrera. $12,500

Jly 18-739Aqu Ⓣ1 1/16 1:45 fm 2 ▲112 45 2½ 2½ 32¾ MapleE6 15000 78 ⒻF'stT'keoff114 Pricelyn M'm'leAlice 7
Jly 10-739Aqu Ⓣ1 1:36⅖fm 5½ 112 68¼ 63 43 33 C'd'oAJr7 16000 96 ⒻS'ly leS'c120 Amb'rn'ka M'dm'eAl'e 9
Jly 3-736Aqu Ⓣ 1⅛ 1:52⅖fm 3¼ ▲113 69½ 46 23 2no C'd'oAJr7 13000 74ⒻW'gFl'ter114 Mad'sleAlice LasTr'p's 8
Jun25-739Aqu 1 1-8 1:51⅘ft 7¾ 103* 1h 21 43½ 58½ Cast'daK4 13000 68 ⒻD'pNeckline112 Pric'l'sJew'l Evyne 8
Jun20-739Aqu Ⓣ 1⅛ 1:51 fm 7½ 103* 32 32 31 34 Cas'daK3 11500 76 PeterG.116 P'l'rTr'fic M'dm's'leAlice 8
Jun 7-739Bel Ⓣ 1¼ 2:03⅕shd 5 102* 714 610 58½ 47½ C'st'daK2 20500 86 ⒻS'lly leSec112 Glor'sky MaryBeGood 7
May31-737GS 1 1/16 1:47⅖sl 3 110 39 39 311 416 Bar'raC3 H5000 52 ⒻSmile 110 Brindabella Moon Stitch 6
May16-739Bel Ⓣ 1⅜ 2:18⅗fm 6¼ 101* 75¾ 53½ 2½ 21¼ Cast'daK4 8500 81 LostIdol 118 M'dm'selleAlice Bagoose 10
May10-732Aqu 6½ f 1:19 sy 7 112 64½ 52¾ 42½ 32¾ Velasq'zJ7 7000 79 ⒻG'd'rSt'n102 M'yM'lc'y M'dm'leAl'e 9
July 9 Bel trt 3f ft :37⅗b

Deep Neckline * 114 Dk. b. or br. f (1970), by Controlling—Social Plunge, by Toulouse Lautrec. Breeder, R. C. Ellsworth (Cal.). 1973 16 2 3 4 $19,200
Owner, Little Lou Stable. Trainer, J. Martin. $12,500 1972 13 1 2 4 $6,084

Jly 3-739Aqu Ⓣ1 1/16 1:46⅗fm 3½ 118 811 63¾ 41 2no MapleE4 14000 73 ⒻM'sInt'n'ly105 D'pN'kline Pr'tyB'fly 8
Jun25-739Aqu 1 1-8 1:51⅘ft 10 112 52¾ 44½ 22 12 MapleE1 14000 77 ⒻD'pNeckline112 Pric'l'sJew'l Evyne 8
Jun18-739Aqu 1 1-8 1:52⅖ft 6½ 101 52 31 1h 1h Cast'daK6 9500 74 ⒻD'pNeckline101 Evyne Pricel'ssJ'w'l 6
Jun 4-732Bel Ⓣ 1 1/16 1:43⅗fm 12 114 1019 1015 815 612 Cor'oAJr1 14000 72 ⒻJustC'rious113 FirstPitch T'blingTo 10
May30-735Bel 1 1/16 1:44⅕ft 3¾ 114 79 714 717 417 C'roAJr3 11500 65 ⒻInst'tC'h116 M'trim'n'lC'se P'cOc'n 7
May 3-734Aqu 1 1:37 ft 9 114 1116 1016 710 69 C'd'oAJr6 19000 73 ⒻBl'eSp'g108 M.S.St'r M'trim'n'lC'se 11
Apr27-735Aqu 1 1:38⅘sy 2e 113 711 78½ 56½ 37 MapleE6 15000 66 ⒻM'tr'lC'se116 F'yPr'c's D'pN'ckl'ne 7
Apr16-736Aqu 1 1:38⅗ft 2 ▲116 9¾ 77½ 45½ 21¼ Velas'zJ8 12500 73 ⒻL'tCr'se103 D'pN'kline ImpieEmp'r 9
Apr 5-736Aqu 1 1:39⅕gd 18 109‡ 86¼ 85¾ 57 36¼ ClarkWC4 16000 65 ⒻF'milyPr'n's116 D't'dL've D'pN'kl'e 9
Mar22-736Aqu 1 1-8 1:52⅖ft 4 110 68 614 517 521 VeneziaM5 Alw 53 ⒻD'rAn'e109 Ir'shR'm'ce R'ber'sH'st 7
July 17 Bel trt 4f ft :49b July 12 Bel trt 4f m :48⅗h June 16 Bel trt 4f ft :50⅘b

Klondike Breeze * 112 B. m (1968), by Persian Gold—Arctic Breeze, by Arctic Flyer.
Breeder, E. F. Schoenbern (N. Y.). 1973 15 1 1 3 $7,870
Owner, L. Calderon. Trainer, F. Laboccetta. $10,500 1971 12 1 1 2 $5,412

Jly 5-739Aqu Ⓣ 1⅛ 1:56⅖sf 4¾ 114 67 21 32 36½ Her'dezS5 8250 46 ⒻCount'sV.102 Indict'r Kl'ndikeBr'ze 7
Jun18-739Aqu 1 1-8 1:52⅖ft 9 113 42 2h 59½ 617 He'dezS5 10000 57 ⒻD'pNeckline101 Evyne Pricel'ssJ'w'l 6
May29-739Bel 1 1-8 1:53 gd 3 ▲116 74½ 31 42 42¼ Car'neE10 c7500 64 ⒻPric'l'sJ'w'l 113 T'lystar H'n'yG'l'e 10
May21-738Bel 1 1-8 1:52⅖sy 10 111 85¾ 53 21 2no CardoneE4 7500 69 ⒻN't'eArt106 Kl'dikeBr'ze Pric'l'sJ'l 12
May11-739Aqu 1 1-8 1:52⅕ft 10 106 78½ 2½ 15 13½ CardoneE6 5000 75 KlondikeBreeze106 M'terPiper MiTaj 9
May 2-739Aqu 1 1-8 1:52⅘ft 5½ 111 69½ 68½ 46½ 36½ VeneziaM2 4500 65 ⒻGrapeJelly116 RedFog Kl'dikeBr'ze 7
Apr18-739Aqu 1 1-8 1:53⅖ft 6 112 611 57½ 36 38¾ VeneziaM3 4500 60 ⒻK'pUp109 Sab'la'sN'se K'dykeB'ze 7
Apr13-731Aqu 6 f 1:11⅘ft 21 112 119¼ 89¼ 611 59½ VeneziaM3 6000 74 ⒻEl'n'sC'ce116 M'sC'pric's R'g'r'sR'n 11
Mar27-732Aqu 6½ f 1:19⅖ft 11 116 85¼ 86 46 44 PinedaR6 5000 76 ⒻM'sC'pric's109 G'peJelly Sw'gDuck 8
June 29 Aqu 6f ft 1:17⅖b June 25 Aqu 5f gd 1:04b Jne 13 Aqu 4f ft :48⅘h

Surf Queen 107 Gr. m (1968), by Native Rythm—El Senora byy I Am.
Breeder, Mrs. D. Coleman (N. Y.). 1973 5 2 1 1 $9,600
Owner, Mary Lou Simmons. Trainer, L. H. Hunt. $10,500 1972 5 0 0 0 (——)

Jly 12-738Aqu Ⓣ 1 1:37⅘fm 6½ 102 12 1½ 2½ 33¾ Card'neE2 10500 88 Ifi116 PrimeAction SurfQueen 9
Jun28-732Aqu 6½ f 1:18⅕sy 3½ 121 22 1½ 13 1½ C'roAJr12 c5000 85 ⒻSurfQ'n121 Ren'g'd'sD'gree C'tessV. 14
Jun13-731Bel 6 f 1:11⅕ft 3 ▲115 1½ 13 11 1h Cord'oAJr2 7000 88 ⒻSurfQu'n115 Sw'sPolicy GalaDancer 11
May18-732Bel 6 f 1:10⅖ft 12 111 1h 2½ 54 57½ Arel'noJ9 10500 84 Gl'dysII.113 R'stl'ssPro W't'ngAtH'me 10
May 1-731Aqu 6 f 1:11⅖ft 4¼ 109* 21½ 2½ 1½ 31† AmyJ4 c6250 85 ⒻM'sC'pricious109 M'ryM'c'hy S'fQ'n 9
†Placed second through disqualification.
Mar 9-727Bow 6 f 1:12 ft 31 112 44 76 88 86 Cusim'noG1 Alw 80 ⒻCyamome113 G'nnysdeb Br'veP'p'se 8
Feb25-728Bow 6 f 1:12⅕m 33 112 43½ 23 24 56 WalshE8 Alw 79 ⒻN'ma'sB'l'de112 Pr'm'rk Br'veP'p'e 8
July 18 Bel trt 4f ft :49⅘b July 10 Bel trt 3f ft :36⅗h July 4 Bel trt 4f ft :49b

Foxglow 111 Dk. b. or br. f (1969), by Besomer—How High, by Skyscraper.
Breeder, J. D. Archbold (Va.). 1973 5 M 0 0 (——)
Owner, M. Brous. Trainer, H. Hughes. $12,500 1972 3 M 0 0 (——)

Jly 3-736Aqu Ⓣ 1⅛ 1:52⅖fm 49 109 711 711 411 57 RuaneJ3 12000 67 ⒻW'gFl'ter114 Mad'sleAlice LasTr'p's 8
Jun15-738Bel Ⓣ 1⅜ 2:16⅕fm 31 108 58½ 45 56½ 511 RuaneJ6 7500 83 GreekComedy116 SodaPop Harangue 7
Jun 7-731Bel 1 1:37⅕ft 36 119 97½ 89½ 713 712 R'aneJ2 M14000 74 ⒻArbeeEye113 C'b'l'sC't Dist'tTwil't 11
May 7-731Aqu 7 f 1:26⅗ft 21f 121 118¼ 1211 1214 1113 R'aneJ9 M8000 55 ⒻChefil 114 HenrysGal LovelyLance 14
Apr27-732Aqu 6 f 1:12⅗sy 32 119 811 714 615 616 RuaneJ3 M8000 64 Nu Billing 113 Eulogy Joe Cement 8
Dec 1-722Lrl 1 1:39⅗m 21 116 86¾ 812 1023 1022 P'reWJ8 M5000 57 Roses ofAraby116 M'ch'nin K'g of T's 12
Nov24-722Lrl 6 f 1:13⅕ft 29 117 1012 1010 912 98 P'reWJr9 M5000 76 ValiantWill 120 G'denM'nie Sh'ffJ'hn 12
July 19 Bel 3f ft :36⅖h July 14 Bel 6f ft 1:17⅖bg July 2 Bel 3f ft :36b

Countess V. * **107** **Ch. f (1969), by Cyane—Libby II., by Court Harwell.**
Breeder, Mrs. H. Obre (Md.). 1973 11 2 0 1 $8,400
Owner, R. M. Harmonay. Traner, T. M. Miles. **$11.500** 1972 16 2 2 2 $10,223
Jly 5-739Aqu Ⓣ 1⅛ 1:56⅖sf 5 102**33½ 31½ 1h 11½ MoonL1 8000 53 ⒻCount'sV.102 Indict'r Kl'ndikeBr'ze 7
Jun28-732Aqu 6½ f 1:18⅕sy 12 113 1113 814 66¼ 32½ VeneziaM5 5000 82 ⒻSurfQ'n121 Ren'g'd'sD'gree C'tessV. 14
Jun19-732Aqu 6 f 1:11⅖ft 5¾e 106*109¾ 79½ 47½ 43½ Cast'daK3 5000 82 ⒻRisha115 John'sPatrol SwissPolicy 12
Jun13-731Bel 6 f 1:11⅕ft 21 114 78 910 710 512 RujanoM1 6500 76 ⒻSurfQu'n115 Sw'sPolicy GalaDancer 11
May30-731Bel 6 f 1:12⅖ft 22 113 96 86 65¾ 75½ TurcotteR9 6500 76 ⒻMsC'pric's106 G'llaD'nc'r Divine L't 12
May21-738Bel 1 1-8 1:52⅖sy 10 114 107¼108¼ 812 819 TurcotteR5 7500 50 ⒻN't'eArt106 Kl'dikeBr'ze Pric'l'sJ'l 12
May10-732Aqu 6½ f 1:19 sy 33 114 53 31½ 52¾ 53½ TurcotteR8 7000 78 ⒻG'd'rSt'n102 M'yM'lc'y M'dm'leAl'e 9
Feb26-7310Hia 1 1-8 1:53 ft 4¾ 114 22 812 914 811 Log'cioA2 7000 59 ⒻMaryPat108 LasTropas Amb'rPoint 11
Feb20-736Hia 1 1-8 1:54⅗sl 18 117 11161113 77½ 54¼ Log'rcioA9 6500 58 ⒻM'yp'o114 J'l'sM's R'n'g'd's D'gree 12
June 6 Bel trt 5f ft 1:02h

Priceless Jewel * **114** **Ch. f (1969), by Poppy Jay—Jewel's Dance, by Bolero. Br., Dr.**
W. S. Karutz & Dr. F. Milana (Ky.). 1973 12 2 2 3 $15,520
Owner, N. Usdan. Trainer, J. A. Trovato. **$11.500** 1972 2 1 0 0 $6,000
Jly 3-736Aqu Ⓣ 1⅛ 1:52⅖fm 4¼ 114 43½ 25 511 712 Vel'q'zJ8 12000 62ⒻW'gFl'ter114 Mad'sleAlice LasTr'p's 8
Jun25-739Aqu 1 1-8 1:51⅘ft 3½ 107* 4¾ 11 12 22 WallisT5 12000 75 ⒻD'pNeckline112 Pric'l'sJew'l Evyne 8
Jun18-739Aqu 1 1-8 1:52⅖ft 2½ 111 31½ 42½ 31½ 3nk MapleE1 c9500 74 ⒻD'pNeckline101 Evyne Pricel'ssJ'w'l 6
Jun 7-738Bel 1 1-8 1:51 ft 8-5 ▲117 43 2h 2h 13 Turc'teR7 c7000 76 ⒻPric'l'ssJ'w'l 117 T'lyst'r H'n'yG'l're 8
May29-739Bel 1 1-8 1:53 gd 3½ 113 85½ 51½ 11½ 12 SantiagoA9 7500 66 ⒻPric'l'sJ'w'l 113 T'lystar H'n'yG'l'e 10
May21-738Bel 1 1-8 1:52⅖sy 3¼ 113 64½ 64 33 33 San'goA11 8000 66 ⒻN't'eArt106 Kl'dikeBr'ze Pric'l'sJ'l 12
May14-738Bel 1 1/16 1:43⅗ft 6¾ 107 87¾ 87 97 84¼ Card'neE6 10500 80 ⒻEvyne 116 Swiss Policy Macaero 9
May 8-732Aqu 7 f 1:25 ft 4 116 56 56½ 56½ 56¼ C'st'daM5 13000 70 ⒻVellum111 Pr'yingM'ntis R'stl'ssPro 8
Apr26-732Aqu 6 f 1:12 sy 4¼ 112 56½ 55 43½ 31½ Cas'daM5 13000 81 ⒻAppear116 Mortally PricelessJewel 7
July 14 Bel trt 4f ft :51⅕b

The supreme handicapping factor in grass races is the established ability of the horses to run on the grass. Few of the entrants in this claiming event for fillies have displayed such ability. Only one of them, Countess V., has ever won on the turf. Two others, Madmoiselle Alice and Deep Neckline, have had near misses. The grass form of the rest of the horses in the field ranges from indifferent to abysmal.

Deep Neckline was beaten by a nose in $14,000 company on July 3, but she was racing against a weak group of three-year-olds. A studious handicapper who looked up that field would see that the winner, Miss Intentionally, had been soundly trounced in all four of her prior grass races. Pretty Butterfly, who finished third behind Deep Neckline, is in today's race, and her past performances reveal that she has never been a particularly adept turf runner. So Deep Neckline's second-place finish did not convincingly establish that she is a good grass horse.

Madmoiselle Alice has run well many times on the turf.

But she has never been able to win on the grass, not even at the $8500 level. In a total of twenty-two starts during 1973, she has zero victories, five seconds, and four thirds. She is the quintessential sucker horse.

Countess V., unable to win on the main track for $5000, was tried in an $8000 turf race and won by a length and a half. At a quick glance she looks a bit cheaper than the rivals she is meeting today. But the filly she defeated on July 5, Indicter, came back ten days later and won a $13,000 claiming race on the grass against males. Her victory implies that Countess V. is a legitimate $13,000 animal who was undervalued when she ran for an $8000 price tag and is entered at a proper level today. She couldn't have found an easier spot. All she has to beat is one chronic loser and a group of other horses who have minimal ability on the turf.

NINTH RACE Aqu July 20, 1973 — **1 1/16 MILES (inner turf). (1:41⅕). CLAIMING. Purse $9,000. Fillies and mares. 3-year-olds and upward. 3-year-olds, 114 lbs.; older, 122 lbs. Non-winners of two races at a mile or over since June 9 allowed 2 lbs.; two such races since May 14, 4 lbs.; one such race since July 2, 6 lbs. Claiming price, $12,500; 2 lbs. for each $1,000 to $10,500. (Races where entered for $9,000 or less not considered.) 3-year-olds which have never won at a mile or over allowed 3 lbs.; older, 5 lbs.**

Value to winner $5,400; second, $1,980; third, $1,080; fourth, $540. Mutuel Pool, $261,903. Off-track betting, $158,988.

Last Raced	Horse	EqtAWt	PP	St	¼	½	¾	Str	Fin	Jockeys	Owners	Odds to $1
7- 5-73^{9} Aqu^{1}	Countess V.	4 107	8	5	$3^{1\frac{1}{2}}$	3^{h}	4^{2}	2^{2}	$1^{1\frac{1}{4}}$	LMoon	R M Harmonay	16.20
7- 3-73^{9} Aqu^{2}	Deep Neckline	b3 114	4	3	6^{3}	5^{2}	$3^{\frac{1}{2}}$	3^{1}	2^{2}	EMaple	Little Lou Stable	1.70
7-12-73^{8} Aqu^{3}	Surf Queen	b5 107	6	1	1^{7}	1^{6}	1^{3}	1^{h}	$3^{1\frac{1}{2}}$	ECardone	Mary Lou Simmcns	4.80
7-10-73^{9} Aqu^{3}	Madmoiselle Alice	b4 114	3	4	7^{5}	7^{3}	6^{4}	5^{2}	$4^{\frac{1}{2}}$	ACorderoJr	L Chang	3.20
7-13-73^{4} Aqu^{7}	Pretty Butterfly	b3 104	1	2	2^{4}	2^{3}	$2^{\frac{1}{2}}$	$4^{1\frac{1}{2}}$	5^{3}	KCastaneda^{5}	Ges Stable	5.60
7- 3-73^{6} Aqu^{7}	Priceless Jewel	b4 114	9	7	4^{h}	$4^{1\frac{1}{2}}$	5^{1}	6^{5}	$6^{2\frac{1}{2}}$	RTurcotte	N Usdan	10.00
7- 3-73^{6} Aqu^{5}	Foxglow	4 111	7	9	$8^{\frac{1}{2}}$	9	8^{4}	8^{10}	7^{3}	JRuane	M Brous	42.30
7- 5-73^{9} Aqu^{3}	Klondike Breeze	b5 113	5	8	9	$8^{1\frac{1}{2}}$	7^{2}	$7^{\frac{1}{2}}$	8^{10}	SHernandez	L Calderon	19.50
7-13-73^{4} Aqu^{9}	Family Princess	b3 107	2	6	$5^{1\frac{1}{2}}$	$6^{\frac{1}{2}}$	9	9	9	TWallis^{5}	M Hache	13.50

Time, :22⅘, :46⅘, 1:11⅖, 1:37, 1:43⅖ (wind in backstretch). Track firm.

$2 Mutuel Prices:			
8-COUNTESS V.	34.40	11.60	6.20
4-DEEP NECKLINE		3.60	2.80
6-SURF QUEEN			3.80

Ch. f, by Cyane—Libby II., by Court Harwell. Trainer, T. M. Miles. Bred by Mrs. H. Obre (Md.).

IN GATE—5:12. OFF AT 5:12 EASTERN DAYLIGHT TIME. Start good. Won driving.

COUNTESS V. moved fast along the inside approaching the stretch, came out for the drive and, after catching SURF QUEEN, held DEEP NECKLINE safe. The latter rallied from the outside leaving the far turn, bumped with PRETTY BUTTERFLY near midstretch and continued on gamely. SURF QUEEN sprinted away to a long lead early, made the pace to midstretch and faltered. MADMOISELLE ALICE rallied from the outside entering the stretch but failed to sustain her bid. PRETTY BUTTERFLY made a bid leaving the far turn but had nothing left for the drive. PRICELESS JEWEL had no excuse.

Overweight—Pretty Butterfly, 4 pounds; Family Princess, 4; Madmoiselle Alice, 3; Klondike Breeze, 1.

Claiming Prices (in order of finish)—$11500, 12500, 10500, 12500, 12500, 11500, 12500, 10500, 12500.

Scratched—Narso.

Countess V. won, as expected. But not even the most optimistic bettor could have imagined that she would pay the astonishing price of $34.40 in such a weak field. This is the sort of race that horseplayers dream about.

6th Pimlico Race Course

MARCH 31, 1973

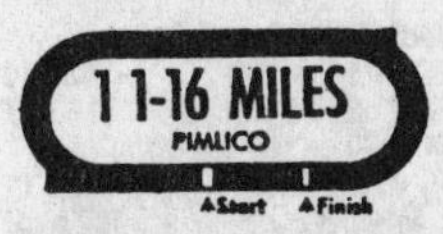

1 1/16 MILES. (1:41). CLAIMING. Purse $6,500. 4-year-olds and upward. Weight, 122 lbs. Non-winners of two races at one mile or over since Feb. 17 allowed 3 lbs.; one such race, 5 lbs.; such a race since Feb. 10, 8 lbs. Claiming price, $9,500: 1 lb. for each $500 to $8,500. (Races where entered for $7,500 or less not considered.)

COUPLED: JALBE and GUNNER'S MATE.

Where Am I — 114

B. c (1969), by Mustato—Blanc de Chine, by Nashua.
Breeler. Mrs. T. M. Waller (N. Y.). — 1973: 1 0 0 0 (—)
Owner, G. A. Freed. Trainer, H. F. Bowyer. $9.500 — 1972: 13 3 1 3 $14,001

Date/Race	Dist.	Time/Track	Odds	Wt					Jockey	Class	Sp.	Top Three	Field
Mar23-73 7GS	6 f	1:14 1/5 ft	28	117	5 6½	7 10	6 9½	7 13	Tich'norW2	5000	60	Valtone112 CreoleWar'r Fant'sticEgo	10
Jun 2-72 5Del	Ⓣ 1	1:38 3/5 fm	7-5	▲114	3 3	1 1½	1 1	1 1	Jim'nezC1	13500	82	WhereAmI 114 Killough Br'ne'leCh't'u	7
May27-72 9GS	Ⓣ 1 1/16	1:43 1/5 fm	8¼	107	4 4	5 7	6 8	6 9	Iann'lliF6	H5000	80	Ray's Rebel 116 Fiendish Lad Petrous	9
May 8-72 5Pim	Ⓣ 5f	:58 4/5 fm	13	112	9 8½	6 7½	8 10	8 9¼	JimenezC9	Alw	84	Mongo'sImage112 Verace Exhortation	9
Apr28-72 9Pim	Ⓣ 1	1:41 2/5 yl	21	112	1 1	1 1	1 2	2½	Jim'ezC2	15500	77	EmJay 114 Where Am I Field House	12
Apr 5-72 7Pim	1 1/16	1:44 ft	15	112	5 7½	6 7½	7 12	7 12	McCar'nG7	Alw	78	Tony'sLuck112 Octet Americ'nH'rit'ge	12
Mar27-72 7Pim	1 1/16	1:44 ft	14	114	3 3½	2 h	1½	1 nk	Jim'n'zC8	10500	90	Wh'eAmI114 Am'r'c'nH'[illegible]'ge Vic'yRise	12
Mar14-72 9Pim	1 1/16	1:46 sy	10	119	2½	2½	2½	3 3¼	T'c'teRL6	c7500	77	Circle ofLove 114 Midimin WhereAm I	8

March 29 Lrl 4f gd :49 2/5 b — Feb 26 Bow 3f ft :39b — Feb 22 Bow 7f ft 1:24b

Broken Thumb * — 113

B. g (1968), by Seven Corners—Mike's Gertie, by Colonel Mike.
Breeder, R. Kahoe (Md.). — 1973: 4 1 0 0 $3,480
Owner, R. F. Kahoe. Trainer, H. Ravich. $9,000 — 1972: 12 1 5 2 $7,820

Date/Race	Dist.	Time/Track	Odds	Wt					Jockey	Class	Sp.	Top Three	Field
Mar24-73 5Pim	1 1/16	1:47 2/5 ft	5¼	114	12 12	7 7	5 1¾	5 3¼	Br'aleVJr9	9000	65	BuffaloRun114 G'nner'sMate Surfac'd	12
Mar 5-73 6Bow	1 1/16	1:47 1/5 gd	5	112	5 5	5 7½	2 h	1 3	Bra'leVJr3	7000	72	Bro[illegible]Thumb[illegible] ClaraFay[illegible]P'ce	7
Feb23-73 9Bow	1 1/16	1:47 3/5 ft	6½	114	6 9¼	8 11	6 7	5 8¾	Cesp'desR7	7500	61	Co[illegible] [illegible]ed Das[illegible]Bitters	8
Feb 3-73 5Bow	1 1/16	1:49 1/5 m	6	112	9 13	9 9¼	8 3¾	6 4¾	Cus'noG5	H4000	57	Wi[illegible]t'ge[illegible] [illegible]'tTrain[illegible]rum	12
Dec23-72 4Lrl	1 3/16	2:04 1/5 m	4	111	5 9½	4 9½	4 4½	5 1½	PilarH4	H5000	62	Ch[illegible]ing119 VeryTouchy TacaroBoy	6
Dec16-72 4Lrl	1 1-8	1:55 1/5 sl	8¾	110	4 3½	4 3	2 2	2 2½	PilarH4	H5000	68	Channeling117 BrokenThumb Interw'd	7

March 29 Pim 5f ft 1:05b — March 21 Pim 4f ft :50 2/5 b — March 17 Pim 5f sy 1:04b

Russell's Rullah * — 113

Ch. g (1966), by Martins Rullah—Hi Delight, by High Bandit.
Breeder, R. L. Buyck (Md.). — 1973: 2 0 0 0 (—)
Owner, R. Gallo. Trainer, D. H. Barr. $9.000 — 1972: 3 0 0 0 (—)

Date/Race	Dist.	Time/Track	Odds	Wt					Jockey	Class	Sp.	Top Three	Field
Mar24-73 5Pim	1 1/16	1:47 2/5 ft	7½	114	9 8½	9 7¼	8 4	7 4½	McC'onG11	9000	63	BuffaloRun114 G'nner'sMate Surfac'd	12
Mar 2-73 7Bow	6 f	1:11 1/5 ft	20	112	8 14	8 17	8 13	7 9	KurtzJ4	13500	78	Gil[illegible] Sa[illegible]Bolero Supercut	8
May25-72 6Pim	1 1/16	1:45 ft	4¼	114	2 1½	3 3	5 10	5 8	KurtzJ6	13500	77	Rhigo[illegible]119 Shy M[illegible]ent Honey Taylor	6
Apr24-72 9Pim	1 1/16	1:46 sy	5½	114	6 6	8 12	9 22	9 26	ShukN2	25000	54	Priv[illegible]eT[illegible]es113 [illegible]Blair El'tedPrince	10
Apr10-72 6Pim	6 f	1:12 4/5 gd	7¾	113	7 11	7 11	6 11	5 6	KurtzJ2	20500	76	Gs Silver A. 117 Gilzo Ground War	7
Nov23-71 6Lrl	1	1:39 2/5 ft	4¼	120	1 1	1 1½	1 4	1 2	McC'r'nG2	20000	80	R's'll'sR'll'h120 B'rkl'yC'rn'r Gr'y Id'l	7

March 19 Bow 1m gd 1:49b — Mar 1 Bow 3f ft :37 2/5 b — Feb 25 Bow 5f ft 1:03b

Formal Count * — 118

Dk. b. or br. h (1968), by Count Amber—Formal Affair, by Frosty Mr.
Breeder, C. B. Fischbach (Ky.). — 1973: 4 1 0 1 $4,140
Owner, Audley Farm Stable. Trainer, J. B. Dodson. $9,000 — 1972: 13 0 1 1 $3,205

Date/Race	Dist.	Time/Track	Odds	Wt					Jockey	Class	Sp.	Top Three	Field
Mar22-73 4Pim	1 1/16	1:46 2/5 ft	8½	114	9 12	7 7¼	2 h	1 2½	JimenezC1	8000	73	FormalCount114 Templar Jandymar	9
Mar 5-73 6Bow	1 1/16	1:47 1/5 gd	5	114	7 9½	6 9	5 3¼	5 5¾	Jim'nezC6	8000	66	Br[illegible]mb[illegible] [illegible]aFaye[illegible]P'ce	7
Jan10-73 9Bow	1 1/16	1:44 2/5 ft	7e	114	11 14	9 16	7 12	7 8¼	Jim'nezC10	7500	78	Ch[illegible]syC[illegible]117 S'[illegible]nk'g [illegible]Love	11
Jan 3-73 4Bow	1 1/16	1:46 2/5 ft	7½	114	7 10	7 3½	2 2½	3½	JimenezC1	7500	75	C[illegible]C[illegible]k114 G[illegible]M'te [illegible]ount	7
Nov 4-72 9Lrl	1 1/16	1:46 gd	8½e	116	10 18	9 14	7 6¾	6 9	BlackAS10	8000	74	Vic's Pick 116 Greybrook JoySmoke	10
Oct20-72 5Lrl	1	1:40 1/5 m	34	114	12 17	6 2¾	4 4½	5 5½	Jim'ezC11	10000	70	StellarShot112 JaipurII. ScotchBroth	12

March 21 Pim 4f ft :51b — Feb 24 Bow 5f ft 1:02 3/5 b — Jan 31 Bow 4f ft :50b

(cont'd on next page)

Old Stoneface * **114** B. g (1968), by Lord Quillo—Rock Day, by Roc du Diable.
Br., Gardiner Farm Limited (Can.). 1973 6 0 0 2 $1,290
Owner, G. R. Gardiner. Trainer, P. Boutiguer. $9,500 1972 10 2 1 2 $7,865
Mar17-732GP 1 1/16 1:44⅖sy 14 114 89½ 79½1011 918 KellyJ3 12000 63 Check List 118 He's Got It Sinu 12
Mar 6-7310GPⓉa1 1/16 1:45⅕fm 8¼e 116 33½ 9141122 1115 KellyJ9 13000 73 TabbyGray116 Sw'tM'nh't'n S'p'rR'ky 12
Feb12-735Hia Ⓣa1⅛ 1:49⅖fm 6e 117 1114121810181015 Tur'teR12 15000 80 T.V.Doubletalk117 Br'dyM'n Up'rp'se 12
Feb 7-7310Hia 1 1-8 1:51⅕ft 4½ 113 91411161110 87½ Vel'ezJ5 16500 71 Roji 115 HasamsHoney Love andPeace 11
Jan27-732Hia 1 1-8 1:51 ft 6¾ 117 8191015 78¾ 4¾† Velas'zJ7 14000 79 Ride the Curl 112 Mariuco Ray Davis 12
†Placed third through disqualification.
Jan18-7310Hia 1 1-8 1:50⅕sy 17 113 21½ 22 36 38½ Tur'teR7 14000 75 Shin'gSw'd117 L've andP'ce OldSt'f'e 12
March 4 Crc 3f ft :37b Feb 24 GP 5f 1:03⅖b

Curious George **114** Dk. b. or br. c (1969), Telekinesis—Dandy Pat, by Gain A' Foot.
Breeder, J. L. Skinner (Pa.). 1973 10 0 0 3 $3,810
Owner, H. Schifrin. Trainer, R. Zimmer. $9,500 1972 25 5 1 5 $16,517
Mar17-739Pim 1 1/16 1:47⅘sm 15 114 98¾ 77¼ 54 33¼ BlackAS10 9500 63 FiveStitches110 G'ner'sM'te C'r'sG'ge 11
Mar12-737Bow 6 f 1:12⅘sl 11 114 78¾ 79¾ 54¾ 48 BlackAS9 10500 71 Big [illegible]114 [illegible] [illegible] 11
Feb24-734Bow 1 1/16 1:47⅘ft 9 113 77¾ 911 98 910 McC'onG8 10500 59 Br'[illegible]14 Mi[illegible]Bully [illegible] 9
Feb20-737Bow 7 f 1:26⅕ft 13 112 66½ 87¼ 34 44¼ McC'onG7 12500 70 Si[illegible] Dip 114 [illegible] Ou[illegible] 12
Feb10-735Bow 6 f 1:11⅕ft 13 114 1011 911 86¾ 63¾ PlattsR8 13000 83 NoMystery117 PopularAct PastHenry 12
Feb 2-737Bow 6 f 1:13 sy 20 114 49½ 48 55¼ 3nk PlattsR8 12500 78 Tr'sureChart114 Rad'tzky C'riousG'ge 9
March 27 Pim 5f sl 1:04b March 11 Bow 3f sl :38b

Tim **114** B. h (1967), by Tim Tam—Sweet Alyssum, by Alycidon.
Breeder, H. A. Love (Md.). 1973 5 0 0 0 (——)
Owner. A. Adamopoulos. Trainer, C. A. Adamopoulos. $9,500 1972 21 1 3 4 $11,025
Mar20-737Pim 1 1/16 1:46⅖ft 85 114 1015 716 65¾ 69¼ KurtzJ10 11500 64 Beriberi114 AmbiHula St.LouisC'ntry 10
Mar 3-732Bow 1 1/16 1:46 ft 40 114 94½ 98½ 810 814 AlbertsB6 11500 64 Za[illegible] [illegible] Ga[illegible] 9
Feb22-735Bow 1 1/16 1:48 ft 43 114 66 715 711 79¾ KurtzJ5 14500 58 Flig[illegible]geon1[illegible] Bac[illegible]lid'g [illegible] 7
Feb13-736Bow 1 1/16 1:45⅗ft 9¼ 114 612 620 518 519 KurtzJ3 14500 61 B'c[illegible]114 [illegible]a Flig[illegible] 6
Feb 2-737Bow 6 f 1:13 sy 24 114 918 917 912 86½ KurtzJ4 13500 71 Tr'sureChart114 Rad'tzky C'r[illegible]ge 9
Dec 2-728Suf 1 1/16 1:48 gd 6¾ 112 814 87¾ 74¾ 63 MineauG7 Hcp0 66 John Hunt 111 Rādiclib Mung 9
March 28 Lrl 4f sl :50⅘b March 26 Lrl 4f sy :50⅗b Feb 11 Lrl 4f fr :49⅗b

Gunner's Mate **114** Ch. g (1969), by Royal Gunner—Jody Belle, by Nasrullah.
Breeder, Ford Stables (Md.). 1973 9 1 4 0 $9,510
Owner, Mrs. John J. Ries. Trainer, Barbara M. Kees. $9,500 1972 25 5 4 2 $17,986
Mar24-735Pim 1 1/16 1:47⅖ft 3e 114 1111 87¼ 62 21¾ YorkR12 9000 66 BuffaloRun114 G'nner'sMate Surfac'd 12
Mar17-739Pim 1 1/16 1:47⅘sm 8½ 112 12 1h 21½ 22¼ Cu'manoB3 8500 64 Five[illegible]110 [illegible]M'te [illegible] 11
Mar 6-737Bow 1 1/16 1:45⅕sm 7 114 35 47 46 414 Cusim'oG2 9500 68 Ri[illegible]114 [illegible]ed [illegible] 9
Feb26-736Bow 1 1/16 1:48 ft 2½ 114 68 66½ 67½ 52¾ YorkR6 9000 65 Sa[illegible]tz114 [illegible] Don't[illegible] 7
Feb17-735Bow 1 1/16 1:46⅕ft 4 114 913 917 814 916 McCa'nG9 11500 61 Gay Fellow 114 Feel Free A Verdict 10
Jan29-736Bow 1 1/16 1:46⅗sl 4¾ 114 712 87 76¾ 612 Wri'tDR1 13500 63 WiseMisty119 Backsliding PatrolPr'ce 8
Feb 13 Lrl 3f ft :37⅗b

The horses in this field are an evenly matched, uninspiring lot. Formal Count, who has the top figure of 87, is a slow-breaking plodder with only one victory in the last two years. Curious George, who earned an 82 in his last start, is winless in ten starts. Gunner's Mate and Broken Thumb also have figures in the 80s, with no other notable handicapping virtues. There is no way to judge which of these in-and-outers will feel like beating the others today.

Two unknown quantities are also entered in this field. Old

Stoneface, who has come to Maryland from Florida, ran well for $14,000 in January, but his form since then has been dismal. Where Am I made his only start of the year in New Jersey, where he was buried in a $5000 claiming race.

What is Where Am I doing in a $9500 race today? His record bears further scrutiny. The horse was a solid $10,000 campaigner last year. He was laid off for nearly a year, probably because of physical problems, which might explain the drop to $5000.

Where Am I was training steadily at Bowie, as his workout line indicates, but instead of running him in Maryland trainer Henry Bowyer went to the trouble and expense of vanning him to Garden State Park. Why? His six-furlong race there was probably just a prep since Where Am I is a router by nature. And there are plenty of $5000 races in Maryland.

There is one possible explanation for Bowyer's actions. When a horse runs once for $5000, he becomes eligible for starter-handicap races that are offered at all the Maryland tracks, and a solid $10,000 animal running in starter handicaps can win a lot of money. Perhaps Bowyer decided to take a gamble and enter his horse for $5000, figuring that he was less likely to be claimed at an out of town track where nobody knew him. Having gotten away with this gamble, he could return Where Am I to Maryland and run him where he belongs.

This interpretation may seem a bit too ingenious, but unless Bowyer is an utter madman it is the only way to explain his horse's past performances and his presence in a $9500 race. Proud of my brilliant deduction, I decided to bet Where Am I strongly, and my convictions were fortified when the horse received strong betting action that knocked his odds down to 5 to 1.

SIXTH RACE Pim 1$\frac{1}{16}$ MILES. (1:41). CLAIMING. Purse $6,500. 4-year-olds and upward. Weight, 122 lbs. Non-winners of two races at one mile or over since Feb. 17 allowed 3 lbs.; one such race, 5 lbs.; such a race since Feb. 10, 8 lbs. Claiming price, $9,500; 1 lb. for each $500 to $8.500. (Races where entered for $7,500 or less not considered.)

March 31, 1973

Value to winner $3,900; second, $1,430; third, $780; fourth, $390. Mutuel Pool, $157,507.

Last Raced	Horse	EqtAWt	PP	St	¼	½	¾	Str	Fin	Jockeys	Owners	Odds to $1
3-17-73^{2} GP^{9}	Old Stoneface	5 114	5	4	2^{3}	$2^{1\frac{1}{2}}$	2^{3}	1^{h}	1^{nk}	JBaboolal	G R Gardiner	11.50
3-23-73^{7} GS^{7}	Where Am I	4 114	1	1	1^{1}	1^{1}	1^{h}	2^{3}	2^{3}	JKurtz	G A Freed	5.50
3-24-73^{5} Pim^{7}	Russell's Rullah	b7 113	3	2	3^{h}	3^{h}	$5^{1\frac{1}{2}}$	3^{1}	$3^{\frac{3}{4}}$	GMcCarron	R Gallo	4.40
3-22-73^{4} Pim^{1}	Formal Count	5 118	4	5	8	7^{1}	7^{1}	$6^{1\frac{1}{2}}$	4no	WHartack	Audley Farm Stable	4.90
3-24-73^{5} Pim^{7}	Broken Thumb	5 113	2	3	6^{1}	6^{h}	$6^{1\frac{1}{2}}$	$5^{1\frac{1}{2}}$	5^{1}	VBraccialeJr	R F Kahoe	6 60
3-17-73^{9} Pim^{3}	Curious George	4 114	6	6	$5^{1\frac{1}{2}}$	$4^{\frac{1}{2}}$	3^{h}	4^{h}	$6^{\frac{3}{4}}$	WJPassmore	H Schifrin	5.30
3-24-73^{5} Pim^{2}	Gunner's Mate	b4 114	8	7	4^{4}	5^{6}	$4^{\frac{1}{2}}$	7^{3}	7^{2}	RYork	Mrs J J Ries	2.90
3-27-73^{7} Pim^{6}	Tim	6 116	7	8	$7^{1\frac{1}{2}}$	8	8	8	8	BAlberts	A Adamopoulos	19.80

Time, :23⅘, :48, 1:13⅕, 1:40, 1:46⅘. Track sloppy.

$2 Mutuel Prices:			
5-OLD STONEFACE	25.00	12.20	8.00
1-WHERE AM I		9.00	6.20
3-RUSSELL'S RULLAH			5.40

B. g, by Lord Quillo—Rock Day, by Roc du Diable. Trainer, P. Buttigieg. Bred by Cardiner Farm Limited (Can.).

IN GATE—3:30. OFF AT 3:30 EASTERN STANDARD TIME. Start good. Won driving.

OLD STONEFACE, hustled to the clubhouse turn, was rated in closest attendance to the pace and wore down WHERE AM I. The latter set the pace under rating and continued gamely when tiring through the stretch. RUSSELL'S RULLAH showed an even effort. BROKEN THUMB passed tired rivals. CURIOUS GEORGE, possibly best, pulled his rider into a blind switch approaching the far turn, was taken up strongly a couple of times and then did not respond when clear. GUNNER'S MATE was through early.

Overweight—Tim, 2 pounds.

Old Stoneface claimed by Audley Farm Stable, trainer J. B. Dodson. Gunner's Mate claimed by J. D. Marsh, trainer J. Tammaro.

Claiming Prices (in order of finish)—$9500, 9500, 9000, 9000, 9000, 9500, 9500, 9500.

Scratched—Jalbe, Irish Tenor, Joy Smoke.

My reasoning had been correct, and Where Am I ran an excellent race, beating all the logical contenders. But Where Am I had the misfortune to be facing a horse who was trained by a slightly sharper conniver than Bowyer. Old Stoneface, the Florida invader who had been trounced in his last four starts, came to life, battled Where Am I head-and-head through most of the race, and won by a neck. Nobody ever said this was an easy game.

Appendix

ONE-TURN SPEED RATINGS

5 FUR.		5½ FUR.		6 FUR.		6½ FUR.		7 FUR.		1 MILE	
:56	131	1:02	133	1:08	135	1:15	124	1:21	127	1:34	124
-1	127	-1	130	-1	132	-1	121	-1	125	-1	122
-2	124	-2	126	-2	129	-2	119	-2	122	-2	120
-3	120	-3	123	-3	126	-3	116	-3	120	-3	117
-4	117	-4	120	-4	123	-4	113	-4	118	-4	115
:57	113	1:03	117	1:09	120	1:16	111	1:22	115	1:35	113
-1	110	-1	114	-1	118	-1	108	-1	113	-1	111
-2	106	-2	110	-2	115	-2	106	-2	110	-2	109
-3	103	-3	107	-3	112	-3	103	-3	108	-3	107
-4	99	-4	104	-4	109	-4	100	-4	105	-4	105
:58	96	1:04	101	1:10	106	1:17	98	1:23	103	1:36	103
-1	92	-1	98	-1	103	-1	95	-1	101	-1	101
-2	89	-2	95	-2	100	-2	92	-2	98	-2	99
-3	85	-3	92	-3	98	-3	90	-3	96	-3	97
-4	82	-4	89	-4	95	-4	87	-4	93	-4	95
:59	79	1:05	86	1:11	92	1:18	85	1:24	91	1:37	92
-1	75	-1	83	-1	89	-1	82	-1	89	-1	90
-2	72	-2	79	-2	86	-2	80	-2	86	-2	88
-3	68	-3	76	-3	83	-3	77	-3	84	-3	86
-4	65	-4	73	-4	81	-4	74	-4	81	-4	84
1:00	62	1:06	70	1:12	78	1:19	72	1:25	79	1:38	82
-1	58	-1	67	-1	75	-1	69	-1	77	-1	80
-2	55	-2	64	-2	72	-2	67	-2	74	-2	78
-3	52	-3	61	-3	70	-3	64	-3	72	-3	76
-4	49	-4	58	-4	67	-4	62	-4	70	-4	74
1:01	45	1:07	55	1:13	64	1:20	59	1:26	67	1:39	72
-1	42	-1	52	-1	61	-1	57	-1	65	-1	70
-2	39	-2	49	-2	59	-2	54	-2	63	-2	68
-3	35	-3	46	-3	56	-3	52	-3	60	-3	66
-4	32	-4	43	-4	53	-4	49	-4	58	-4	64
1:02	29	1:08	40	1:14	51	1:21	47	1:27	56	1:40	62
-1	26	-1	38	-1	48	-1	44	-1	54	-1	60
-2	23	-2	35	-2	45	-2	42	-2	51	-2	58
-3	19	-3	32	-3	42	-3	39	-3	49	-3	56
-4	16	-4	29	-4	40	-4	37	-4	47	-4	54
1:03	13	1:09	26	1:15	37	1:22	35	1:28	44	1:41	52
				-1	34	-1	32	-1	42	-1	50
				-2	32	-2	30	-2	40	-2	48
				-3	29	-3	27	-3	38	-3	46
				-4	26	-4	25	-4	35	-4	44
				1:16	24	1.23	22	1.29	33	1:42	42

TWO-TURN SPEED RATINGS

1 MILE		1-70		1 1/16		1 1/8		1 1/4	
1:34	133	1:38	134	1:40	137	1:47	132	2:00	133
−1	131	−1	132	−1	135	−1	130	−1	131
−2	129	−2	130	−2	133	−2	128	−2	130
−3	126	−3	128	−3	131	−3	126	−3	128
−4	124	−4	126	−4	129	−4	124	−4	126
1:35	122	1:39	124	1:41	127	1:48	122	2:01	125
−1	120	−1	122	−1	125	−1	120	−1	123
−2	118	−2	120	−2	123	−2	119	−2	122
−3	116	−3	118	−3	121	−3	117	−3	120
−4	114	−4	116	−4	119	−4	115	−4	118
1:36	112	1:40	114	1:42	117	1:49	113	2:02	117
−1	110	−1	112	−1	115	−1	111	−1	115
−2	108	−2	110	−2	113	−2	108	−2	113
−3	106	−3	108	−3	111	−3	106	−3	112
−4	103	−4	106	−4	109	−4	105	−4	110
1:37	101	1:41	104	1:43	107	1:50	104	2:03	108
−1	99	−1	102	−1	106	−1	102	−1	107
−2	97	−2	100	−2	104	−2	100	−2	105
−3	95	−3	98	−3	102	−3	99	−3	104
−4	93	−4	96	−4	100	−4	97	−4	102
1:38	91	1:42	94	1:44	98	1:51	95	2:04	100
−1	89	−1	92	−1	96	−1	93	−1	99
−2	87	−2	90	−2	94	−2	90	−2	97
−3	85	−3	88	−3	92	−3	88	−3	96
−4	83	−4	86	−4	90	−4	87	−4	94
1:39	81	1:43	84	1:45	88	1:52	86	2:05	92
−1	79	−1	82	−1	86	−1	84	−1	91
−2	77	−2	80	−2	84	−2	82	−2	89
−3	75	−3	78	−3	83	−3	81	−3	88
−4	73	−4	76	−4	81	−4	79	−4	86
1:40	71	1:44	74	1:46	79	1:53	77	2:06	84
−1	69	−1	73	−1	77	−1	75	−1	83
−2	67	−2	71	−2	75	−2	74	−2	81
−3	65	−3	69	−3	73	−3	72	−3	80
−4	63	−4	67	−4	71	−4	70	−4	78
1:41	61	1:45	65	1:47	69	1:54	68	2:07	76
−1	59	−1	63	−1	68	−1	67	−1	75
−2	57	−2	61	−2	66	−2	65	−2	73
−3	55	−3	59	−3	64	−3	63	−3	72
−4	53	−4	57	−4	62	−4	61	−4	70
1:42	51	1:46	55	1:48	60	1:55	60	2:08	69
−1	49	−1	54	−1	58	−1	58	−1	67
−2	47	−2	52	−2	56	−2	56	−2	66
−3	45	−3	50	−3	55	−3	54	−3	64
−4	43	−4	48	−4	53	−4	53	−4	62
1:43	41	1:47	46	1:49	51	1:56	51	2:09	61
−1	39	−1	44	−1	49	−1	49	−1	59
−2	38	−2	42	−2	47	−2	47	−2	58
−3	36	−3	40	−3	45	−3	46	−3	56
−4	34	−4	39	−4	44	−4	44	−4	55
1:44	32	1:48	37	1:50	42	1:57	42	2:10	53

BEATEN LENGTHS ADJUSTMENTS

Margin	5F	5½F	6F	6½F	7F	Mile	1-70	1¹⁄₁₆	1⅛	1¼
neck	1	1	1	1	1	0	0	0	0	0
½	1	1	1	1	1	1	1	1	1	1
¾	2	2	2	2	2	1	1	1	1	1
1	3	3	2	2	2	2	2	2	2	1
1¼	4	4	3	3	3	2	2	2	2	2
1½	4	4	4	3	3	3	3	3	2	2
1¾	5	5	4	4	4	3	3	3	3	3
2	6	6	5	5	4	4	3	3	3	3
2¼	7	6	6	5	5	4	4	4	4	3
2½	7	7	6	6	5	4	4	4	4	4
2¾	8	7	7	6	6	5	5	5	5	4
3	9	8	7	7	6	5	5	5	5	4
3¼	9	9	8	7	7	6	5	5	5	5
3½	10	10	9	8	7	6	6	6	6	5
3¾	11	10	9	9	8	7	6	6	6	5
4	12	11	10	9	8	7	7	7	6	5
4¼	12	12	10	10	9	8	7	7	7	6
4½	13	12	11	10	9	8	8	8	7	7
4¾	14	13	11	11	10	9	8	8	8	7
5	15	14	12	11	11	9	9	8	8	7
5½	17	15	13	13	12	10	10	9	9	8
6	18	17	15	14	13	11	10	10	9	9
6½	20	18	16	15	14	12	11	11	10	9
7	21	19	17	16	15	13	12	12	11	10
7½	23	21	18	17	16	14	13	13	12	11
8	24	22	20	18	17	14	14	13	13	11
8½	26	23	21	19	18	15	15	14	13	12
9	27	24	22	20	19	16	16	15	14	13
9½	29	26	24	22	20	17	17	16	15	14
10	30	28	25	23	21	18	17	17	16	14
11	33	30	28	25	24	20	19	18	18	16
12	36	33	30	27	26	22	21	20	19	17
13	39	36	33	30	28	24	22	22	21	19
14	42	39	35	32	30	25	24	24	23	20
15	45	41	38	34	32	27	26	26	25	21

Par Figures

These are the average winning figures — or pars — for various classes at certain major racetracks. They are pars for older male horses and are not applicable to races limited to 2- or 3-year-olds. The claiming pars apply only to unrestricted races — not to ones that are limited to state-breds or horses who meet certain eligibility conditions, such as "nonwinners of a race in the last six months." MSW denotes maiden-special-weight races. Allowance categories represent the most common conditions for those races: N1OT refers to those for nonwinners of one race other than maiden or claiming. **The pars for races limited to fillies and mares will typically be eight points lower than for males.** No pars are listed for classes where the data was either insufficient or too erratic to derive a meaningful average. When the *Daily Racing Form*'s data base has a larger accumulation of our speed figures, we will have much more extensive par figures.

Track	4000	5000	6000 7400	7500 9000	10000 14000	15000 20000	21000 34000	35000 49000	50000 75000	MSW	ALW N1OT	ALW N2OT	ALW N3OT
AQU BEL SAR					85	90	92	95	98	88	95	98	102
AQU (inner)					85	90	92	95	98	77	94	96	99
AP HAW	72	73	76	80	83	85	88			76	85	87	89
BM GG			78	80	85	90	93			79	87	90	96
CD	69	73	75	77	79	83	85			79	84	91	
CRC		76	80	82	84	86	89	92			90	91	93
DET	65	69	71	71	74	77				56	68	76	80
DMR HOL SA					85	90	93	96	98	90	98	101	102
FG LAD		75	77		83	87	91			64	76	87	91
GP				79	85	89	91	93	97	75	93		
GRD		65	69	76	77	79	83						
GS	65	68	73	75	81	83				75	81	85	91
KEE		72		76	78	83	86						
LRL PIM		73	75	78	83	85	89	91	95	74	84	87	91
MED		74	76	81	84	89	89	91	94		85	87	90
MTH		74	78	80	84	87	91				85	87	90
OP		76	79	82	83	88	90	94		81	91	95	97
PHA	68	68	75	75	80	86	91			75	81	85	91
RP	65	68	72	74	77	82				62	73	82	83
SPT	67	68	70	75	80	83					76	81	85
TDN	66	68	73	75	77						66	74	78
TP	69	72	76	80	85	86				67	84	85	94
TUP	71	73	74	75	77	84							
WO				70	77	82	87			75	85	88	91

Claiming Pars at Smaller Tracks

At smaller racetracks, the vast majority of races will be conditioned claiming events, which restrict the eligibility of the entrants to horses who have not won a certain number of races in a certain period of time. The chart below shows the pars for both open and conditioned races in the lower claiming categories.

	2000	2000 COND	2500	2500 COND	3000	3000 COND	4000	4000 COND	5000	6000 7400	7500 9000	10000 14000
AKS			65	61	67	63			69		70	74
ALB, RUI, SUN, SFE			60	57	65	61	67	62	69	71	72	76
ASD			59	57	61		63		65	70	71	73
ATL							67	66	72	75		80
BEU					61	56	64		65			
BND	54	51	55	52	59	56			62			
BRD			55	55			61	57	63	64		
CLS, FON, LNN			57	57	62	59		60	63			
CT			59	51	61	57			62			
EVD			62	57		60	68					
FE					58	58	64	59	65	70		
FER, PLN, SAC, STK, SR							66	64		74	77	80
FL					66	58	67		68			75
FP					62	56	57	63	67	69	76	
JND				59		59			69			
PRE	55	52	57		60	52						
PEN			64	57	68	57	72		74			
PM			60	55	63	61	64	61	65			
RKM					69	63	69		74	75		
SUF							70	66	73	77	80	84
TAM					69	64	71		74	76	80	
TRM			61	58	62	59	64		66			
YM			64	58	65		67	65	69	70	71	